BUILD IT, MAKE IT, DO IT, PLAY IT!

Recent Titles in the
Children's and Young Adult Literature Reference Series
Catherine Barr, Series Editor

Literature Links to American History, K–6: Resources to Enhance and Entice
Lynda G. Adamson

Celebrating Cuentos: Promoting Latino Children's Literature and Literacy in Classrooms and Libraries
Jamie Campbell Naidoo, Editor

The Family in Literature for Young Readers: A Resource Guide for Use with Grades 4 to 9
John T. Gillespie

Best Books for High School Readers, Grades 9–12: Supplement to the Second Edition
Catherine Barr

Best Books for Middle School and Junior High Readers, Grades 6–9:
Supplement to the Second Edition
Catherine Barr

Rainbow Family Collections: Selecting and Using Children's Books with Lesbian, Gay, Bisexual, Transgender, and Queer Content
Jamie Campbell Naidoo

A to Zoo: Subject Access to Children's Picture Books, Supplement to the 8th Edition
Rebecca L. Thomas

Best Books for Children: Preschool Through Grade 6, Supplement to the 9th Edition
Catherine Barr

Best Books for Middle School and Junior High Readers, Grades 6–9: Third Edition
Catherine Barr

Best Books for High School Readers, Grades 9–12: Third Edition
Catherine Barr

A to Zoo: Subject Access to Children's Picture Books, Ninth Edition
Rebecca L. Thomas

Diversity Programming for Digital Youth: Promoting Cultural Competence in the Children's Library
Jamie Campbell Naidoo

BUILD IT, MAKE IT, DO IT, PLAY IT!

Subject Access to the Best How-To Guides for Children and Teens

Catharine Bomhold

and

Terri Elder

Children's and Young Adult Literature Reference
Catherine Barr, Series Editor

 **LIBRARIES UNLIMITED**

AN IMPRINT OF ABC-CLIO, LLC
Santa Barbara, California • Denver, Colorado • Oxford, England

Library of Congress Cataloging-in-Publication Data

Bomhold, Catharine, 1966–
  Build it, make it, do it, play it! : subject access to the best how-to guides for children and teens / Catharine R. Bomhold and Terri Elder.
      pages cm — (Children's and young adult literature reference)
  Includes bibliographical references and index.
  ISBN 978-1-59884-391-0 (hardback) — ISBN 978-1-59884-392-7 (ebook)
  1. Creative activities and seat work—Bibliography. 2. Handicraft—Bibliography. 3. Activity programs in education—Bibliography. 4. Do-it-yourself work—Bibliography. I. Elder, Terri E. II. Title. III. Title: Subject access to the best how-to guides for children and teens.
  Z6151.B66B85 2014
  [LB1027.25]
  016.3713—dc23   2014005177

ISBN: 978-1-59884-391-0
EISBN: 978-1-59884-392-7

18 17 16 15 14   1 2 3 4 5

This book is also available on the World Wide Web as an ebook.
Visit www.abc-clio.com for details.

Libraries Unlimited
An Imprint of ABC-CLIO, LLC

ABC-CLIO, LLC
130 Cremona Drive, P.O. Box 1911
Santa Barbara, California 93116-1911

This book is printed on acid-free paper ∞
Manufactured in the United States of America

8/14

Contents

Acknowledgments

The author would like to thank the following people for their help bringing this project to fruition. To Rex Bomhold, without whose technical assistance this never would have happened. I would put you on as co-author, my dear, if it didn't subvert my plans for promotion. To the SLIS graduate assistants, Catherine Smith, Michelle Finerty, and Sarah Himel for making copies, diverting phone calls, transcribing contents pages, and "other duties as required." Thanks also to my colleagues at the University of Southern Mississippi School of Library and Information Science for their invaluable feedback, brainstorming, and positive encouragement. Finally, my deepest appreciation and admiration goes to my infinitely patient editor, Catherine Barr.

Catharine Bomhold

Introduction

~~~~~~

For a reference librarian working in a children's department

"How do I . . . " is a frequent beginning to a child's reference question. Whether it is learning a new skill or taking on a new hobby, children are often in need of explanatory material. But in the plethora of books on the nonfiction shelves, many are descriptive rather than instructional, and finding a source with step-by-step instructions can be a challenge. Library catalogs, most librarians' first choice for searching, do not differentiate between books that inform a child about a subject and those that tell them how to do it themselves. The purpose of this index is to provide subject access to books that provide such instructions, and the books were selected on the basis of subject, coverage, and format.

Books were chosen by publication date (2007 or later), by the way the subject or task was covered, and by format. The instructions must be clear and thorough and, with the exception of those that clearly state that they are "advanced" or "expert," do not assume previous knowledge by the user. Books included feature incremental instructions detailed enough that a child in the designated age range would have a reasonable chance of accomplishment. The availability of a glossary of terms, as well as an explanation of techniques, was also considered. Titles that were not included were primarily descriptive, the instructions were too brief or too complicated for the age group, or the user needed previous knowledge of the subject to begin. In addition, titles that were out of print or had minimal availability were not included. Books in formats inappropriate to library collections, such as spiral bindings or containing consumable parts were also not considered.

Most books indexed are on a single topic such as how to play baseball, or how to knit or to cook. A few titles, however, stood out as being worthy to be indexed by chapter. Those titles, on multiple topics, provided either unique coverage of a particular topic, or especially clear and concise instruction. In the Subject Index these titles are listed below the monograph titles, and include the chapter heading and page number within the book.

Calligraphy 286, 662, 1665
    756, *Making a quill pen*, p. 85
    1244, *Creative lettering*, p. 30

The following books were indexed by chapter:

5, *Go out and play! Favorite outdoor games from KaBOOM!* (Candlewick 2012)

17, *My art book.* (DK Publishing, 2011)

104, *The kids' guide to classic games.* (Capstone Press, 2009)

199, *The adventurous boy's handbook.* (Skyhorse Publishing, 2009)

200, *The adventurous girl's handbook: for ages 9 to 99.* (Skyhorse Publishing, 2009)

217, *The daring book for girls.* (Collins, 2007)

218, *The pocket daring book for girls: things to do.* (Collins, 2008)

363, *The games book.* (Scholastic, 2009)

441, *The boys' book: how to be the best at everything.* (Scholastic, 2007)

498, *The girls' book: how to be the best at everything.* (Scholastic, 2007)

755, *The dangerous book for boys.* (Collins, 2007)

756, *The pocket dangerous book for boys: things to do.* (Collins, 2008)

1244, *Crafty activities: over 50 fun and easy things to make.* (Search Press, 2007)

1504, *Show off: how to do absolutely everything one step at a time.* (Candlewick Press, 2009)

The books indexed for this volume fall into four broad categories; Arts and Crafts, Social Science, Sports and Recreation, and Science and Technology. The Arts and Crafts titles include those tasks in which there is a tangible output, where making something is the primary purpose. Conversely, Sports and Recreation books are those where the output is physical (as in any sport) or mental (as in games). Science and Technology includes projects of a broad nature, while science experiments, indexed separately, are focused on methods and results. The index of science experiment books provides full titles, giving quick access for users seeking specific topics.

This volume contains several sections in order to provide the user with the greatest amount of access to the material: Subject Headings, Subject Index, Bibliography, Titles by Series, and Keyword Index.

The list of **Subject Headings** provides a compact, browsable list of topics used in the index.

The **Subject Index** is an expanded list of Subject Headings, with numbers of relevant books corresponding to the Bibliography. In instances where there is relevant information in a title that was indexed by chapter, that information is provided below the main list of book numbers. In this case, the book number is provided, followed by the chapter name in italics and the page number.

The **Bibliography** is a comprehensive list of all titles indexed. Organized alphabetically, books without personal authors are listed first by title. Each entry includes basic bibliographic information (author, title, publication information, and ISBN), as well as series, grade level, and basic contents when available. The targeted grade levels include lower elementary (K–3rd grade), elementary (3rd–6th grade), middle school (6th–9th grade), and high school (9th grade and above). While every effort was made to provide accurate age groups, many titles span a group of ages and are indicated as such. Users are encouraged to preview titles before purchasing to ensure age-appropriateness.

Bibliographic entries also include a series title when applicable. Publishers create series based on a wide range of parameters that can include subject, page layout, instructional design, or a combination of any of these. The list of Titles by Series located at the back of the book can be used to investigate a general subject further or to find books of a similar format or age level.

Finally, whenever available, an adapted list of relevant contents is provided in the bibliographic list. For brevity, content references to introductions, glossaries, and indexes have been removed. An index to select keywords is at the end of the text to provide access to even more specific subjects than is allowed through the index.

The list of **Titles by Series** allows the user to find other titles listed in the Bibliography that are within the same series. Since series can be based upon multiple factors, not all titles within one series may meet the parameters for inclusion in this book. Therefore, users are encouraged to check with the series publisher for more titles within the series. Some series and individual titles have both U.S. and U.K. publishers. Whenever possible the U.S. edition was included. U.K. titles were included when there was no U.S. alternative or when they covered a unique topic.

The **Keyword Index** is provided to give users additional access to topics by listing important keywords from the titles and available contents.

Following this Introduction is "Makerspaces and How-To Projects," which discusses this growing movement that emphasizes everything from arts and crafts to tinkering, experimenting, and creative thinking. How-to books are invaluable to librarians collaborating with patrons in makerspaces, but sometimes technology moves faster than the publishing cycle. This section recommends some useful resources.

Makerspaces and How-To Projects

Makerspaces are community-oriented workspaces, often library-based, that allow people to share knowledge and collaborate on creative projects that often involve computers, technology, science, art, and crafts. One of the advantages of makerspaces is the ability they afford to librarians to offer passive programming, or programming that needs little or no supervision. As the popularity of makerspaces grows, librarians are looking for activities that will make these areas attractive to a wide range of patrons, particularly youth.

This guide to how-to books for K–12 students provides a wealth of ideas for activities that can be offered in makerspaces and the materials that may be needed there. Popular options such as fashion, building and woodworking, stamping and printing, drawing, scrapbooking, and environmental projects are all covered here. Books for K–12 students on newer technologies such as 3-D printing tend to focus more on exciting finished projects than on step-by-step instructions. Therefore, librarians may find magazines and the Internet a rewarding source for learning more about these new technologies.

The following is a selected list of resources that focus on the how-to aspects of makerspaces, some articles of interest to librarians setting up makerspaces, and examples of makerspaces for kids. The potential for using how-to books in identifying activities for makerspaces is rich and it is our desire that this guide will facilitate in the planning of these spaces.

BOOKS

BAGLEY, CAITLIN. *Makerspaces: Top Trailblazing Projects, a LITA Guide.* ALA TechSource (2014). ISBN: 978-1-55570-990-7.
A sourcebook for makerspaces around the United States, this text includes a discussion of the movement, considerations that need to be undertaken prior to beginning one, and profiles of exemplary makerspaces.

WEB SITES

Edutopia

http://www.edutopia.org/

> "Designing a School Makerspace" by Jennifer Cooper is just one of the useful posts on the Education Trends blog. Another is "Teaching Physics with Felt" by Mary Beth Hertz, an account of integrating LEDs into a sewing project.

Instructables

http://www.instructables.com/

> Want to design 3-D printed glasses? Or a 3-D printed toy car? Instructables gives clear, illustrated instructions for everything from these to building a treehouse and using wooden pallets in a variety of inventive projects.

LEGO®

http://education.lego.com/

> LEGO® is popular in many makerspaces, but there are not many books for K–12 students showing step-by-step instructions for LEGO® projects. At this site you will find downloadable instructions for building projects suitable for preschool, lower primary, upper primary, and secondary students.

Make it @ your library

http://makeitatyourlibrary.org/

> With sections focusing on ages 1 to 10, 11 to 18, and adults, this is a rich and well-organized collection of makerspace projects. A recent visit featured items ranging from recycled paper baskets, tie-dyed Easter eggs, and DIY body scrub to a simple sail car, a water rocket, a vibrobot, and 3-D scanning with Skanect.

MakerKids

http://www.makerkids.ca/about/

> MakerKids is a nonprofit agency based in Toronto, Canada, that offers workshop space, materials, and programming for youth. The website is a helpful place to find out more about the wide-ranging possibilities of the makerspace movement.

Makerspace

http://makerspace.com/

> With a blog, a free *Makerspace Playbook*, and a directory of makerspaces around the world, this site provides links to many successful ideas.

Makerspaces

http://youthserviceslibrarianship.wikispaces.com/Makerspaces

> Part of the Youth Services Librarianship wiki, this is an extensive and growing article on makerspaces, programming, and projects for youth in libraries. It also includes ideas on funding such projects.

Pinterest

http://www.pinterest.com/ebrpl/makerspace/

> Many of the projects here can be found elsewhere, but this site provides a starting place for students seeking interesting ideas and step-by-step instructions.

MAGAZINES AND JOURNALS

"Low Tech, High Gains: Starting a Maker Program Is Easier Than You Think." By Karyn M. Peterson. *School Library Journal* (Oct. 10, 2013). Accessed May 17, 2014, at http://www.thedigitalshift.com/2013/10/k-12/low-tech-high-gains-knitting-arts-and-crafts-bike-repair-anyingall-are-maker-activities/.

> A brief article stressing that makerspaces need not be high-tech lab affairs and that the spirit of DIY and learning is more important. Includes examples of key activities and of sources of inspiration.

Make:

http://makezine.com/

> Robotics, high-tech DIY, drones, and 3-D printing are among the topics explored in recent issues of this magazine. The website details projects in the areas of electronics, workshop, craft, science, home, and art and design. The Maker Shed sells tools, kits, books, and other items, and a blog regularly discusses topics of interest to K–12 educators. *Craft:* magazine is a sister product.

"Makerspaces in the School Library Learning Commons and the uTEC Maker Model." By David B. Loertscher, Leslie Preddy, and Bill Derry. *Teacher Librarian* (Dec. 2013), pp. 48–51.

> Discusses the new makerspace movement and the benefits of the uTEC (using, tinkering, experimenting, and creating) approach to creative thinking.

"Manufacturing Makerspaces." *American Libraries* (Feb. 6, 2013). Accessed May 16, 2014, at http://www.americanlibrariesmagazine.org/article/manufacturing-makerspaces.

> As well as looking at three successful makerspace models, this article includes an interview with writer Cory Doctorow and a list of "Cool Stuff to Outfit Your Makerspace."

Subject Headings

General works always precede more specific topics. Otherwise, topics are in alphabetical order.

ARTS AND CRAFTS

General arts & crafts books
- Fantasy and mythology
- Holidays and celebrations
  - General celebrations
  - Birthday
  - Christmas
  - Easter
  - Father's Day
  - Halloween
  - Hanukkah
  - Independence Day
  - Kwanzaa
  - Mother's Day
  - Thanksgiving
  - Valentine's Day
- Pets
- Seasonal
- Transportation and machinery

Bookmaking

Building toys and models

Calligraphy

Candlemaking

Collage

Cooking
- General works
- Baking and desserts
- Holidays and celebrations
  - General celebrations
  - Christmas

Halloween
Thanksgiving
International
- Africa and the Middle East
  - Afghanistan
  - Egypt
  - Ethiopia
  - Kenya
  - South Africa
- Asia
  - General works
  - China
  - India
  - Indonesia
  - Japan
  - Korea
- Australia
- Europe
  - General works
  - France
  - Germany
  - Ireland
  - Italy
  - Scandinavia
  - Spain
- The Americas
  - Brazil
  - Caribbean
  - Chile
  - Cuba
  - Mexico

Peru
United States
Snacks
Special diets
Themed menus
Vegetarian
Décor
Drawing
General works
Animals and nature
General works
Dinosaurs and reptiles
Insects
Mammals
General works
Cats
Dogs
Farm animals
Horses
Nature
Sea life
Cartoons and graphic novels
Fantasy and mythology
Fashion
Historical people and landmarks
Holidays and celebrations
Christmas
Halloween
Independence Day
Thanksgiving
Licensed characters
Disney
Other licensed characters
Manga and anime
People
Transportation and machinery
Duct tape
Eco-crafts
Fashion and accessories
General works
Accessories
Clothing
Fashion
Hair, teeth, and nails
Shoes
Fiber arts
General works
Applique
Batik

Crocheting
Felting
Knitting
Needlework
Quilting
Sewing
Jewelry and beading
Beading
Jewelry
Masks
Painting
Paper crafts
General works
Card making
Holidays and celebrations
Chinese New Year
Christmas
Day of the Dead
Easter
Halloween
Independence Day
Kwanzaa
Mardi Gras
Thanksgiving
Valentine's Day
Origami and kirigami
Paper folding
Paper making
Papier-mâché
Pop-ups
Party crafts and planning
Photography
Puppets
Scrapbooking

Sculpture
General works
Clay
Mosaics
Sand
Wood
Stamping and printing
Writing and research
Electronic publishing
Nonfiction
Research
Writing
Fiction and poetry

Graphic novels and comic books
Mechanics
Nonfiction
Other types of writing

SOCIAL SCIENCE

General works
Chronological subdivisions
   Age of exploration
   American Civil War
   American Revolution
   Colonial America
   Medieval times
   Pioneers
   United States
      19th century
      20th century
   Wild West
Cultural groups
   Ancient China
   Ancient Egypt
   Ancient Greece
   Ancient India
   Ancient Islam
   Ancient Japan
   Ancient Rome
   Arab American
   Asian American
   Aztecs
   Celts
   Inca
   Indian
   Inuit
   Knights
   Maya
   Mesopotamian
   Native American
   Pirates
   Vikings
Geographical subdivisions
   Africa
   China
   Japan
   Mexico
   North America
   South America
   United States

SPORTS AND RECREATION

Archery
Assorted skills and hobbies
   General works
   Animal skills and training
   Balloon twisting
   Darts
   Jumping rope
   Noise making
   Palm reading
   Skipping stones
   Yo-yos
Badminton
Baseball
Basketball
Boating
   Canoeing and kayaking
   Navigation
   Rowing
   Sailing
Bowling
Codes and cyphers
Cricket
Cycling
Dance
   Choreography
   Folk and traditional dances
   Individual dances
      Ballet
      Capoeira
      Contemporary
      Modern dance
      Tap
   Partner or group dances
      Ballroom
      Contemporary
      Modern dance
Entrepreneurship
Fencing
First aid and rescue
Football
Games (indoor)
   General works
   Chess and checkers
   Deciders
   Party games
   Singing and circle games

String, card, and paper games
Word and memory games
Games (outdoor)
    General works
    Ball and throwing games
    Chasing and hiding games
    Circle games
    Jump rope
    Kites
    Other physical games
    Race games
    Sidewalk games
    Team games
Golf
Gymnastics
Health, fitness and exercise
    Beginning fitness
    Healthy living
    Running and general fitness
    Sports training
Hockey
Horsemanship
Juggling
Lacrosse
Magic, pranks, and tricks
    General works
    Mind tricks
    Pranks and practical jokes
    Small tricks and sleight of hand
        General works
        Card tricks
        Coin tricks
        Other small tricks
    Stand-up magic and illusions
        General works
        Illusions
Martial arts
    General works
    Aikido
    Judo and jujitsu
    Karate
    Kendo
    Kickboxing
    Kung fu
    Tae kwon do
Motocross
Music writing
Musical instruments

General instruments (performance)
    Brass
    Percussion
    Strings
    Winds
Netball
Paintball
Pilates
Rugby
Self-defense
Skateboarding
Skiing, skating, and snowboarding
    Skating
    Skiing
Soccer
Softball
Swimming and water sports
    Jumping, diving, and snorkeling
    Swimming
    Water games and sports
    Water safety
Tai chi
Tennis
Theater and performance
    General works
    Costumes and make-up
    Performance skills
    Props, illusions, and staging
    Sound and music
Track and field
Video production
Volleyball
Wilderness and survival skills
    General works
    Campfires and activities
    Camping and shelters
    Climbing and rappelling
    Cooking and finding food and water
    Fishing
        General works
        Catfish
        Fly fishing
        Freshwater fishing
        Ice fishing
        Saltwater
    Hiking and orienteering
    Hunting, tracking, and shooting

Orienteering
Ropework
Survival skills
Wrestling
Yoga

SCIENCE AND TECHNOLOGY

General works
  Science projects
Anatomy, physiology, and nutrition
  Genetics
    Science projects
  Science projects
  Senses
Astronomy
  Science projects
Biology
  Science projects
Botany
  General works
    Science projects
  Gardening
Chemistry
  General works
    Science projects
  Food science
    Science projects
  Water
    Science projects
Engineering
  General works
    Science projects
  Electrical
  Mechanical
    Science projects
  Robotics
    Science projects
  Structural
Environment, conservation, and recycling
  General works
    Science projects
  Conservation and sustainability
    Science projects
  Ecosystems and lifecycles

Science projects
  Recycling
Forensics and criminology
  Science projects
Geography
Geology
  General works
    Science projects
  Natural disasters
    Science projects
  Rocks and minerals
    Science projects
  Soil and erosion
    Science projects
  Water
    Science projects
Mathematics
  Science projects
Physics
  General works
    Science projects
  Electricity and magnetism
    Science projects
  Energy and heat
    Science projects
  Force and motion
    Science projects
  Light, optics, and sound
    Science projects
  Weather
    Science projects
Zoology
  General works
    Science projects
  Dinosaurs
  Fish and amphibians
    Science projects
  Insects
    Science projects
  Invertebrates
    Science projects
  Mammals
    Science projects
  Reptiles and birds
    Science projects

Subject Index

SOCIAL SCIENCE BOOKS

755, *First aid*, p. 129

Football 6, 388, 584, 600, 1072, 1559

Games (indoor)

    General works 1290

        756, *Games*, p. 1

    Chess and checkers 359, 793, 1017, 1660

        755, *The game of chess*, p. 233

    Deciders

        104, *Rock, paper, scissors*, p. 11

        363, *Dips*, p. 8

        363, *Rock, paper, scissors*, p. 12

        363, *Spuds*, p. 11

    Party games

        5, *Dance freeze*, p. 81

        5, *Follow the leader*, p. 80

        5, *Limbo*, p. 84

        5, *Rhythm detective*, p. 82

        5, *Scavenger hunt*, p. 38

        5, *Simon says*, p. 79

        5, *Sleeping lions*, p. 78

        104, *Coin collector*, p. 18

        104, *Sculptor*, p. 17

        104, *Spiderweb*, p. 10

        218, *Slumber party games*, p. 102

        363, *Adder's nest*, p. 40

        363, *Charades*, p. 22

        363, *Follow the leader*, p. 36

        363, *Hotter, colder*, p. 17

        363, *Musical bumps*, p. 31

        363, *Musical chairs*, p. 26

        363, *Musical statues*, p. 31

        363, *Simon says*, p. 28

        363, *Sleeping lions*, p. 21

        363, *Sly fox*, p. 34

        363, *Statues*, p. 30

        363, *Wink murder*, p. 19

    Singing and circle games

        218, *Handclap games*, p. 223

        363, *In and out the dusty bluebells*, p. 87

        363, *Kingy*, p. 94

        363, *Knots*, p. 89

        363, *Pat-a-cake*, p. 50

        363, *Queenie*, p. 92

        363, *Sevens*, p. 98

    String, card, and paper games

        104, *Box it up*, p. 6

        104, *Old maid*, p. 16

        104, *Paper football*, p. 26

        104, *Ping pong soccer*, p. 19

Chasing and hiding games

Circle games

Jump rope

218, *Chinese jump rope*, p. 25
218, *Double Dutch jump rope*, p. 27
218, *Hopscotch, tetherball, jump rope*, p. 32
363, Chinese jump rope 46
363, *Double Dutch*, p. 48

Kites

498, *How to make a kite*, p. 10
1504, *Design a kite*, p. 81
1504, *Fly a kite*, p. 82

Other physical games

5, *Giant dominoes*, p. 83
5, *Hop 'n' freeze*, p. 76
5, *Leapfrog*, p. 77
5, *Spinning statues*, p. 75
104, *Ringer*, p. 24
363, *Leapfrog*, p. 42
1504, *Hang a tire swing*, p. 222

Race games

5, *Egg and spoon race*, p. 66
5, *Mother may I?*, p. 70
5, *Obstacle course*, p. 67
5, *Red light, green light*, p. 65
5, *Run if*, p. 71
5, *Sack race*, p. 64
5, *What time is it, Mr. Wolf?*, p. 68
363, *What time is it, Mr. Fox?*, p. 38

Sidewalk games

5, *Four square*, p. 50
5, *Hopscotch*, p. 48
5, *Snail*, p. 51
217, *Hopscotch*, p. 118
218, *Four square*, p. 19
218, *Hopscotch, tetherball, jump rope*, p. 32
218, *Jacks*, p. 260
363, *Hopscotch*, p. 44
363, *Jacks*, p. 52
363, *Marbles*, p. 54
755, *Marbles*, p. 27
756, *Conkers*, p. 145
756, *Marbles*, p. 158

Team games

5, *Big base kickball*, p. 40
5, *Capture the flag*, p. 39
5, *Crab soccer*, p. 43
5, *Pony express*, p. 44
5, *Red rover*, p. 42
5, *Steal the bacon*, p. 45
104, *Red rover*, p. 15
104, *Tug of war*, p. 20

Campfires and activities 216, 437, 849

Camping and shelters 267, 776, 810, 994, 1014, 1459, 1526

Climbing and rappelling 269, 1048, 1285

Cooking and finding food and water

Fishing

    General works 495, 888, 1042, 1252, 1336, 1461, 1510, 1638

Insects 1205, 1327, 1539, 1666
  Science projects 626, 629, 1023, 1692
Invertebrates
  Science projects 846
Mammals 682, 1538
  Science projects 1231
Reptiles and birds 364, 1651
  Science projects 845

SCIENCE EXPERIMENT BOOKS

General science experiment books

The book of potentially catastrophic science: 50 experiments for daring young scientists, 323

The book of totally irresponsible science: 64 daring experiments for young scientists, 324

The brilliant book of experiments, 685

Cool spy supplies: fun top secret science projects, 101

Eat your science homework: recipes for inquiring minds, 1063

The everything kids' easy science experiments book: explore the world of science through quick and fun experiments, 1112

Fire bubbles and exploding toothpaste: more unforgettable experiments that make science fun, 1484

46 science fair projects for the evil genius, 177

Gross science projects, 1654

Janice VanCleave's big book of play and find out science projects: easy activities for young childen, 1624

Material world: the science of matter, 697

Mythbusters: confirm or bust! Science fair book #2, 1019

Mythbusters science fair book, 1018

Naked eggs and flying potatoes: unforgettable experiments that make science fun, 1485

101 hands-on experiments, 1223

Plant and animal science fair projects, revised and expanded using the scientific method, 238

Potato chip science: 29 incredible experiments, 865

The science behind magic science projects, 554

Science experiments that surprise and delight, 109

Science rocks!, 615

See for yourself: more than 100 amazing experiments for science fairs and school projects, 311

Super science lab: bright ideas, 656

Time for kids big book of science experiments, 19

Yikes! Wow! Yuck! fun experiments for your first science fair, 684

Anatomy, physiology, and nutrition

Ace your exercise and nutrition science project: great science fair ideas, 522

Ace your food science project: great science fair ideas, 523

Ace your human biology science project: great science fair ideas, 525

Chemistry science fair projects using inorganic stuff, revised and expanded using the scientific method, 537

Cool dry ice devices: fun science projects with dry ice, 738

Crazy concoctions: a mad scientist's guide to messy mixture, 211

Environmental chemistry, 414

Junior scientists: experiment with liquids, 1161

Junior scientists: experiment with solids, 637

Kitchen chemistry, 477

Kitchen science experiments: how does your mold garden grow? 60

Organic chemistry science fair projects, revised and expanded using the scientific method, 549

Plastics and polymers science fair projects, revised and expanded using the scientific method, 612

Science experiments that explode and implode, 1655

Science experiments that fizz and bubble, 1656

Science experiments with food, 871

Science experiments with liquid, 873

Solids, liquids, and gases experiments using water, air, marbles, and more: one hour or less science experiments, 558

Step-by-step experiments with matter, 647

Step-by-step science experiments in chemistry, 1627

Super cool science experiments: compounds and mixtures, 1444

Super cool science experiments: water, 1446

Super simple things to do with water: fun and easy science for kids, 396

Why is milk white? And 200 other curious chemistry questions, 312

Engineering and computer science

Computer science experiments, 1639

Cool distance assistants: fun science projects to propel things, 737

Electric motor experiments, 1467

The physics of toys and games science projects, 551

Radio-controlled car experiments, 1469

Robot experiments, 1470

Science experiments that fly and move, 945

Simple experiments with inclined planes, 1214

Simple experiments with pulleys, 1215

Simple experiments with wheels and axles, 1216

Simple machine experiments using seesaws, wheels, pulleys, and more: one hour or less science experiments, 555

Step-by-step experiments with simple machines, 648

Stomp rockets, catapults, and kaleidoscopes: 30+ amazing science projects you can build for less than $1, 516

Super simple things to do with balloons: fun and easy science for kids, 391

Wheels! Science projects with bicycles, skateboards, and skates, 614

Environment, conservation, and recycling

Ace your ecology and environmental science project: great science fair ideas, 521

Air: green science projects for a sustainable planet, 533

Physics: General works

Ace your physical science project: great science fair ideas, 527

Energy experiments using ice cubes, springs, magnets, and more: one hour or less science experiments, 541

Matter and materials, 1105

Motion, magnets and more: the big book of primary physical science, 1038

Super cool science experiments: states of matter, 1165

Super simple things to do with bubbles: fun and easy science for kids, 392

Physics: Electricity and magnetism

Electricity and magnetism experiments using batteries, bulbs, wires, and more: one hour or less science experiments, 539

Electricity and magnetism science fair projects, revised and expanded using the scientific method, 540

Electricity and magnets, 45

Experiments with electricity and magnetism, 1676

Explore electricity! With 25 great projects, 1622

How to make a universe with 92 ingredients: an electrifying guide to the elements, 385

Junior scientists: experiment with magnets, 1541

Science experiments with magnets, 874

Step-by-step experiments with electricity, 645

Step-by-step experiments with magnets, 646

Super cool science experiments: electricity, 978

Super cool science experiments: magnets, 1543

Physics: Energy and heat

Catch the wind harness the sun: 22 super-charged science projects for kids, 237

Energy: green science projects for a sustainable planet, 542

Experiments with heat and energy, 1015

Hot stuff: the science of heat and cold, 695

Junior scientists: experiment with heat, 976

Junior scientists: experiment with solar energy, 1542

Solar cell and renewable energy experiments, 1471

Step-by-step science experiments in energy, 1630

Super cool science experiments: solar energy, 1544

Super simple things to do with temperature: fun and easy science for kids, 395

Physics: Force and motion

Ace your forces and motion science project: great science fair ideas, 524

Ace your sports science project: great science fair ideas, 610

Cool gravity activities: fun science projects about balance, 739

Experiments with force and motion, 1616

Forces and motion, 46

Goal! Science projects with soccer, 611

Home run! Science projects with baseball and softball, 178

Motion, 925

The physics of sports science projects, 550

Push and pull: the science of forces, 698

Bibliography

1   *Button crafts*. 2009, American Girl (ISBN: 9781593695774).

   GRADE LEVEL: Elementary

   CONTENTS: Button tops—shoe jewelry—socks—barrettes—bangles—bobby blooms—stack ring—earrings—button bag—necklace—necklace—button chain—cushions—art station—lamp shade—on-off buttons—clips—bulletin buttons—picture perfect—trendy trash—button greetings—button bags—key chain—theme tins—ornaments—flowers

2   *Cook it step by step*. 2013, DK (ISBN: 9781409366225). 128 p.

   GRADE LEVEL: Upper elementary

   CONTENTS: Eggy bread—four ways with eggs—fruity cereal—fruit smoothies—fruit bars—tomato and couscous salad—tuna and bean salad—picnic salad—tomato soup—butternut squash soup—basic bread—Italian bread—sunflower loaves—cornbread—pizza dough—four ways with pizzas—club sandwich—pitta pockets—vegetable platter—four ways with starters—lamb hotspot—sausage hotspot—beef pasta—fresh tomato pasta—vegetable lasagna—rice balls—jambalaya—potato salad—fishcakes—mashed potato pies—chilli con carne—mini-burgers—BBQ chicken—four ways with kebabs—vegetable tart—tomato and aubergine layers—four ways with sauces—mixed bean stir-fry—rainbow beef—marinated chicken—four ways with roast vegetables—roast chicken—griddled chicken—strawberry tarts—four ways with cookies—cupcakes—sponge—gingerbread—brownies—carrot and orange muffins—frozen yogurt—mint chocolate pots—fridge cake—meringues—blueberry cherry—oaty crumble—planning a party—a three-course meal—picnic

3   *Craft sale: earn money making and selling fun easy crafts*. 2008, American Girl (ISBN: 9781593693442).

   SERIES: American Girl do-it yourself

   GRADE LEVEL: Elementary

   CONTENTS: Bitty bobbies—flowers—garden greetings—bookmark—pencils—cat grass—tacks—something fishy—coasters—button bugs—books—scrunchies—rings—going batty—frames—candy cane forest—gifts—charms—pencil toppers—photo clips

4   *Faith, food, & fun: a Faithgirlz cookbook*. 2012, Zonderkidz (ISBN: 9780310723165).

GRADE LEVEL: Upper elementary – middle school

CONTENTS: Munchies—drinks—salads—main courses—sweets—holidays

5 *Go out and play! Favorite outdoor games from KaBOOM!* 2012, Candlewick (ISBN 9780763655303.). 96 p.

GRADE LEVEL: Elementary

CONTENTS: N/A

6 *How to—football: a step-step guide to mastering the skills.* 2011, DK (ISBN: 9781405363389).

SERIES: How to—

GRADE LEVEL: Upper elementary

CONTENTS: N/A

7 *How to—soccer: a step-by-step guide to mastering the skills.* 2011, DK (ISBN: 9780756675813).

SERIES: How to—

GRADE LEVEL: Upper elementary

CONTENTS: Ball control—dribbling—passing—crossing the ball—clean tackle—defending—heads up—shooting—attacking—safe hands—super save—distribution—teamwork—playing as a team—dead ball—tricks and turns

8 *Just add water: science projects you can sink, squirt, splash, sail.* 2008, Children's Press (ISBN: 9780531185452). 32p.

SERIES: Experiment with science

GRADE LEVEL: Upper elementary – middle school

CONTENTS: Hard or soft—meltdown—liquid—boat—fish—volcano—drip—humidity—rainmaker

9 *Learn to draw Disney celebrated characters collection: including your Disney/Pixar favorites!* 2009, Walter Foster (ISBN: 9781600581441). 143 p.

SERIES: Learn to draw

GRADE LEVEL: Upper elementary – middle school

CONTENTS: Mickey Mouse and his friends—Winnie the Pooh—the world of Cars—Ratatouille—favorite Disney-Pixar characters—Wall-E—Finding Nemo—Lilo and Stitch—The Lion King

10 *Learn to draw Disney princesses: favorite princesses featuring Tiana, Cinderella, Ariel, Snow White, Belle and other characters!* 2010, Walter Foster (ISBN: 9781600581458). 144 p.

SERIES: Learn to draw

GRADE LEVEL: Upper elementary – middle school

CONTENTS: N/A

11 *Learn to draw Disney/Pixar Cars: draw your favorite characters, step by simple step.* 2012, Walter Foster (ISBN: 9781936309320). 32 p.

SERIES: Learn to draw

GRADE LEVEL: Upper elementary – middle school

CONTENTS: N/A

12   *Learn to draw Disney/Pixar Toy Story*. 2010, Walter Foster (ISBN: 9781600581892). 32 p.
   SERIES: Learn to draw
   GRADE LEVEL: Upper elementary – middle school
   CONTENTS: N/A

13   *Learn to draw Disney/Pixar Toy Story: featuring favorite characters from Toy Story 2 and Toy Story 3!* 2011, Walter Foster (ISBN: 9781936309009). 32 p.
   GRADE LEVEL: Upper elementary – middle school
   CONTENTS: N/A

14   *Learn to draw Disney/Pixar WALL-E*. 2008, Walter Foster (ISBN: 9781600580765). 32 p.
   SERIES: Learn to draw
   GRADE LEVEL: Upper elementary – middle school
   CONTENTS: N/A

15   *Learn to draw the fairies of Pixie Hollow*. 2011, Walter Foster (ISBN: 9781936309054). 31 p.
   SERIES: Learn to draw
   GRADE LEVEL: Upper elementary – middle school
   CONTENTS: N/A

16   *Learn to draw your favorite Disney/Pixar characters*. 2011, Walter Foster (ISBN: 9781936309221). 32 p.
   SERIES: Learn to draw
   GRADE LEVEL: Upper elementary – middle school
   CONTENTS: N/A

17   *My art book*. 2011, DK (ISBN 9780756675820.). 80 p.
   GRADE LEVEL: Elementary
   CONTENTS: N/A

18   *Tiana's cookbook: recipes for kids*. 2009, Disney Press (ISBN: 9781423125402).
   GRADE LEVEL: Upper elementary
   CONTENTS: Beignets—egg in a nest—coffee cake—banana French toast—muffuletta sandwich—po'boy sandwich—PB&J blossom sandwiches—fruit salad—jambalaya—gumbo—red beans and rice—chicken and biscuits—fish fillets—macaroni and cheese—skillet cornbread—green beans—potato wedges—swamp-water smoothie—minty iced tea—juleps—sugar cookies—cupcakes—mud pie—alligator cake—cobbler—bread pudding

19   *Time for kids big book of science experiments*. 2011, Time for Kids Books (ISBN: 9781603208932). 192 p.
   GRADE LEVEL: Elementary
   CONTENTS: N/A

20   **ADAMS, I.** *Drumming*. 2012, PowerKids Press (ISBN: 9781448852840). 32 p.
   SERIES: Master this!

GRADE LEVEL: Upper elementary – middle school

CONTENTS: Types of drum kit—drumming equipment—setting up—sitting and gripping—theory and rhythm—building up rhythms—drumming rudiments—coordination basics—top techniques—grooves and styles—rhythms

21 **ADAMSON, T. *Bowhunting*.** 2011, Capstone (ISBN: 9781429648080). 32 p.
    SERIES: Wild outdoors
    GRADE LEVEL: Lower elementary
    CONTENTS: On the hunt—be prepared—skills and techniques—safety—take on the challenge

22 **ADAMSON, T. *Deer hunting*.** 2011, Capstone (ISBN: 9781429648073). 32 p.
    SERIES: Wild outdoors
    GRADE LEVEL: Lower elementary
    CONTENTS: Waiting for the right shot—equipment—skills and techniques—safety—outdoor adventure

23 **ADAMSON, T. *Duck hunting*.** 2011, Capstone (ISBN: 9781429648097). 32 p.
    SERIES: Wild outdoors
    GRADE LEVEL: Lower elementary
    CONTENTS: Take aim—getting ready—skills and techniques—be safe—bag some duck

24 **AIKINS, D. *Watch me draw Dora's favorite adventures*.** 2012, Walter Foster (ISBN: 9781936309764). 24 p,
    SERIES: Watch me draw
    GRADE LEVEL: Upper elementary
    CONTENTS: N/A

25 **AIKMAN, L. *Pilates step-by-step*.** 2011, Rosen Central (ISBN: 9781448815494). 96 p.
    SERIES: Skills in motion
    GRADE LEVEL: Upper elementary – middle school
    CONTENTS: First connection—creating energy—core dynamics—final release

26 **AKASS, S. *My quilting book: 35 easy and fun quilting, patchwork, and applique projects for children aged 7 years+*.** 2012, Cico Kidz (ISBN: 9781908170842).
    GRADE LEVEL: Upper elementary – middle school
    CONTENTS: Kitty purse—iPod holder—braid bracelets—pencil case—phone case—brooch—hairband—pendant—pencil roll—recorder bag—wooden-handled bag—scarf—drawstring bag—sachet—jewelry basket—bunting—pet toy—summer quilt—appliqué cushion—needle case—pincushion—sleepover roll—wall hanging—hot water bottle cover—flower—doll's pillow—patchwork purse—ribbon and button lavender bags—egg cozy—trivet—notebook cover—doll's quilt—mug cover—peg doll sleeping bag—Valentine's day heart

27 **ALDERTON, D. *How to look after your guinea pig: a practical guide to caring for your pet, in step-by-step photographs*.** 2012, Armadillo (ISBN: 9781843227687). 20 p.
    GRADE LEVEL: Elementary
    CONTENTS: N/A

28   **ALDERTON, D.** *How to look after your pet dog: a practical guide to caring for your pet, in step-by-step photographs*. 2012, Armadillo (ISBN: 9781843228394). 20 p.
GRADE LEVEL: Elementary
CONTENTS: N/A

29   **ALEXANDER, C.** *Difficult origami*. 2009, Capstone (ISBN: 9781429620222). 32 p.
SERIES: Origami
GRADE LEVEL: Elementary
CONTENTS: N/A

30   **ALEXANDER, C.** *Sort-of-difficult origami*. 2009, Capstone (ISBN: 9781429620239). 32 p.
SERIES: Origami
GRADE LEVEL: Elementary
CONTENTS: Fox mask—waterbomb—ornament—tulip and stem—Masu box and insert

31   **ALEXANDER, H.** *Easy desserts from around the world*. 2012, Enslow (ISBN: 9780766037656). 48 p.
SERIES: Easy cookbooks for kids
GRADE LEVEL: Elementary
CONTENTS: Celebration cookies—akwadu/banana coconut bake—apple pie—toscakaka/almond caramel cake—coconut sticky rice with mango—shortbread cookies—strawberries Romanoff—Anzac biscuits—lemon granita—kolaczki cookies—baklava—maple butter tarts—lebkuchen—alfajores

32   **ALEXANDER, H.** *Easy main dishes from around the world*. 2012, Enslow (ISBN: 9780766037663). 48 p.
SERIES: Easy cookbooks for kids
GRADE LEVEL: Elementary
CONTENTS: Köttbollar—sweet and sour shrimp—Jollof rice—spaghetti al pomodoro e basilico—Wiener schnitzel—tacos de pescado—papaya chicken and coconut milk—shepherd's pie—baked fish with bread crumbs—beef or chicken satay—quiche Lorraine

33   **ALEXANDER, H.** *Easy snacks from around the world*. 2012, Enslow (ISBN: 9780766037670). 48 p.
SERIES: Easy cookbooks for kids
GRADE LEVEL: Elementary
CONTENTS: Bruschetta—cold sesame noodles—Caribbean fruit smoothie—tzatziki—banana bread—welsh rarebit—granola bars—guacamole—hummus—paprika cheese sticks—edamame

34   **ALI, D.** *Hands-on history! Ancient India: discover the rich heritage of the Indus Valley and the Mughal Empire, with 15 step-by-step projects and 340 pictures*. 2013, Armadillo (ISBN: 9781843228233). 64 p.
SERIES: Hands-on history!
GRADE LEVEL: Upper elementary
CONTENTS: N/A

35   ALTER, A. *What can you do with an old red shoe? A green activity book about re-use*. 2009, Henry Holt (ISBN: 9780805082906). 32p.

   GRADE LEVEL: Lower elementary

   CONTENTS: Flip-flop—t-shirt—shower curtain—shoe—blanket—berry baskets—odds and ends—tin cans—old crayons—calendar—wrapping paper—toys—sewing tips

36   AMARA, P. *So, you want to be a comic book artist? The ultimate guide on how to break into comics*. 2012, Aladdin (ISBN: 9781582703572).

   GRADE LEVEL: Middle school – high school

   CONTENTS: The studio and tools of the trade—draw—illustration tips and tricks—character creation—creating stellar scripts—putting it all together—copy-shop comics—getting publicity—portfolios—Hollywood directing and video game designing—recommended industry info—comic book terminology

37   AMERICAN ACADEMY OF PEDIATRICS, EDITORS. *BLAST: babysitter lessons and safety training*. 2007, Jones and Bartlett (ISBN: 763735167).

   GRADE LEVEL: Middle school

   CONTENTS: Sitter qualities—prepare to answer questions—be a good guest—ages and stages—safety first—before saying "yes" to a job—important points—strangers—house rules and routines—safety rules—fire—sitter basics: diapering—bottle feeding—burping a baby—spoon feeding a baby or toddler—crying—getting ready for bed—behavior problems—discipline—sitter's checklist—first aid: what to do for an injured or sick child—what is not an emergency—what is an emergency—calling 9-1-1—cpr—choking—bleeding and shock—bone—joint—and muscle injuries—breathing difficulty—burns—diabetic emergencies—diarrhea—dog bite—electrocution—eye injuries—fever—head injuries—insect stings—nosebleed—poisoning—seizures or convulsions—tooth knocked out—vomiting—first aid kit—recommended supplies—sitter's busy bag

38   AMES, L. *Draw 50 princesses: the step-by-step way to draw Snow White, Sleeping Beauty, Cinderella, and many more*. 2008, Broadway Books (ISBN: 9780767927970).

   SERIES: Draw 50

   GRADE LEVEL: Elementary

   CONTENTS: Cinderella – fairy godmother—Cinderella – nasty stepsisters—magic mirror—evil stepmother—glass slipper—royal coach—sire—lost slipper—Sir Lancelot—Guinevere—Lancelittle—dragon—Merlin—magic wand—King Arthur – goblet—ice queen—Native American princess—fairy princess—teenage princess—Eliza—the handmaiden—Snow White—Seven Dwarfs—poisoned apple—royal crown—throne—young princess—castle—Japanese princess—kneeling princess—Romeo – Juliet—warlock—Rapunzel—Princess Lilybet—queen—King Goodhart—lighting—palace jester—dancing prince—squire—lady-in-waiting—frog prince—prince—Indian princess—Queen Nefertiti—Prince Charming—Sleeping Beauty—African princess

39   ANCONA, G. *Capoeira: game! dance! martial art!* 2007, Lee and Low Books (ISBN: 9781584302681).

   GRADE LEVEL: Elementary

   CONTENTS: N/A

40 ANDERSON, J. *The history and activities of ancient China*. 2007, Heinemann (ISBN: 9781403479228). 32 p.
SERIES: Hands-on ancient history
GRADE LEVEL: Elementary
CONTENTS: Moon cakes—abacus—paper—the tiger walk

41 ANDERSON, L. *No-bake gingerbread houses for kids*. 2010, Gibbs Smith (ISBN: 9781423605904).
GRADE LEVEL: Elementary
CONTENTS: Candy cottage—lollipop lane—sweetheart cottage—fairy tree house—bunny house—mermaid palace—cabin—windmill—tiki hut—red barn—bungalow—fire house—chalet—dollhouse—gnome home—igloo—Seven Dwarfs' cottage—haunted mansion—Santa's castle—Dracula's castle—polka-dot house—pink castle

42 ANDERSON, M. *Explore spring! 25 great ways to learn about spring*. 2007, Nomad Press (ISBN: 9780978503741). 96 p.
SERIES: Explore your world
GRADE LEVEL: Upper elementary
CONTENTS: N/A

43 ANDERSON, M. *Explore winter! 25 great ways to learn about winter*. 2007, Nomad Press (ISBN: 9780978503758). 96 p.
SERIES: Explore your world
GRADE LEVEL: Upper elementary
CONTENTS: Science journal—the spin—winter sun—long shadows—how far can you go—hibernation den—how warm is your form—feathers—fat—shoes—camouflage peek—camouflage hide—bird food tracker—menu—ice spikes—water—salt water—salt water study—ice cream—prism—snowflakes—snowflake fossils—sugar crystals—salt crystals—wet snow—toasty snow—barometer—anemometer

44 ANDERSON, M. *Great Civil War projects you can build yourself*. 2012, Nomad Press (ISBN: 9781936749454). 128 p.
SERIES: Build it yourself
GRADE LEVEL: Upper elementary – middle school
CONTENTS: Bugle—drum—pinhole camera—Fort Sumter flag—ironclad ship—lean-to—steamboat—periscope—vittles—telegraph—kepi—fez—handmade paper—quilt block—pillow or wall hanging—corn husk doll—rag doll—molasses taffy—fruit dehydrator—rock candy—fan—tambourine—banjo—railroad lantern

45 ANGLISS, S. *Electricity and magnets*. 2013, Kingfisher (ISBN: 9780753467848). 32 p.
SERIES: Hands-on science
GRADE LEVEL: Upper elementary
CONTENTS: Tingle—wire—thick and thin—go with the flow—powerhouse—the big push—pole to pole—magnetic art—magnets—map—power

46 ANGLISS, S. *Forces and motion*. 2013, Kingfisher (ISBN: 9780753469729). 32 p.
SERIES: Hands-on science
GRADE LEVEL: Upper elementary

CONTENTS: Forces—squeezing and twisting—gravity—balancing—pressure—floating and sinking—faster—measuring—friction—force—gears—motion

47 **ANGLISS, S.** *Sound and light*. 2013, Kingfisher (ISBN: 9780753433683). 32 p.
SERIES: Hands-on science
GRADE LEVEL: Upper elementary
CONTENTS: Sound—light—sound travels—light travels—music and tone—white light—coloured light—hearing sound—seeing light—mirror—bending light—lenses

48 **ANNISS, M.** *Dj-ing*. 2011, PowerKids Press (ISBN: 9781615325962). 32 p.
SERIES: Master this!
GRADE LEVEL: Upper elementary – middle school
CONTENTS: N/A

49 **ANNISS, M.** *Make a podcast!* 2013, Arcturus (ISBN: 9781848585720). 32 p.
SERIES: Find your talent
GRADE LEVEL: Middle school – high school
CONTENTS: Find your talent—the podcast story—what's your big idea?—get the gear—perfect planning—start recording—credit to the edit—from s series—going live—spread the word!—guest stars—vodcast dreams—step up a gear

50 **ANNISS, M.** *Start a band!* 2013, Arcturus (ISBN: 9781848585713). 32 p.
SERIES: Find your talent
GRADE LEVEL: Middle school – high school
CONTENTS: Find your talent—find your inspiration—who do you think you are?—bandmates wanted—band basics—sort the sessions—go your own way—write a bit—going live—get the gig—room for improvement—do a demo—step up a gear

51 **ANNISS, M.** *Start a blog!* 2013, Arcturus (ISBN: 978184409605). 32 p.
SERIES: Find your talent
GRADE LEVEL: Middle school – high school
CONTENTS: Welcome to the blogosphere—blogging for beginners—the plan—start it up—what is it all about?—get the look—find your voice—picture perfect—make it multimedia—we have liftoff—going social

52 **ANTRAM, D.** *How to draw cartoons*. 2011, PowerKids Press (ISBN: 9781448815760). 32 p.
SERIES: How to draw
GRADE LEVEL: Middle school
CONTENTS: Making a start—perspective—drawing tools—materials—drawing a figure—heads—expressions—characters—figure work—figure in costume—monster—rats—bulldog—man on a donkey

53 **ANTRAM, D.** *How to draw fairies*. 2012, PowerKids Press (ISBN: 9781448845132). 32 p.
SERIES: How to draw
GRADE LEVEL: Middle school

CONTENTS: Tools—perspective—fairy fashion—adventurous fairies—naughty fairies—punk fairies—musical fairies—fairy friends—fairy toadstools—flying fairies—fairy godmother—woodland fairies

54   ANTRAM, D. *How to draw fantasy castles*. 2012, PowerKids Press (ISBN: 9781448864614). 32 p.
SERIES: How to draw
GRADE LEVEL: Middle school
CONTENTS: Basic castle—underwater castle—Dracula's castle—ice castle—medieval tower—cliff-top castle—pirate skull castle—fairy tale castle

55   ANTRAM, D. *How to draw pirates*. 2012, PowerKids Press (ISBN: 9781448845156). 32 p.
SERIES: How to draw
GRADE LEVEL: Middle school
CONTENTS: Materials—hats—Blackbeard—flags—pirate trio—buccaneer—ships—pirate with parrot—pirates in action—treasure maps—pirate in the rigging

56   ARETHA, D. *Top 25 baseball skills, tips, and tricks*. 2012, Enslow (ISBN: 9780766038592). 48 p.
SERIES: Top 25 sports skills, tips, and tricks
GRADE LEVEL: Elementary
CONTENTS: N/A

57   ATHA, A. *Fitness for young people: step-by-step*. 2010, Rosen Central (ISBN: 9781435833647). 96 p.
SERIES: Skills in motion
GRADE LEVEL: Upper elementary – middle school
CONTENTS: Fitness—strength and endurance—flexibility

58   ATWOOD, L. *The cookbook for kids: great recipes for kids who love to cook*. 2010, WeldonOwen (ISBN: 9781616280185). 127 p.
GRADE LEVEL: Elementary
CONTENTS: Breakfast—lunch—snacks—sweets

59   BALCHIN, J. *Bumper book of crafty activities*. 2012, Search Press (ISBN: 9781844487935).
GRADE LEVEL: Elementary
CONTENTS: Natural wrapping paper and gift tag—sea monster game—Chinese pencil pot—gecko t-shirt—Aztec birthday card—Egyptian dominoes—modern art socks—mosaic chalk board—Asian cushion—primitve clay picture—rocket birthday card—balloon party invitation—alien door plaque—illuminated bookmark—personlized paper—Snow White poster—hobby box—school project folder—insect greetings card—African mask—knight in armour picture—Indian elephant shoebag—Egyptian eagle necklace—maths biscuit—Grecian coaster—seaside pebble frame—celestial pot—Aztec book cover—Celtic goblet—Indian frame—Native American headdress—Mexican bowl—Gothic mirror—Egyptian cat—Aztec necklace—Roman

box—African pencil pot—origami bases—layered fan—secrets folder—paper penguin—picture frame—Japanese card—obi bookmark—folded flower—space rocket—flapping bird—blow-up box—Nazca birds—fantasy planets—Matisse collage—it's a goal!—spooky wood—funky fish—smiling sunflower—pop-up dinosaur—jazzy guitar—winter window—sea scene—butterflies—Roman mosaic—creepy crawlies—sunflower card—fairy card—junk truck—Egyptian god—leaf card—alien—wobbly pot—fat cat—swinging tiger—flower pot—squiggly bowl—fish tile—treasure box—pencil holder—lion dish—bonsai tree—Indian wall hanging—Egyptian picture frame—fish pen toppers—Native American shaker—gecko key ring—rainbow sun catcher—astronaut puppet—Aztec game—bumble bee spoon—rosy gift box—sun wall hanging—patchwork sweet jar—padlocked money box—tiger paperweight—fruity flower pot—monster egg—Picasso mirror—sparkly birthday card—fancy folder—personal paper—feather bookmarks—magic picture frame—string-along book—funny face lampshade—pulp painting—patterned paper—pirate hat—glider plane—spinning windmill—twisted pot—bat mobile—pleated picture frame—bird and worm card—treasure chest—elephant mask

60 **BARDHAN-QUALLEN, S.** *Kitchen science experiments: how does your mold garden grow?* 2010, Sterling (ISBN: 9781402724138). 64 p.
SERIES: Mad science
GRADE LEVEL: Elementary
CONTENTS: Alive—bacteria—fungus—chemistry

61 **BARDHAN-QUALLEN, S.** *Nature science experiments: what's hopping in a dust bunny?* 2010, Sterling (ISBN: 9781402724121). 64 p.
SERIES: Mad science
GRADE LEVEL: Elementary
CONTENTS: Be a scientist—life—bacteria—protists—mites—worms—carnivorous plants

62 **BARDOS, L.** *Amazing math projects you can build yourself.* 2010, Nomad Press (ISBN: 9781934670583). 128 p.
SERIES: Build it Yourself
GRADE LEVEL: Upper elementary – middle school
CONTENTS: Abacus—dial—fibonacci—ratio—angles—parabola—ellipses—cone—paths—walk—shoelace—polygons—triangles—stars—circles—mobius—solids—tetrahedron—icosahedron—pyramids—domes—hyperboloid—paraboloid—string—bubbles—snowflakes—images—tiling

63 **BARNHART, N.** *Amazing magic tricks.* 2009, Capstone (ISBN: 9781429629164).
GRADE LEVEL: Middle school
CONTENTS: N/A

64 **BARNHART, N.** *Amazing magic tricks: apprentice level.* 2009, Capstone (ISBN: 9781429619431).
SERIES: Magic tricks
GRADE LEVEL: Elementary
CONTENTS: Phoenix balloon—amazing brain-e-o—Ricky the Wonder Rabbit—Happy New Year!—message from a ghost—freaky mind weld—Where's Rover?—amazing sports prediction—magic monster—puzzling puzzle

65   **BARNHART, N.** *Amazing magic tricks: beginner level*. 2009, Capstone (ISBN: 9781429619424).

SERIES: Magic tricks

GRADE LEVEL: Elementary

CONTENTS: Magical sailor's knot—tricky treats—find the magic rabbit—jack—the incredible card—wonderful appearing wand—invisible magic glue—amazing appearing ball—fantastic flower—mysterious car trick—Zarcon, the invisible hero—fast rabbit and the ace

66   **BARNHART, N.** *Amazing magic tricks: expert level*. 2009, Capstone (ISBN: 9781429619455).

SERIES: Magic tricks

GRADE LEVEL: Elementary

CONTENTS: Magic hanky—Sunday comics hero—magic mag-nee-to man—escaping coin—zooming moon rock—tricky leprechaun—multiplying money—mystic snowflake—crazy comical sock—magic penny bank

67   **BARNHART, N.** *Amazing magic tricks: master level*. 2009, Capstone (ISBN: 9781429619448).

SERIES: Magic tricks

GRADE LEVEL: Elementary

CONTENTS: Impossible coin—tricky lizard—magic ace—Tommy—the trained ping-pong ball—number one fan—coin multiplying book—spooky spoon—magic matchbox bank—egg-straordinary egg—healing rope

68   **BARNHART, N.** *Fantastically funny tricks*. 2014, Capstone (ISBN: 9781476501369).

SERIES: Magic manuals

GRADE LEVEL: Upper elementary – middle school

CONTENTS: Make them laugh—have a chip—funny flower—excellent flying eggs—party in a box—washday wonder—ping-pong surprise—phooey shoey—key of mystery—dancing hanky

69   **BARNHART, N.** *Marvelous money tricks*. 2014, Capstone (ISBN: 9781476501345).

SERIES: Magic manuals

GRADE LEVEL: Upper elementary – middle school

CONTENTS: Money magic—Leaping Lincoln—Lucky Leprechaun—a fist full of dollars—mysterious vanishing coin—double your money—the vanishing president—coupon cash-in—big surprise prize—pirate's treasure

70   **BARNHART, N.** *Stunning stage tricks*. 2014, Capstone (ISBN: 9781476501352).

SERIES: Magic manuals

GRADE LEVEL: Upper elementary – middle school

CONTENTS: Stupendous stage magic—Dr. Freeze—Super Magno Man—floating assistant—the teleporting bunny—rainbow hanky—instant vacation—super stretcho—astounding card appearance—the living doll

71   **BARR, G.** *The history and activities of the Islamic Empire*. 2007, Heinemann Library (ISBN: 9781403479266). 32 p.

SERIES: Hands-on ancient history

GRADE LEVEL: Elementary

CONTENTS: Pancakes—tughra—decorate a tray—pachisi

72 **BARTH, K.** *Learning volleyball*. 2007, Meyer & Meyer Verlag (ISBN: 9781841261973). 151 p.
GRADE LEVEL: Middle school – high school
CONTENTS: N/A

73 **BASEL, J.M.** *A Christmas drawing wonderland*. 2014, Capstone (ISBN: 9781476530925). 32 p.
SERIES: Holiday sketchbook
GRADE LEVEL: Elementary
CONTENTS: N/A

74 **BASEL, J.M.** *A Halloween drawing spectacular*. 2014, Capstone (ISBN: 9781476530918). 32 p.
SERIES: Holiday sketchbook
GRADE LEVEL: Elementary
CONTENTS: N/A

75 **BASEL, J.M.** *A Thanksgiving drawing feast*. 2014, Capstone (ISBN: 9781476530932). 32 p.
SERIES: Holiday sketchbook
GRADE LEVEL: Elementary
CONTENTS: N/A

76 **BAUER, H.** *Beethoven for kids: his life and music with 21 activities*. 2011, Chicago Review Press (ISBN: 9781569767115). 144 p.
SERIES: For kids
GRADE LEVEL: Middle school
CONTENTS: Hornbook and quill pen—play blind and bell—your own variation—silhouette picture—Viennese waltz—apple pancakes—letter of introduction—create a CD cover—model eardrum—music critic—thumb piano—sew your own notebook—create music—discover the key—diorama—picture the music—plaster life mask—ear trumpet—sign language—liner notes—how your lungs work

77 **BAUER, H.** *Verdi for kids: his life and music*. 2013, Chicago Review Press (ISBN: 9781613745007). 144 p.
SERIES: For kids
GRADE LEVEL: Middle school
CONTENTS: Listen to a compostion—stained glass window—opera word search—water purifier—read music—CD cover for nabucco—clay map of Italy—sing like a diva—panpipe—write a letter to someone you admire—bocce ball—carnival mask—debate and vote—design and sew a flag—paint a poster—pizza party invitations—tomato sauce garden—sketch a costume design

78 **BAUGH, S.** *Learn to draw Tinker Bell*. 2008, Walter Foster (ISBN: 9781600580581). 31 p.
SERIES: Learn to draw

GRADE LEVEL: Upper elementary – middle school
CONTENTS: N/A

79   **BEAK, N. *How to bend balloons: 25 brilliant ways to bend, fold and twist balloons!***
2013, Armadillo (ISBN: 9781843228646). 64p.
GRADE LEVEL: Upper elementary – middle school
CONTENTS: N/A

80   **BEAUMONT, S. *Drawing Diplodocus and other plant-eating dinosaurs.*** 2010,
PowerKids Press (ISBN: 9781615319022). 32 p.
SERIES: Drawing dinosaurs
GRADE LEVEL: Elementary
CONTENTS: Diplodocus—Iguanodon—Parasaurolophus

81   **BEAUMONT, S. *Drawing dragons and other cold-blooded creatures.*** 2011,
PowerKids Press (ISBN: 9781448833245). 32 p.
SERIES: Drawing legendary monsters
GRADE LEVEL: Elementary
CONTENTS: Dragon—basilisk—Medusa

82   **BEAUMONT, S. *Drawing Giganotosaurus and other giant dinosaurs.*** 2010,
PowerKids Press (ISBN: 9781615319053). 32 p.
SERIES: Drawing dinosaurs
GRADE LEVEL: Elementary
CONTENTS: Giganotosaurus—Spinosaurus—Argentinosaurus

83   **BEAUMONT, S. *Drawing griffins and other winged wonders.*** 2011, PowerKids Press
(ISBN: 9781448832538). 32 p.
SERIES: Drawing legendary monsters
GRADE LEVEL: Elementary
CONTENTS: Pegasus—harpy—griffin

84   **BEAUMONT, S. *Drawing Plesiosaurus and other ocean dinosaurs.*** 2010, PowerKids
Press (ISBN: 9781615319039). 32 p.
SERIES: Drawing dinosaurs
GRADE LEVEL: Elementary
CONTENTS: Plesiosaurus—Ichthyosaurus—Liopleurodon

85   **BEAUMONT, S. *Drawing Pteranodon and other flying dinosaurs.*** 2010, PowerKids
Press (ISBN: 9781615319046). 32 p.
SERIES: Drawing dinosaurs
GRADE LEVEL: Elementary
CONTENTS: Pteranodon—Archaeopteryx—Tropeognathus

86   **BEAUMONT, S. *Drawing T. Rex and other meat-eating dinosaurs.*** 2010, PowerKids
Press (ISBN: 9781615319077). 32 p.
SERIES: Drawing dinosaurs
GRADE LEVEL: Elementary
CONTENTS: Tyrannosaurus Rex—Velociraptor—Oviraptor

87   BEAUMONT, S. *Drawing the kraken and other sea monsters*. 2011, PowerKids
Press (ISBN: 9781448832521). 32 p.
SERIES: Drawing legendary monsters
GRADE LEVEL: Elementary
CONTENTS: N/A

88   BEAUMONT, S. *Drawing the minotaur and other demihumans*. 2011, PowerKids
Press (ISBN: 9781448832507). 32 p.
SERIES: Drawing legendary monsters
GRADE LEVEL: Elementary
CONTENTS: Centaur—sphinx—minotaur

89   BEAUMONT, S. *Drawing Triceratops and other armored dinosaurs*. 2010,
PowerKids Press (ISBN: 9781615319060). 32 p.
SERIES: Drawing dinosaurs
GRADE LEVEL: Elementary
CONTENTS: Triceratops—Ankylosaurus—Stegosaurus

90   BEAUMONT, S. *Drawing unicorns and other mythical beasts*. 2011, PowerKids
Press (ISBN: 9781448832514). 32 p.
SERIES: Drawing legendary monsters
GRADE LEVEL: Elementary
CONTENTS: Cerberus—unicorn—Chimera

91   BEAUMONT, S. *Drawing werewolves and other gothic ghouls*. 2011, PowerKids
Press (ISBN: 9781448832545). 32 p.
SERIES: Drawing legendary monsters
GRADE LEVEL: Elementary
CONTENTS: Vampire—werewolf – zombie

92   BEAUMONT, S. *How to draw magical kings and queens*. 2008, PowerKids Press
(ISBN: 9781404238602). 32 p.
SERIES: Drawing fantasy art
GRADE LEVEL: Upper elementary
CONTENTS: Basic construction—good king—evil king—good queen—equipment—evil
queen

93   BEAUMONT, S. *How to draw orcs, elves and dwarves*. 2008, PowerKids Press
(ISBN: 9781404238596). 32 p.
SERIES: Drawing fantasy art
GRADE LEVEL: Upper elementary
CONTENTS: Faces—dwarf—warrior orc—goblin orc—female elf—male elf

94   BEAUMONT, S. *How to draw warriors*. 2008, PowerKids Press (ISBN:
9781404238589). 32 p.
SERIES: Drawing fantasy art
GRADE LEVEL: Upper elementary
CONTENTS: Faces—hands and feet—male warrior—female warrior—warrior on
horseback—warrior gallery

95 BEAUMONT, S. *How to draw witches and wizards*. 2008, PowerKids Press (ISBN: 9781404238572). 32 p.
SERIES: Drawing fantasy art
GRADE LEVEL: Upper elementary
CONTENTS: Faces—good witch—evil witch—good wizard—evil wizard

96 BEAVER, J. *Simple machines*. 2010, Mark Twain Media (ISBN: 9781580375238). 80p.
SERIES: Expanding science skills
GRADE LEVEL: Upper elementary – middle school
CONTENTS: N/A

97 BECK, E. *Cool crime scene basics: securing the scene*. 2008, ABDO (ISBN: 9781604534849). 32 p.
SERIES: Cool CSI
GRADE LEVEL: Upper elementary – middle school
CONTENTS: CSI kit—map—more maps—pattern—crime scene

98 BECK, E. *Cool eyewitness encounters: how's your memory?* 2009, ABDO (ISBN: 9781604535856). 32 p.
SERIES: Cool CSI
GRADE LEVEL: Upper elementary – middle school
CONTENTS: Seeing—listening—remembering—eye witness—alibi

99 BECK, E. *Cool odor detectors: fun science projects about smells*. 2008, ABDO (ISBN: 9781599289090). 32 p.
SERIES: Cool science
GRADE LEVEL: Upper elementary
CONTENTS: Stink fest—sweet—temperature—smelling—bodyworks—family

100 BECK, E. *Cool sensory suspense: fun science projects about senses*. 2008, ABDO (ISBN: 9781599289106). 32 p.
SERIES: Cool science
GRADE LEVEL: Upper elementary
CONTENTS: Eye—supertaster—sound—taste test—nose know—sensitivity—senses

101 BECK, E. *Cool spy supplies: fun top secret science projects*. 2008, ABDO (ISBN: 9781599289113). 32 p.
SERIES: Cool science
GRADE LEVEL: Upper elementary
CONTENTS: Talk—ink—periscope—gear—game—alarming

102 BECKER, H. *Magic up your sleeve: amazing illusions, tricks, and science facts you'll never believe*. 2010, Owlkids Books (ISBN: 9781897349762). 64 p.
GRADE LEVEL: Upper elementary
CONTENTS: Optical illusions—read their minds—science stunners—math magic—magician's survival guide—show-stopping science—science concepts

103 BELL-REHWOLDT, S. *The kids' guide to building cool stuff*. 2009, Capstone (ISBN: 9781429622769). 32 p.

SERIES: Kids' guides

GRADE LEVEL: Elementary

CONTENTS: Boat—volcano—rocks—launcher—rocket—bird feeder—kite—dog—hovercraft—bridge—butter

104 **BELL-REHWOLDT, S.** *The kids' guide to classic games*. 2009, Capstone (ISBN: 9781429622738). 32 p.

GRADE LEVEL: Elementary

CONTENTS: N/A

105 **BELL-REHWOLDT, S.** *The kids' guide to duct tape projects*. 2012, Capstone (ISBN: 9781429660105). 32 p.

SERIES: Kids' guides

GRADE LEVEL: Upper elementary – middle school

CONTENTS: Book cover—cell phone pouch—wallet—flower power—frame it!—checkerboard—vest—cap—keep taping

106 **BELL-REHWOLDT, S.** *The kids' guide to jumping rope*. 2011, Capstone (ISBN: 9781429654432). 32 p.

SERIES: Kids' guides

GRADE LEVEL: Elementary

CONTENTS: The rope—safety basics—jumping solo—advanced jumps—jumping with pals—tandem tricks—jumping in rhyme—team turning—double dutch it—double dutch turning—tricks and tips—jump to it

107 **BELL-REHWOLDT, S.** *The kids' guide to pranks, tricks, and practical jokes*. 2009, Capstone (ISBN: 9781429622752). 32 p.

SERIES: Kids' guides

GRADE LEVEL: Elementary

CONTENTS: Drippy—say cheese—let 'er rip—beach bomb—shake—rattle—and roll—you snooze—you lose—laughing through the tears—psst! here's the poop!—gag-o-barf-o-rama—scared ya!—it's a gusher—pee yeeeww!—secret letters—it's all in the fold—dive-bombing egg—jumping aces—going up!—icy deal

108 **BELL-REHWOLDT, S.** *Maya: amazing inventions you can build yourself with 25 projects*. 2012, Nomad Press (ISBN: 9781936749607). 128 p.

SERIES: Build it yourself

GRADE LEVEL: Upper elementary – middle school

CONTENTS: Sand art picture—burial mask—musical gourds—clay figures—hot chocolate—tortillas—rainstick—loom and cloth—spindle whorl—atole—replica child's toy—buli—ball—play pok-a-tok—paper—codex—soap carving—flash cards—numbers—calendar wheel—dates—ruins map—model pyramid—clay cup—jaguar cape—necklace

109 **BELL-REHWOLDT, S.** *Science experiments that surprise and delight*. 2011, Capstone (ISBN: 9781429654289). 32 p.

SERIES: Fun projects for curious kids

GRADE LEVEL: Elementary

CONTENTS: Raisins—straws—separator—apple—bottle—liquid or solid—paper—lemon—egg—milk—layer

110 BELL-REHWOLDT, S. *Speaking secret codes*. 2011, Capstone (ISBN: 978429645690).
SERIES: Making and breaking codes
GRADE LEVEL: Upper elementary – middle school
CONTENTS: Language is code—about language—codes in history—working codes—fun with codes

111 BENBOW, A. *Master the scientific method with fun life science projects*. 2010, Enslow (ISBN: 9780766031517). 48p.
GRADE LEVEL: Lower elementary
CONTENTS: N/A

112 BENBOW, A. *Sensational human body science projects*. 2010, Enslow (ISBN: 9780766031494). 48p.
GRADE LEVEL: Lower elementary
CONTENTS: N/A

113 BERENDES, M. *Birthday crafts*. 2011, Child's World (ISBN: 9781609542313). 24 p.
GRADE LEVEL: Lower elementary
CONTENTS: N/A

114 BERENDES, M. *Independence Day crafts*. 2011, Child's World (ISBN: 9781609542351). 24 p.
GRADE LEVEL: Lower elementary
CONTENTS: N/A

115 BERGIN, M. *You can draw boats*. 2013, Gareth Stevens (ISBN: 9781433974656). 24 p.
SERIES: You can draw
GRADE LEVEL: Lower elementary
CONTENTS: Laser—racing boat—US Coast Guard—powerboat—RHIB—sailing boat—tugboat—fishing boat—yacht

116 BERGIN, M. *You can draw cars*. 2013, Gareth Stevens (ISBN: 9781433974687). 24 p.
SERIES: You can draw
GRADE LEVEL: Lower elementary
CONTENTS: VW-Beetle—Bugatti—Aleen S7—dragster—Chrysler—Cadillac—NASCAR—hot rod—Formula 1

117 BERGIN, M. *It's fun to draw ghosts and ghouls*. 2012, Windmill Books (ISBN: 9781615336005). 32 p.
SERIES: It's fun to draw
GRADE LEVEL: Lower Elementary
CONTENTS: Bat—witch—dragon—monster—ghost—igor—mummy—scarecrow—vampire—werewolf—witch on broomstick—witch's cat—wizard—skeleton

118 BERGIN, M. *How to draw cars*. 2009, PowerKids Press (ISBN: 97814358252087900). 32 p.
SERIES: How to draw

GRADE LEVEL: Middle school

CONTENTS: Honda Civic R—Aston Martin DBS—Ford GT—Subaru Impreza—NASCAR—Bentley Speed 8—Ferrari FXX—Ferrari F1—Thrust SSC

119 **BERGIN, M.** *How to draw dinosaurs and other prehistoric creatures*. 2009, PowerKids Press (ISBN: 9781435825178). 32 p.

SERIES: How to draw

GRADE LEVEL: Middle school

CONTENTS: Ankylosaurus—Iguanodon—Liopleurodon—Parasaurolophus—Pteranodon—Styracosaurus—Stegosaurus—Brachiosaurus—Velociraptor—Tyrannosaurus Rex

120 **BERGIN, M.** *How to draw dragons*. 2011, PowerKids Press (ISBN: 9781448815807). 32 p.

SERIES: How to draw

GRADE LEVEL: Middle school

CONTENTS: Dragon head—birth of a dragon—sleeping dragon—fire-breathing dragon—the wise dragon—perched dragon—flying dragon—battling dragons—dragon and slayer—fire and ice dragons

121 **BERGIN, M.** *How to draw fantasy art*. 2011, PowerKids Press (ISBN: 9781448815784). 32 p.

SERIES: How to draw

GRADE LEVEL: Middle school

CONTENTS: Man beasts—Amazon warrior—warrior queen—barbarian—ogre—undead warrior—winged avenger—war wizard—goblin—goblin vs. warrior

122 **BERGIN, M.** *How to draw knights and castles*. 2012, PowerKids Press (ISBN: 9781448845149). 32 p.

SERIES: How to draw

GRADE LEVEL: Middle school

CONTENTS: Castle keep and towers—gatehouse and drawbridge—how castles developed—castle detail—knights through the ages—knight—knight on the attack—jousting knight—traveling knight—knights in battle

123 **BERGIN, M.** *How to draw magical creatures and mythical beasts*. 2009, PowerKids Press (ISBN: 9781435825185). 32 p.

SERIES: How to draw

GRADE LEVEL: Middle school

CONTENTS: Centaur—dragon—gryphon—Hydra—minotaur—Pegasus—phoenix—troll—unicorn

124 **BERGIN, M.** *How to draw pets*. 2012, PowerKids Press (ISBN: 9781448845118). 32 p.

SERIES: How to draw

GRADE LEVEL: Middle school

CONTENTS: Materials—perspective—heads—paws—and claws—using photos—dog—cat—hamster—rabbit—fish—parrot—mouse—snake—bearded dragon

125 **BERGIN, M.** *How to draw planes*. 2009, PowerKids Press (ISBN: 9781435825192). 32 p.

SERIES: How to draw
GRADE LEVEL: Middle school
CONTENTS: N/A

126 BERGIN, M. *How to draw robots*. 2009, PowerKids Press (ISBN: 9781435825215). 32 p.
SERIES: How to draw
GRADE LEVEL: Middle school
CONTENTS: Security droid—giant mecha—flying mecha—explorer robot—combat mecha—human mecha—land walker—mutant mecha—fantasy mecha

127 BERGIN, M. *How to draw science fiction*. 2012, PowerKids Press (ISBN: 9781448845163). 32 p.
SERIES: How to draw
GRADE LEVEL: Middle school
CONTENTS: Perspective—places and planets—spacecraft—vehicles—space stations—human characters—robots and droids—space machinery—alien characters—cartoon aliens—spaceman and robots—cartoon scene

128 BERGIN, M. *How to draw ships*. 2011, PowerKids Press (ISBN: 9781448815777). 32 p.
SERIES: How to draw
GRADE LEVEL: Middle school
CONTENTS: Drawing sails—sketching—speedboat—racing yachts—rowboat—topsail schooner—ocean tanker—fishing boat—ocean liner—lifeboat—harbor scene

129 BERGIN, M. *How to draw vampires, zombies, and other monsters*. 2012, PowerKids Press (ISBN: 9781448845125). 32 p.
SERIES: How to draw
GRADE LEVEL: Middle school
CONTENTS: Materials—creating characters—drawing movement—vampire—zombie—ghoul—werewolf—ghost—witch—Frankenstein's monster—scarecrow—grim reaper

130 BERGIN, M. *It's fun to draw dinosaurs*. 2012, Windmill Books (ISBN: 9781615333493). 32 p.
SERIES: It's fun to draw
GRADE LEVEL: Lower Elementary
CONTENTS: Diplodocus—Tyrannosaurus Rex—Ankylosaurus—Pteranodon—Dimetrodon—Parasaurolophus—Pachycephalosaurus—Stegosaurus—Iguanodon—Liopleurodon—Styracosaurus—Velociraptor—Triceratops—Corythosaurus

131 BERGIN, M. *It's fun to draw fairies and mermaids*. 2013, Sky Pony Press (ISBN: 9781620871126). 32 p.
SERIES: It's fun to draw
GRADE LEVEL: Lower Elementary
CONTENTS: N/A

132 BERGIN, M. *It's fun to draw farm animals*. 2012, Windmill Books (ISBN: 9781615335992). 32 p.
SERIES: It's fun to draw

GRADE LEVEL: Lower Elementary

CONTENTS: Chicken—cow—donkey—mallard—farm cat—goat—duck—horse—owl—pig—rabbit—sheep—sheepdog—turkey

133   **BERGIN, M.** *It's fun to draw knights and castles*. 2013, Windmill Books (ISBN: 9781620871133). 32 p.

SERIES: It's fun to draw

GRADE LEVEL: Lower Elementary

CONTENTS: Castle guard—Eagleford Castle—Norman knight—axe knight—archer—Ravenswood Castle—jousting knight—jousting tent—the joust—mace knight—Hawkbury Castle—Arabian knight—spearman—battling knight

134   **BERGIN, M.** *It's fun to draw monsters*. 2012, Windmill Books (ISBN: 9781615336012). 32 p.

SERIES: It's fun to draw

GRADE LEVEL: Lower Elementary

CONTENTS: N/A

135   **BERGIN, M.** *It's fun to draw pets*. 2012, Windmill Books (ISBN: 9781615335978). 32 p.

SERIES: It's fun to draw

GRADE LEVEL: Lower Elementary

CONTENTS: Cat—dog—fish—parakeet—guinea pig—horse—lizard—parrot—rabbit—rat—snake—stick insect—spider—tortoise

136   **BERGIN, M.** *It's fun to draw pirates*. 2012, Windmill Books (ISBN: 9781615336029). 32 p.

SERIES: It's fun to draw

GRADE LEVEL: Lower Elementary

CONTENTS: Barnacle Boris—Sharktooth Jack—Redbeard—Scurvy Jim—Squid-lips Sid—Starboard Steve—monkey—Captain Clunk—Sophie Storm—One-eyed John—Pete the Plank—Sharkbait George—Gunpowder Billy—Captain Black

137   **BERGIN, M.** *It's fun to draw princesses and ballerinas*. 2012, Windmill Books (ISBN: 9781615333516). 32 p.

SERIES: It's fun to draw

GRADE LEVEL: Lower Elementary

CONTENTS: Princess Anna—Louise—Henrietta—Princess Margot—Princess Lisa—Marina—Princess Helena—Princess Melissa—Jennifer—Princess Nicole—Princess Heather—Amanda—Kirsten—Fiona

138   **BERGIN, M.** *It's fun to draw robots and aliens*. 2012, Windmill Books (ISBN: 9781615333530). 32 p.

SERIES: It's fun to draw

GRADE LEVEL: Lower Elementary

CONTENTS: N/A

139   **BERGIN, M.** *It's fun to draw safari animals*. 2011, Windmill Books (ISBN: 9781615333486). 32 p.

SERIES: It's fun to draw
GRADE LEVEL: Lower Elementary
CONTENTS: N/A

140 BERGIN, M. *It's fun to draw sea creatures*. 2013, Sky Pony Press (ISBN: 9781620875353). 32 p.
SERIES: It's fun to draw
GRADE LEVEL: Lower Elementary
CONTENTS: N/A

141 BERGIN, M. *You can draw planes*. 2013, Gareth Stevens (ISBN: 9781433974717). 24 p.
SERIES: You can draw
GRADE LEVEL: Lower elementary
CONTENTS: Learjet—Bleriot—F-16—Gee Bee—Mustang—glider—Bell X-1—seaplane—Pitts special

142 BERGIN, M. *You can draw rockets*. 2013, Gareth Stevens (ISBN: 9781433974748). 24 p.
SERIES: You can draw
GRADE LEVEL: Lower elementary
CONTENTS: Mercury-Redstone—Saturn V—Apollo CSM—X-2—Blue Flame—space shuttle—X-15
—Ariane—Spaceshipone

143 BERGIN, M. *You can draw trains*. 2013, Gareth Stevens (ISBN: 9781433974779). 24 p.
SERIES: You can draw
GRADE LEVEL: Lower elementary
CONTENTS: Stourbridge Lion—Cog train—LNER class A4—TGV—steam train—tank engine—intercity-express—diesel train—Union Pacific

144 BERGIN, M. *You can draw trucks*. 2013, Gareth Stevens (ISBN: 9781433974809). 24 p.
SERIES: You can draw
GRADE LEVEL: Lower elementary
CONTENTS: Concrete mixer—truck—snowplow—racing truck—monster truck—pickup truck—digger—fire truck—earthmover

145 BERKENKAMP, L. *Discover the Amazon: the world's largest rainforest*. 2008, Nomad Press (ISBN: 9781934670279). 96p.
SERIES: Discover your world
GRADE LEVEL: Upper elementary – middle school
CONTENTS: Eye—pattern—cairns—sun—compass—raft—fruit—meal—spear/fish weir—fish—water—water safety—knots—tracks—fires

146 BERKENKAMP, L. *Discover the oceans: the world's largest ecosystem*. 2009, Nomad Press (ISBN: 9781934670385). 96p.
SERIES: Discover your world

GRADE LEVEL: Upper elementary – middle school

CONTENTS: Salt—sodium—cal.c—net—spear—bell—sounding device—compass—polaris—mask—colors—insulation—dehydration—water—still—conservation

147 **BERRY, B.** *Learn to draw ancient times: step-by-step instructions for 18 ancient characters and civilizations*. 2013, Walter Foster (ISBN: 9781600583100). 32 p.

SERIES: Learn to draw

GRADE LEVEL: Upper elementary – middle school

CONTENTS: Caveman—mammoth—saber-toothed tiger—Great Pyramid—Sphinx of Gaza—mummy—pharaoh—Lighthouse of Alexandria—horus statue—chariot—Hercules—Colossus of Rhodes—gladiator—Mayan temple—Mayan king—castle—knight—Sword in the Stone

148 **BERRY, B.** *Learn to draw pirates, Vikings, and ancient civilizations: step-by step instructions for drawing ancient characters, civilizations, creatures, and more!* 2013, Walter Foster (ISBN: 9781600583421). 32 p.

SERIES: Learn to draw

GRADE LEVEL: Upper elementary – middle school

CONTENTS: Pirate—pirate ship—pirate maiden—first mate—monkey—parrot—Davy Jones—sunken city—kraken—Leif Eriksson—Viking longship—sea serpent—Thor—Aegir—Sir Francis Drake—Moby Dick—Leviathan—Sinbad the Sailor—cannon—Marco Polo—castle—knight—princess—Beowulf—chariot—gladiator—Hercules—Nero—Trojan horse—mummy—pharaoh—caveman—mammoth—saber-toothed tiger

149 **BESLEY, A.** *The outdoor book for adventurous boys: essential skills and activities for boys of all ages*. 2008, Lyons Press (ISBN: 9781599213415). 224 p.

GRADE LEVEL: Elementary

CONTENTS: N/A

150 **BIDNER, J.** *The kids' guide to digital photography: how to shoot, save, play with and print your digital photos*. 2011, Sterling (ISBN: 9781402780394). 96 p.

GRADE LEVEL: Elementary

CONTENTS: Basics—your camera—take pictures—software—the Internet—printing—ideas and projects

151 **BIRKEMOE, K.** *Strike a pose*. 2007, Kids Can Press (ISBN: 9781553370048). 96 p.

SERIES: Planet girl

GRADE LEVEL: Middle school – high school

CONTENTS: Why do yoga – getting it right—what you need—getting started: beginner's sequence: rowing the boat—cat—swaying palm tree—lying full spinal twist—tree—downward facing dog—thunderbolt—corpse—going further: more advanced sequence: forward bend—cobra—triangle—twisting squad—warrior—balancing stick—dancer—locust—bridge—lion—lotus

152 **BJORKLUND, R.** *Aikido*. 2012, Marshall Cavendish Benchmark (ISBN: 9780761449317). 47 p.

SERIES: Martial arts in action

GRADE LEVEL: Upper elementary – middle school

CONTENTS: N/A

153 BLAKE, S. *Bread and pizzas*. 2009, PowerKids Press (ISBN: 9781435828582). 24 p.

SERIES: Make and eat

GRADE LEVEL: Upper elementary

CONTENTS: About bread and pizza—soda bread—cornbread—whole-wheat bread—cottage bread—garlic focaccia—fruity buns—pizza—tasty calzone

154 BLAKE, S. *Cookies and cakes*. 2009, PowerKids Press (ISBN: 9781435828599). 24 p.

SERIES: Make and eat

GRADE LEVEL: Upper elementary

CONTENTS: Cookies and cakes—oat bars—chocolate chip cookies—cheesy cookies—layer cake—banana and fig muffins—candy cookies—marshmallow fingers—vanilla cupcakes

155 BLAKE, S. *Sandwiches and snacks*. 2009, PowerKids Press (ISBN: 9781435828575). 24 p.

SERIES: Make and eat

GRADE LEVEL: Upper elementary

CONTENTS: Sandwiches and snacks—creamy raita—hummus wrap—classic egg salad—bruschetta—quesadilla wedges—chunky wedges and dip—chicken pita pocket—tuna melt

156 BLAKE, S. *Vegetarian food*. 2009, PowerKids Press (ISBN: 9781435828605). 24 p.

SERIES: Make and eat

GRADE LEVEL: Upper elementary

CONTENTS: Vegetarian food—tasy hummus—tricolore salad—scrambled eggs—tofu kebabs—couscous salad—minestrone soup—baked potato with chili—chunky pasta

157 BLAXLAND, W. *American food*. 2012, Smart Apple Media (ISBN: 9781599206677). 32 p.

SERIES: I can cook!

GRADE LEVEL: Elementary

CONTENTS: Blueberry muffins—hamburgers—peanut butter and jelly sandwich—corn on the cob—pancakes—homemade lemonade—apple pie—American food: Thanksgiving

158 BLAXLAND, W. *Chinese food*. 2012, Smart Apple Media (ISBN: 9781599206714). 32 p.

SERIES: I can cook!

GRADE LEVEL: Elementary

CONTENTS: Tea eggs—spring rolls—tomato egg flower soup—Chinese dumplings—chicken and cashew stir-fry—sweet orange tea—glazed bananas—a Chinese food celebration: Chinese New Year

159 BLAXLAND, W. *French food*. 2012, Smart Apple Media (ISBN: 9781599206691). 32 p.

SERIES: I can cook!

GRADE LEVEL: Elementary

CONTENTS: Croque Monsieur—omelette—carrot salad—mini-crepes—chocolate-dipped strawberries—grenadine—a French picnic—a French food celebration: Bastille Day

160 **BLAXLAND, W.** *Italian food*. 2012, Smart Apple Media (ISBN: 9781599206707). 32 p.

SERIES: I can cook!

GRADE LEVEL: Elementary

CONTENTS: Bruschetta—melon and prosciutto antipasto—spaghetti bolognese—mushroom risotto—chocolate salami—raspberry granita—pizza margherita—an Italian food celebration

161 **BLAXLAND, W.** *Mexican food*. 2012, Smart Apple Media (ISBN: 9781599206684). 32 p.

SERIES: I can cook!

GRADE LEVEL: Elementary

CONTENTS: Huevos rancheros—refried beans—guacamole—burritos—Mexican fruit salad—hot chocolate—Pan de Muertos—Mexican food celebration: Día de los Muertos

162 **BLAXLAND, W.** *Middle Eastern food*. 2012, Smart Apple Media (ISBN: 9781599206721). 32 p.

SERIES: I can cook!

GRADE LEVEL: Elementary

CONTENTS: Dolmas—hummus—tabouli—lamb shish kebabs—chicken and couscous—orange sharbat—Turkish delight—a Middle Eastern food celebration: Eid al-Fitr

163 **BLOBAUM, C.** *Explore gravity! With 25 great projects*. 2014, Nomad Press (ISBN: 9781619302075). 96 p.

SERIES: Explore your world

GRADE LEVEL: Upper elementary

CONTENTS: Journal—lights—switch—static electricity—electricity—electricity again—electroscope—watts—voltaic pile—conductors and insulators—battery—breaker box—circuit—switch—nightlight—art—moving compass—compass—electromagnet—pinwheel—motor—electrophorus—anemometer—oven—protector

164 **BLOBAUM, C.** *Explore night science! With 25 great projects*. 2012, Nomad Press (ISBN: 9781619301566). 96 p.

SERIES: Explore your world

GRADE LEVEL: Upper elementary

CONTENTS: Light—night—length—color—open—shut—shadows—hoot—frog—katydids—ears—sound—bag and bug—moth—garden—smells—touch—dew—light—night light—moons—stardome—compass—light—firefly—mad lib

165 **BOASE, P.** *Brilliant badges to make yourself: 25 amazing step-by-step badge-making projects*. 2013, Armadillo (ISBN: 9781843228288).

GRADE LEVEL: Elementary

CONTENTS: N/A

166 **BOCHNER, A.** *The new totally awesome business book for kids: with twenty super businesses you can start right now!* 2007, Newmarket Press (ISBN: 9781557047571).

GRADE LEVEL: Middle school – high school

CONTENTS: Eye for business—the body of a business: corporations, partnerships, and sole proprietorships—business purpose and idea—the home of a business—the heart of a business: people—the conscience of a business—two big businesses for kids—seven old standbys—an idea—set up a home consulting business

167 BODDEN, V. *Hiking*. 2009, Creative Education (ISBN: 9781583416983). 24 p.
SERIES: Active sports
GRADE LEVEL: Elementary
CONTENTS: N/A

168 BOEKHOFF, P. *Nifty thrifty space crafts*. 2008, Enslow (ISBN: 9780766027831). 32 p.
SERIES: Nifty thrifty crafts for kids
GRADE LEVEL: Elementary
CONTENTS: Space—star finder—moon—supply holder—glider—colony—planet—greetings—night—comet—flying saucer

169 BOLTE, M. *All-American girl style: fun fashions you can sketch*. 2013, Capstone (ISBN: 9781620650394). 32 p.
SERIES: Drawing fun fashions
GRADE LEVEL: Middle school – high school
CONTENTS: N/A

170 BOLTE, M. *Girly-girl style: fun fashions you can sketch*. 2013, Capstone (ISBN: 9781620650356). 32 p.
SERIES: Drawing fun fashions
GRADE LEVEL: Middle school – high school
CONTENTS: Embroidered edges—radiant romper—beach boutique—pretty prints—lacy layers—crocheted cutie—timeless trend—relaxed Romantic—flowers—style at sea—cool weather cool—a vintage affair—on the runway

171 BOLTE, M. *Harajuka style: fun fashions you can sketch*. 2013, Capstone (ISBN: 9781620650349). 32 p.
SERIES: Drawing fun fashions
GRADE LEVEL: Middle school – high school
CONTENTS: N/A

172 BOLTE, M. *Hollywood style: fun fashions you can sketch*. 2013, Capstone (ISBN: 9781620650370). 32 p.
SERIES: Drawing fun fashions
GRADE LEVEL: Middle school – high school
CONTENTS: Belle of the disco—short and sweet—red carpet ruffles—smooth metals—star-studded sheath—21st century princess—floral formal—Hollywood glam—hall of famer—glitz and gauze—backstage glam—think pink

173 BOLTE, M. *Rock star style: fun fashions you can sketch*. 2013, Capstone (ISBN: 9781620650363). 32 p.
SERIES: Drawing fun fashions
GRADE LEVEL: Middle school – high school
CONTENTS: N/A

174 BOLTE, M. *Skater chic style: fun fashions you can sketch*. 2013, Capstone (ISBN: 9781620650387). 32 p.

SERIES: Drawing fun fashions

GRADE LEVEL: Middle school – high school

CONTENTS: Vert style—punk you out—street league style—skater prep—surf skater—hanging with the homies—standing out—top deck style—overall impression—supertech sparkle—winter wear—the park

175 BONADDIO, T. *Stick it! 99 D.I.Y. duct tape projects*. 2009, R.P. Kids (ISBN: 9780762434947).

GRADE LEVEL: High school

CONTENTS: Wallets—wrist wearables—rings—necklaces—bags and purses—other wild wearables—decor for wherever you are—paper goods

176 BONE, E. *Recycling things to make and do*. 2009, Usborne (ISBN: 9780794526757). 31 p.

GRADE LEVEL: Elementary

CONTENTS: Bits and pieces—shiny bugs—robot collage—tube people—newspaper chains—paper gift bags—printed flowers—notebook covering—dangly mobile—gift tags—patterned boxes—birds in a tree—castle desk tidy—truck collage—ribbon houses—paper decorations—plastic bag beads—material heads—collage faces—dragon puppet

177 BONNET, B. *46 science fair projects for the evil genius*. 2008, McGraw Hill (ISBN: 9780071600279). 209p.

SERIES: Evil genuis

GRADE LEVEL: Upper elementary – middle school

CONTENTS: Water—birds' nests—lighthouses—pendulum—melody—sound—salt—noise—wind—struts—stocks—beef—insect collecting—nocturnal insects—sugar—vitamin C—zenith—environment—sample size—choices—oxygen—mountains—goldfish—bracing—plant acid—stock market strategy—mold—electromagnetism—chlorophyll—lemons—evaporating rainwater—pesticide—olfactory—bacteria—instructions—artificial gravity—evaporating water and alcohol—bread mold—fungi—search engines—house plants—crickets—picnic pests—technology—television—sunlight—radishes

178 BONNET, R. *Home run! Science projects with baseball and softball*. 2009, Enslow (ISBN: 9780766033658). 104 p.

SERIES: Score! Sports science projects

GRADE LEVEL: Middle school – high school

CONTENTS: Wind and a ball—rain and a ball—a wet field and the ground ball—a bat's weight—a ball's hardness—hands on the bat—hitting the ball—sampling—batting average—shoes and speed—spinning ball—a batting glove—bat weight—timing the swing—bat control—strike zone—throwing the ball—pitching—game

179 BOONYADHISTARN, T. *Beading: bracelets, barrettes, and beyond*. 2007, Capstone (ISBN: 736864725). 32 p.

SERIES: Crafts

GRADE LEVEL: Elementary

CONTENTS: Your style—pliers and wires—pin it down—get wired—beads to the rescue—bead it and bag it—wild and wacky beads—charmed

180   BOONYADHISTARN, T. *Fingernail art: dazzling fingers and terrific toes*. 2007, Capstone (ISBN: 9780736864749). 32 p.

SERIES: Crafts

GRADE LEVEL: Elementary

CONTENTS: No more plain polish—ready—set—prep—polka dots—starry, starry night—flower girl—show stripes—emotions—princess

181   BOONYADHISTARN, T. *Origami: the fun and funky art of paper folding*. 2007, Capstone (ISBN: 9780736864763). 32 p.

SERIES: Crafts

GRADE LEVEL: Elementary

CONTENTS: N/A

182   BOONYADHISTARN, T. *Stamping art: imprint your designs*. 2007, Capstone (ISBN: 9780736864770). 32 p.

SERIES: Crafts

GRADE LEVEL: Elementary

CONTENTS: N/A

183   BOONYADHISTARN, T. *Valentines: cards and crafts from the heart*. 2007, Capstone (ISBN: 9780736864756). 32 p.

SERIES: Crafts

GRADE LEVEL: Elementary

CONTENTS: Valentine—message in a bottle—bouquet of hearts—fortune in Valentines—my heart's on a chain—munch to the message—display of affection

184   BORDESSA, K. *Great Medieval projects you can build yourself*. 2008, Nomad Press (ISBN: 9780979226809). 128 p.

SERIES: Build it yourself

GRADE LEVEL: Upper elementary – middle school

CONTENTS: Jester hat—juggling sticks—knight's shield—chain mail—helmet—trebuchet—marshmallow cannon—tapestry—trencher—mead—potage—pokerounce—almond milk—butter—insect repellent—thatched roof—hennin—spiced almonds—pretzels—clapper—grail—reliquary—pilgrim's badge—sign language—clay pot bell—illuminated letter—stained glass

185   BORGENICHT, D. *The worst-case scenario survival handbook: extreme junior edition*. 2008, Chronicle (ISBN: 9780811865685).

GRADE LEVEL: Elementary

CONTENTS: Survive at sea—survive in the mountains—survive in the desert—survive in the jungle—survive in the arctic—survive on safari

186   BOURSIN, D. *Folding for fun*. 2007, Firefly Books (ISBN: 9781554072538).

GRADE LEVEL: Lower elementary

CONTENTS: N/A

187   BRECKE, N. *Airplanes and ships you can draw*. 2010, Millbrook Press (ISBN: 9780761341666). 32 p.

SERIES: Ready, set, draw!

GRADE LEVEL: Elementary

CONTENTS: Submarine—fighter jet—speedboat—tugboat—747 airplane—biplane—helicopter—pirate ship

188 **BRECKE, N.** *Cars, trucks, and motorcycles you can draw*. 2010, Millbrook Press (ISBN: 9780761341628). 32 p.

SERIES: Ready, set, draw!

GRADE LEVEL: Elementary

CONTENTS: Convertible—monster truck—Ferrari—dirt bike—semitruck—Jeep—motorcycle—Indy car

189 **BRECKE, N.** *Cats you can draw*. 2010, Millbrook Press (ISBN: 9780761341611). 32 p.

SERIES: Ready, set, draw!

GRADE LEVEL: Elementary

CONTENTS: Maine Coon—Ragdoll—Persian—Birman—Sphynx—American shorthair—Abyssinian—Siamese

190 **BRECKE, N.** *Cool boy stuff you can draw*. 2010, Millbrook Press (ISBN: 9780761341635). 32 p.

SERIES: Ready, set, draw!

GRADE LEVEL: Elementary

CONTENTS: Ogre—giant—dragon—superhero—villain—baseball player—football player—skateboarder

191 **BRECKE, N.** *Cool girl stuff you can draw*. 2010, Millbrook Press (ISBN: 9780761341642). 32 p.

SERIES: Ready, set, draw!

GRADE LEVEL: Elementary

CONTENTS: Castle—unicorn—fairy—ballerina—singing star—soccer player—figure skater—snowboarder

192 **BRECKE, N.** *Dinosaurs and other prehistoric creatures you can draw*. 2010, Millbrook Press (ISBN: 9780761341697). 32 p.

SERIES: Ready, set, draw!

GRADE LEVEL: Elementary

CONTENTS: Apatosaurus—Triceratops—Supercroc—Ichthyosaurus—Tyrannosaurus Rex—Pterodactylus—Stegosaurus—Ankylosaurus

193 **BRECKE, N.** *Dogs you can draw*. 2010, Millbrook Press (ISBN: 9780761341598). 32 p.

SERIES: Ready, set, draw!

GRADE LEVEL: Elementary

CONTENTS: Dachshund—poodle—German shepherd—boxer—Yorkshire terrier—Labrador retriever—beagle—golden retriever

194 **BRECKE, N.** *Extinct and endangered animals you can draw*. 2010, Millbrook Press (ISBN: 9780761341659). 32 p.

SERIES: Ready, set, draw!

GRADE LEVEL: Elementary

CONTENTS: Quagga—Panamanian golden frog—rhinoceros—saber-toothed cat—gorilla—dodo bird—wooly mammoth—giant panda

195 BRECKE, N. *Horses you can draw*. 2010, Millbrook Press (ISBN: 9780761341604). 32 p.

SERIES: Ready, set, draw!

GRADE LEVEL: Elementary

CONTENTS: Clydesdale—Lipizzan—Shetland pony—American Quarter Horse—Arabian—mustang—Appaloosa—American paint horse

196 BRECKE, N. *Insects you can draw*. 2010, Millbrook Press (ISBN: 9780761341703). 32 p.

SERIES: Ready, set, draw!

GRADE LEVEL: Elementary

CONTENTS: Madagascar hissing cockroach—ant—goliath beetle—grasshopper—honeybee—monarch butterfly—dragonfly—praying mantis

197 BRECKE, N. *Sea creatures you can draw*. 2010, Millbrook Press (ISBN: 9780761341680). 32 p.

SERIES: Ready, set, draw!

GRADE LEVEL: Elementary

CONTENTS: Stingray—killer whale—walrus—hammerhead shark—clown fish—bottlenose dolphin—sea turtle—crab

198 BRECKE, N. *Spaceships, aliens, and robots you can draw*. 2009, Millbrook Press (ISBN: 9780761341673). 32 p.

SERIES: Ready, set, draw!

GRADE LEVEL: Elementary

CONTENTS: UFO—alien—robotic dog—cyborg—giant robot—astronaut—Mars rover—space shuttle orbiter

199 BRENNAN, S. *The adventurous boy's handbook*. 2008, Skyhorse (ISBN: 9781602392229). 224 p.

GRADE LEVEL: Elementary

CONTENTS: N/A

200 BRENNAN, S. *The adventurous girl's handbook: for ages 9 to 99*. 2009, Skyhorse (ISBN: 9781602396357). 186 p.

GRADE LEVEL: Elementary

CONTENTS: N/A

201 BRIGNELL, R. *The Pilates handbook*. 2010, Rosen (ISBN: 9781435853614). 256 p.

SERIES: A young woman's guide to health and well-being

GRADE LEVEL: Middle school – high school

CONTENTS: The eight principles of Pilates—preparation—stretching and warming up—the exercises—intermediate program—advanced program—swiss-ball exercises—Pilates during pregnancy—machine exercises

202 BROWN, C. *Amazing kitchen chemistry projects you can build yourself*. 2008, Nomad Press (ISBN: 9780979226823). 128 p.

SERIES: Build it yourself

GRADE LEVEL: Upper elementary – middle school

CONTENTS: Buckyball—bookmark—rocket—shapes—pennies necklace—volcano—eggs—messages—crystals—candy—glass house—waves—liquids—diver—bottled egg—explosion—taffy—ice cream—oobleck—goop—cookies—paper—bending water—bubbles

203 BROWN, C. *Discover national monuments: national parks*. 2009, Nomad Press (ISBN: 9781934670286). 96 p.

SERIES: Discover your world

GRADE LEVEL: Upper elementary – middle school

CONTENTS: Transpiration—cavern—stalactites—fossil—petroglyph—canyon—volcano—rift zone—columns—igneous rocks—sand dunes—crevasses—glacier—sorting—evaporite—naked eggs

204 BROWN, C. *Explore rocks and minerals! 25 great projects, activities, experiments*. 2010, Nomad Press (ISBN: 9781934670613). 96 p.

SERIES: Explore your world

GRADE LEVEL: Upper elementary

CONTENTS: Egg—earth—mineral—salt—diamond—lava—basalt—cookies—rocks—sed-sandwich—sedimentary rock—stalactites—evaporite—folded rocks—ig—sed—meta—metamorphic bars—fossil—time—display—treasure hunt

205 BROWN, C. *Geology of the desert Southwest: investigate how the Earth was formed with 15 projects*. 2011, Nomad Press (ISBN: 9781936313402). 128 p.

SERIES: Build it yourself

GRADE LEVEL: Upper elementary – middle school

CONTENTS: Rift—basin—volcano—San Andreas—liquid action—earthquakes—cracking eggs—canyon—oven—bricks—swamp—water supply—lake—cactus—terrarium—pure water—oil

206 BROWN, C. *Geology of the eastern coast: investigate how the Earth was formed with 15 projects*. 2012, Nomad Press (ISBN: 9781936313877). 128 p.

SERIES: Build it yourself

GRADE LEVEL: Upper elementary – middle school

CONTENTS: Basalts—mountains—weather—earthquakes—fracking—oil—caves—kettle—big storms—pressure—waterfall—rafts—eggs—lighthouses—Coriolis

207 BROWN, C. *Geology of the Great Plains and Mountain West: investigate how the Earth was formed with 15 projects*. 2011, Nomad Press (ISBN: 9781936313839). 128 p.

SERIES: Build it yourself

GRADE LEVEL: Upper elementary – middle school

CONTENTS: Time travel—popcorn—mountains—liquid action—geysers—kettle—crystals—climate—tornados—floods—hoops—tree—sunflower—temperature—dunes

208 BROWN, C. *Geology of the Pacific Northwest: investigate how the Earth was formed with 15 projects*. 2011, Nomad Press (ISBN: 9781936313389). 128 p.

SERIES: Build it yourself

GRADE LEVEL: Upper elementary – middle school

CONTENTS: Boundaries—formation—mountains—glacier—volcano—mounds—tsunami—columns—plumes—rain—fog—water wheel—river—fungi—terrarium—sorting—coastline

209   BROWN, C. *Mapping and navigation: explore the history and science of finding your way with 20 projects*. 2013, Nomad Press (ISBN: 9781619301948). 128 p.

SERIES: Build it yourself

GRADE LEVEL: Upper elementary – middle school

CONTENTS: N/A

210   BROWN, H. *How to improve at gymnastics*. 2009, Crabtree (ISBN: 9780778735731). 48 p.

SERIES: How to improve at

GRADE LEVEL: Elementary

CONTENTS: Equipment—what to wear and training—warming up and stretching—vault—handspring vault—floor—cartwheels and back handsprings—parallel bars—basket swing—rings—basic swing—rings—asymmetric bars—glide kip—pommel horse—beam—high bar—backward hip circle—competition—diet and mental attitude

211   BROWN, J. *Crazy concoctions: a mad scientist's guide to messy mixture*. 2011, Imagine (ISBN: 9781936140510). 24p.

GRADE LEVEL: Upper elementary – middle school

CONTENTS: Ooze—slime—puke—boogers—blood—boom—pop rocks—raisins—eruption—blobs—rainbow—color—blue—acid or base—glows—muffins—chocolate cake—biscuits—pickle slices

212   BROWN, L. *How to create spectacular Halloween costumes*. 2011, Capstone (ISBN: 9781429654227). 32 p.

SERIES: Halloween extreme

GRADE LEVEL: Upper elementary

CONTENTS: Don't feed the sharks—shadow of death—walk all over me—call of the wild—raggedy ruckus—operation disaster—fanged rocker—good enough to eat

213   BROWN, T. *Costume crafts*. 2010, Gareth Stevens (ISBN: 9781433935558). 32 p.

SERIES: Creative crafts for kids

GRADE LEVEL: Elementary

CONTENTS: Cowgirl chaps—gold watch—football helmet—treasure chest—spring bonnet—sheriff's star—candy wrapper crown—funky phones—bubblewrap wings—flower garlands—pirate's parrot—bouncy antennas

214   BROWN, T. *Staging and choreography*. 2012, Rosen (ISBN: 9781448868742). 64 p.

SERIES: Glee club

GRADE LEVEL: Upper elementary – middle school

CONTENTS: Dance—keeping in step—staging—teamwork, teamwork, teamwork

215   BROWNING, L. *Babysitting basics: caring for kids*. 2007, Capstone (ISBN: 736864628).

SERIES: Babysitting

GRADE LEVEL: Middle school

CONTENTS: Babysitters here—keeping kids safe—entertaining everyone—time to eat—washing up—it's potty time—curing the crying—misbehavior—putting kids to bed—checklist—glossary—quick tips—read more—internet sites—about the author—index

216 BRUNELLE, L. *Camp out! The ultimate kids' guide, from the backyard to the backwoods*. 2007, Workman (ISBN: 9780761141228). 32 p.

GRADE LEVEL: Upper elementary – middle school

CONTENTS: Plan and pack—setting up camp—fun food—knots—getting around—staying found—the weather—the night sky—experiments and projects—arts and crafts—fun and games—animal tracks and scat—the singing camper's book of silly songs

217 BUCHANAN, A. *The daring book for girls*. 2007, Collins (ISBN: 9780061472572). 279 p.

GRADE LEVEL: Elementary

CONTENTS: N/A

218 BUCHANAN, A. *The pocket daring book for girls: things to do*. 2008, Collins (ISBN: 9780061673078). 211 p.

GRADE LEVEL: Elementary

CONTENTS: N/A

219 BUCKLEY, C. *Start to embroider*. 2009, Search Press (ISBN: 9781844483907). 48 p.

SERIES: Start to

GRADE LEVEL: Upper elementary – middle school

CONTENTS: Peacock—picture—funky book cover—magic bag—heart purse—lucky charms

220 BULL, J. *Made by me*. 2009, DK (ISBN: 9780756651633). 63 p.

GRADE LEVEL: Upper elementary – middle school

CONTENTS: Picture stitches—t-shirt—stitch directory—pixel pics—cross-stitch—pouches—lavender bags—pocket lockets—hanging softies—felt flowers—bags of ribbons—cupcakes—dolly—doll's face and clothes—knitting dolls—krazy knits—knitted purses—woolen hats

221 BULL, J. *Make it*. 2008, DK (ISBN: 9780756638375).

GRADE LEVEL: Elementary

CONTENTS: N/A

222 BULL, J. *Make it! Don't throw it away — create something amazing*. 2013, DK (ISBN: 9781409325772).

GRADE LEVEL: Lower elementary

CONTENTS: N/A

223 BULL, P. *Quick draw cats and dogs*. 2008, Kingfisher (ISBN: 9780753462003). 32 p.

SERIES: Quick draw

GRADE LEVEL: Lower elementary

CONTENTS: N/A

224   BULL, P. *Quick draw creepy crawlies*. 2008, Kingfisher (ISBN: 9780753461983). 32 p.

SERIES: Quick draw

GRADE LEVEL: Lower elementary

CONTENTS: Caterpillar—dragonfly—scorpion—snail—earthworm—ant—earwig—spider—fly—ladybird—beetle—bee—butterfly—grasshopper

225   BULL, P. *Quick draw fairies and princesses*. 2008, Kingfisher (ISBN: 9780753462010). 32 p.

SERIES: Quick draw

GRADE LEVEL: Lower elementary

CONTENTS: N/A

226   BULL, P. *Quick draw transportation*. 2008, Kingfisher (ISBN: 9780753462737). 32 p.

SERIES: Quick draw

GRADE LEVEL: Lower elementary

CONTENTS: N/A

227   BULL, P. *Quick draw under the sea*. 2008, Kingfisher (ISBN: 9780753461990). 32 p.

SERIES: Quick draw

GRADE LEVEL: Lower elementary

CONTENTS: Starfish—jellyfish—puffer fish—walrus—dolphin—electric ray—humpback whale—giant clam—shark—gulper eel—octopus—clown fish—crab—lobster

228   BULLARD, L. *Ace your oral or multimedia presentation*. 2009, Enslow (ISBN: 9780766033917). 48 p.

SERIES: Ace it! Information literacy series

GRADE LEVEL: Elementary

CONTENTS: So you have to give a presentation—choose your topic—explore your topic—draft and revise—visual aids and multimedia—take the stage—after the applause

229   BULLARD, L. *Crocheting for fun!* 2009, Compass Point (ISBN: 9780756538613). 48 p.

SERIES: For fun!

GRADE LEVEL: Elementary

CONTENTS: N/A

230   BUNKERS, T. *Print it!* 2012, QEB (ISBN: 9781609922771).

SERIES: Art smart

GRADE LEVEL: Upper elementary

CONTENTS: N/A

231   BURKE, L. *I'm a scientist: backyard*. 2010, DK (ISBN: 9780756663063). 24 p.

SERIES: I'm a scientist

GRADE LEVEL: Lower elementary

CONTENTS: Flower—roots—bug house—snail—worm—rain gauge—windmill flower—parachutes—shower caps—fish

232   **BURKE, L.** *I'm a scientist: in the kitchen*. 2010, DK (ISBN: 9780756663070). 24 p.
SERIES: I'm a scientist
GRADE LEVEL: Lower elementary
CONTENTS: Density—a bottle—force—bridges and ridges—structures—apples—surprise—magnet—compass—goo—fruit freeze—meltdown—eggs—liquid to solid—lantern—straws

233   **BURKE, L.** *I'm a scientist: my body*. 2011, DK (ISBN: 9780756682170). 24 p.
GRADE LEVEL: Lower elementary
CONTENTS: N/A

234   **BURKE, L.** *I'm a scientist: water fun*. 2011, DK (ISBN: 9780756682187). 24 p.
SERIES: I'm a scientist
GRADE LEVEL: Lower elementary
CONTENTS: Boat—life jacket—submarine—starburst—water—cubes—hot and cold—volcano—meltdown—ice—waterwheel—bulging water—pond skater—music

235   **BURNS, B.** *Basketball step-by-step*. 2010, Rosen Central (ISBN: 9781435833609). 96 p.
SERIES: Skills in motion
GRADE LEVEL: Upper elementary – middle school
CONTENTS: N/A

236   **BURTON, B.** *You can draw Star Wars*. 2007, DK (ISBN: 9780756623432). 96 p.
GRADE LEVEL: Elementary
CONTENTS: N/A

237   **CADUTO, M.** *Catch the wind harness the sun: 22 super-charged science projects for kids*. 2011, Storey (ISBN: 9781603429719). 224p.
GRADE LEVEL: Upper elementary – middle school
CONTENTS: Enlightenment—simluation—marsh bubbles—ohms & watts—trees—countries—writing—campfire—drying clothes—sun cooking—sun test—solar heat—solar power—wind maker—wind gauge—sail away—windmill power—static balloons—north—pedals—board game

238   **CALHOUN, Y.** *Plant and animal science fair projects, revised and expanded using the scientific method*. 2010, Enslow (ISBN: 9780766034211). 160 p.
GRADE LEVEL: Upper elementary – middle school
CONTENTS: Biological diversity—survival needs—responses—adaptations

239   **CAMPBELL, G.** *The boys' book of survival: survive anything, anywhere*. 2009, Scholastic (ISBN: 9780545085366).
GRADE LEVEL: Elementary
CONTENTS: Group expedition—survival pack—be a leader—avoid piranhas—survive a tornado—spend the night in the wilderness—falling off a horse—duel—alien invasion—bully—shark attack—make a ladder—attacked by a polar bear—long car journey—read a compass—cope without a compass—make a compass using the sun—haunting—tricky situations—radiation—swarm of honeybees—catch a fish with your bare hands—gut a fish—get rid of leeches—the recovery position—land an airplane—avalanche—bear country—survival shelter—abominable snowman—

quick-release knot—S.O.S.—zombie invasion—quicksand—track an animal—make a tracking stick—stage a jailbreak—make a getaway—survive a school dance—make a catapult—survive a huge pimple—carry someone to safety—make an underwater escape—survive the bubonic plague—shopping expedition—hungry hippos—tie a sling—essay crisis—stuck in an elevator—snakebite—man-eating tiger—predict rain—igloo—make fresh water from seawater—light a fire—survive a family Christmas—wade through running water—dugout canoe—be a modest hero—survive your teachers

240   **CAPPELLI, F.** *The clarinet: an illustrated step-by-step instructional guide.* 2007, Eldorado Ink (ISBN: 9781932904123). 112 p.

SERIES: Learn to play

GRADE LEVEL: High school

CONTENTS: Getting started—reading music—let's play

241   **CAPPELLI, F.** *The flute: an illustrated step-by-step instructional guide.* 2007, Eldorado Ink (ISBN: 9781932904130). 112 p.

SERIES: Learn to play

GRADE LEVEL: High school

CONTENTS: Reading music—getting ready to play—let's play

242   **CAPPELLI, F.** *The guitar: an illustrated step-by-step instructional guide.* 2007, Eldorado Ink (ISBN: 9781932904147). 112 p.

SERIES: Learn to play

GRADE LEVEL: High school

CONTENTS: Choosing the guitar—amplifier—holding the guitar—hand techniques—strumming—the strings—tuning—changing strings—making music—reading a chord diagram—the G and D chords—reading music—time signature—rhythmic notes—basic warm-up—G and G exercises—tablature—C and F—E—EM—and E7—A—B7—playing the chords you know—beyond chords—the rest of the basics—the notes—clef symbols—time signature—more chords—the sharp and flat signs—string notation—E and its notes—B string and its notes—G string and its notes—D string and its notes—A string and its notes—E string and its notes—songs: Kumbaya—My Bonnie—Cielito Lindo—Bingo—On Top of Old Mmokey—The Gate of Heaven—This Old Man—Red River Valley

243   **CAPPELLI, F.** *The piano: an illustrated step-by-step instructional guide.* 2007, Eldorado Ink (ISBN: 9781932904154). 112 p.

SERIES: Learn to play

GRADE LEVEL: High school

CONTENTS: Choosing a piano—staff and notes—treble clef—bass clef—time signature—sharp and flat symbols—the notes on the keyboard—right hand—left hand—right and left hand together—C chord—treble clef—using both hands—F chord—G chord—C scale—scales and other exercises—more chording options—major chords in C: the i—iv—and v chords—basic piano care—tips

244   **CAPPELLI, F.** *The trumpet: an illustrated step-by-step instructional guide.* 2007, Eldorado Ink (ISBN: 9781932904161). 112 p.

SERIES: Learn to play

GRADE LEVEL: High school

CONTENTS: Trumpet basics—getting ready to play—let's play!—songs and exercises

245 **CAPPELLI, F. *The violin: an illustrated step-by-step instructional guide*.** 2007, Eldorado Ink (ISBN: 9781932904178). 112 p.

SERIES: Learn to play

GRADE LEVEL: High school

CONTENTS: Getting started—reading music—let's play—songs

246 **CAPSEY, S. *Cars*.** 2011, Windmill Books (ISBN: 9781615332632). 32 p.

SERIES: Let's draw

GRADE LEVEL: Upper elementary

CONTENTS: Materials—basic shapes—car parts—shading—texture and color—action—Mini—dragster—4x4—custom car—Saloon—Porsche—Smart car—Lamborghini—stock car—Aston Martin—Jeep—Ferrari—Mercedes—rally car—F1 racing car

247 **CARLSON, L. *Harry Houdini for kids: his life and adventures with 21 magic tricks and illusions*.** 2009, Chicago Review Press (ISBN: 9781556527821). 144 p.

SERIES: For kids

GRADE LEVEL: Middle school

CONTENTS: Step through a note card—odd number trick—star is born—linking paper rings—lift a person with one hand—four against one—balls or coins trick—becoming the handcuff king—dissolving rings trick—magic knot trick—mind reading with secret code—crowd goes wild—magic key—make a magic box—going to extremes—milk can escape—measure volume displacement—build a box kite—aviator—actor-spy?—magical money trick—write an invisible message—make a secret spy safe—crack a secret code—ghostbuster—make some slimy ectoplasm—make a talking board—create ghostly handprints

248 **CARLSON, M. *Crazy clay creations*.** 2013, Impact (ISBN: 9781440322211). 64 p.

SERIES: Kids DIY

GRADE LEVEL: Upper elementary

CONTENTS: N/A

249 **CARSON, M. *Beyond the solar system: explaining galaxies, black holes, alien planets, and more: a history with 21 activities*.** 2013, Chicago Review Press (ISBN: 9781613745441). 144 p.

SERIES: For kids

GRADE LEVEL: Middle school

CONTENTS: Polaris—Ptolemy—astrolabe—star watch—lenses—reflecting telescope—white light—3-D starscape—milky way—sky distances—t-shirt—a toy—space-time—balloon—interference—radio picture—pulsar—black hole—galaxy clusters—galactic group—exoplanets

250 **CARSON, M. *Exploring the solar system: a history with 22 activities*.** 2008, Chicago Review Press (ISBN: 9781556527159). 168 p.

GRADE LEVEL: Upper elementary

CONTENTS: Evening star—orbits—telescope—spectroscope—rocket—Pluto—satellite watching—moon's surface—astronaut—kitchen craters—warm-up—organic—

eggs—code—earth greetings—comet nucleus—metric—falling stars—a probe—Mars in 3-d—Mars' mission—mission patch

251 CARSON, M. *Weather projects for young scientists: experiments and science fair ideas*. 2007, Chicago Review Press (ISBN: 9781435208858). 144p.
GRADE LEVEL: Upper elementary – middle school
CONTENTS: Atmosphere—air—balloons—pressure—barometer—hurricane—sun—telling time—prints—seasons—strength—absorbing heat—thermometer—hot air—hothouse—water cycle—changes—rain gauge—rainbow—sleet and snow—snow globes—rain—dew point—frost—psychrometer—clouds—tracking weather—static—weather testing—wind—anemometer—chilly feeling—wind vane—wind power—poems—tornado—invert air—pollution trap—weather station—forecast—weather mapping—weather warnings—warming water

252 CASTALDO, N. *Keeping our earth green: over 100 hands-on ways to help save the earth*. 2008, Williamson (ISBN: 9781439579879). 128 p.
SERIES: Kids can!
GRADE LEVEL: Elementary
CONTENTS: Air—water—land—energy

253 CATTERALL, C. *The hot air balloon book: build and launch kongming lanterns, solar tetroons, and more*. 2013, Chicago Review Press (ISBN: 9781613740965). 240 p.
SERIES: Science in motion
GRADE LEVEL: Middle school – high school
CONTENTS: Balloon—lantern—Montgolfiere—Khom loi—UFO—solar tetroon

254 CECERI, K. *Around the world crafts: great activities for kids who like history, math, art, science, and more*. 2008, Crafts for Learning (ISBN: 9781438278001). 76 p.
GRADE LEVEL: Elementary
CONTENTS: N/A

255 CECERI, K. *Discover the desert: the driest place on Earth*. 2009, Nomad Press (ISBN: 9781934670460). 96p.
SERIES: Discover your world
GRADE LEVEL: Upper elementary – middle school
CONTENTS: Bottle—salt crystals—pendant—pet triops—dish garden—gaiters—transport—mirage—solar still—morning dew—plant moisture—hat—anchor—shelter

256 CECERI, K. *Robotics: discover the science and technology of the future with 20 projects*. 2012, Nomad Press (ISBN: 9781936749768). 128 p.
SERIES: Build it Yourself
GRADE LEVEL: Upper elementary – middle school
CONTENTS: Vibrobot—robot skin—solar wobblebot—solenoid—mini-walker—robotic hand—robotic arm—robotic gripper—tilt sensor—pressure sensor—logo program (#1)—logo program (#2)—logo program (#3)—bead jewelry

257 CECERI, K. *The silk road: explore the world's most famous trade routes*. 2011, Nomad Press (ISBN: 9781934670620). 128 p.
SERIES: Build it yourself

GRADE LEVEL: Upper elementary – middle school

CONTENTS: N/A

258   CECERI, K. *World myths and legends: 25 projects you can build yourself.* 2010, Nomad Press (ISBN: 9781934670439). 128 p.

SERIES: Build it yourself

GRADE LEVEL: Upper elementary – middle school

CONTENTS: Window hanging—clay tablet—zodiac starfinder—mummy—allusions collage—triangle with compass and ruler—odyssey whirlpool—flower hair wreath—Celtic armband—sword in the stone—runic stones and pouch—thunder drum—adinkra cloth—Rangoli design—stone stupa—magic square—tiger kite—egg doll—indoor boomerang—Maya ball game—Calavera—quipa—Three Sisters garden—succotash—kachina doll

259   CERATO, M. *You can draw construction vehicles.* 2012, Picture Window Books (ISBN: 9781404868076). 24 p.

SERIES: You can draw

GRADE LEVEL: Lower elementary

CONTENTS: N/A

260   CERATO, M. *You can draw dinosaurs.* 2011, Picture Window Books (ISBN: 9781404862807). 24 p.

SERIES: You can draw

GRADE LEVEL: Lower elementary

CONTENTS: N/A

261   CERATO, M. *You can draw dragons, unicorns, and other magical creatures.* 2012, Picture Window Books (ISBN: 9781404868090). 24 p.

SERIES: You can draw

GRADE LEVEL: Lower elementary

CONTENTS: N/A

262   CERATO, M. *You can draw flowers.* 2011, Picture Window Books (ISBN: 9781404862791). 24 p.

SERIES: You can draw

GRADE LEVEL: Lower elementary

CONTENTS: N/A

263   CHALLONER, J. *Sound and light.* 2013, Kingfisher (ISBN: 9780753469743). 32 p.

SERIES: Hands-on science

GRADE LEVEL: Upper elementary

CONTENTS: Getting started—sound sources—light sources—traveling sound—traveling light—sound tones—musical sounds—white light—colored light—hearing sound—seeing light—reflecting sound—reflecting light—mirrors—bending light—lenses—recording sound and light

264   CHAMPION, N. *Camping and hiking.* 2011, PowerKids Press (ISBN: 9781448832958). 32 p.

SERIES: Get outdoors

GRADE LEVEL: Upper elementary

CONTENTS: Camping and hiking—walking for fitness—get started—equipment—packing—walk—planning—choosing a site—food—water—and cooking—hazards—first aid

265   **CHAMPION, N. *Finding your way*.** 2011, Amicus (ISBN: 9781607530381). 32 p.

SERIES: Survive alive

GRADE LEVEL: Upper elementary – middle school

CONTENTS: Lost—into the unknown—ancient skills—using the sun—night—reading a map—get your bearings—gadgets—danger—smart skills—real-life navigators—out and about

266   **CHAMPION, N. *In an emergency*.** 2011, Amicus (ISBN: 9781607530404). 32 p.

SERIES: Survive alive

GRADE LEVEL: Upper elementary – middle school

CONTENTS: Disaster strikes—using your head—first aid skills—extreme cold—extreme heat—lost—dangerous places—angry animals—wild weather – fire—hunger and thirst—getting help

267   **CHAMPION, N. *Making shelter*.** 2011, Amicus (ISBN: 9781607530411). 32 p.

SERIES: Survive alive

GRADE LEVEL: Upper elementary – middle school

CONTENTS: Emergency homes—natural shelters—choosing a site—building basics—forest huts—jungle shelters—snow caves and graves—making an igloo—desert shelters—prairie homes—stone—sod—and log huts—taking a tent

268   **CHAMPION, N. *Orienteering*.** 2010, PowerKids Press (ISBN: 9781435830448). 32 p.

SERIES: Get outdoors

GRADE LEVEL: Upper elementary

CONTENTS: Sport for all—equipment—the map—using a compass—training body and mind—developing skills—techniques—when something goes wrong—competitive orienteering

269   **CHAMPION, N. *Rock climbing*.** 2010, PowerKids Press (ISBN: 9781435830431). 32 p.

SERIES: Get outdoors

GRADE LEVEL: Upper elementary

CONTENTS: Equipment—safety chain—warming up and stretching—indoor climbing walls—real rock—technique and movement skills—strength and endurance—using holds well—abseiling

270   **CHAMPION, N. *Tools and crafts*.** 2011, Amicus (ISBN: 9781607530428). 32 p.

SERIES: Survive alive

GRADE LEVEL: Upper elementary – middle school

CONTENTS: All kinds of wood—wooden crafts—bark—branches and grass—making rope—know your knots—stones—bones—and shells—clay crafts—fishing tools—keeping clean—wilderness sense

271   **CHANCELLOR, D. *Maps and mapping*.** 2010, Kingfisher (ISBN: 9780753464502). 56 p.

SERIES: Discover science

GRADE LEVEL: Elementary

CONTENTS: N/A

272 **CHANCELLOR, D.** *Planet Earth*. 2011, Kingfisher (ISBN: 9780753466049). 56 p.

SERIES: Discover science

GRADE LEVEL: Elementary

CONTENTS: Volcano—rain gauge—windmill—forest

273 **CHARNEY, S.** *Amazing tricks with everyday stuff*. 2011, Capstone (ISBN: 9781429645171). 24 p.

SERIES: Easy magic tricks

GRADE LEVEL: Lower elementary

CONTENTS: Loony balloony—tipsy soda can—disappearing toothpick—karate finger—don't worry, be happy—a banana for two—lolli-pop!—having a ball

274 **CHARNEY, S.** *Awesome coin tricks*. 2011, Capstone (ISBN: 9781429645140). 24 p.

SERIES: Easy magic tricks

GRADE LEVEL: Lower elementary

CONTENTS: Flipped out—coin drop—bottled up—Joe's mom—elbow coin snatch—funny bone magic—making change—disappearing crayon

275 **CHARNEY, S.** *Cool card tricks*. 2011, Capstone (ISBN: 9781429645157). 24 p.

SERIES: Easy magic tricks

GRADE LEVEL: Lower elementary

CONTENTS: Flip-flop—bubble cards—key cards—magic fingers—two piles—one card—four pirates—fingerprints

276 **CHARNEY, S.** *Incredible tricks at the dinner table*. 2011, Capstone (ISBN: 9781429645164). 24 p.

SERIES: Easy magic tricks

GRADE LEVEL: Lower elementary

CONTENTS: Shaker taker—balancing act—last straw—really cool trick—sticky fingers—great grape—new-again napkin—clink drink

277 **CHARNEY, S.** *The kids' guide to magic tricks*. 2013, Capstone (ISBN: 9781429684521). 32 p.

SERIES: Kids' guides

GRADE LEVEL: Upper elementary – middle school

CONTENTS: What's your number?—ring and rope—a hearty assistance—poking washington's eye—the magic shoelace—hatful of water—shrinking ads—cups and balls—beam me up—squirmy wormy

278 **CHAUFFE, E.** *Kids show kids how to make balloon animals*. 2009, Casy Shay Press (ISBN: 9780984187904).

GRADE LEVEL: Elementary

CONTENTS: Getting started—bee—sword and belt—dog—giraffe—elephant—twist hat—candy cane—wreath—crown

279 **CHRYSSICAS, M.** *Breathe: yoga for teens*. 2007, DK (ISBN: 9780756626617). 160 p.
GRADE LEVEL: Middle school – high school
CONTENTS: Why yoga?—creating energy—warm up—confidence builders—commanding respect—cool to be me—powerful posture—athleticism—creativity—what's right for your body—savasana—practices—your yoga journal

280 **CIVARDI, A.** *Bags and purses: craft ideas from around the world*. 2011, Sea to Sea (ISBN: 9781445101590).
SERIES: World of design
GRADE LEVEL: Elementary
CONTENTS: Drawstring bag—perfect pouch—envelope bag—wallet beltbag—disco-box bag—applique bag

281 **CIVARDI, A.** *Bowls and boxes: craft ideas from around the world*. 2011, Sea to Sea (ISBN: 9781445101583).
SERIES: World of design
GRADE LEVEL: Elementary
CONTENTS: Clay coil pot—pulpy paper holder—pumpkin lantern—paper basket—recycled wrapper bowl—shiny star box

282 **CIVARDI, A.** *Festival decorations: craft ideas from around the world*. 2010, Sea to Sea (ISBN: 9781597712088).
SERIES: World of design
GRADE LEVEL: Elementary
CONTENTS: Paper piñata—gingerbread people—making a Diwali lamp—eye of god—corn dolly—bird headdress

283 **CLARK, T.** *How to improve at playing guitar*. 2010, Crabtree (ISBN: 9780778735786). 48 p.
SERIES: How to improve at
GRADE LEVEL: Elementary
CONTENTS: Tuning—playing positions—strumming and picking—musical notation—warming up—basic skills: open chords—chords and single notes—rhythm—time signatures—basic plucking—palm muting—major and minor scales—play-along songs—intermediate skills: spot of revision—hammer-ons—pull-offs—legato and staccato—building up speed—fingerpicking—barre chords—more scales exercises—musical styles—play-along songs—advanced skills: blues scale—alternate picking—major pentatonic scales—minor pentonic scales—soloing techniques—blues melodies—rock melodies

284 **CLAY, K.** *Ballet dancing*. 2010, Capstone (ISBN: 9781429640022). 24 p.
SERIES: Dance, dance, dance
GRADE LEVEL: Lower elementary
CONTENTS: N/A

285 **CLAY, K.** *Hip-hop dancing*. 2010, Capstone (ISBN: 9781429640039). 24 p.
SERIES: Dance, dance, dance
GRADE LEVEL: Lower elementary
CONTENTS: What to wear—sweet steps—ready to dance

286   CLAY, K. *How to draw amazing letters*. 2009, Capstone (ISBN: 9781429623056). 32 p.
SERIES: Drawing fun
GRADE LEVEL: Elementary
CONTENTS: N/A

287   CLAY, K. *How to draw cool kids*. 2009, Capstone (ISBN: 9781429623049). 32 p.
SERIES: Drawing fun
GRADE LEVEL: Elementary
CONTENTS: N/A

288   CLAY, K. *How to draw cute animals*. 2010, Capstone (ISBN: 9781429634052). 32 p.
SERIES: Drawing fun
GRADE LEVEL: Elementary
CONTENTS: Rabbit—duckling—kangaroo and joey—kitten—koala—meerkat—panda—puppy—sea lion—red-eyed tree frog—penguin family

289   CLAY, K. *How to draw horses*. 2009, Capstone (ISBN: 9781429623063). 32 p.
SERIES: Drawing fun
GRADE LEVEL: Elementary
CONTENTS: Head study—Clydesdale—foal—grazing horse—horse resting—braided beauty—bucking bronco—dancing Lipizzan—racing Arabian—Appaloosa—Thoroughbred and rider

290   CLAY, K. *How to draw mythical creatures*. 2009, Capstone (ISBN: 9781429623070). 32 p.
SERIES: Drawing fun
GRADE LEVEL: Elementary
CONTENTS: Fairy—genie—mermaid—dragon—good witch—woodland elf—Medusa—Pegasus—garden pixie—unicorn—magical friends

291   CLAY, K. *Jazz dancing*. 2010, Capstone (ISBN: 9781429640046). 24 p.
SERIES: Dance, dance, dance
GRADE LEVEL: Lower elementary
CONTENTS: Getting ready—sweet steps—ready to dance

292   CLAY, K. *Tap dancing*. 2010, Capstone (ISBN: 9781429640053). 24 p.
SERIES: Dance, dance, dance
GRADE LEVEL: Lower elementary
CONTENTS: Equipment—sweet steps—ready to dance

293   CLAYBOURNE, A. *Accessories for all*. 2013, Smart Apple Media (ISBN: 9781599206943). 32 p.
SERIES: Be creative
GRADE LEVEL: Upper elementary – middle school
CONTENTS: N/A

294   CLAYBOURNE, A. *Bedroom makeover*. 2013, Smart Apple Media (ISBN: 9781599206950). 32 p.

SERIES: Be creative

GRADE LEVEL: Upper elementary – middle school

CONTENTS: Little birds—bedroom bunting—pillow cover—decorated pillow—panel curtain—handy pocket—big bedspread—patchwork projects—photo frame—writing on the wall—wall stencils—waste paper basket

295 **CLAYBOURNE, A. *Cards, wraps, and tags*.** 2013, Smart Apple Media (ISBN: 9781599206967). 32 p.

SERIES: Be creative

GRADE LEVEL: Upper elementary – middle school

CONTENTS: N/A

296 **CLAYBOURNE, A. *Customize your clothes*.** 2013, Smart Apple Media (ISBN: 9781599206936). 32 p.

SERIES: Be creative

GRADE LEVEL: Upper elementary – middle school

CONTENTS: T-shirt picture—ribbons and trimmings—felt flowers—jazz up your jeans—corsage—pants to shorts—cuffs—beads and buttons—footwear—sandals—applique—advanced applique

297 **CLAYBOURNE, A. *Ear-splitting sounds and other vile noises*.** 2013, Crabtree (ISBN: 9780778709510). 32 p.

SERIES: Disgusting & dreadful science

GRADE LEVEL: Upper elementary

CONTENTS: Bang—sound—ears—boom—ultrasound—sounds—grunts—growls—squeaks and shrieks—ear-splitting science—instruments—inventions—playback—sounds nasty—the future

298 **CLAYBOURNE, A. *Electric shocks and other energy evils*.** 2013, Crabtree (ISBN: 9780778709534). 32 p.

SERIES: Disgusting & dreadful science

GRADE LEVEL: Upper elementary

CONTENTS: Zap—wires—electricity—shocka—static—lightning—sparks—life—medicine—monster—the future

299 **CLAYBOURNE, A. *Glaring light and other eye-burning rays*.** 2013, Crabtree (ISBN: 9780778709558). 32 p.

SERIES: Disgusting & dreadful science

GRADE LEVEL: Upper elementary

CONTENTS: Flash—stretch—time travel—slime—eyeballs—dark and spooky—seeing—sparks—inventions—spectrum—beasts

300 **CLAYBOURNE, A. *Gut-wrenching gravity and other fatal forces*.** 2013, Crabtree (ISBN: 9780778709572). 32 p.

SERIES: Disgusting & dreadful science

GRADE LEVEL: Upper elementary

CONTENTS: Force—gravity—splat—deadly gravity—g-forces—falling—spaghetti—gravity—friction—magnets—floating—flying—gravity-defying—crawling—vomit comet

301 **CLAYBOURNE, A.** *Make it bang!* 2013, Wayland (ISBN: 9780750277310). 32 p.
SERIES: Whizzy science
GRADE LEVEL: Elementary
CONTENTS: N/A

302 **CLAYBOURNE, A.** *Make it change!* 2013, Wayland (ISBN: 9780750277341). 32 p.
SERIES: Whizzy science
GRADE LEVEL: Elementary
CONTENTS: N/A

303 **CLAYBOURNE, A.** *Make it glow!* 2013, Wayland (ISBN: 9780750277334). 32 p.
SERIES: Whizzy science
GRADE LEVEL: Elementary
CONTENTS: N/A

304 **CLAYBOURNE, A.** *Make it grow!* 2013, Wayland (ISBN: 9780750277365). 32 p.
SERIES: Whizzy science
GRADE LEVEL: Elementary
CONTENTS: N/A

305 **CLAYBOURNE, A.** *Make it splash!* 2013, Wayland (ISBN: 9780750277358). 32 p.
SERIES: Whizzy science
GRADE LEVEL: Elementary
CONTENTS: N/A

306 **CLAYBOURNE, A.** *Make it zoom!* 2013, Wayland (ISBN: 9780750277327). 32 p.
SERIES: Whizzy science
GRADE LEVEL: Elementary
CONTENTS: N/A

307 **CLUNES, R.** *Drawing creepy crawlies.* 2012, Gareth Stevens (ISBN: 9781433959387). 32 p.
SERIES: Drawing is fun!
GRADE LEVEL: Elementary
CONTENTS: Scorpion—praying mantis—fly—caterpillar—snail—grasshopper—butterfly—ladybug—dragonfly—centipede—stag beetle—moth—ant—bumblebee

308 **CLUNES, R.** *Drawing dinosaurs.* 2012, Gareth Stevens (ISBN: 9781433959424). 32 p.
SERIES: Drawing is fun!
GRADE LEVEL: Elementary
CONTENTS: Apatosaurus—Tyrannosaurus Rex—Pteranodon—Triceratops—Archaeopteryx—Stegosaurus—Deinonychus—Parasaurolophus—Allosaurus—Brachiosaurus—Spinosaurus—Elasmosaurus—Einiosaurus—Velociraptor

309 **CLUNES, R.** *Drawing sea creatures.* 2012, Gareth Stevens (ISBN: 9781433959462). 32 p.
SERIES: Drawing is fun!
GRADE LEVEL: Elementary

CONTENTS: Clown fish—turtle—killer whale—seahorse—walrus—jellyfish—sea otter—sailfish—lobster—hammerhead shark—octopus—sea lion—crab

310 **CLUNES, R.** *Drawing speed machines*. 2012, Gareth Stevens (ISBN: 9781433959509). 32 p.
SERIES: Drawing is fun!
GRADE LEVEL: Elementary
CONTENTS: Bullet train—racing car—speedboat—jet ski—stealth plane—ATV—fighter plane—snowmobile—private jet—kart—scooter—motorbike and sidecar—stunt plane—sports car

311 **COBB, V.** *See for yourself: more than 100 amazing experiments for science fairs and school projects*. 2010, Skyhorse (ISBN: 9781616080839). 192p.
GRADE LEVEL: Upper elementary – middle school
CONTENTS: N/A

312 **COELHO, A.** *Why is milk white? And 200 other curious chemistry questions*. 2013, Chicago Review Press (ISBN: 9781613744529). 288p.
GRADE LEVEL: Lower elementary
CONTENTS: N/A

313 **COHEN, R.** *Catfish fishing*. 2012, Rosen Central (ISBN: 9781448846023). 62 p.
SERIES: Fishing tips and techniques
GRADE LEVEL: Upper elementary
CONTENTS: N/A

314 **COHN, J.** *The ancient Chinese*. 2013, Gareth Stevens (ISBN: 9781433976971). 48 p.
SERIES: Crafts from the past
GRADE LEVEL: Upper elementary – middle school
CONTENTS: N/A

315 **COHN, J.** *The ancient Eyptians*. 2013, Gareth Stevens (ISBN: 9781433977015). 48 p.
SERIES: Crafts from the past
GRADE LEVEL: Upper elementary – middle school
CONTENTS: N/A

316 **COHN, J.** *The ancient Greeks*. 2012, Gareth Stevens (ISBN: 9781433977053). 48 p.
SERIES: Crafts from the past
GRADE LEVEL: Upper elementary – middle school
CONTENTS: N/A

317 **COHN, J.** *The ancient Indians*. 2013, Gareth Stevens (ISBN: 9781433977183). 48 p.
SERIES: Crafts from the past
GRADE LEVEL: Upper elementary – middle school
CONTENTS: N/A

318 **COHN, J.** *The ancient Romans*. 2013, Gareth Stevens (ISBN: 9781433977091). 48 p.
SERIES: Crafts from the past

GRADE LEVEL: Upper elementary – middle school

CONTENTS: N/A

319 **COHN, J.** *The Aztecs*. 2013, Gareth Stevens (ISBN: 9781433977138). 48 p.
SERIES: Crafts from the past
GRADE LEVEL: Upper elementary – middle school
CONTENTS: N/A

320 **COLEMAN, L.** *Girls' basketball: making your mark on the court*. 2007, Capstone (ISBN: 9780736868211). 32 p.
SERIES: Girls got game
GRADE LEVEL: Elementary
CONTENTS: Slam dunk—hitting the court—get in the game—becoming the best

321 **COLEMAN, L.** *Girls' soccer: going for the goal*. 2007, Capstone (ISBN: 9780736868235). 32 p.
SERIES: Girls got game
GRADE LEVEL: Elementary
CONTENTS: On the field—the rules—soccer in action—becoming the best

322 **CONNOLLY, S.** *The book of perfectly perilous math: 24 death-defying challenges for young mathematicians*. 2012, Workman (ISBN: 9780761163749). 240 p.
GRADE LEVEL: Upper elementary – middle school
CONTENTS: Pendulum—pizza—spending—gallon—sage—the solution—the desert—make it last—secret code—quick change—pyramid—buried alive—rope bridge—punk prank—tornado—the long way—sands of time—final countdown—vampires—lost at sea—the bends—escape—treasure—which door

323 **CONNOLLY, S.** *The book of potentially catastrophic science: 50 experiments for daring young scientists*. 2010, Workman (ISBN: 9780761156871). 306 p.
GRADE LEVEL: Upper elementary – middle school
CONTENTS: Chopper—Fahrenheit 451 experiment—bow and arrow—wheel and axle—superbike—skyscraper—North star—earthquake—fireworks—lunar eclipse—telescope—Jupiter moons—friction—third law of motion—lightning mouth—charged balloon—hair-raising experiment—battery—trash bag—ping pong experiment—water microscope—germ—parachute—steam can—bobbin elevator—fossil—x-ray vision—x-ray machine—carbon dating—aerodynamics—flying machine—magical atom—motion—rocket—helicopter—airfoil—chain reaction—sonic boom—rocket sled—deceleration—DNA—laser oven—flashlight beam—orbit—balloon thrust—water—stethoscope—heartbeat—avalanche—hadron collider

324 **CONNOLLY, S.** *The book of totally irresponsible science: 64 daring experiments for young scientists*. 2008, Workman (ISBN: 9780761150206). 205 p.
GRADE LEVEL: Upper elementary – middle school
CONTENTS: Geyser—Vesuvius—bomb—balloon—beacon—hold—lightning—weather—slime—air cannon—ice—smokescreen—gun—hand—bungee jump—milk to stone—breakfast cereal—spoon—ice cream—rice—eggs—marshmallows—milk—straw—peas—eggs—sandwich—salt—first aid—water—rocket—moon bounce—mothballs—hovercraft—rocket—ball—funeral—little ball—unpoppable balloon—hot air balloon—last straw—balloon—pond-life—chicken bone—solid liquid or

liquid solid—sandwich bag—rose—plant—exposure—blubber—overflowing cup—bottomless pit—microphone—non-leak leak—the truth—banshee—bubble child—gravity—magic napkin—cash or charge?—non-drip document—alchemy—head for lights

325 **COOK, C.** *Glee club style: choosing costumes, makeup, sets, and props*. 2012, Rosen (ISBN: 9781448868766). 64 p.
SERIES: Glee club
GRADE LEVEL: Upper elementary – middle school
CONTENTS: Gleeful costumes—makeup—sets—props—the performance

326 **COOK, D.** *The kids' multicultural cookbook: food and fun from around the world*. 2008, Williamson (ISBN: 9780824968175). 157 p.
SERIES: Kids can!
GRADE LEVEL: Elementary
CONTENTS: N/A

327 **COOK, T.** *Drawing manga*. 2011, Gareth Stevens (ISBN: 9781433950674). 32 p.
SERIES: Drawing is fun!
GRADE LEVEL: Elementary
CONTENTS: N/A

328 **COOK, T.** *Drawing pets and farm animals*. 2011, Gareth Stevens (ISBN: 9781433950711). 32 p.
SERIES: Drawing is fun!
GRADE LEVEL: Elementary
CONTENTS: N/A

329 **COOK, T.** *Drawing sports figures*. 2011, Gareth Stevens (ISBN: 9781433950742). 32 p.
SERIES: Drawing is fun!
GRADE LEVEL: Elementary
CONTENTS: N/A

330 **COOK, T.** *Drawing vehicles*. 2011, Gareth Stevens (ISBN: 9781433950773). 32 p.
SERIES: Drawing is fun!
GRADE LEVEL: Elementary
CONTENTS: Viking ship—jet plane—train—bus—bicycle—helicopter—steamroller—car—pirate ship—backhoe—tractor—cruise ship—truck—motorcycle

331 **COOK, T.** *Drawing wild animals*. 2011, Gareth Stevens (ISBN: 9781433950797). 32 p.
SERIES: Drawing is fun!
GRADE LEVEL: Elementary
CONTENTS: Camel—dolphin—lion—giraffe—rhinoceros—gorilla—leopard—shark—tiger—polar bear—elephant—hippopotamus—orangutan—penguin

332 **CORFEE, S.** *Fashion design workshop: stylish step-by-step projects and drawing tips for the up-and-coming designers*. 2011, Walter Foster (ISBN: 9781936309856).

GRADE LEVEL: Middle school – high school

CONTENTS: Proportions—poses—head & face—eyes & lips—hairstyles—arms & hands—legs & feet—mannequins—tips & tricks—tops—tees & tanks—jeans—pants & shorts—skirts—dresses & gowns—sweater—jackets & outerwear—hats—shoes & handbags—chic & trendy—girly & romantic—fun & casual—confident & classic—athletic & sporty—bohemian & eclectic—rebellious & daring—skate dude—'40s swing—'50s rock 'n' roll—'60s mod squad—'70s disco—'80s new wave—renaissance era—blushing bride

333 COURT, R. *How to draw aircraft*. 2007, Child's World (ISBN: 9781592968039). 32 p.
SERIES: Doodle books
GRADE LEVEL: Elementary
CONTENTS: N/A

334 COURT, R. *How to draw cars and trucks*. 2007, Child's World (ISBN: 159296804X). 32 p.
SERIES: Doodle books
GRADE LEVEL: Elementary
CONTENTS: N/A

335 COURT, R. *How to draw Christmas things*. 2007, Child's World (ISBN: 9781592968053). 32 p.
SERIES: Doodle books
GRADE LEVEL: Elementary
CONTENTS: N/A

336 COURT, R. *How to draw dinosaurs*. 2007, Child's World (ISBN: 9781592968060). 32 p.
SERIES: Doodle books
GRADE LEVEL: Elementary
CONTENTS: N/A

337 COURT, R. *How to draw flowers and trees*. 2007, Child's World (ISBN: 9781592968077). 32 p.
SERIES: Doodle books
GRADE LEVEL: Elementary
CONTENTS: N/A

338 COURT, R. *How to draw food*. 2008, Child's World (ISBN: 9781592969531). 32 p.
SERIES: Doodle books
GRADE LEVEL: Elementary
CONTENTS: Apple—grapes—carrot—corn—bread—muffin—hamburger—hotdog—pizza—spaghetti—cookie—cake—pie—ice cream

339 COURT, R. *How to draw Halloween things*. 2007, Child's World (ISBN: 9781592968084). 32 p.
SERIES: Doodle books
GRADE LEVEL: Elementary
CONTENTS: N/A

340 **COURT, R.** *How to draw Independence Day things*. 2008, Child's World (ISBN: 9781592969548). 32 p.

SERIES: Doodle books

GRADE LEVEL: Elementary

CONTENTS: Flag—stars—eagle—Uncle Sam—sparkler—fireworks—watermelon—apple pie—picnic—Liberty Bell—Statue of Liberty—White House—Mount Rushmore—Washington monument

341 **COURT, R.** *How to draw jungle animals*. 2008, Child's World (ISBN: 9781592969555). 32 p.

SERIES: Doodle books

GRADE LEVEL: Elementary

CONTENTS: N/A

342 **COURT, R.** *How to draw people*. 2007, Child's World (ISBN: 9781592968091). 32 p.

SERIES: Doodle books

GRADE LEVEL: Elementary

CONTENTS: N/A

343 **COURT, R.** *How to draw sports things*. 2008, Child's World (ISBN: 9781592969562). 32 p.

SERIES: Doodle books

GRADE LEVEL: Elementary

CONTENTS: N/A

344 **COURT, R.** *How to draw underwater animals*. 2007, Child's World (ISBN: 9781592968107). 32 p.

SERIES: Doodle books

GRADE LEVEL: Elementary

CONTENTS: N/A

345 **COURT, R.** *How to draw watercraft*. 2008, Child's World (ISBN: 9781592969586). 32 p.

SERIES: Doodle books

GRADE LEVEL: Elementary

CONTENTS: Rowboat—sailboat—motorboat—personal watercraft—yacht—canoe—raft—kayak—tugboat—barge—catamaran—pontoon—submarine—tall ship

346 **CRESPO, S.** *Learn to draw the best of Nickelodeon*. 2013, Walter Foster (ISBN: 9781936309214).

GRADE LEVEL: Upper elementary – middle school

CONTENTS: Spongebob Squarepants—Patrick Star—Plankton—Mr. Krabs—Gary—Tommy Pickles—Chuckie Finster—Timmy—Cosmo—Wanda—Jimmy Neutron—Leonardo—Raphael—Michelangelo—Donatello—Aang—Katara—Sokka

347 **CRISFIELD, D.** *Winning soccer for girls*. 2010, Checkmark Books (ISBN: 9780816077144). 164 p.

SERIES: Winning sports for girls

GRADE LEVEL: Middle school – high school
CONTENTS: N/A

348 **CRISFIELD, D. *Winning volleyball for girls*.** 2010, Chelsea House (ISBN: 9780816077205). 189 p.
SERIES: Winning sports for girls
GRADE LEVEL: Middle school – high school
CONTENTS: N/A

349 **CROCKETT, S. *Fly fishing*.** 2012, Capstone (ISBN: 9781429648110). 32 p.
SERIES: Wild outdoors
GRADE LEVEL: Lower elementary
CONTENTS: N/A

350 **CURTO, R. *Draw the magic blue fairy*.** 2013, Enslow (ISBN: 9780766042650). 35 p.
SERIES: Draw the magic fairy
GRADE LEVEL: Upper elementary – middle school
CONTENTS: N/A

351 **CURTO, R. *Draw the magic green fairy*.** 2014, Enslow (ISBN: 9780766042681). 35 p.
SERIES: Draw the magic fairy
GRADE LEVEL: Upper elementary – middle school
CONTENTS: N/A

352 **CURTO, R. *Draw the magic pink fairy*.** 2013, Enslow (ISBN: 9780766042667). 35 p.
SERIES: Draw the magic fairy
GRADE LEVEL: Upper elementary – middle school
CONTENTS: N/A

353 **CURTO, R. *Draw the magic red fairy*.** 2014, Enslow (ISBN: 9780766042674). 35 p.
SERIES: Draw the magic fairy
GRADE LEVEL: Upper elementary – middle school
CONTENTS: N/A

354 **CURTO, R. *Fun and easy drawing at sea*.** 2013, Enslow (ISBN: 9780766060395). 35 p.
SERIES: Fun and easy drawing
GRADE LEVEL: Elementary
CONTENTS: N/A

355 **CURTO, R. *Fun and easy drawing fantasy characters*.** 2013, Enslow (ISBN: 9780766060418). 35 p.
SERIES: Fun and easy drawing
GRADE LEVEL: Elementary
CONTENTS: N/A

356 **CURTO, R. *Fun and easy drawing on the farm*.** 2013, Enslow (ISBN: 9780766060371). 35 p.
SERIES: Fun and easy drawing

GRADE LEVEL: Elementary

CONTENTS: N/A

357   CURTO, R. *Fun and easy drawing storybook characters*. 2013, Enslow (ISBN: 9780766060432). 35 p.

SERIES: Fun and easy drawing

GRADE LEVEL: Elementary

CONTENTS: N/A

358   CUXART, B. *Modeling clay: animals*. 2010, Barron's (ISBN: 9780764145797). 95 p.

GRADE LEVEL: Lower elementary

CONTENTS: N/A

359   DALBY, E. *The Usborne complete book of chess*. 2007, EDC (ISBN: 9780794524203). 96 p.

GRADE LEVEL: Upper elementary

CONTENTS: Playing chess—writing chess down—king—queen—rooks—bishops—knights—pawns—values—sacrifices and exchanges—piece puzzles—opening—opening sequences—Italian-Giuoco Piano—Spanish-Rye Lopez—queen's gambit—more white openings—Caro-Kann defense—Sicilian defense—French defense—king's indian defense—thinking in the middlegame—board in the middlegame—middlegame puzzles—tactical tricks—tactical trick puzzles—making plans—combination puzzles—defense techniques—sacrifice puzzles—endgame—endgame puzzles—attacking the king—king is dead-checkmate—checkmate puzzles—drawn games—chess tournaments—drawn game puzzles—chess words—puzzle solutions

360   DALY, M. *87 ways to party*. 2011, Zest Books (ISBN: 9780981973395).

GRADE LEVEL: High school

CONTENTS: Star-sign soiree—super surprise party—old-school slumber party—classic costume party—birth year bash—piece-of-cake party—the big give—heroes and villains party—haunted hotel party—murder mystery party—pumpkin-carving party—blood bash—Christmukkah party—naughty or nice party—winter solstice party—winter wonderland party—global warming party—Mardi Gras party—black and white ball—Rock-Around-the-Clock party—time travel party—candy-for-strangers party—nuts and bolts party—truth or dare party—anti-Valentine's day party—Sadie Hawkins day party—pre-prom cocktail and photo party—after prom pajama party—alterna-prom—fortune-telling party—bonfire party—grad night shut-in—off-to-college goodbye party—parlor game night—ultimate scavenger hunt—Trivial Pursuit party—ice-breaker party—outdoor movie night—sleepaway camp night—south beach pool party—meteor show viewing party—Fourth of July party—desert island party—blackout party—classic dinner party—the perfect picnic—top chef cook-off—fondue party—stone soup soiree—tasting party—ice age party—toga party—old Hollywood party—'60s Woodstock party—'80s teen movie party—clothing swap—just-the-girls spa night—extreme room makeover—mystery tour—Vegas-inspired night—obscure holiday part—initiation party—pre-game carbo loading party—ultimate tailgate party—powder puff party—move-it-or-lose it party—Super Bowl party—Oscar night soiree—season premiere/finale party—karaoke party—Rocky Horror Picture Show party—film festival—character soundtrack party—clip show party—grafitti party—ultimate cast party—scrapbooking party—open mic night—fashion statement party—Thailand:

Full Moon party—Scandinavia: Midsummer party—Brazil: carnaval drumming and dance party—Mexico: Cinco de Mayo fiesta—Ireland: St. Patrick's Day party—China: Chinese New Year bash—Spain: La Tomatina party—India: Diwali fest

361 D'ARCY, S. *Freestyle soccer street moves: tricks, stepovers, passes*. 2010, Firefly Books (ISBN: 9781554075836). 128 p.
GRADE LEVEL: Upper elementary – middle school
CONTENTS: N/A

362 DARDIK, H. *Embroidery for Little Miss Crafty: projects and patterns to create and embellish*. 2009, Walter Foster (ISBN: 9781600585982). 96 p.
GRADE LEVEL: Upper elementary
CONTENTS: N/A

363 DAVIES, H. *The games book*. 2009, Scholastic (ISBN: 9780545134033). 118 p.
GRADE LEVEL: Elementary
CONTENTS: N/A

364 DAVIES, N. *Birds*. 2012, Kingfisher (ISBN: 9780753467770). 56 p.
SERIES: Discover science
GRADE LEVEL: Elementary
CONTENTS: N/A

365 DAVIES, N. *Desert*. 2012, Kingfisher (ISBN: 9780753468364). 56 p.
SERIES: Discover science
GRADE LEVEL: Elementary
CONTENTS: N/A

366 DAVIES, N. *Oceans and seas*. 2011, Kingfisher (ISBN: 9780753466025). 56 p.
SERIES: Discover science
GRADE LEVEL: Elementary
CONTENTS: Sea slug—waves—fish—starfish—jellyfish—underwater scape

367 DAVIS, J. *How to draw Garfield and Friends*. 2009, Walter Foster (ISBN: 9781600581465). 32 p.
GRADE LEVEL: Upper elementary
CONTENTS: N/A

368 DAVIS, N. *Grow your own monsters*. 2010, Frances Lincoln (ISBN: 9781845078331). 32 p.
GRADE LEVEL: Elementary
CONTENTS: Cucumber—lily—banana—cardoon—cabbage—fly trap—pitcher plant—echium—lychee

369 D'CRUZ, A. *Make your own books*. 2009, PowerKids Press (ISBN: 9781435828551). 24 p.
SERIES: Do it yourself projects!
GRADE LEVEL: Lower elementary
CONTENTS: Button holder—folding book—palm-leaf book—lift the flaps—pop-up book—address book—photo album—eco-notebook

370 D'CRUZ, A. *Make your own masks*. 2009, PowerKids Press (ISBN: 9781435828537). 24 p.

SERIES: Do it yourself projects!

GRADE LEVEL: Lower elementary

CONTENTS: Aztec skull—khon mask—carnival jester—Bwa sun mask—Kenyan giraffe—Egyptian mask—Greek medusa—Viking mask

371 D'CRUZ, A. *Make your own musical instruments*. 2009, PowerKids Press (ISBN: 9781435828544).

SERIES: Do it yourself projects!

GRADE LEVEL: Lower elementary

CONTENTS: Spanish castanets—simple flute—bongo drums—jazz washboard—African thumb piano—hand drum—shaking maracas—Egyptian harp

372 D'CRUZ, A. *Make your own puppets*. 2009, PowerKids Press (ISBN: 9781435828513). 24 p.

SERIES: Do it yourself projects!

GRADE LEVEL: Lower elementary

CONTENTS: N/A

373 D'CRUZ, A. *Make your own purses and bags*. 2009, PowerKids Press (ISBN: 9781435828568). 24 p.

SERIES: Do it yourself projects!

GRADE LEVEL: Lower elementary

CONTENTS: Didgeridoo pencil case—parfleche—wallet—MP3 player bag—Halloween bag—drawstring gym bag—magic wallet—magazine bag

374 D'CRUZ, A. *Make your own slippers and shoes*. 2009, PowerKids Press (ISBN: 9781435828520). 24 p.

SERIES: Do it yourself projects!

GRADE LEVEL: Lower elementary

CONTENTS: Leaf shoes—Roman sandals—flip-flops—clogs—fur boots—lotus shoes—jutti slippers—Native American moccasins

375 D'CRUZ, A. *Puppets*. 2007, Wayland (ISBN: 9780750250542). 24 p.

SERIES: Make and use

GRADE LEVEL: Upper elementary

CONTENTS: N/A

376 DEANE-PRATT, A. *Musical instruments: how things work*. 2012, PowerKids Press (ISBN: 9781448852802).

SERIES: How things work

GRADE LEVEL: Elementary

CONTENTS: Cardboard guitar—panpipes—drum—oboe

377 DELL, P. *Paintball for fun!* 2009, Compass Point (ISBN: 9780756538637). 48 p.

SERIES: For fun!

GRADE LEVEL: Elementary

CONTENTS: N/A

378   DELL, P. *Stamping for fun!* 2009, Compass Point (ISBN: 9780756538620). 48 p.
SERIES: For fun!
GRADE LEVEL: Elementary
CONTENTS: The best stamps—treat your stamps right—all about inks—paint and pens—additional tools to use—things to think about—surfaces: where to make your mark—homemade stamps—basic techniques—special techniques—projects

379   DENNIS, Y. *A kid's guide to Arab American history: more than 50 activities*. 2013, Chicago Review Press (ISBN: 9781613740170). 224 p.
SERIES: A kid's guide
GRADE LEVEL: Upper elementary – middle school
CONTENTS: Shadow puppet show—Helen Zughaib's style—fashion designer—tabbouleh salad—derbekke drum—national safety month paper—olive oil soap—The Famous Four—book in Arabic and English—wood inlay box—play mancala—Sarma embroidered scarf—a riq—say it in Syrian—hummus—sidewalk art—notebook cover—Naomi Shihab Nye—say it in Jordanian—fatoosh salad—vest for the dabkeh line dance—a game of senet—a harp—tile hot plate—light a lantern—falafel—sew a kaftan—say it in Egyptian—cuff bracelet—play el'quirkat—copper pendant—bandora tomato salad—count in Kurdish—birdbath with arabesque design—say it in Iraqi—frieze designs—melon baal canaf melon with wings—oh hillcock—say it in Yemeni—camel friend—karakebs—say it in Moroccan—Belgha slippers—Zaida Benyusuf's style—dried-flower searing plate—couscous—comic book hero—play the hunter—date candy—worry beads—say it in Kuwaiti—Girgian candy bag—puffy pancakes—banner for Arab American heritage month

380   DEUTSCH, J. *Downhill skiing for fun!* 2009, Compass Point (ISBN: 9780756540289). 48 p.
SERIES: For fun!
GRADE LEVEL: Elementary
CONTENTS: N/A

381   DEUTSCH, J. *Running for fun!* 2008, Compass Point (ISBN: 9780756536299). 48 p.
SERIES: For fun!
GRADE LEVEL: Elementary
CONTENTS: Indoor and outdoor—cross-country—road running—equipment—getting started—sprints—distance running—technique—the lower limbs—drills—safety—checking progress—competitions—starts and finishes—relays

382   DICKINS, R. *The Usborne complete book of riding and pony care*. 2009, Usborne (ISBN: 9781409507635).
GRADE LEVEL: Elementary
CONTENTS: N/A

383   DICKINSON, G. *Crafts for kids*. 2013, Hamlyn (ISBN: 9780600625148).
SERIES: Craft Library
GRADE LEVEL: Elementary
CONTENTS: Mother's Day—Father's Day—Valentine's day—Easter—Halloween—Thanksgiving & harvest festival—Christmas—birthdays—carnivals—festivals around the world

384 DICKINSON, R. *Great pioneer projects you can build yourself*. 2007, Nomad Press (ISBN: 9780978503765). 128 p.

SERIES: Build it yourself

GRADE LEVEL: Upper elementary – middle school

CONTENTS: Dough map—treasure hunt—pemmican—broadside—covered wagon—butter—pictograph—journal—frontier pouch—cross-stitch sampler—train engine—sod house—log cabin—root vegetables—johnnycakes—straw hat—prairie bonnet—four-patch block quilt—braided rug—hand-dipped candles—spatterware crock—molasses taffy—ball and cup game—dried apple doll—salt dough oranaments—miniature teepee—pinhole camera—silhouette—newspaper

385 DINGLE, A. *How to make a universe with 92 ingredients: an electrifying guide to the elements*. 2013, Owlkids Books (ISBN: 9781771470087). 96p.

GRADE LEVEL: Upper elementary – middle school

CONTENTS: N/A

386 DOBSON, C. *Wind power: 20 projects to make with paper*. 2010, Firefly Books (ISBN: 9781554077496). 96 p.

GRADE LEVEL: Middle school – high school

CONTENTS: Wind—wind power—wind principles—limits—hawts and vawts—experiments—turbines with horizontal axis—turbines with vertical axis—wind power future

387 DODD, C. *How to be brilliant at ballet*. 2009, Franklin Watts (ISBN: 9780749693459). 32 p.

GRADE LEVEL: Elementary

CONTENTS: N/A

388 DOEDEN, M. *Play football like a pro: key skills and tips*. 2011, Capstone (ISBN: 9781429648257). 32 p.

SERIES: Play like the pros

GRADE LEVEL: Upper elementary – middle school

CONTENTS: A clean snap—complete a pass—hang onto the ball—make an explosive run—run routes—make a great catch—block on the line—make a great tackle—rush a passer—cover a receiver—placekick—punt

389 DOLPHIN, C. *Cool exercise: healthy and fun ways to get your body moving*. 2013, ABDO (ISBN: 9781617834271). 32 p.

SERIES: Cool health and fitness

GRADE LEVEL: Elementary

CONTENTS: N/A

390 DOUDNA, K. *The kid's book of simple everyday science*. 2013, Scarletta Kids (ISBN: 9781938063343). 112 p.

GRADE LEVEL: Elementary

CONTENTS: N/A

391 DOUDNA, K. *Super simple things to do with balloons: fun and easy science for kids*. 2011, ABDO (ISBN: 9781617146725). 24 p.

SERIES: Super simple science

GRADE LEVEL: Elementary

CONTENTS: Repulse—go crazy!—motion—jet—Attract—water balloons—nail bed

392 DOUDNA, K. *Super simple things to do with bubbles: fun and easy science for kids*. 2011, ABDO (ISBN: 9781617146732). 24 p.
SERIES: Super simple science
GRADE LEVEL: Elementary
CONTENTS: Square—aisin—toothpaste—lala-ly—soap—gas

393 DOUDNA, K. *Super simple things to do with plants: fun and easy science for kids*. 2011, ABDO (ISBN: 9781617146749). 24 p.
SERIES: Super simple science
GRADE LEVEL: Elementary
CONTENTS: Beans—plants—the point—seeds—botany—shrivel—carnations

394 DOUDNA, K. *Super simple things to do with pressure: fun and easy science for kids*. 2011, ABDO (ISBN: 9781617146756). 24 p.
SERIES: Super simple science
GRADE LEVEL: Elementary
CONTENTS: Science made simple—pressure—scientist—stopper—rise and fall—ketchup—potato—can crusher—balloons and bottles—microwave

395 DOUDNA, K. *Super simple things to do with temperature: fun and easy science for kids*. 2011, ABDO (ISBN: 9781617146763). 24 p.
SERIES: Super simple science
GRADE LEVEL: Elementary
CONTENTS: Hot and cold—insulation—heat—stretch it—passion—top and bottom

396 DOUDNA, K. *Super simple things to do with water: fun and easy science for kids*. 2011, ABDO (ISBN: 9781617146770). 24 p.
SERIES: Super simple science
GRADE LEVEL: Elementary
CONTENTS: Bottles—siphon—pack and expand—seal—straws

397 DOUGHERTY, T. *Girls' skateboarding: skating to be the best*. 2008, Capstone (ISBN: 9781429601344). 32 p.
SERIES: Girls got game
GRADE LEVEL: Elementary
CONTENTS: On the edge—you and the board—dropping in anywhere—skating to the top

398 DOWNEY, T. *Filmmaking*. 2010, PowerKids Press (ISBN: 9781615325979). 32 p.
SERIES: Master this!
GRADE LEVEL: Upper elementary – middle school
CONTENTS: N/A

399 DOYLE, J. *A young scientist's guide to defying disasters: includes 20 experiments for the sink, bathtub, and backyard*. 2012, Gibbs Smith (ISBN: 9781423624400). 160 p.

GRADE LEVEL: Middle school

CONTENTS: Seas—eruptions—tidal waves—water spouts—bores—volcanoes—quicksand—mountains—icebergs—deserts—mass movements—bombs—surprises underground—poles—earthquakes—lava—tornado—raining cats and dogs—blowing dust—hurricanes—droughts—lightning—floods—fires—bees—jellyfish—alligators and crocodiles—large whale—frog poison—abdominable snowman

400 **DOYLE, J.** *A young scientist's guide to faulty freaks of nature: including 20 experiments for the sink, bathtub and backyard.* 2013, Gibbs Smith (ISBN: 9781423624554). 128p.

GRADE LEVEL: Middle school

CONTENTS: Hobbits—lyre—dinosaur—fears—funny science-words—dangerous foods—neanderthals—extreme sports—evolution—fatbergs—smog—methane—omz—chemistry—coral—funny chemical names—bad scientist—global warning—animal groupings—strange coffee—tigons—pollination—biodiversity—trees—north pole—diseases—vanishing sea—slimy sea animals—alien predator—silence—faking—dumb ideas—grim reaper

401 **DOYLE, J.** *The Zombie catcher's handbook.* 2013, Gibbs Smith (ISBN: 9781423634171). 160 p.

GRADE LEVEL: Middle school

CONTENTS: Caution—Kinemortophobia—the undead—paper—fact vs. fiction: figures—bacteria—decay—survival—read a map—signal for help—goo—weaponry: catcher shield—dress a wound—fireman's carry—dress like a zombie—skin wound—a trap—night watchman's pendulum—role model catcher—choosing a catcher companion—zombie catcher speak: secret messages—houses—rope skills—base camp: pumpkins—campfire: fire extinguisher—guts sack—clothing—blood splatter—knots—water filter—apocalypse—the basics—zombie brain jell-0

402 **DREW, S.** *Junk-box jewelry: 25 DIY low cost (or no cost) jewelry projects.* 2012, Zest Books (ISBN: 9780982732267).

GRADE LEVEL: High school

CONTENTS: Retro-bauble bracelet—braided collar—ring—royal jewels necklace—lace choker—sea-jewel pendant—recycled necklace—charm bracelet—cuff—sea-jewel cuff—necklace—earrings—art nouveau pendant—jeweled branches necklace—newsstand notice—toolbox bracelet—customized cuff—Juliet tiara—so-quirky-it's-cool necklace—Billie Holiday headband—sparkle-and-chain necklace—art deco bracelet—vines headband—lace headband—tiara

403 **DREWETT, J.** *How to improve at basketball.* 2008, Crabtree (ISBN: 9780778735663). 48 p.

SERIES: How to improve at

GRADE LEVEL: Elementary

CONTENTS: Dribbling—ball handling—passing—shooting—rebounding—defending—advanced skills and drills—advanced dribbling—fake and drive—tip off—advanced shooting—fast break drills—fouls—warming up and stretching

404 **DREWETT, J.** *How to improve at soccer.* 2008, Crabtree (ISBN: 9780778735694). 48 p.

SERIES: How to improve at

GRADE LEVEL: Elementary

CONTENTS: Control—kicking—control—passing—shooting—heading—defending—throw-ins—crosses and corners—goalkeeping—shot-stopping—distribution—advanced control—advanced shooting—warming up and stretching—diet

405 DREWETT, J. *How to improve at tennis*. 2008, Crabtree (ISBN: 9780778735717). 48 p.

SERIES: How to improve at

GRADE LEVEL: Elementary

CONTENTS: Body position—grips—rules of play—warming up—forehand strokes—backhand strokes—groundstrokes—serve—service returns—volley—lob—smash—drop shot

406 DUFFIELD, K. *California history for kids: missions, miners, and moviemakers in the Golden State; includes 21 activities*. 2012, Chicago Review Press (ISBN: 9781569765326). 144 p.

SERIES: For kids

GRADE LEVEL: Middle school

CONTENTS: Archaeological dig—rock painting—hoop-and-pool game—astrolabe—Spanish galleon—diseno—brand—your flag—hardtack snack—letter sheet—Morse code—railroad cipher—orange muffins—grow a shasta daisy—earthquake preparedness kit—backyard scientist—produce a movie—Hollywood handprints—a photo essay—air pollution logbook

407 DUKE, S. *Step-by-step experiments with plants*. 2012, Child's World (ISBN: 9781609735913). 32 p.

SERIES: Step-by-step experiments

GRADE LEVEL: Lower elementary

CONTENTS: Plants—science steps—seed—moving—water

408 DUKE, S. *Step-by-step experiments with the water cycle*. 2012, Child's World (ISBN: 9781609736156). 32 p.

SERIES: Step-by-step experiments

GRADE LEVEL: Lower elementary

CONTENTS: Water cycle—science steps—on the move—from the air—rain—see it

409 DUPERNEX, A. *Start to knit*. 2009, Search Press (ISBN: 9781844483884). 48 p.

SERIES: Start to

GRADE LEVEL: Upper elementary – middle school

CONTENTS: Rhubarb and custard scarf—mermaid's purse—rosy bag—jazzy jewellery—cool beanie—flower belt—big bag

410 DURKIN, K. *Paint it!* 2012, QEB (ISBN: 9781609922757).

SERIES: Art smart

GRADE LEVEL: Lower Elementary

CONTENTS: N/A

411 DYBVIK, T. *Cute clothes for the crafty fashionista*. 2012, Capstone (ISBN: 9781429665537). 32 p.

SERIES: FashionCraft studio

GRADE LEVEL: Elementary

CONTENTS: N/A

412 DYBVIK, T. *Trendy jewelry for the crafty fashionista*. 2012, Capstone (ISBN: 9781429665490). 32 p.

SERIES: FashionCraft studio

GRADE LEVEL: Elementary

CONTENTS: N/A

413 EAGEN, R. *Body care chemistry*. 2011, Crabtree (ISBN: 9780778752820). 32 p.

SERIES: Chemstastrophe!

GRADE LEVEL: Upper elementary – middle school

CONTENTS: Accidents—matter—method and means—day-to-day chemistry—bathroom chemistry—test it—tornado—acid or base—eureka, amazing—chemists—learn more

414 EAGEN, R. *Environmental chemistry*. 2011, Crabtree (ISBN: 9780778752851). 32 p.

SERIES: Chemstastrophe!

GRADE LEVEL: Upper elementary – middle school

CONTENTS: Matter—method—chemistry—enviro chemistry—theories—slimeball—cleaner—eureka!—chemists—chemistry today—learn more

415 EBERT, M. *Photography for kids! A fun guide to digital photography*. 2011, Rocky Nook (ISBN: 9781933952765). 159 p.

GRADE LEVEL: Elementary

CONTENTS: The camera—get started—look—snap—see—subjects—a picture of me—everyone loves animals—around the world—pictures without color—making small subjects look bigger—vacation: tons of time for pictures—bring your camera along for a swim—a sea of moving lights—happy birthday—pictures of me—my hometown—what to do with your pictures

416 EDWARDS, M. *Start to quilt*. 2009, Search Press (ISBN: 9781844483891). 48 p.

SERIES: Start to

GRADE LEVEL: Upper elementary – middle school

CONTENTS: Notebook cover—fun phone pouch—sashiko bag—beady bag—cat wall hanging

417 EICK, J. *Christmas crafts*. 2011, Child's World (ISBN: 9781609542320). 24 p.

GRADE LEVEL: Elementary

CONTENTS: N/A

418 EICK, J. *Easter crafts*. 2011, Child's World (ISBN: 9781609542337). 24 p.

GRADE LEVEL: Elementary

CONTENTS: Paper eggs—egg strings—bunny—bunny basket—egg holders—Easter cards—envelopes

419 EICK, J. *Halloween crafts*. 2011, Child's World (ISBN: 9781609542344). 24 p.

GRADE LEVEL: Elementary

CONTENTS: Spiders—pumpkin cutouts—masks—painted pumpkins—treat bags—Halloween cards—envelopes

420 **EICK, J. *Mother's Day crafts*.** 2011, Child's World (ISBN: 9781609542368). 24 p.
GRADE LEVEL: Elementary
CONTENTS: Happy Mother's Day—let's begin—pipe-cleaner flowers—tissue flowers—painted pots—pencil holder—flower vase—Mother's Day cards—envelopes—activities

421 **EICK, J. *Thanksgiving crafts*.** 2011, Child's World (ISBN: 9781609542375). 24 p.
GRADE LEVEL: Elementary
CONTENTS: Handprint turkey—paper-bag turkey—napkins—napkin holders—table runner—Thanksgiving cards—envelopes

422 **EICK, J. *Valentine's Day crafts*.** 2010, Child's World (ISBN: 9781609542795). 24 p.
GRADE LEVEL: Elementary
CONTENTS: Pipe-cleaner hearts—paper hearts—heart flowers—heart treasures—heart bookmark—Valentine's day cards—envelopes

423 **EINHORN, N. *Close-up magic*.** 2011, Rosen Central (ISBN: 9781435894532). 64 p.
SERIES: Inside magic
GRADE LEVEL: Upper elementary – middle school
CONTENTS: Pen-go—let there be light—coin through coaster—ring on a string—Chinese coin off string—rising ring on pencil—gravity-defying ring—dissolving coin version 1—dissolving coin version 2—coin through ring—vanishing coin in handkerchief—the bermuda triangle—magic papers—marked coin in ball of yarn—coin cascade—Concorde coin version 1—Concorde coin version 2—the coin test—universal vanish—gravity vanish—unlinking safety pins—pin-credible—safety pin-a-tration—domi-no-way—straw penetration—banana splitz—kiss me quick—escaping jack—card on wall—swapping checkers—indestructible string—magnetic cards—picture perfect—beads of mystery—sweet tooth—ping-pong balance—zero gravity—enchanted ball—what a mug!—mugged again!—magnetic credit cards—the shirt off your back—unburstable balloon—obedient handkerchief

424 **EINHORN, N. *Presto change-o! Jaw-dropping magic with dinner table objects*.**
2013, Rosen Central (ISBN: 9781448892204). 64 p.
SERIES: Inside magic
GRADE LEVEL: Upper elementary – middle school
CONTENTS: Rolling straw—clinging cutlery—bending knife vesion 1—bending knife version 2—bouncing bread roll—vanishing glass—torn and restored knapkin—sugar rush uncovered—all sugared up—two in the hand—knife and paper trick—the cup and balls—cut and re-strawed—jumping rubber band—string through arm version 1—string through arm version 2—string through ring—rope through neck—rope through neck again!—hunter bow knot—impossible knot—slip knot—cut and restored rope version 1—cut and restored rope version 2—rope through apple—coin under bottle caps—whispering jack—"x" marks the spot—dice divination—human calculator—impossible prediction—four card poker—tri-thought—face value—you find it!—1089: book test—double book test—the big prediction—black magic—temples of wisdom

425 **EINHORN, N.** *Stand-up magic and optical illusions*. 2011, Rosen Central (ISBN: 9781435894525). 64 p.

SERIES: Inside magic

GRADE LEVEL: Upper elementary – middle school

CONTENTS: Production tube—blended skills version 1—magic photo album—needles through balloon—vanishing glass of liquid—going into liquidation—liquidated assets—multiplication sensation—square circle production—mini flip-flap production box—silk through glass version 1—silk through glass version 2—switching bag—blended silks version 2—candy caper—escapologist—lord of the rings—magic circles—crazy spots!—parade of colors—paper balls over the head—incredible prediction—vanishing mug of liquid—incredible blindfold act—watch this!—second sight—excalibur's cup—anti-gravity glasses—common optical illusions shrinking pen—floating sausage—hole in hand—ship in a bottle—Emily's illusion—stretching arm—pinkie down—thumb stretch—thumb off—impossible!—boomerang cards—stamp it

426 **EINHORN, N.** *Stunts, puzzles, and stage illusions*. 2011, Rosen Central (ISBN: 9781435894549). 64 p.

SERIES: Inside magic

GRADE LEVEL: Upper elementary – middle school

CONTENTS: Follow the leader—still following the leader—hypnotic—magnetic fingers—wand twist—floating arms—pepper-sepper-ation—table lock—broom suspension—time for a shower—coin through hole—rising tube mystery—suspended animation—straw bottle—immovable—card flick—the rice lift—try to stand up!—surefire bet—lift me if you can—superman—coin con—riddle me this—letter of resignation—bullseye—total this sum—impossible numbers!—calculation sensation—hide and seek—hide and seek solo—topsy-turvy mugs—x-ray vision—penny pincher—invisible traveler—the trapdoor card—walking through a postcard—a cutting problem—quickness of hand—salt and pepper separation—crazy corks—interlocked—impossible link—comedy levitation—mini me—Houdini outdone!—flip-flap production—bowl vanish—victory cartons illusion—cutting a person in two—metamorphosis—tip over box—out of thin air—inverted glass trick

427 **EJAZ, K.** *Recipe and craft guide to India*. 2011, Mitchell Lane (ISBN: 9781584159384). 63 p.

SERIES: World crafts and recipes

GRADE LEVEL: Upper elementary – middle school

CONTENTS: Recipes: paapad—dhokla—mach bhaja—chicken karhai—aaloo matar tamaatar—chanay (chickpeas)—matar chaawal—payasam—besan ke laddoo—sharbat—crafts: flower garland—block print—henna—doli—punkha (fan)—chakri (pinwheel)—sehra (headdress)—rangoli—raakhi—diya

428 **ELDREDGE, K.** *Amazing pet tricks*. 2009, Wiley (ISBN: 9780470410837).

SERIES: ASPCA kids

GRADE LEVEL: Elementary

CONTENTS: The trick is in the click—the magic touch—classic dog tricks—trickier tricks—spectacular skits—fantastic felines—down on the farm—weird and wacky

429 **ELISH, D.** *Fiction*. 2012, Marshall Cavendish (ISBN: 9781608704972). 96 p.

SERIES: Craft of writing

GRADE LEVEL: Middle school

CONTENTS: A short story—the big picture—things to think about—from start to finish—writing exercises

430 **ELISH, D. *Plays*.** 2012, Marshall Cavendish (ISBN: 9781608704996). 95 p.

SERIES: Craft of writing

GRADE LEVEL: Middle school

CONTENTS: The big picture—things to think about—your play—from beginning to end—writing exercises

431 **ELISH, D. *Screenplays*.** 2012, Marshall Cavendish (ISBN: 9781608705016). 95 p.

SERIES: Craft of writing

GRADE LEVEL: Middle school

CONTENTS: The big picture—things to think about—the screenplay—from beginning to end—writing exercises

432 **ELLAR, S. *Survival skills: survive in the wild*.** 2012, Capstone (ISBN: 9781429668842). 48 p.

SERIES: Velocity

GRADE LEVEL: Upper elementary – middle school

CONTENTS: Why become a survival skills expert?—clothing for the wild—equipment for the wild—preparing a fire—now light a fire—Bear Grylls: survival expert—shelter building for survival—build a debris hut—water collection and safety—make your own survival tin—tracking wild animals—never get lost—use nature to navigate—SOS—survival fishing—get knotted!—leave no trace—survival food

433 **ELLENWOOD, E. *Woodcarving*.** 2009, Fox Chapel (ISBN: 9781565233669). 121 p.

SERIES: Kid crafts

GRADE LEVEL: Upper elementary – middle school

CONTENTS: About wood—woodcarving supplies—tools—soap boat—snowman ornament—wooden whistle—arrowhead—name plaque—eagle head—frog

434 **ELLIS, C. *Judo and jujitsu*.** 2012, Marshall Cavendish Benchmark (ISBN: 9780761449331). 47 p.

SERIES: Martial arts in action

GRADE LEVEL: Upper elementary – middle school

CONTENTS: N/A

435 **ELLIS, C. *Kendo*.** 2011, Marshall Cavendish Benchmark (ISBN: 9780761449355). 47 p.

SERIES: Martial arts in action

GRADE LEVEL: Upper elementary – middle school

CONTENTS: History of kendo and other sword arts—kendo basics—kendo and you

436 **ELLIS, C. *Wrestling*.** 2011, Marshall Cavendish Benchmark (ISBN: 9780761449416). 47 p.

SERIES: Martial arts in action

GRADE LEVEL: Upper elementary – middle school

CONTENTS: N/A

437   ENCARNACION, E. *The girls' guide to campfire activities*. 2008, Applesauce Press (ISBN: 9781604330038). 122 p.
GRADE LEVEL: Elementary
CONTENTS: N/A

438   ENGEL, P. *10-fold origami: fabulous paperfolds you can make in just 10 steps!* 2009, Tuttle (ISBN: 9784805310694). 96 p.
GRADE LEVEL: Middle school – high school
CONTENTS: Traditionals—delectables—for the romantic—wild kingdom—just for fun

439   ENNIS, E. *The American Civil War*. 2008, Evan-Moor Corp. (ISBN: 9781596732599). 96 p.
SERIES: History pockets
GRADE LEVEL: Elementary
CONTENTS: N/A

440   ENNIS, E. *The American Revolution*. 2008, Evan-Moor Corp. (ISBN: 9781596732605). 96 p.
SERIES: History pockets
GRADE LEVEL: Elementary
CONTENTS: N/A

441   ENRIGHT, D. *The boys' book: how to be the best at everything*. 2007, Scholastic (ISBN: 9780545016285). 118 p.
GRADE LEVEL: Elementary
CONTENTS: N/A

442   ENZ, T. *Build it: invent new structures and contraptions*. 2012, Capstone (ISBN: 9781429676359). 32p.
SERIES: Invent it
GRADE LEVEL: Upper elementary
CONTENTS: Solutions—pulley—fort—trash grabber—sorter—pet waterer—raft—parachute—bridge

443   ENZ, T. *Build your own car, rocket, and other things that go*. 2011, Capstone (ISBN: 9781429654371). 32 p.
SERIES: Build it yourself
GRADE LEVEL: Upper elementary – middle school
CONTENTS: Helicopter launcher—box kite—boat—rocket—flyer—car—race car

444   ENZ, T. *Build your own fort, igloo, and other hangouts*. 2011, Capstone (ISBN: 9781429654364). 32 p.
SERIES: Build it yourself
GRADE LEVEL: Upper elementary – middle school
CONTENTS: Hideout—fort—teepee—garden fort—tent—hut—snow castle—igloo

445   ENZ, T. *Build your own mini golf course, lemonade stand, and other things to do*. 2011, Capstone (ISBN: 9781429654388). 32 p.
SERIES: Build it yourself

GRADE LEVEL: Upper elementary – middle school

CONTENTS: Build something—stilts—golf course—boomerang—tree swing—kaleidoscope—lemonade stand—pop gun

446   **ENZ, T. *Build your own periscope, flashlight, and other useful stuff*.** 2011, Capstone (ISBN: 9781429654395). 32 p.

SERIES: Build it yourself

GRADE LEVEL: Upper elementary – middle school

CONTENTS: Telephone—crayon candle—compass—telescope—burglar alarm—snowshoes—flashlight

447   **ENZ, T. *Harness it: invent new ways to harness energy and nature*.** 2012, Capstone (ISBN: 9781429676335). 32 p.

SERIES: Invent it

GRADE LEVEL: Upper elementary

CONTENTS: Battery—marshmallow roaster—water filter—garden—trip wire—windmill—message

448   **ENZ, T. *Repurpose it: invent new uses for old stuff*.** 2012, Capstone (ISBN: 9781429676366). 32 p.

SERIES: Invent it

GRADE LEVEL: Upper elementary

CONTENTS: Compost bin—cooler—still—bug bot—safe—lawn chair—poncho

449   **ENZ, T. *Zoom it: invent new machines that move*.** 2012, Capstone (ISBN: 978429676342). 32p.

SERIES: Fact finders. Invent it

GRADE LEVEL: Upper elementary

CONTENTS: Spider—boat—cannon—car—catapult—shoes—boat

450   **EPPARD, J. *Aircraft*.** 2013, Bellwether Media (ISBN: 9781600148088). 24 p.

SERIES: You can draw it

GRADE LEVEL: Upper elementary – middle school

CONTENTS: N/A

451   **EPPARD, J. *Big cats*.** 2013, Bellwether Media (ISBN: 9781600148095). 24 p.

SERIES: You can draw it

GRADE LEVEL: Upper elementary – middle school

CONTENTS: Bobcat—mountain lion—cheetah—caracal—leopard—lion—snow leopard—tiger

452   **EPPARD, J. *Dogs*.** 2013, Bellwether Media (ISBN: 9781600148101). 24 p.

SERIES: You can draw it

GRADE LEVEL: Upper elementary – middle school

CONTENTS: Pug—Saint Bernard—beagle—Labrador retriever—Dalmatian—Doberman pinscher—German shepard—chihuahua

453   **EPPARD, J. *Horses*.** 2013, Bellwether Media (ISBN: 9781600148118). 24 p.

SERIES: You can draw it

GRADE LEVEL: Upper elementary – middle school

CONTENTS: N/A

454 EPPARD, J. *Manga*. 2013, Bellwether Media (ISBN: 9781600148125). 24 p.

SERIES: You can draw it

GRADE LEVEL: Upper elementary – middle school

CONTENTS: Girl figure—girl portrait—guy figure—guy portrait—villain figure—villain portrait—Chibi—mecha

455 EPPARD, J. *Monsters*. 2013, Bellwether Media (ISBN: 9780531220245). 24 p.

SERIES: You can draw it

GRADE LEVEL: Upper elementary – middle school

CONTENTS: Chupacabra—Frankenstein's monster—goblin—mummy—Loch Ness Monster—werewolf—zombie—Bigfoot

456 EVANS, K. *Cool crafts for hip kids*. 2012, Price Stern Sloan (ISBN: 9780843170627).

GRADE LEVEL: Elementary

CONTENTS: Lace-pressed brooch—paper beads—button rings—bunting—owl canvas—frog purse—lavender cocoons—pincushions—leaf mobile—wreath—picture hanger—paper lanterns—pony friend—cat bookmark—puppet—little mat

457 FANDEL, J. *Picture yourself writing nonfiction: using photos to inspire writing*. 2012, Capstone (ISBN: 9781429661256). 32 p.

SERIES: Fact finders. See it, write it

GRADE LEVEL: Middle school – high school

CONTENTS: Nothing but the truth—detailing the facts—people—the action—the truth

458 FANDEL, J. *You can write a terrific opinion piece*. 2013, Capstone (ISBN: 9781429684095). 24 p.

SERIES: You can write

GRADE LEVEL: Elementary

CONTENTS: For or against—take a stand: position—why write?: purpose—the starting line: introduction—hear the other side: listening—build support: proof—take a closer look: examples—no right or wrong: being fair—say it again: conclusion

459 FANDEL, J. *You can write an amazing journal*. 2013, Capstone (ISBN: 9781429684088). 24 p.

SERIES: You can write

GRADE LEVEL: Elementary

CONTENTS: A place of your own—getting started—free to be—making time—taking notes—facts—saving things—storytelling—safekeeping

460 FANDEL, J. *You can write awesome stories*. 2012, Capstone (ISBN: 9781429676151). 24 p.

SERIES: You can write

GRADE LEVEL: Elementary

CONTENTS: Tell me a story—characters—details—setting—plot—scene—mood—dialogue—ending

461   **FANDEL, J.** *You can write cool poems*. 2012, Capstone (ISBN: 9781429679619). 24 p.
     SERIES: You can write
     GRADE LEVEL: Elementary
     CONTENTS: Art of poetry—details—free verse—imagery—being new—strong verbs—repeating sounds—formal poetry—revising

462   **FARRELL, R.** *All about drawing horses and pets*. 2008, Walter Foster (ISBN: 9781600585807). 80 p.
     GRADE LEVEL: Elementary
     CONTENTS: N/A

463   **FARRELL, R.** *All about drawing sea creatures and animals*. 2011, Walter Foster (ISBN: 9781936309085). 80 p.
     GRADE LEVEL: Elementary
     CONTENTS: N/A

464   **FARRELL, R.** *Learn to draw horses and ponies: learn to draw and color 25 favorite horse and pony breeds, step by easy step, shape by simple shape!* 2011, Walter Foster (ISBN: 9781936309160). 32 p.
     SERIES: Learn to draw
     GRADE LEVEL: Upper elementary – middle school
     CONTENTS: N/A

465   **FARRELL, R.** *Learn to draw sea creatures: learn to draw and color 25 favorite ocean animals, step by easy step, shape by simple shape!* 2011, Walter Foster (ISBN: 9781936309191). 40 p.
     SERIES: Learn to draw
     GRADE LEVEL: Upper elementary – middle school
     CONTENTS: N/A

466   **FATHER, H.** *Learn to draw Disney/Pixar Ratatouille (rat-a-too-ee)*. 2007, Walter Foster (ISBN: 1600580297). 31 p.
     SERIES: Learn to draw
     GRADE LEVEL: Upper elementary – middle school
     CONTENTS: N/A

467   **FAUCHALD, N.** *Chocolate chill-out cake and other yummy desserts*. 2008, Picture Window Books (ISBN: 9781404839977). 32 p.
     SERIES: Kids dish
     GRADE LEVEL: Elementary
     CONTENTS: Slush—ice cream—frozen yogurt—malts—trifle—ice cream cake—granola cookies—crumble bars—cheesecake pie—cherry crisp—cobbler—banana bread pudding—applesauce cake—chocolate cherry cake

468   **FAUCHALD, N.** *Funky chicken enchiladas and other Mexican dishes*. 2009, Picture Window Books (ISBN: 9781404851894). 32 p.
     SERIES: Kids dish
     GRADE LEVEL: Elementary

CONTENTS: Fiesta tortilla chips—watermelon agua fresca—salsa verde—cheesy quesadillas—pico de gallo—chili-cheese corn on the cob—giant taco empanadas—wrap-no-roll burritos—funky chicken enchiladas—crispy fish tacos—guacamole-filled tomato bowls—wedding cookies—tres leches cake

469   FAUCHALD, N. *Holy guacamole! And other scrumptious snacks*. 2008, Picture Window Books (ISBN: 9781404839953). 32 p.

SERIES: Kids dish

GRADE LEVEL: Elementary

CONTENTS: Trail mix—soda pop—monkey milkshakes—tortilla chips—chili-cheese popcorn—pita chips with hummus—pineapple-yogurt freezer pops—quesadilla bites—mini pepperoni pizzas—raisiny applesauce—maple-yogurt fruit kabobs—pimento cheese dip—holy guacamole!—gooey granola bars

470   FAUCHALD, N. *Indoor s'mores and other tasty treats for special occasions*. 2008, Picture Window Books (ISBN: 9781404840003). 32 p.

SERIES: Kids dish

GRADE LEVEL: Elementary

CONTENTS: Lemonade stand—popcorn—indoor smores—ice cream soda social—party punch—hot chocolate—banana boats—cookie decorating party—chocolate fondue—chicken noodle soup—brownies—holiday snowflakes—fudge—cupcakes

471   FAUCHALD, N. *Keep on rollin' meatballs and other delicious dinners*. 2008, Picture Window Books (ISBN: 9781404839984). 32 p.

SERIES: Kids dish

GRADE LEVEL: Elementary

CONTENTS: Salad bar—shapes pizza—bread bowl chili—couscous—lasagna—peas and carrots penne—tortilla taco casserole—lemon and pesto fish—pork chops with apples—mini turkey meatloaves—baked meatballs—stuffed potatoes—chicken tenders

472   FAUCHALD, N. *On-the-go schwarmas and other Middle-Eastern dishes*. 2010, Picture Window Books (ISBN: 9781404851924). 32 p.

SERIES: Kids dish

GRADE LEVEL: Elementary

CONTENTS: Poppin' pepper hummus—couscous—party pita chips—super-sweet hamentaschen—coconut nibbles—chlada fakya—schwarmas—kebabs—falafel—tabbouleh—salad—baba ghanouj—baklava

473   FAUCHALD, N. *Puffy popovers and other get-out-of-bed breakfasts*. 2008, Picture Window Books (ISBN: 9781404839960). 32 p.

SERIES: Kids dish

GRADE LEVEL: Elementary

CONTENTS: Shake—sundaes—smoothies—quiche—bagel sandwiches—microwave scrambled eggs—blueberry pancake—popovers and jam—oatmeal—muffins—eggs in toast—peanut butter and chocolate chip scones—granola—baked French toast

474   FAUCHALD, N. *Roly-poly ravioli and other Italian dishes*. 2009, Picture Window Books (ISBN: 9781404851863). 32 p.

SERIES: Kids dish

GRADE LEVEL: Elementary

CONTENTS: Insalata mista—strawberry semifreddo—salad Caprese—basil pesto with penne—tuna bruschetta—baked prosciutto and mozzarella panini—intermediate—lemon granita—breakfast strata—ricotta ravioli—cheesy spinach lasagna—spaghetti and meatballs—advanced—stromboli—pizza margherita

475 FAUCHALD, N. *Walk-around tacos and other likeable lunches*. 2008, Picture Window Books (ISBN: 9781404839991). 32 p.

SERIES: Kids dish

GRADE LEVEL: Elementary

CONTENTS: Smoothie—salad with homemade dressing—cole slaw—tacos—hero sandwich—rollups—nutty butter triangles—lettuce wraps—pitas—stuffed tomatoes—club sandwich—crescent rolls—chicken wraps—bean burritos—hoagies

476 FAUCHALD, N. *Wrap-n-bake egg rolls and other Chinese dishes*. 2010, Picture Window Books (ISBN: 9781404851832). 32 p.

SERIES: Kids dish

GRADE LEVEL: Elementary

CONTENTS: Five-spice broccoli—birthday noodles—eight treasures pudding—Sichuan bold beans—Hoisin chicken lettuce wraps—sticky sesame wings—not-fried rice—dim sum dumplings—egg drop soup—honey-hoisin barbecued ribs—fortune cookies—wrap-n-bake egg rolls—spiky meatballs

477 FIELD, J. *Kitchen chemistry*. 2011, Crabtree (ISBN: 9780778753032). 32 p.

SERIES: Chemstastrophe!

GRADE LEVEL: Upper elementary – middle school

CONTENTS: N/A

478 FIELDS, J. *You can write excellent reports*. 2012, Capstone (ISBN: 9781429676144). 24 p.

SERIES: You can write

GRADE LEVEL: Elementary

CONTENTS: What is a report—topic—research—taking notes—outline—introduction—body and conclusion—revision—bibliography

479 FIELDS, J. *You can write great letters and e-mails*. 2012, Capstone (ISBN: 9781429676137). 24 p.

SERIES: You can write

GRADE LEVEL: Elementary

CONTENTS: Formal or friendly—heading and greeting—formal—friendly—closing and signature—email parts—internet safety—sending e-mails and letters

480 FINNEY, S. *The yoga handbook*. 2010, Rosen (ISBN: 9781435853591). 256 p.

SERIES: A young woman's guide to health and well-being

GRADE LEVEL: Middle school – high school

CONTENTS: Yoga schools and styles—what is yoga?—paths of yoga—hatha yoga physical postures—yoga nidra deep relaxation—pranayama breathing practices—dhyana meditation—yogic diet—yoga all day and every day

481 FIORENZA, S. *Jewelry crafting with kids: 35 creative jewelry projects for children to make and wear*. 2012, Ryland Peters & Small (ISBN: 9781849752145).
GRADE LEVEL: Upper elementary – middle school
CONTENTS: N/A

482 FISHER, D. *All about drawing dinosaurs and reptiles*. 2008, Walter Foster (ISBN: 9781600585791). 80 p.
GRADE LEVEL: Elementary
CONTENTS: N/A

483 FISHER, D. *Learn to draw animals: learn to draw and color 26 wild creatures, step by easy step, shape by simple shape!* 2011, Walter Foster (ISBN: 9781936309207). 40 p.
SERIES: Learn to draw
GRADE LEVEL: Upper elementary – middle school
CONTENTS: N/A

484 FISHER, D. *Learn to draw dogs and puppies: learn to draw and color 25 favorite dog breeds, step by easy step, shape by simple shape!* 2011, Walter Foster (ISBN: 9781936309184). 40 p.
SERIES: Learn to draw
GRADE LEVEL: Upper elementary – middle school
CONTENTS: N/A

485 FISHER, D. *Learn to draw reptiles & amphibians: learn to draw and color 29 reptiles and amphibians, step by easy step, shape by simple shape!* 2012, Walter Foster (ISBN: 9781936309504). 32 p.
SERIES: Learn to draw
GRADE LEVEL: Upper elementary – middle school
CONTENTS: N/A

486 FISHER, D. *Rockin' crafts: everything you need to become a rock-painting craft star!* 2009, Walter Foster (ISBN: 9781600586019). 64 p.
SERIES: Craft star
GRADE LEVEL: Elementary
CONTENTS: N/A

487 FISHER, V. *Explore colonial America! 25 great projects, activities, experiments*. 2009, Nomad Press (ISBN: 9781934670378). 96 p.
SERIES: Explore your world!
GRADE LEVEL: Elementary
CONTENTS: Map of the 13 colonies—soap boat—and eat a log cabin—candle—recreate colonial feast—johnnycakes—colonial butter—cornstick muffins—rock candy—plant herb garden—clay pots—wampum necklace—hold trading post day—colonial wig—tea sandwiches and party—pomander ball—hornbook—marbles—play ring taw—colonial journal—static electricity—scavenger hunt—feather pen

488 FLYNN, M. *The ultimate survival guide*. 2010, Macmillan Children's (ISBN: 9780330467254). 138 p.

SERIES: The science of

GRADE LEVEL: Upper elementary

CONTENTS: N/A

489 FLYNN, N. *Jeaneology: crafty ways to reinvent your old blues*. 2007, Zest Books (ISBN: 9780977266036).

GRADE LEVEL: High school

CONTENTS: Bohemian chic—skirt—shorts—flares—embellish it—distressed—necktie—headband—MP3 player and cell phone pocket—handbag—belt bag—wallet—pencil pouch—belt—slippers—earrings—bracelet—flower choker—laundry bag—place mat—coaster—pot holder—cushions—book jacket—key fob

490 FOLLET, V. *How to make friendship bracelets*. 2010, Search Press (ISBN: 9781844485420). 64 p.

GRADE LEVEL: Upper elementary – middle school

CONTENTS: N/A

491 FONTICHIARO, K. *Learning and sharing with a wiki*. 2013, Cherry Lake (ISBN: 9781624311321). 24 p.

SERIES: Information explorer junior

GRADE LEVEL: Elementary

CONTENTS: N/A

492 FONTICHIARO, K. *Speak out: creating podcasts and other audio recordings*. 2013, Cherry Lake (ISBN: 9781624310225). 24 p.

SERIES: Information explorer junior

GRADE LEVEL: Elementary

CONTENTS: What is podcasting—planning—recording—adding music or sound effects—editing—exporting—sharing

493 FONTICHIARO, K. *Starting your own blog*. 2013, Cherry Lake (ISBN: 9781624311338). 24 p.

SERIES: Information explorer junior

GRADE LEVEL: Elementary

CONTENTS: N/A

494 FORBES, S. *How to make a planet: a step-by-step guide to building the Earth*. 2014, Kids Can Press (ISBN: 9781894786881). 64 p.

GRADE LEVEL: Elementary

CONTENTS: N/A

495 FORD, M. *Fishing*. 2009, Wayland (ISBN: 9780750258333). 32 p.

SERIES: Master this!

GRADE LEVEL: Upper elementary – middle school

CONTENTS: N/A

496 FOREST, C. *Play soccer like a pro: key skills and tips*. 2011, Capstone (ISBN: 9781429648271). 32 p.

SERIES: Play like the pros

GRADE LEVEL: Upper elementary – middle school

CONTENTS: Dribble—pass—assist—legally slide tackle—beat a defender—power shot—make an accurate shot—stop a shot—throw in—defend a shot—head the ball—free kicks

497 FORMICHELLI, L. *Timekeeping: explore the history and science of telling time with 15 projects*. 2012, Nomad Press (ISBN: 9781619300330). 128 p.

SERIES: Build it yourself

GRADE LEVEL: Upper elementary – middle school

CONTENTS: Seasons from a shadow—time stick—quadrant—sundial—sandglass—the hours—time in the stars—sundial—candle clock—escapement—longitude—pendulum power—a day—timing reflex—quarter in a haystack—dawn

498 FOSTER, J. *The girls' book: how to be the best at everything*. 2007, Scholastic (ISBN: 9780545016292). 119 p.

GRADE LEVEL: Elementary

CONTENTS: N/A

499 FRANCHINO, V. *Junior scientists: experiment with soil*. 2011, Cherry Lake (ISBN: 9781602798373). 32 p.

SERIES: Science explorer junior

GRADE LEVEL: Lower elementary

CONTENTS: Soil—soil size—stop it

500 FRANCHINO, V. *Super cool science experiments: soil*. 2010, Cherry Lake (ISBN: 9781602795266). 32 p.

SERIES: Science explorer

GRADE LEVEL: Elementary

CONTENTS: Dirty science—soil—soil size—stop it!—don't wash it away—feeding your soil—do it yourself

501 FRANKLIN, C. *How to draw big cats*. 2009, PowerKids Press (ISBN: 9781435825161). 32 p.

SERIES: How to draw

GRADE LEVEL: Middle school

CONTENTS: Tiger—lion—panther—tiger's head—leopard—lynx—cheetah—lion cubs—puma

502 FREDERICK, S. *Badminton for fun!* 2009, Compass Point (ISBN: 9780756540258). 48 p.

SERIES: For fun!

GRADE LEVEL: Elementary

CONTENTS: Where to play—racket—shuttle—clothes—rules—serving—shots—strategy—etiquette—types of games—need for speed

503 FREDERICK, S. *Speed training for teen athletes: exercises to take your game to the next level*. 2012, Capstone (ISBN: 9781429679992).

SERIES: Sports Illustrated kids

GRADE LEVEL: High school

CONTENTS: Jump rope—shuttle run—speed ladder—ickey shuffle—sprint intervals—lateral jumps—bounds—squat jumps—strong core—quick rotation—lunges—hip crossover—wood chops—medicine ball chest pass—bicep curls—push-ups—bear crawls

504 FREDERICK, S. *Stamina training for teen athletes: exercises to take your game to the next level*. 2012, Capstone (ISBN: 9781429680011).
   SERIES: Sports Illustrated kids
   GRADE LEVEL: High school
   CONTENTS: Interval training—fartleks—killers—vertical jump—depth jump—jump rope—medicine ball chest pass—chest pass with resistance bands—overhead press with resistance bands—medicine ball push-ups—crunches—superhero—medicine ball twists

505 FREDERICK, S. *Trap and skeet shooting for fun!* 2009, Compass Point (ISBN: 9780756538651). 48 p.
   SERIES: For fun!
   GRADE LEVEL: Elementary
   CONTENTS: N/A

506 FREESE, J. *Ballroom dancing*. 2008, Capstone (ISBN: 9781429601238). 32 p.
   SERIES: Dance
   GRADE LEVEL: Elementary
   CONTENTS: N/A

507 FREESE, J. *Hip-hop dancing*. 2008, Capstone (ISBN: 9781429601214). 32 p.
   SERIES: Dance
   GRADE LEVEL: Elementary
   CONTENTS: Old school—hip-hop world—moving with style—putting it together

508 FRIDAY, M. *Green crafts: become an earth-friendly craft star, step by easy step!* 2009, Walter Foster (ISBN: 9781600586026). 64 p.
   SERIES: Craft star
   GRADE LEVEL: Elementary
   CONTENTS: N/A

509 FRIDAY, M. *Pet crafts: everything you need to become your pet's craft star!* 2009, Walter Foster (ISBN: 9781600586002). 64 p.
   SERIES: Craft star
   GRADE LEVEL: Elementary
   CONTENTS: iPet—pet bandana—tiny tee—paw print plaque—pet carpet—critter crawlspace—pet treats tin—disco ball—bird swing—pet announcement—pet tutu—pet products—pet lover's agreement

510 FUJIMOTO, N. *Cool jewels: beading projects for teens*. 2007, Kalmbach (ISBN: 9780871162472). 95 p.
   GRADE LEVEL: Middle school – high school
   CONTENTS: N/A

511 FULLMAN, J. *Card tricks*. 2008, QEB (ISBN: 9781595666048). 32 p.
SERIES: Magic handbook
GRADE LEVEL: Elementary
CONTENTS: Magic of cards—abracadabra—presto—ace trick—mind reading—aces high—elastic band trick—odds and evens—peek—force—pocket—vanishing card—magic shoe—lift

512 FULLMAN, J. *Celts: eat, write, and play just like the Celts*. 2010, QEB (ISBN: 9781595662477). 32 p.
SERIES: Hands-on history
GRADE LEVEL: Elementary
CONTENTS: N/A

513 FULLMAN, J. *Coin and rope tricks*. 2009, Firefly Books (ISBN: 9781554075706). 32 p.
SERIES: Magic handbook
GRADE LEVEL: Elementary
CONTENTS: N/A

514 FULLMAN, J. *Mind tricks*. 2008, QEB (ISBN: 9781595666079). 32 p.
SERIES: Magic handbook
GRADE LEVEL: Elementary
CONTENTS: N/A

515 FULLMAN, J. *Sleight of hand*. 2009, Firefly Books (ISBN: 9781554075720). 32 p.
SERIES: Magic handbook
GRADE LEVEL: Elementary
CONTENTS: N/A

516 GABRIELSON, C. *Stomp rockets, catapults, and kaleidoscopes: 30+ amazing science projects you can build for less than $1*. 2008, Chicago Review Press (ISBN: 9781556527371). 177 p.
GRADE LEVEL: Upper elementary – middle school
CONTENTS: Light circuit—crane—car—electrostatics—spinner—solenoid and speaker—bird and cuica—saxophone—harmonica—guitar—bull roarer—oboe—and sucker—xylophone and marimba—kaleidoscope—thaumatrope—balancing—catapult—spinner—mini-bot—racer—birdmen of Papantla—airplanes—fish—helicopters—butterfly—rockets—toilet—tornado—eye—fingers—heart—lung—divers—oil on water—gak and oobleck

517 GAINES, A. *Ace your internet research*. 2009, Enslow (ISBN: 9780766033924). 48 p.
SERIES: Ace it! Information literacy series
GRADE LEVEL: Elementary
CONTENTS: What is the web anyway—a lot of information—search engines—pictures—movies—music—more—is this site good—using what you find

518 GAINES, A. *Ace your research project*. 2009, Enslow (ISBN: 9780766033900). 48 p.
SERIES: Ace it! Information literacy series
GRADE LEVEL: Elementary

CONTENTS: Understand your assignment—choose your topic—research—make an outline—ready, set, write—draft and revise—peer review and publication

519 GARDNER, R. *Ace your animal science project: great science fair ideas*. 2010, Enslow (ISBN: 9780766032200). 128 p.

SERIES: Ace your biology science project

GRADE LEVEL: Upper elementary – middle school

CONTENTS: Dog conditioning—measuring the smallest animal—hydras—the shape of feather—using scales to find the age of a fish—spiders trap insects—finding direction—walk straight—darkness and balance—owl pellet—sow bugs—earthworms—mealworms—goldfish respiration and temperature—bird feeders

520 GARDNER, R. *Ace your chemistry science project: great science fair ideas*. 2010, Enslow (ISBN: 9780766032279). 128 p.

SERIES: Ace your science project

GRADE LEVEL: Upper elementary – middle school

CONTENTS: Bleach and stains—vinegar and galvanized nails—galvanized metal—density—finding acids and bases—natural indicators—mixing acids and bases—concentration of an acid—testing acids and bases—potato pole indicator—air temperature—air pressure—depth and pressure?—water and air barometer—pipette—testing air pressure—electrical conductivity of solids and gases—thermal conductivity of solids—electrical conductivity of liquids and gases—gases, liquids and temperature—temperature and solids—behavior of water—convection—aspirin—aspirin substitutes—distillation—making soap—testing blood

521 GARDNER, R. *Ace your ecology and environmental science project: great science fair ideas*. 2009, Enslow (ISBN: 9780766032163). 128 p.

SERIES: Ace your science project

GRADE LEVEL: Upper elementary – middle school

CONTENTS: N/A

522 GARDNER, R. *Ace your exercise and nutrition science project: great science fair ideas*. 2010, Enslow (ISBN: 9780766032187). 128 p.

SERIES: Ace your biology science project

GRADE LEVEL: Upper elementary – middle school

CONTENTS: Heart rate—breathing rate—blood pressure—body temperature—position of body—heart rate conditioning and exercise—breathing rate conditioning and exercise—blood pressure conditioning—body temperature conditioning and exercise—maintaining temperature—weight and perspiration—vital capacity and conditioning—basal metabolic rate—total metabolic rate—energy requirements and diet—food label nutritional facts—daily calcium requirements and diet—weight—body mass index—different types of milk—food nutritional value—calories in food—sugar in food—vitamin C in food—sunblock and sunscreen—antibacterial cream—how does hand soap work?—antibacterial soap—toothpaste—shampoo

523 GARDNER, R. *Ace your food science project: great science fair ideas*. 2010, Enslow (ISBN: 9780766032286). 128 p.

SERIES: Ace your science project

GRADE LEVEL: Upper elementary – middle school

CONTENTS: N/A

524 **GARDNER, R.** *Ace your forces and motion science project: great science fair ideas*. 2010, Enslow (ISBN: 9780766032224). 128 p.
SERIES: Ace your physics science project
GRADE LEVEL: Upper elementary – middle school
CONTENTS: An object in motion—bowling alley—friction—acceleration—action and reaction—buoyancy—submarines—balances and scales—making a scale—Coriolis—Hero's engine—moving shower curtain—motion transfer—accelerometer—acceleration and force—weight and acceleration—spinning objects and acceleration—centripetal force—rocket boat—testing for friction—wheels on a hill—marbles on a hill—gravity and hills—defy gravity—gravity and brakes on a hill—repulsing magnets—repulsing springs—ride safely—bicycles and friction—ball bearings—force and pedal position—bicycle brakes—centrifuge

525 **GARDNER, R.** *Ace your human biology science project: great science fair ideas*. 2010, Enslow (ISBN: 9780766032194). 128 p.
SERIES: Ace your biology science project
GRADE LEVEL: Upper elementary – middle school
CONTENTS: Body temperature and skin—your skeleton—joints—chicken wing dissection—inside bones—your muscles—a heartbeat—a pulse—breathing—your lungs—starch in the mouth—digestive tract—reflexes—the body and temperature changes—nerve receptors—chromosomes—family tree—PTC tasting—inheritance—blood types and inheritance—introvert or extrovert—inkblots tests—conditioning—learning in a maze—doing the alphabet backward—numbers and active memory—Stroop

526 **GARDNER, R.** *Ace your math and measuring science project: great science fair ideas*. 2010, Enslow (ISBN: 9780766032248). 128 p.
SERIES: Ace your physics science project
GRADE LEVEL: Upper elementary – middle school
CONTENTS: N/A

527 **GARDNER, R.** *Ace your physical science project: great science fair ideas*. 2010, Enslow (ISBN: 9780766032255). 128 p.
SERIES: Ace your physics science project
GRADE LEVEL: Upper elementary – middle school
CONTENTS: States of matter—volume of matter—mass in matter—density of liquids and solids—density and floating—solutions—effect of temperature on solubility—liquids in liquids—emulsions—viscosity—solid or liquid?—needle—surface tension—cohesion and adhesion—pouring water down a string—water flowing upward—siphon—capillary action—"empty" jar—air pushing water—carbon dioxide air mass—mass of water—mass of gases—density of carbon dioxide—disappearing solids—reappearing solids—reappearing liquids and appearing gas—temperature and disappearing liquids—disappearing solids and appearing liquids and vice versa—appearing liquids in a chemical reaction—diffusion of liquids and gases—sugar affects the freezing point of water—salt affects carbonated beverages—phosphoric acid affects metal oxides

528 **GARDNER, R.** *Ace your plant science project: great science fair ideas*. 2009, Enslow (ISBN: 9780766032217). 128 p.
SERIES: Ace your biology science project

GRADE LEVEL: Upper elementary – middle school

CONTENTS: N/A

529   **GARDNER, R.** *Ace your science project about the senses: great science fair ideas*. 2010, Enslow (ISBN: 9780766032170). 128 p.

SERIES: Ace your biology science project

GRADE LEVEL: Upper elementary – middle school

CONTENTS: N/A

530   **GARDNER, R.** *Ace your science project using chemistry magic and toys: great science fair ideas*. 2010, Enslow (ISBN: 9780766032262). 128 p.

SERIES: Ace your science project

GRADE LEVEL: Upper elementary – middle school

CONTENTS: Balloon—a funnel—a bottle—with air pressure—crushing air pressure—geyser—gravity defying ping-pong ball—submarine—raisins—genie in a bottle—dragon's blood—bubbles—magic red to green to red—iron to copper—oil into ink—written secrets—flame that jumps—blue bottle—disappearing ink—disappearing glass—comeback toy—balancing toy—frictionless toy air car—forces on the frictionless toy air car—electric and magnetic forces on the frictionless toy air car—toy electric motor—toy telephone—toy top—electrical balloons: charged up—hot and cold balloons—balloon in a bottle or a rocket launcher—mysterious balloons—throwing curves with a beach ball—bouncing ball—speed of a falling object—projectile?—playground physics—speed and running surface

531   **GARDNER, R.** *Ace your space science project: great science fair ideas*. 2009, Enslow (ISBN: 9780766032309). 128 p.

SERIES: Ace your science project

GRADE LEVEL: Upper elementary – middle school

CONTENTS: Astrolabe—sundial—seasons—path of the moon—planets—the solar system—sky clock—spectroscope—parallax—sizes of the earth and sun—solar eclipse—lunar eclipse—directions and the sun—shadow clock—magnetic fields—observing the moon—the sun, moon and earth—size of the moon—viewing with binoculars—air resistance—moon orbit—balloon rocket—weightlessness—weight in space

532   **GARDNER, R.** *Ace your weather science project: great science fair ideas*. 2010, Enslow (ISBN: 9780766032231). 128 p.

SERIES: Ace your physics science project

GRADE LEVEL: Upper elementary – middle school

CONTENTS: Barometer—atmospheric pressure—air temperature—temperature and angle of the sun—humidity—absolute humidity—evaporation—cooling and evaporation—cooling and the rate of evaporation—rain—clouds—pressure—measuring storm distance—how much rainfall—water evaporation—the water cycle—measuring raindrops—raindrop shape—raindrops splash—acid rain—formation of a rainbow—raindrops reflect light—raindrops refract light—temperature and clouds—pressure and clouds—cold and warm fluids—dew point—snowfall—melting snow—snowflakes—how to melt snow faster—how to stop snow from melting

533 **GARDNER, R.** *Air: green science projects for a sustainable planet.* 2011, Enslow (ISBN: 9780766036468). 128 p.

SERIES: Team green science projects

GRADE LEVEL: Upper elementary – middle school

CONTENTS: Air—aneroid barometer—air weight—Archimedes—air and buoyancy—aneroid barometer—altitude and air pressure—air pressure effects—electricity from light—heating air with a solar collector—heating and air—reduce heat loss reduction—air leaks—polluting particles in air—cold air mass—smog—rubber and air pollution—acid rain—salt in rain?—car fuel efficiency—tire pressure and friction—weight and friction—an electric motor as a generator—generating electricity with air

534 **GARDNER, R.** *Astronomy projects with an observatory you can build.* 2008, Enslow (ISBN: 9780766028081). 128 p.

SERIES: Build-a-lab! Science experiments

GRADE LEVEL: Upper elementary – middle school

CONTENTS: Observatory—finding north—magnetic compass problem—instruments for observatory—star locating—moon—planet—constellations and stars—earth—planet and the sun—measure width of earth—distance to the moon—moon observation—moon phases—moon and earth model—where does the moon rise?—harvest moon—does the moon change size?—sunrise and sunset location—path of the sun—altitude of the sun—seasons—absorbing sunlight—time measurement—time using the sun—time using a clock—analemma—size of the sun—Foucault—number of stars—latitude—starlight—Venus—Venus phases—moons of Jupiter

535 **GARDNER, R.** *Atoms and molecules experiments using ice, salt, marbles, and more.* 2013, Enslow (ISBN: 9780766039612). 48 p.

SERIES: Last-minute science projects

GRADE LEVEL: Upper elementary

CONTENTS: Molecule—gases—temperature—salt crystals—exchanging atoms—atoms and molecules—conducting electricity—separating atoms from molecules—colliding molecules—chemical reaction—combined atoms—states of matter—atoms are mostly empty—water molecules—tiny molecules—squeezing molecules—molecules and electrical charges—evaporation—temperature—and molecular speed

536 **GARDNER, R.** *Chemistry projects with a laboratory you can build.* 2008, Enslow (ISBN: 9780766028050). 128 p.

SERIES: Build-a-lab! Science experiments

GRADE LEVEL: Upper elementary – middle school

CONTENTS: Balance—measure mass—does mass change with freezing water—using density to identify liquids—identifying solids using density—gas weight—gas density—water and seltzer—source of gas in seltzer—chemical knowledge—reaction speed—catalyst—reaction with oxidation-reduction—electric current and ions—iron rust—starch test—precipitate from a slow reaction—litmus to identify acids and bases—indicators of acids and bases—neutralization—measuring acidity—fun trick with blood and water—raisins rise and fall—bottle with a genie—pushing with air—bubble magic—ink that disappears—writing invisible words—jumping flame

537 GARDNER, R. *Chemistry science fair projects using inorganic stuff, revised and expanded using the scientific method*. 2010, Enslow (ISBN: 9780766034136). 160 p.
GRADE LEVEL: Upper elementary – middle school
CONTENTS: Substances—conservation—chemical reactions and reaction speeds—energy—electric cell

538 GARDNER, R. *Earth's cycle: green science projects for a sustainable planet*. 2011, Enslow (ISBN: 9780766036444). 128 p.
SERIES: Team green science projects
GRADE LEVEL: Upper elementary – middle school
CONTENTS: Shadow cast by the midday sun—finding north-south line—two cycles with sunrise and sunset—path of the sun—apparent cycles of the sun—the sun and season cycles—carbon and decomposition—testing for starch—photosynthesis—stored food and leaves—carbon dioxide and photosynthesis—demonstration of photosynthesis and carbon dioxide—photosynthesis in light and darkness—plants adapt to receive maximum light—test for carbon dioxide—properties of carbon dioxide—lungs and carbon dioxide—carbon dioxide preparation and density—the water cycle—ocean water evaporation—what affects evaporation—isolating nitrogen—cycle of population—world population

539 GARDNER, R. *Electricity and magnetism experiments using batteries, bulbs, wires, and more: one hour or less science experiments*. 2013, Enslow (ISBN: 9780766039605). 48 p.
SERIES: Last-minute science projects
GRADE LEVEL: Upper elementary
CONTENTS: North and south poles—magnetic—electricity—series circuit—magnetic field—parallel circuit—current meter—magnetic coils—generate electricity—electricity and magnetism—electromagnet—electric motor—fruit and nails battery—can magnetism be felt?—nonmagnet into a magnet—magnetic motor—compass—water bending

540 GARDNER, R. *Electricity and magnetism science fair projects, revised and expanded using the scientific method*. 2010, Enslow (ISBN: 9780766034181). 160 p.
GRADE LEVEL: Upper elementary – middle school
CONTENTS: N/A

541 GARDNER, R. *Energy experiments using ice cubes, springs, magnets, and more: one hour or less science experiments*. 2013, Enslow (ISBN: 9780766039599). 48 p.
SERIES: Last minute science projects
GRADE LEVEL: Upper elementary
CONTENTS: N/A

542 GARDNER, R. *Energy: green science projects for a sustainable planet*. 2011, Enslow (ISBN: 9780766036437). 128 p.
SERIES: Team green science projects
GRADE LEVEL: Upper elementary – middle school
CONTENTS: Sea ice and glaciers melting—are you powerful—solar energy—electricity from sunlight—heat from sunlight—solar energy absorption—generating electricity—electric motor as a generator—electricity from wind—water density

and temperature—appliances power ratings—wattage and an immersion heater—lightbulb experiment—heat law demonstration—heat conduction—heat flow—cooling curve—surface area and heat loss—infiltration—insulation and heat flow

543   GARDNER, R. *Experimenting with plants science projects*. 2013, Enslow (ISBN: 9780766041448). 128 p.

SERIES: Exploring hands-on science projects

GRADE LEVEL: High school

CONTENTS: Collecting seeds—looking at seeds—water—food—cloning—germination—germinating seeds—air and germination—more air and germination—freezing temperatures—light and germination—bean seeds without cotyledons—seedlings and cotyledons—growth—depth of planting—growing grass—sand—leaves and light—leaves and veins—carbon dioxide—growing grass—stomates—transpiration—transpiration—stems—upward goes the water—growth on the stem—growth on the root—removing the tip of a root—upside down seedlings—twigs and buds—dissection—flower hunt—flowers and daylight—wildflowers—life cycle—crowded plants—dandelions—light and young plants—hydroponic—Van Helmont

544   GARDNER, R. *Experimenting with sound science projects*. 2013, Enslow (ISBN: 9780766041486). 128 p.

SERIES: Exploring hands-on science projects

GRADE LEVEL: High school

CONTENTS: Vibrations and sound—other sources of vibrations and sound—sound and air—feeling sound—sound and resonance—air and a vacuum—sound and distance—sound and strings—pulse of air—multiple air pulses and molecular model—waves—transverse waves—sound waves and a horn—back-and-forth motion—waves on a rope—water waves—transmission of sound—the speed of sound—the speed of sound in another medium—sounding board—reflection of sound—refraction of sound—diffraction of sound—Doppler effect—hose telephone—pipes of pan—insulating sound—sound intensity—sound filter—a wire harp—wind chimes—animal sounds—common sounds—sound effects—closed tubes and water—panpipe—trombone—bottle or glass band—stringed instruments

545   GARDNER, R. *Forensic science projects with a crime lab you can build*. 2008, Enslow (ISBN: 9780766028067). 128 p.

SERIES: Build-a-lab! Science experiments

GRADE LEVEL: Upper elementary – middle school

CONTENTS: Fingerprints—glass analysis—document analysis—forensic chemistry—sight observations—other senses—eyewitnesses—records of fingerprints—fingerprint classification—identification with fingerprints—getting fingerprints—view fingerprints with cyanoactylate—prints from lips—checking footprints—checking voiceprints—white solids—pieces of glass—glass evidence and density—refractivity and glass evidence—refractivity by immersion—solving crimes with teeth—solving crimes with bone—drowning and microbes—decomposition—temperature and time of death—DNA—evidence and blood—splashed blood drops—evidence and hair—evidence and fibers—counterfeit—indented writing—handwiring evidence—evidence in ink—reconstruction—hidden writing—breaking codes

546   GARDNER, R. *Genetics and evolution science fair projects: revised and expanded using the scientific method*. 2010, Enslow (ISBN: 9780766034228). 160 p.
GRADE LEVEL: Upper elementary – middle school
CONTENTS: Objects—evolution—missing links—evolution through time—Mendel—genetics—genes

547   GARDNER, R. *Human body experiments using fingerprints, hair, muscles, and more: one hour or less science experiment*. 2013, Enslow (ISBN: 9780766039582). 48 p.
SERIES: Last-minute science projects
GRADE LEVEL: Upper elementary
CONTENTS: Lever—clothes—reflexes—fingerprints—hairs on a human head—muscles—cells—breathing—air—touch—gravity—after images—cataracts—blind spot—your heart—the valves—taking pulses

548   GARDNER, R. *Meteorology projects with a weather station you can build*. 2008, Enslow (ISBN: 9780766028074). 128 p.
SERIES: Build-a-lab! Science experiments
GRADE LEVEL: Upper elementary – middle school
CONTENTS: N/A

549   GARDNER, R. *Organic chemistry science fair projects, revised and expanded using the scientific method*. 2010, Enslow (ISBN: 9780766034143). 160 p.
GRADE LEVEL: Upper elementary – middle school
CONTENTS: Organic chemistry—carbon—polar and nonpolar compounds—food—baking

550   GARDNER, R. *The physics of sports science projects*. 2013, Enslow (ISBN: 9780766041462). 128 p.
SERIES: Exploring hands-on science projects
GRADE LEVEL: High school
CONTENTS: Base paths—ice—the outfield—passes—hockey puck—pass the puck or ball—kick a football—speed and running—basketball and Newton's first law of motion—more sports and Newton's first law of motion—sports and the second part of Newton's first law of motion—sports and Newton's second law of motion—sports and newton's third law of motion—sports and forces perpendicular to an object's motion—making circles on ice—curveballs—an object's center of gravity—your center of gravity—sports and center of gravity—a football's center of gravity and passing—a football's center of gravity and kicking—a baseball or softball bat—cog—why do baseball and softball players slide—friction and football cleats—friction and "English" indicates experiments that offer ideas for science fair projects—follow-through and momentum—impulse and catching—collisions between surfaces and balls—rules—collisions—protection from collisions—another model—another model—a less elastic model—soccer balls—hockey—hockey goalie—basketball and shooting—shooting distances—lefties and distance to first base

551   GARDNER, R. *The physics of toys and games science projects*. 2013, Enslow (ISBN: 9780766041431). 128 p.
SERIES: Exploring hands-on science projects
GRADE LEVEL: High school

CONTENTS: Comeback toy—balancing toy—frictionless toy air car—forces and the frictionless toy air car—electric and magnetic forces and your frictionless toy air car—toy electric motor—toy telephone—spinning top—toy cars on hills—marbles and balls on hills—gravity on hills—gravity defying cars that loop-the-loop—gravity—magnetic cars—cars with springs—safety on a toy car—electrical balloons—balloons—ping pong ball and Bernoulli—hot and cold balloon—balloon in a bottle—superball—throwing curves with beach ball—speed and range of water projectiles—water bombs—ascending rockets—marble in orbit—circling wagons—pulling wagons—wind-up walking toy—how does a Push-n-Go® toy work—dipping bird—aluminum cans—soap bubble—bubbles that float

552   **GARDNER, R.** *Physics projects with a light box you can build*. 2007, Enslow (ISBN: 9780766028104). 128 p.
   SERIES: Build-a-lab! Science experiments
   GRADE LEVEL: Upper elementary – middle school
   CONTENTS: N/A

553   **GARDNER, R.** *Recycle: green science projects for a sustainable planet*. 2011, Enslow (ISBN: 9780766036482). 128 p.
   SERIES: Team green science projects
   GRADE LEVEL: Upper elementary – middle school
   CONTENTS: Diaper polymers—numbered plastics—liquids—solids—sink or float to demonstration density—using density to identifying—burning plastics—pollution—landfills—soil decomposers—decay—water and decay—Redi—electric generator—composting—composting with earthworms—surface area and volume—measuring polluting substances—separating cans—paper fibers—recycling paper—separating trash to recycle—natural resources trapped in solid waste—litter removal squad—beachcombing—entanglement—packaging—recycling in your city—recycling at school—recycling in the classroom—waste-free lunch—choosing a good one-use cup?

554   **GARDNER, R.** *The science behind magic science projects*. 2013, Enslow (ISBN: 9780766041479). 128 p.
   GRADE LEVEL: Middle school
   CONTENTS: N/A

555   **GARDNER, R.** *Simple machine experiments using seesaws, wheels, pulleys, and more: one hour or less science experiments*. 2013, Enslow (ISBN: 9780766039575). 48 p.
   SERIES: Last minute science projects
   GRADE LEVEL: Upper elementary
   CONTENTS: N/A

556   **GARDNER, R.** *Slam dunk! Science projects with basketball*. 2010, Enslow (ISBN: 9780766033665). 104 p.
   SERIES: Score! Sports science projects
   GRADE LEVEL: Middle school – high school
   CONTENTS: Measuring a ball—using a basketball to weigh air—bouncing a basketball—counting bounces—compression during a bounce—Galileo—Newton—circular motion—friction—more about friction—impulse—momentum—"soft hand"—

shooting layups—mass center—model of mass center—floating layup—set shot angles—distance and shooting percentages—maximum distance and passing angle—risk and long passes—vectors and passes—work

557 GARDNER, R. *Soil: green science projects for a sustainable planet*. 2011, Enslow (ISBN: 9780766036475). 128 p.

SERIES: Team green science projects

GRADE LEVEL: Upper elementary – middle school

CONTENTS: Layers of soil—soil particles—source of soil—weathering a rock—chemical weathering—solids and temperature change—animals in soil—wormarium—leaves make soil—water-holding capacity of soil—reaching an aquifer—space between soil particles—soil particle size—percolation—capillarity—capillarity experiment—best soils for plants—germinate seeds without soil—soil acidity—soil erosion—splashing raindrops on soil—agriculture on a hillside—soil erosion—local erosion—glacial erosion—dark soil—soil erosion and solar energy—erosion caused by a river—erosion caused by the wind—reducing erosion by the wind—beaches and wave erosion—sources of salt—soil compaction—creating compost

558 GARDNER, R. *Solids, liquids, and gases experiments using water, air, marbles, and more: one hour or less science experiments*. 2013, Enslow (ISBN: 9780766039629). 48 p.

SERIES: Last-minute science projects

GRADE LEVEL: Upper elementary

CONTENTS: Solids—liquids—gases—electricity—heat and solids—volume and weight—thickness of fluids—liquid and solid density—two liquids density—Archimedes—behavior of water—volume and surface area—expansion of a gas—fluids mixing—liquid climbing—drop of water volume—air weight—water cohesion—liquid expansion—mutual expansion

559 GARDNER, R. *Sound projects with a music lab you can build*. 2008, Enslow (ISBN: 9780766028098). 32 p.

SERIES: Build a lab! Science experiments

GRADE LEVEL: Upper elementary – middle school

CONTENTS: Vibrations—roar—sound—frequency—pitch—traveling sound—trumpet—solids and liquids—strings—standing waves—harmonics—octaves—music—math—telephone with a string—column of air—resonance—tubes of air—stringed instrument—string instrument construction—piano with wide keys—piano with twang—guitar with one string—banjo—bass—guitar with shoe box—horn with a hose—pipe organ—fluty horn—band of bottles—panpipe—horns from reeds—xylophone—bells—woodwinds and bells—chimes—flowerpot bells—wood chimes—percussion instruments

560 GARDNER, R. *Super science projects about Earth's soil and water*. 2008, Enslow (ISBN: 9780766027350). 48 p.

SERIES: Rockin' Earth science experiments

GRADE LEVEL: Upper elementary

CONTENTS: Disappearing water—cycle of water—soil—soil and water—soil settling—water underground—aquifer—plants—raising water—water moving soil

561 GARDNER, R. *Tundra experiments: 14 science experiments in one hour or less.* 2014, Enslow (ISBN: 9780766059429). 48 p.
SERIES: Last minute science projects
GRADE LEVEL: Upper elementary
CONTENTS: N/A

562 GARDNER, R. *Water: green science projects for a sustainable planet.* 2011, Enslow (ISBN: 9780766036451). 128 p.
SERIES: Team green science projects
GRADE LEVEL: Upper elementary – middle school
CONTENTS: Water on the earth—water footprint—polarity of water—surface tension—universal solvent—capillarity and surface tension—boiling water—melting ice—water becomes a gas and changes volume—behavior of freezing water—heat capacity—heat capacities of water and sand—water cycle—formation of raindrops—rain acidity—aquifer—working an aquifer—mixing seawater and freshwater—space between soil particles—transpiration—flow of water—wetland plants and animals—conserve water—is your home leaking—find the leaks in your home—shower or bath

563 GARDNER, R. *Who can solve the crime? Science projects using detective skills.* 2011, Enslow (ISBN: 9780766032477). 48 p.
SERIES: Who dunnit? Forensic science experiments
GRADE LEVEL: Elementary
CONTENTS: Observing—investigating a crime scene—using touch sound and smell—believing what you see—effects of color and light—believing what you hear—communicating with codes—remembering what you see

564 GARDNER, R. *Who forged this document? Crime solving science projects.* 2011, Enslow (ISBN: 9780766032460). 48 p.
SERIES: Who dunnit? Forensic science experiments
GRADE LEVEL: Elementary
CONTENTS: Indented—manuscript—chromatography—writing invisible words—paper—torn pages—counterfeit—fake checks

565 GARDNER, R. *Whose bones are these? Crime solving science projects.* 2011, Enslow (ISBN: 9780766032484). 48 p.
SERIES: Who dunnit? Forensic science experiments
GRADE LEVEL: Elementary
CONTENTS: Blood splatters—blood types—crime scene blood—body temperature and time of death—measuring bones to find height—studying bone—why spin a bullet—evidence from bullet holes—matching bullets to a gun

566 GARDNER, R. *Whose fingerprints are these? Crime solving science projects.* 2011, Enslow (ISBN: 9780766032453). 48 p.
SERIES: Who dunnit? Forensic science experiments
GRADE LEVEL: Elementary
CONTENTS: Fingerprints—fingerprint records—solving a crime—lifting fingerprints—latent fingerprint—lip prints—tooth prints—tracks—footprints

567   GARNER, L. *African crafts: fun things to and do from West Africa*. 2008, Chicago Review Press (ISBN: 9781556527487). 48 p.
GRADE LEVEL: Upper elementary – middle school
CONTENTS: Print adinkra cloth—coil pots—making mask—drum—kente strip

568   GAROFOLI, W. *Breakdancing*. 2008, Capstone (ISBN: 9781429601221). 32 p.
SERIES: Dance
GRADE LEVEL: Elementary
CONTENTS: N/A

569   GAROFOLI, W. *Dance team*. 2008, Capstone (ISBN: 9781429601207). 32 p.
SERIES: Dance
GRADE LEVEL: Elementary
CONTENTS: dancing together—training for tryouts—dancing machine—T is for team

570   GAROFOLI, W. *Hip-hop dancing volume 1: the basics*. 2011, Capstone (ISBN: 9781429654845). 48 p.
SERIES: Velocity
GRADE LEVEL: Middle school
CONTENTS: N/A

571   GAROFOLI, W. *Hip-hop dancing volume 2: breaking*. 2011, Capstone (ISBN: 9781429654852). 48 p.
SERIES: Velocity
GRADE LEVEL: Middle school – high school
CONTENTS: Toprock and uprock—drops—floor works—freezes—power moves

572   GAROFOLI, W. *Hip-hop dancing volume 3: popping, locking, and everything in between*. 2011, Capstone (ISBN: 9781429654869). 48 p.
SERIES: Velocity
GRADE LEVEL: Middle school – high school
CONTENTS: Popping moves—locking moves—the robot—waving and tutting—gliding—floating—sliding

573   GAROFOLI, W. *Hip-hop dancing volume 4: dancing with a crew*. 2011, Capstone (ISBN: 9781429654876). 48 p.
SERIES: Velocity
GRADE LEVEL: Middle school – high school
CONTENTS: Practicing with a crew—expanding a crew—performing with a crew—dress it up

574   GAROFOLI, W. *Irish step dancing*. 2008, Capstone (ISBN: 1429613513). 32 p.
SERIES: Dance
GRADE LEVEL: Elementary
CONTENTS: Irish dance at a glance—getting started—different dances—let's dance—getting good

575   GAROFOLI, W. *Modern dance*. 2008, Capstone (ISBN: 9781429613538). 32 p.
SERIES: Dance

GRADE LEVEL: Elementary

CONTENTS: N/A

576 **GAROFOLI, W.** *Swing dancing*. 2008, Capstone (ISBN: 9781429613507). 32 p.

SERIES: Dance

GRADE LEVEL: Elementary

CONTENTS: N/A

577 **GEORGE, J.** *Pocket guide to the outdoors*. 2009, Dutton Children's Books (ISBN: 9780525421634). 138 p.

GRADE LEVEL: Upper elementary – middle school

CONTENTS: What to take—camping—shelters—fire—water—fishing—roadkill and bugs—outdoor cooking—edible wild plants—poisonous plants—medicine plants— useful knots—animal tracking—birdsongs—falconry—hiking and trailblazing— finding your way—outdoor fun—outdoor safety—recipes

578 **GERASOLE, I.** *The Spatulatta cookbook*. 2007, Scholastic (ISBN: 9780439022507). 128 p.

GRADE LEVEL: Upper elementary – middle school

CONTENTS: N/A

579 **GIBSON, K.** *Native American history for kids: with 21 activities*. 2010, Chicago Review Press (ISBN: 9781569762806). 144 p.

SERIES: For kids

GRADE LEVEL: Middle school

CONTENTS: Pictographs—tool time—Three Sisters garden—weaving—tell a story— communicate without speaking—build a community—ball-and-triangle—trading post—jerky—totem pole—fry bread—journaling—decipher a code—numbers— names—a family tree

580 **GIFFORD, C.** *Badminton*. 2010, Sea to Sea (ISBN: 9781597712156). 30 p.

SERIES: Know your sport

GRADE LEVEL: Upper elementary

CONTENTS: N/A

581 **GIFFORD, C.** *Basketball*. 2009, PowerKids Press (ISBN: 9781404244443).

SERIES: Personal best

GRADE LEVEL: Elementary

CONTENTS: Stance and pivoting—passing—dribbling—court movement—screening— defending—fouls and free throws—jump and hook shots—layups—jumping and rebounding—team plays

582 **GIFFORD, C.** *Basketball*. 2010, Sea to Sea (ISBN: 9781597712149). 30 p.

SERIES: Know your sport

GRADE LEVEL: Upper elementary

CONTENTS: N/A

583 **GIFFORD, C.** *Field athletics*. 2010, Sea to Sea (ISBN: 9781597712200). 30 p.

SERIES: Know your sport

GRADE LEVEL: Upper elementary

CONTENTS: Equipment and clothing—shot put—javelin—discus—hammer—high jump—the pole vault—long jump—triple jump

584 GIFFORD, C. *Football*. 2010, Franklin Watts (ISBN: 9781445101378). 30 p.
SERIES: Know your sport
GRADE LEVEL: Upper elementary
CONTENTS: N/A

585 GIFFORD, C. *Golf*. 2010, Sea to Sea (ISBN: 9781597712170). 30 p.
SERIES: Know your sport
GRADE LEVEL: Upper elementary
CONTENTS: N/A

586 GIFFORD, C. *Golf: from tee to green: the essential guide for young golfers*. 2010, Kingfisher (ISBN: 9780753463994). 64 p.
GRADE LEVEL: Elementary
CONTENTS: N/A

587 GIFFORD, C. *Hockey*. 2008, Franklin Watts (ISBN: 9780749678371). 30 p.
SERIES: Know your sport
GRADE LEVEL: Upper elementary
CONTENTS: N/A

588 GIFFORD, C. *Materials*. 2012, Kingfisher (ISBN: 9780753467817). 56 p.
SERIES: Discover science
GRADE LEVEL: Elementary
CONTENTS: Slalom—balloon—crispies

589 GIFFORD, C. *Netball*. 2007, Franklin Watts (ISBN: 9780749674083). 30 p.
SERIES: Know your sport
GRADE LEVEL: Upper elementary
CONTENTS: N/A

590 GIFFORD, C. *Rugby*. 2008, Franklin Watts (ISBN: 9780749678333). 30 p.
SERIES: Starting sport
GRADE LEVEL: Lower elementary
CONTENTS: N/A

591 GIFFORD, C. *Skiing*. 2011, PowerKids Press (ISBN: 9781448832989). 32 p.
SERIES: Get outdoors
GRADE LEVEL: Upper elementary
CONTENTS: The gear—skis—boots—and bindings—on the slopes—get moving— your first runs—traversing and turning—building experience—ski safety—alpine competition skiing—cross-country and freestyle skiing

592 GIFFORD, C. *Soccer*. 2009, Sea to Sea (ISBN: 9781597711524). 30 p.
SERIES: Know your sport
GRADE LEVEL: Upper elementary

CONTENTS: Training—ball control—passing—on the ball—attacking—goal scoring—defending—tackling—goalkeeping

593 GIFFORD, C. *Swimming*. 2012, Wayland (ISBN: 9780750263702). 32 p.
SERIES: Sporting skills
GRADE LEVEL: Elementary
CONTENTS: N/A

594 GIFFORD, C. *Tennis*. 2009, Sea to Sea (ISBN: 9781597711531). 30 p.
SERIES: Know your sport
GRADE LEVEL: Upper elementary
CONTENTS: Ready to play—forehand drive—backhand drive—volleys—courtcraft—learning to serve—serving and receiving—advanced shots—playing doubles

595 GIFFORD, C. *Track and field*. 2009, PowerKids Press (ISBN: 9781404244429).
SERIES: Personal best
GRADE LEVEL: Elementary
CONTENTS: Training and preparation—sprint start—sprinting—relay running—hurdling—distance running—long jump—high jump—throwing the javelin—shot putting—discus throwing—other events

596 GIFFORD, C. *Track athletics*. 2009, Sea to Sea (ISBN: 9781597711548). 30 p.
SERIES: Know your sport
GRADE LEVEL: Upper elementary
CONTENTS: Training—competition—sprints 1—sprints 2—relay racing—hurdles—middle-distance running—long-distance running—marathon and race walking—the big competitions

597 GILBERT, S. *Write your own article: newspaper, magazine, online*. 2009, Compass Point (ISBN: 9780756538552). 64 p.
SERIES: Write your own
GRADE LEVEL: Upper elementary – middle school
CONTENTS: Getting the story—people—viewpoint—story development—winning words—scintillating speech

598 GILLIS, J. *Ballroom dancing for fun!* 2008, Compass Point (ISBN: 9780756532857). 48 p.
SERIES: For fun!
GRADE LEVEL: Elementary
CONTENTS: Basics—from castles to dance halls—in the 21st century—competition—first steps—what to wear—doing it—warming up—position—do's and don'ts—waltz—foxtrot—tango—rumba—cha-cha—East Coast swing

599 GIOFFRÈ, R. *Fun with French cooking*. 2010, PowerKids Press (ISBN: 9781435834545). 32 p.
SERIES: Let's get cooking!
GRADE LEVEL: Upper elementary – middle school
CONTENTS: Croque-Monsieur—ham and cheese crêpes—macaroni with béchamel—tomato omelette—quiche Lorraine—salade niçoise—chicken skewers—la fête de

rois—ground beef and potato pie—sole meunière—strawberry tart—chocolate mousse—profiteroles—crème brûlée

600 GITLIN, M. *Football skills*. 2009, Enslow (ISBN: 9780766032033). 48 p.
SERIES: How to play like a pro
GRADE LEVEL: Upper elementary
CONTENTS: Football pregame—passing—rushing and receiving—blocking—defense—special teams

601 GLASER, J. *Batter*. 2011, Gareth Stevens (ISBN: 9781433946202). 48 p.
SERIES: Play ball: baseball
GRADE LEVEL: Elementary
CONTENTS: Carry a big stick—baseball becomes a big hit—the kings of swing—batter on deck

602 GLASER, J. *Catcher*. 2011, Gareth Stevens (ISBN: 9781433944840). 48 p.
SERIES: Play ball: baseball
GRADE LEVEL: Elementary
CONTENTS: The man behind the mask—ever more dangerous—playing catcher

603 GLASER, J. *Infielders*. 2011, Gareth Stevens (ISBN: 9781433944888). 48 p.
SERIES: Play ball: baseball
GRADE LEVEL: Elementary
CONTENTS: N/A

604 GLASER, J. *Pitcher*. 2011, Gareth Stevens (ISBN: 9781433944963). 48 p.
SERIES: Play ball: baseball
GRADE LEVEL: Elementary
CONTENTS: Today's hero—pitching's past—historic hurlers—playing as a pitcher—superstar pitchers

605 GOLA, M. *Winning softball for girls*. 2010, Chelsea House (ISBN: 9780816077168). 220 p.
SERIES: Winning sports for girls
GRADE LEVEL: Middle school – high school
CONTENTS: N/A

606 GOLD, R. *Eat fresh food: awesome recipes for teen chefs*. 2009, Bloomsbury (ISBN: 978159990282). 160 p.
GRADE LEVEL: Upper elementary – middle school
CONTENTS: Bread—butter and breakfast—soup and pasta—sandwiches—burgers and pizza—salads—big and small—dinner specials with vegetables—side dishes—desserts and drinks

607 GOLDBERG, B. *Watch me draw Spongebob's underwater escapades*. 2012, Walter Foster (ISBN: 9781936309757). 24 p.
SERIES: Watch me draw
GRADE LEVEL: Upper elementary
CONTENTS: N/A

608   **GOLDSMITH, M.** *Light and sound*. 2012, Kingfisher (ISBN: 9780753467794). 56 p.
   SERIES: Discover science
   GRADE LEVEL: Elementary
   CONTENTS: Puppets—clock—xylophone—telephone

609   **GOLDSMITH, M.** *Solar system*. 2010, Kingfisher (ISBN: 9780753464472). 56 p.
   SERIES: Discover science
   GRADE LEVEL: Elementary
   CONTENTS: N/A

610   **GOODSTEIN, M.** *Ace your sports science project: great science fair ideas*. 2010,
   Enslow (ISBN: 9780766032293). 128 p.
   SERIES: Ace your physics science project
   GRADE LEVEL: Upper elementary – middle school
   CONTENTS: Physical condition—exercise—heart rate—anaerobic exercise—muscles—
      base paths—throwing speed—fast passes—kick a football—center of gravity—center
      of gravity and passing—bat's sweet spot—shooting positions—follow through—
      soft hands—rebound rating of a ball—rules—protection from collisions—Magnus
      effect?—Bernoulli's principle—spin and the tennis ball—rebound angle without
      spin—rebound angle with spin—air resistance of a golf ball—golf clubs—baseball—
      launch angle—controlling a basketball's bounce—topspin and backspin—getting the
      basketball in the basket—spin on a basketball—the football—football pass with and
      without spin—punting a football

611   **GOODSTEIN, M.** *Goal! Science projects with soccer*. 2009, Enslow (ISBN:
   9780766031067). 104 p.
   SERIES: Score! Sports science projects
   GRADE LEVEL: Middle school – high school
   CONTENTS: Soccer ball—ground and the ball—energy—energy of deformation—
      compound motion—soccer ball—standing kick versus running kick—conservation
      of momentum—pass or dribble—controlling angles—kicking accuracy—offside—air
      drag—air drag and height—smooth versus turbulent airflow—kicking a ball off-
      center—the side kick—Bernoulli's principle—the Magnus effect

612   **GOODSTEIN, M.** *Plastics and polymers science fair projects, revised and
   expanded using the scientific method*. 2010, Enslow (ISBN: 9780766034129). 160 p.
   GRADE LEVEL: Upper elementary – middle school
   CONTENTS: Plastics and polymers—properties of polymers—testing plastics—natural
      rubber

613   **GOODSTEIN, M.** *Water science fair projects: revised and expanded using the
   scientific method*. 2010, Enslow (ISBN: 9780766034112). 160 p.
   GRADE LEVEL: Elementary
   CONTENTS: Water—states of matter of water—surface—tension—adhesion—cohesion
      of liquid water—chemical properties

614   **GOODSTEIN, M.** *Wheels! Science projects with bicycles, skateboards, and skates*.
   2009, Enslow (ISBN: 9780766031074). 104 p.
   SERIES: Score! Sports science projects

GRADE LEVEL: Middle school – high school

CONTENTS: The wheel—Galileo and Newton's First Law—friction—bearings—center of gravity—center of gravity—how to fall on skates—Third Law of Motion and skates—in-line skates—muscular energy—the Law of Conservation—the law of conservation of energy—unweighting—ollie—turning in midair—balance a bicycle—turning a bicycle—bicycle gears—air—drafting

615 **GRAHAM, I. *Science rocks!*** 2011, DK (ISBN: 9780756671983). 144 p.

GRADE LEVEL: Upper elementary – middle school

CONTENTS: Changed state—ice cloud—ice bubbles—mega bubble—crystal—bigger bubbles—liquid layers—density—boat—diver—fountain—slime—plastic—butter—holding it together—centrifuge—colors—oxidation—rotten apple—toothpaste—turn water pink—cabbage—volcano—copper plating—silver—dome—bottle rocket—water—pendulums—eggs—balancing—dart—glider—hovercraft—drag racer—can crusher—fountain—eggs—under pressure—suck it to them—soda shoot—two-stage rocket—hydraulic lifter—weightlifting—spreading the load—convection currents—solar oven—metal through ice—chill out—full steam ahead—sunbeam—rainbow—spectroscope—gelatin—periscope—telescope—camera—microphone—tune—charm a snake—lightning—static charge—flashlight—lighten up—circuit—citrus current—radio—metal detector—meteorites—breakfast—electromagnet—motor—under pressure—wind whizzer—cloud—sow a seed—light—starch—flower—carrot—eggs—rapid response—DNA—germs

616 **GRAIMES, N. *The ultimate children's cookbook*.** 2009, DK (ISBN: 9781405351898). 304 p.

GRADE LEVEL: Upper elementary

CONTENTS: N/A

617 **GRANT, A. *The silver spoon for children: favorite Italian recipes*.** 2009, Phaidon (ISBN: 9780714857565). 99 p.

GRADE LEVEL: Upper elementary – middle school

CONTENTS: N/A

618 **GRAVES, K. *Ballet dance*.** 2008, Capstone (ISBN: 9781429601191). 32 p.

SERIES: Dance

GRADE LEVEL: Elementary

CONTENTS: Ballet basics—the first leap—the barre—your dream

619 **GRAVES, K. *Tap dancing*.** 2008, Capstone (ISBN: 1429601248). 32 p.

SERIES: Dance

GRADE LEVEL: Elementary

CONTENTS: N/A

620 **GRAY, P. *How to draw butterflies and other insects*.** 2013, PowerKids Press (ISBN: 9781477714096). 32 p.

SERIES: How to draw animals

GRADE LEVEL: Upper elementary

CONTENTS: N/A

621 GRAY, P. *How to draw cats and dogs, and other pets*. 2013, PowerKids Press (ISBN: 9781445118758). 32 p.
SERIES: How to draw animals
GRADE LEVEL: Upper elementary
CONTENTS: N/A

622 GRAY, P. *How to draw crocodiles and other reptiles*. 2013, PowerKids Press (ISBN: 9781477714133). 32 p.
SERIES: How to draw animals
GRADE LEVEL: Upper elementary
CONTENTS: N/A

623 GRAY, P. *How to draw dolphins and other sea creatures*. 2013, PowerKids Press (ISBN: 9781477713020). 32 p.
SERIES: How to draw animals
GRADE LEVEL: Upper elementary
CONTENTS: N/A

624 GRAY, P. *How to draw horses and ponies*. 2013, PowerKids Press (ISBN: 9781445118765). 32 p.
SERIES: How to draw animals
GRADE LEVEL: Upper elementary
CONTENTS: N/A

625 GRAY, P. *How to draw tigers and other big cats*. 2013, PowerKids Press (ISBN: 9781445118772). 32 p.
SERIES: How to draw animals
GRADE LEVEL: Upper elementary
CONTENTS: N/A

626 GRAY, S. *Junior scientists: experiment with bugs*. 2011, Cherry Lake (ISBN: 9781602798427). 32 p.
SERIES: Science explorer junior
GRADE LEVEL: Lower elementary
CONTENTS: Damp or dry—bugs and light—worms—do it yourself

627 GRAY, S. *Junior scientists: experiment with plants*. 2011, Cherry Lake (ISBN: 9781602798397). 32 p.
SERIES: Science explorer junior
GRADE LEVEL: Lower elementary
CONTENTS: Roots and shoots—light or dark—how plants drink

628 GRAY, S. *Junior scientists: experiment with seeds*. 2011, Cherry Lake (ISBN: 9781602798359). 32 p.
SERIES: Science explorer junior
GRADE LEVEL: Lower elementary
CONTENTS: Seeds' needs—scarred—roots

629 **GRAY, S.** *Super cool science experiments: bugs*. 2010, Cherry Lake (ISBN: 9781602795211). 32 p.

SERIES: Science explorer

GRADE LEVEL: Elementary

CONTENTS: Classroom—first things first—damp or dry—bugs and light—worms—mealworms and maggots—wiggly worms—do it yourself

630 **GRAY, S.** *Super cool science experiments: plants*. 2010, Cherry Lake (ISBN: 9781602795228). 32 p.

SERIES: Science explorer

GRADE LEVEL: Elementary

CONTENTS: Not so creepy!—first things first—roots and shoots—light versus dark—being green—more than meets the eye—how plants drink?—do it yourself

631 **GRAY, S.** *Super cool science experiments: seeds*. 2010, Cherry Lake (ISBN: 9781602795143). 32 p.

SERIES: Science explorer

GRADE LEVEL: Elementary

CONTENTS: No mad scientists here!—first things first—seeds' needs—heat—scarred—roots—can roots be fooled?—do it yourself

632 **GREEN, G.** *The kids' guide to projects for your pets*. 2012, Capstone (ISBN: 9781429676625). 32 p.

SERIES: Kids' guides

GRADE LEVEL: Upper elementary

CONTENTS: Treat container—liver treats—pet environment—cat toy—fraid-e-braids—dog t-shirt—funhouse—sleeping mat—collar decoration—cage and crate cover

633 **GREEN, G.** *Paper artist: creations kids can fold, tear, wear, or share*. 2013, Capstone (ISBN: 9781623700041). 32 p.

SERIES: Paper creations

GRADE LEVEL: Upper elementary

CONTENTS: N/A

634 **GREEN, G.** *Pretty presents: paper creations to share*. 2013, Capstone (ISBN: 9781620650417). 32 p.

SERIES: Paper creations

GRADE LEVEL: Middle school – high school

CONTENTS: Totally tubular frame—better-than-new vase—fluttering butterfly gift bag—quilled nameplate—forever bouquet—swimming in tissue—"I heart you" card—spiraling out—stack 'em up photo cubes—sweet owl—corrugated bookends—box it up—paper tile mosaic

635 **GREEN, J.** *Hands-on history! Eskimo, Inuit, Saami & Arctic peoples: learn all about the inhabitants of the frozen north, with 15 step-by-step projects and over 350 exciting pictures*. 2013, Armadillo (ISBN: 9781843229940). 64 p.

SERIES: Hands-on history!

GRADE LEVEL: Upper elementary

CONTENTS: N/A

636   GREGORY, J. *Breaking secret codes*. 2011, Capstone (ISBN: 9781429645683).
SERIES: Making and breaking codes
GRADE LEVEL: Upper elementary – middle school
CONTENTS: The queen's code crackers—transposition codes—substitution codes—book ciphers and beyond—what was the secret message?

637   GREGORY, J. *Junior scientists: experiment with solids*. 2011, Cherry Lake (ISBN: 9781602798458). 32 p.
SERIES: Science explorer junior
GRADE LEVEL: Lower elementary
CONTENTS: Mix it—meltdown—space

638   GREGORY, J. *Making secret codes*. 2011, Capstone (ISBN: 9781429645676).
SERIES: Making and breaking codes
GRADE LEVEL: Upper elementary – middle school
CONTENTS: Codes—cryptography—codes throughout history—code play

639   GREGSON, S. *Cyber literacy: evaluating the reliability of data*. 2008, Rosen Central (ISBN: 9781404213531).
SERIES: Cyber citizenship and cyber safety
GRADE LEVEL: Upper elementary – middle school
CONTENTS: Round and round the world wide web we go—the truth—the whole truth—and nothing but the truth?—the good—the bad—the totally untrue—get your information the smart way—when the www spills into the real world

640   GRIMSHAW, M. *Make it!* 2012, QEB (ISBN: 9781609922740).
GRADE LEVEL: Lower elementary
CONTENTS: Gift box—woven mobile—space pillowcase—pocket organizer—hair tie bird—get well card—doorstop—sock snake—patchwork picture—burlap pot wrap—bird—puppet

641   GUNDERSON, J. *Bowhunting for fun!* 2009, Compass Point (ISBN: 9780756538644). 48 p.
SERIES: For fun!
GRADE LEVEL: Elementary
CONTENTS: N/A

642   GUNDERSON, J. *Snorkeling for fun!* 2009, Compass Point (ISBN: 9780756540340). 48 p.
SERIES: For fun!
GRADE LEVEL: Elementary
CONTENTS: N/A

643   GUY, L. *Kids learn to crochet*. 2008, Trafalgar Square Books (ISBN: 9781570763953). 96 p.
GRADE LEVEL: Lower elementary
CONTENTS: N/A

644   HAAB, S. *Clay so cute! 21 polymer clay projects for cool charms, itty-bitty animals, and tiny treasures*. 2009, Watson-Guptill (ISBN: 9780823098996).
> **GRADE LEVEL:** Upper elementary – middle school
>
> **CONTENTS:** Swirly beads—bangles—necklace—rings—bracelet—bubble rings—bottle cap necklaces—ponytail holders—monogram jewelry—mermaid jewelry—wishing stone jewelry—chocolate and marshmallows—banana split—cupcake charms—choco-licious bracelet—licorice dangles—luggage tags—mirror in my purse—treasure tins—itty-bitty critters—claybots

645   HAGLER, G. *Step-by-step experiments with electricity*. 2012, Child's World (ISBN: 9781609733384). 32 p.
> **SERIES:** Step-by-step experiments
>
> **GRADE LEVEL:** Lower elementary
>
> **CONTENTS:** Electricity—seven steps—circuit—conducting—electric hair—battery

646   HAGLER, G. *Step-by-step experiments with magnets*. 2012, Child's World (ISBN: 9781609735890). 32 p.
> **SERIES:** Step-by-step experiments
>
> **GRADE LEVEL:** Lower elementary
>
> **CONTENTS:** Magnets—seven steps—magic—magnetic—do opposites attract—compass

647   HAGLER, G. *Step-by-step experiments with matter*. 2012, Child's World (ISBN: 9781609735906). 32 p.
> **SERIES:** Step-by-step experiments
>
> **GRADE LEVEL:** Lower elementary
>
> **CONTENTS:** Matter—steps—ice and heat—frosty—salt—balloon—freezing

648   HAGLER, G. *Step-by-step experiments with simple machines*. 2012, Child's World (ISBN: 9781609735869). 32 p.
> **SERIES:** Step-by-step experiments
>
> **GRADE LEVEL:** Lower elementary
>
> **CONTENTS:** Simple machines—seven steps – soap-up—a finger's touch

649   HAGLER, G. *Step-by-step experiments with soils*. 2012, Child's World (ISBN: 9781609735920). 32 p.
> **SERIES:** Step-by-step experiments
>
> **GRADE LEVEL:** Lower elementary
>
> **CONTENTS:** Soils—seven steps—critters—air—heavy or light

650   HAGLER, G. *Step-by-step experiments with sound*. 2012, Child's World (ISBN: 9781609735937). 32 p.
> **SERIES:** Step-by-step experiments
>
> **GRADE LEVEL:** Lower elementary
>
> **CONTENTS:** Sounds—steps—wave—hearing—knocking

651   HALL, P. *5 steps to drawing aircraft*. 2012, Child's World (ISBN: 9781609731939). 32 p.
> **SERIES:** 5 steps to drawing
>
> **GRADE LEVEL:** Elementary

CONTENTS: Biplane—jumbo jet—hang glider—seaplane—helicopter—fighter jet—hot air balloon—blimp

652 **HALL, P.** *5 steps to drawing dinosaurs*. 2012, Child's World (ISBN: 9781609731953). 32 p.
SERIES: 5 steps to drawing
GRADE LEVEL: Elementary
CONTENTS: N/A

653 **HALL, P.** *5 steps to drawing farm animals*. 2012, Child's World (ISBN: 9781609731991). 32 p.
SERIES: 5 steps to drawing
GRADE LEVEL: Elementary
CONTENTS: N/A

654 **HALL, P.** *5 steps to drawing people*. 2012, Child's World (ISBN: 9781609732035). 32 p.
SERIES: 5 steps to drawing
GRADE LEVEL: Elementary
CONTENTS: Baseball player—surfer girl—baby—doctor—rock star—pilot—movie star—president

655 **HAMMOND, R.** *Super science lab*. 2009, DK (ISBN: 9780756655501). 96 p.
GRADE LEVEL: Elementary
CONTENTS: Hovercraft—racing spool—boomerang—crown—rocket—pictures—3-D—Mobius—pixels—optical illusions—quizzes—flavors—trick—crackers and balls 'n' tights—bottle—farting—eyes—pen—prints—intruder—DNA—quizzes

656 **HAMMOND, R.** *Super science lab: bright ideas*. 2009, DK (ISBN: 9780756658403). 48 p.
GRADE LEVEL: Upper elementary – middle school
CONTENTS: Throwies—light—crystal—metal detectors—shades—lamp—marshmallows—rainbow—bulb—kaleidoscope—electric—gel

657 **HANEY, J.** *Capoeira*. 2012, Marshall Cavendish Benchmark (ISBN: 9780761449324). 47 p.
SERIES: Martial arts in action
GRADE LEVEL: Upper elementary – middle school
CONTENTS: N/A

658 **HANEY-WITHROW, A.** *Tae kwon do*. 2012, Marshall Cavendish Benchmark (ISBN: 9780761449409). 47 p.
SERIES: Martial arts in action
GRADE LEVEL: Upper elementary – middle school
CONTENTS: N/A

659 **HANLEY, V.** *Seize the story: a handbook for teens who like to write*. 2008, Cottonwood Press (ISBN: 9781877673818). 213 p.
GRADE LEVEL: Middle school – high school

CONTENTS: Imagination—characters—beginnings—setting—the heart of a writer—writing dialogue—showing and telling—plotting and scheming—conflicts—middles and ends—polishing your writing—point of view

660 HANSEN, J. *How to draw dragons*. 2008, PowerKids Press (ISBN: 9781404238565). 32 p.

SERIES: Drawing fantasy art

GRADE LEVEL: Upper elementary

CONTENTS: Perspective—meet the dragons—Western dragon—Eastern dragon—North American dragon

661 HANSEN, J. *How to draw superheroes*. 2008, PowerKids Press (ISBN: 9781404238558). 32 p.

SERIES: Drawing fantasy art

GRADE LEVEL: Upper elementary

CONTENTS: Styles—construction—equipment—cartoon style—head—expressions—body—body in action—different characters/heads—different characters/bodies—screen hero style—teen superheroes—teen superheroes in action—adult superheroes—adult superheroes in action—manga style—head—expressions—female body in action—male body in action

662 HANSON, A. *Cool calligraphy: the art of creativity for kids!* 2009, ABDO (ISBN: 9781604531459). 32 p.

SERIES: Cool art

GRADE LEVEL: Elementary

CONTENTS: Tools—parts of a letter—strokes—decorations—techniques—frames—lowercase italic—uppercase italic—lowercase gothic—uppercase gothic—calligraphy card—letters t-shirt

663 HANSON, A. *Cool collage: the art of creativity for kids!* 2009, ABDO (ISBN: 9781604531466). 32 p.

SERIES: Cool art

GRADE LEVEL: Elementary

CONTENTS: Tools—basic elements—composition—techniques—faces—puppy love—windows—sand and surf—pop-up card—collage battle

664 HANSON, A. *Cool drawing: the art of creativity for kids!* 2009, ABDO (ISBN: 9781604531428). 32 p.

SERIES: Cool art

GRADE LEVEL: Elementary

CONTENTS: Tools—basic elements—composition—techniques—warm-up—mega montage—the blind line—still life—action figures—self-portrait

665 HANSON, A. *Cool painting: the art of creativity for kids!* 2009, ABDO (ISBN: 9781604531435). 32 p.

SERIES: Cool art

GRADE LEVEL: Elementary

CONTENTS: Tools—basic elements—composition—techniques—color theory—painted music—monochrome monster—sea of color—loony landscape—warm and cool

666 HANSON, A. *Cool paper folding: creative activities that make math and science fun for kids!* 2013, Checkerboard Books (ISBN: 9781617838231). 32 p.
   SERIES: Cool art with math & science
   GRADE LEVEL: Upper elementary
   CONTENTS: N/A

667 HANSON, A. *Cool printmaking: the art of creativity for kids*! 2009, ABDO (ISBN: 9781604531473). 32 p.
   SERIES: Cool art
   GRADE LEVEL: Elementary
   CONTENTS: Tools—basic elements—composition—techniques—monoprint—leafy gift wrap—potato people—fish print—what a relief!—sun and moon—stencil style

668 HANSON, A. *Cool sculpture: the art of creativity for kids*! 2009, ABDO (ISBN: 9781604531442). 32 p.
   SERIES: Cool art
   GRADE LEVEL: Elementary
   CONTENTS: Tools—basic elements—composition—techniques—wire frame—superhero—swan song—cast away

669 HARBO, C. *Easy animal origami*. 2011, Capstone (ISBN: 9781429653848). 24 p.
   SERIES: Easy origami
   GRADE LEVEL: Lower elementary
   CONTENTS: Materials—folding techniques and symbols—dog—cat—butterfly—bunny—ladybug—parakeet—swan—origami pets

670 HARBO, C. *Easy holiday origami*. 2011, Capstone (ISBN: 9781429653879). 24 p.
   SERIES: Easy origami
   GRADE LEVEL: Lower elementary
   CONTENTS: N/A

671 HARBO, C. *Easy magician origami*. 2011, Capstone (ISBN: 9781429660006). 24 p.
   SERIES: First facts
   GRADE LEVEL: Lower Elementary
   CONTENTS: Lucky rabbit—wizard's hat—magic want—top hat—lovely dove—monkey bow tie—fortune-teller

672 HARBO, C. *Easy ocean origami*. 2011, Capstone (ISBN: 9781429653855). 24 p.
   SERIES: Easy origami
   GRADE LEVEL: Lower elementary
   CONTENTS: N/A

673 HARBO, C. *Easy origami toys*. 2011, Capstone (ISBN: 9781429653862). 24 p.
   SERIES: Easy origami
   GRADE LEVEL: Lower elementary
   CONTENTS: N/A

674 HARBO, C. *Easy space origami*. 2012, Capstone (ISBN: 9781429660013). 24 p.
   SERIES: Easy origami

GRADE LEVEL: Lower elementary

CONTENTS: N/A

675 HARBO, C. *The kids' guide to paper airplanes*. 2009, Capstone (ISBN: 9781429622745). 32 p.

SERIES: Kids' guides

GRADE LEVEL: Upper elementary – middle school

CONTENTS: Techniques and terms—classic dart—sonic dart—stealth glider—space ring—double arrow—hammerhead—super plane—angry finch—silent huntress—raptor—J-rom bomber

676 HARBO, C. *Paper airplanes: captain*. 2011, Capstone (ISBN: 9781429647441). 32 p.

SERIES: Paper airplanes

GRADE LEVEL: Upper elementary – middle school

CONTENTS: Material—techniques and terms—folding symbols—fighter jet—Warthog—Gliding Grace—Flying Accordion—space bomber—Sparrowhawk—Screech Owl—aircraft carrier

677 HARBO, C. *Paper airplanes: co-pilot*. 2011, Capstone (ISBN: 9781429647410). 32 p.

SERIES: Paper airplanes

GRADE LEVEL: Upper elementary – middle school

CONTENTS: Time to fly—materials—techniques and terms—folding symbols—air shark—wind tunnel—streaking eagle—parakeet—whisper bat—vampire bat—arrowhead—nighthawk—vapor—bulls-eye

678 HARBO, C. *Paper airplanes: flight school*. 2011, Capstone (ISBN: 9781429647410). 32 p.

SERIES: Paper airplanes

GRADE LEVEL: Upper elementary – middle school

CONTENTS: Flight training—materials—techniques and terms—folding symbols—dynamic dart—spinning blimp—whirly—helicopter—flying squirrel—ring wing—tailspin—long ranger—V-wing—schoolyard special—elevator glider—longshot

679 HARBO, C. *Paper airplanes: pilot*. 2011, Capstone (ISBN: 9781429647434). 32 p.

SERIES: Paper airplanes

GRADE LEVEL: Upper elementary – middle school

CONTENTS: Prepare—materials—techniques and terms—folding symbols—liftoff—needle nose—aviator—fang—lazy lander—hang glider—Steady Eddie—D-wing—hang time

680 HARMS, J. *Recipe and craft guide to Italy*. 2011, Mitchell Lane (ISBN: 9781612280837). 63 p.

SERIES: World crafts and recipes

GRADE LEVEL: Upper elementary – middle school

CONTENTS: N/A

681 HARRIS, C. *Weather*. 2012, Kingfisher (ISBN: 9780753468340). 56 p.

SERIES: Discover science

GRADE LEVEL: Elementary

CONTENTS: Wind—colors—swirling winds

682   HARRIS, C. *Whales and dolphins*. 2010, Kingfisher (ISBN: 9780753464489). 56 p.
SERIES: Discover science
GRADE LEVEL: Elementary
CONTENTS: N/A

683   HARRIS, E. *Save the Earth science experiments*. 2008, Lark Books (ISBN: 9781600593222). 112 p.
GRADE LEVEL: Upper elementary – middle school
CONTENTS: Oil substitutes—plants providing power—bright idea—wind work—the sun—methane as fuel—wind power—solar power—the experiment—garbage diet—recycling—buying in bulk—removing waste—heat—no-zone—turn off lights—keep it clean—sewage—hydro power—grass—still and the sun—fertilizers—charts & graphs—sources—keep it green—ecological footprint

684   HARRIS, E. *Yikes! Wow! Yuck! Fun experiments for your first science fair*. 2008, Lark Books (ISBN: 9781579909307). 112 p.
GRADE LEVEL: Elementary
CONTENTS: Red eye—eggs—dough ball—hear—paint—dessert—eyes—stink—taste—game—water—fog—pumpkin—ooze—salt crystals—dominos—soda—bag—candy melt—stretch-o-meter—color—feeling—spin city

685   HARRIS, J. *The brilliant book of experiments*. 2013, Arcturus (ISBN: 9781848583948). 128 p.
GRADE LEVEL: Upper elementary
CONTENTS: N/A

686   HARROD, E. *How to improve at playing piano*. 2010, Crabtree (ISBN: 9780778735793). 48 p.
SERIES: How to improve at
GRADE LEVEL: Elementary
CONTENTS: Rhythm—time signatures—treble notation—bass notation—hands together—shifting hand positions—legato—staccato—taking it further—finger strength—musical signs—the black keys—scales—key signatures—minor scales—chords and arpeggios—sight-reading—train your ears—piano pieces

687   HART, C. *Drawing the new adventure cartoons: cool spies, evil guys, and action heroes*. 2008, Chris Hart Books (ISBN: 9781933027609). 126 p.
GRADE LEVEL: Upper elementary
CONTENTS: Drawing the head—drawing the action body—using body language to convey emotion—communicating attitude—putting characters in motion—funny characters—composition

688   HART, C. *Manga mania romance: drawing shojo girls and bishie boys*. 2008, Chris Hart Books (ISBN: 9781933027432). 147 p.
GRADE LEVEL: Middle school
CONTENTS: Shojo girls: the basics—bishie boys: the basics—manga eyes—costume design—magical girls—cool bishies—ABCs of scene staging—finishing touches

689 HART, C. *You can draw cartoon animals: a simple step-by-step drawing guide*. 2009, Walter Foster (ISBN: 9781600586118). 120 p.
GRADE LEVEL: Lower elementary
CONTENTS: Using guidelines—line thickness—head shapes—body types—big and small together—curves—big animals—small animals—bears—hoofed animals—birds—canines and felines—unusual animals

690 HATTORI, C. *The manga cookbook*. 2007, Japanime Co. (ISBN: 9784921205072).
GRADE LEVEL: Middle school – high school
CONTENTS: Appetizers: usagi ringo (rabbit-shaped apple slices)—tamago tomodachi ("egg buddies")—tako sausage (and more!)—steamed rice for two—obento basics: onigiri (rice balls)—naruto rolls (ham-and-cheese rolls)—nikumake (meat rolls)—jyagatama (potato balls)—rice burgers—soboro bento (minced pork-and-egg)—train bento—garden bento—the main course: oshinko (pickled vegetables)—miso soup (soybean soup)—tamagoyaki (Japanese-style omelette)—sushi rice—California roll—tonkatsu (fried pork cutlet)—karaage (Japanese-style chicken nuggets)—teriyaki sauce—teriyaki chicken—yakitori (chicken kabobs)—gyudon (beef bowl)—okonomiyaki (Japanese-style pizza)—nama udon (raw noodles)—cold udon—hot udon—wagashi: 3-color dango (sweet dumplings)—anko paste (sweet red bean paste)—anko dango—anko cake—anko buns

691 HAUSER, E. *Crafty bags for stylish girls: uniquely chic purses, pouches & pocketbooks*. 2007, Sterling (ISBN: 9781402736544). 112 p.
GRADE LEVEL: Upper elementary
CONTENTS: N/A

692 HAUSER, J. *Little hands celebrate America: learning about the U.S.A. through crafts and activities*. 2012, Williamson (ISBN: 9780824968366). 128 p.
SERIES: Little hands!
GRADE LEVEL: Lower elementary
CONTENTS: N/A

693 HAVERICH, B. *Photography: how to take awesome photos*. 2012, Capstone (ISBN: 9781429668873). 48 p.
SERIES: Instant expert
GRADE LEVEL: Upper elementary – middle school
CONTENTS: Types of cameras—the story of photography—pick a point of interest—keep it simple—consider contrast—Ansel Adams photography—framing—viewpoints—movement—skateboarding photography—diagonals—portraits—self-portraits—landscapes—still life—street photography—color or black and white—digital resolutions—troubleshooting

694 HAWKINS, J. *Bright ideas: the science of light*. 2013, Windmill Books (ISBN: 9781477703205). 32 p.
SERIES: Big bang science experiments
GRADE LEVEL: Upper elementary
CONTENTS: Shine—lenses—kaleidoscope—mirrors—sky—3-D glasses—camera—top—zoetrope—maker—your eyes

695 HAWKINS, J. *Hot stuff: the science of heat and cold*. 2013, Windmill Books (ISBN: 9781477703632). 32 p.
SERIES: Big bang science experiments
GRADE LEVEL: Upper elementary
CONTENTS: N/A

696 HAWKINS, J. *It's alive! The science of plants and living things*. 2013, Windmill Books (ISBN: 9781477703229). 32 p.
SERIES: Big bang science experiments
GRADE LEVEL: Upper elementary
CONTENTS: N/A

697 HAWKINS, J. *Material world: the science of matter*. 2013, Windmill Books (ISBN: 9781477703670). 32 p.
SERIES: Big bang science experiments
GRADE LEVEL: Upper elementary
CONTENTS: N/A

698 HAWKINS, J. *Push and pull: the science of forces*. 2013, Windmill Press (ISBN: 9781477703243). 32 p.
SERIES: Big bang science experiments
GRADE LEVEL: Upper elementary
CONTENTS: Sky!—battle—water—marble—butterfly—compass—toy—parachute—racers—monsters—sled vs. go-kart

699 HAWKINS, J. *Super sonic: the science of sound*. 2013, Windmill Books (ISBN: 9781477703700). 32 p.
SERIES: Big bang science experiments
GRADE LEVEL: Upper elementary
CONTENTS: N/A

700 HAYN, C. *Drawing dragons*. 2013, Windmill Books (ISBN: 9781615336982). 24 p.
SERIES: Drawing monsters step-by-step
GRADE LEVEL: Middle school
CONTENTS: N/A

701 HAYN, C. *Drawing ghosts*. 2013, Windmill Books (ISBN: 9781615337002). 24 p.
SERIES: Drawing monsters step-by-step
GRADE LEVEL: Middle school
CONTENTS: N/A

702 HAYN, C. *Drawing vampires*. 2013, Windmill Books (ISBN: 9781615337026). 24 p.
SERIES: Drawing monsters step-by-step
GRADE LEVEL: Middle school
CONTENTS: N/A

703 HAYN, C. *Drawing werewolves*. 2013, Windmill Books (ISBN: 9781615336920). 24 p.
SERIES: Drawing monsters step-by-step

GRADE LEVEL: Middle school

CONTENTS: N/A

704   **HAYN, C.** *Drawing witches and wizards*. 2013, Windmill Books (ISBN: 9781615336937). 24 p.

SERIES: Drawing monsters step-by-step

GRADE LEVEL: Middle school

CONTENTS: N/A

705   **HAYN, C.** *Drawing zombies*. 2013, Windmill Books (ISBN: 9781615337088). 24 p.

SERIES: Drawing monsters step-by-step

GRADE LEVEL: Middle school

CONTENTS: N/A

706   **HENGEL, K.** *Cool basil from garden to table: how to plant, grow, and prepare basil*. 2012, ABDO (ISBN: 9781617831829). 32 p.

SERIES: Cool garden to table

GRADE LEVEL: Elementary

CONTENTS: Sowing seeds—harvesting—parmesan dip—pizza margherita—tomato basil soup—Thai noodles & basil—grilled cheese & pesto sandwich—basil-lemon cake

707   **HENGEL, K.** *Cool carrots from garden to table: how to plant, grow, and prepare carrots*. 2012, ABDO (ISBN: 9781617831836). 32 p.

SERIES: Cool garden to table

GRADE LEVEL: Elementary

CONTENTS: Sowing seeds—harvesting—carrot dip—carrot sticks—carrot soup—carrots & raisins—carrot bake—carrot muffins

708   **HENGEL, K.** *Cool green beans from garden to table: how to plant, grow, and prepare green beans*. 2012, ABDO (ISBN: 9781617831843). 32 p.

SERIES: Cool garden to table

GRADE LEVEL: Elementary

CONTENTS: Sowing seeds—harvesting—sesame green beans—green bean penne—green bean salad—bean & ham soup—green bean casserole—citrus zest beans

709   **HENGEL, K.** *Cool leaf lettuce from garden to table: how to plant, grow, and prepare leaf lettuce*. 2012, ABDO (ISBN: 9781617831850). 32 p.

SERIES: Cool garden to table

GRADE LEVEL: Elementary

CONTENTS: Sowing seeds—harvesting—sushi rolls—raisin salad—breakfast wrap—vinaigrette salad—BLT sandwich—taco bowl

710   **HENGEL, K.** *Cool potatoes from garden to table: how to plant, grow, and prepare potatoes*. 2012, ABDO (ISBN: 9781617831867). 32 p.

SERIES: Cool garden to table

GRADE LEVEL: Elementary

CONTENTS: Sowing seeds—harvesting—oven fries—potato soup—twice-baked potatoes—onion fingerlings—potato-bacon salad—potato cakes

711 HENGEL, K. *Cool tomatoes from garden to table: how to plant, grow, and prepare tomatoes*. 2012, ABDO (ISBN: 9781617831874). 32 p.

SERIES: Cool garden to table

GRADE LEVEL: Elementary

CONTENTS: Sowing seeds—harvesting—orange salsa—tomato salad—Caprese melt—tomato pasta—bruschetta—tomato pie

712 HENRY, S. *Card making*. 2009, PowerKids Press (ISBN: 9781435825062). 24 p.

SERIES: Make your own art

GRADE LEVEL: Elementary

CONTENTS: Birthday cake—tortoise and hare—stamp designs—badges—birthday clowns—pop-up greetings—paper weaving—opposites—glitter and glue—pirates

713 HENRY, S. *Clay modeling*. 2009, PowerKids Press (ISBN: 9781435825086). 24 p.

SERIES: Make your own art

GRADE LEVEL: Elementary

CONTENTS: Animal parade—house numbers—fridge magnets—leaf dish—fashion beads—friendship bands—picture frame—badge boutique—desk tidy—pencil pals—clay coil pot—pebbles

714 HENRY, S. *Collage*. 2009, PowerKids Press (ISBN: 9781435825093). 24 p.

SERIES: Make your own art

GRADE LEVEL: Elementary

CONTENTS: Textures—gardening—invent a robot—pasta cottage—fish supper—zoo—faces—keep my place—owl—cut and tear

715 HENRY, S. *Drawing*. 2009, PowerKids Press (ISBN: 9781435825109). 24 p.

SERIES: Make your own art

GRADE LEVEL: Elementary

CONTENTS: Portraits—my friend—young animal—still life study—charcoal sketch—cartoons—jungle wildlife—stunt plane—fantasy figure—racing cars—manga faces

716 HENRY, S. *Eco-crafts*. 2011, PowerKids Press (ISBN: 9781448815821). 32 p.

SERIES: Make your own art

GRADE LEVEL: Elementary

CONTENTS: Glow jars—bird feeder—bug box—cat bookends—CD mobile—little alligator—pressed flowers—bookmarks—gift boxes—batik paper—stone family rock band

717 HENRY, S. *Making amazing art! 40 activities using the 7 elements of art design*. 2007, Kids Can Press (ISBN: 9780824967956).

GRADE LEVEL: Elementary

CONTENTS: Linear web design—decorative-line design—magical machine—grid drawing—visual music—kaleidoscope lines—geometric & free-form—shape discovery—cutout collage—stencil shapes—letter & number shapes—shape hunt—texture rubbing—textured-flowers bouquet—3-D texture tapestry—textured-paper bird collage—furry pet portrait—secondary-color surprise—warm & cool ocean scene—complementary-color puzzle design—color explosion—analogous color puzzle—giant ice cream cone—beautiful butterfly—hidden shapes—sock-head sculpture—paper sculpture—dancing mobile—sunflower—perspective collage—3-D shapes—view from the window

718   HENRY, S. *Making masks*. 2011, PowerKids Press (ISBN: 9781448815838). 32 p.

SERIES: Make your own art

GRADE LEVEL: Elementary

CONTENTS: Easy mask—guess the animal—butterfly and moth—robot—super specs—papier-mâché mask—Pirate Pete—fairy star—king—ice queen—carnival time – Halloween

719   HENRY, S. *Making mosaics*. 2011, PowerKids Press (ISBN: 9781448815852). 24 p.

SERIES: Make your own art

GRADE LEVEL: Elementary

CONTENTS: Animal mats—pixel art—pebble pattern—plate picture—planters—frames—school bag—portrait—shell mirror—animal patterns—jewelry box—maze or labyrinth

720   HENRY, S. *Making puppets*. 2011, PowerKids Press (ISBN: 9781448815845). 32 p.

SERIES: Make your own art

GRADE LEVEL: Elementary

CONTENTS: Finger puppets—walking puppets—sock puppets—glove puppet—tinsel clown—shadow dragon—napkin puppets—funny bird—nutty professor—jumping jack—stick puppets

721   HENRY, S. *Origami*. 2011, PowerKids Press (ISBN: 9781448815869). 32 p.

SERIES: Make your own art

GRADE LEVEL: Elementary

CONTENTS: Garden bird—lotus flower—jumping frog—school of fish—duck—windmill—dinosaur—tiger lily—pinwheel—butterfly—flapping crane—water bomb

722   HENRY, S. *Painting*. 2009, PowerKids Press (ISBN: 9781435825116). 24 p.

SERIES: Make your own art

GRADE LEVEL: Elementary

CONTENTS: Self-portrait—simple still life—my own room—landscape—dinosaur—figure painting—creatures—pop art posters—house of wax—magic palace

723   HENRY, S. *Paper folding*. 2009, PowerKids Press (ISBN: 9781435825079). 24 p.

SERIES: Make your own art

GRADE LEVEL: Elementary

CONTENTS: Windmills—gift boxes—high flyers—party hats—paper flowers—zig-zag frame—paper banger—snappers—fortune teller—water bomb—swan mobile

724   HENRY, S. *Papier-mâché*. 2011, PowerKids Press (ISBN: 9781448815876). 32 p.

SERIES: Make your own art

GRADE LEVEL: Elementary

CONTENTS: Piggy bank—maracas—turtle bowl—monster heads—bowling-pin soldiers—fantastic fish—treasure island—painting with paper—paper jewelry—octopus—piñata

725   **HEOS, B.** *Ice fishing*. 2012, Rosen Central (ISBN: 9781448846009). 62 p.
SERIES: Fishing tips and techniques
GRADE LEVEL: Upper elementary
CONTENTS: N/A

726   **HETLAND, K.** *Native Americans: discover the history and cultures of the first Americans*. 2013, Nomad Press (ISBN: 9781619301702). 128 p.
SERIES: Build it yourself
GRADE LEVEL: Upper elementary – middle school
CONTENTS: Carve soap art—archaic toolkit—Algonquian art—syllabary—face paint designs—miniature bullboat—dog travois—create rattle—irrigation—hieroglyphics—Navajo jewelry—x-ray art—family totem pole—play nugluktaq

727   **HETRICK, H.** *Play baseball like a pro: key skills and tips*. 2011, Capstone (ISBN: 9781429648240). 32 p.
SERIES: Play like the pros
GRADE LEVEL: Upper elementary – middle school
CONTENTS: Start with the basics—paint the corners—throw a changeup—sacrifice bunt—hit a curveball—slide into home—break up a double play—defend home plate—throw out a base stealer—turn a double play—hold a runner on base—field a fly ball

728   **HICKS, T.** *Karate*. 2011, Marshall Cavendish Benchmark (ISBN: 9780761449348). 47 p.
SERIES: Martial arts in action
GRADE LEVEL: Upper elementary – middle school
CONTENTS: The way of the empty hand—the history of karate—karate techniques and training—karate in everyday life

729   **HO, J.** *You can draw monsters and other scary things*. 2011, Picture Window Books (ISBN: 9781404862760). 24 p.
SERIES: You can draw
GRADE LEVEL: Lower elementary
CONTENTS: N/A

730   **HO, J.** *You can draw zoo animals*. 2010, Picture Window Books (ISBN: 9781404862753). 24 p.
SERIES: You can draw
GRADE LEVEL: Lower elementary
CONTENTS: N/A

731   **HODGE, S.** *Animals*. 2011, Windmill Books (ISBN: 9781615332694). 32 p.
SERIES: Let's draw
GRADE LEVEL: Upper elementary
CONTENTS: Penguin—frog—shark—bear—dog—parrot—lion—giraffe—horse—cat

732   **HODGE, S.** *Dinosaurs*. 2011, Windmill Books (ISBN: 9781615332649). 32 p.
SERIES: Let's draw
GRADE LEVEL: Upper elementary

CONTENTS: Brachiosaurus—Allosaurus—Ornithomimus—Triceratops—Ankylosaurus—
Velociraptor—Spinosaurus—Compsognathus—Stegosaurus—Tyrannosaurus

733   HOLLIHAN, K. *Isaac Newton and physics for kids: his life and ideas with 21 activities*. 2012, Chicago Review Press (ISBN: 9781556527784). 166 p.
SERIES: For kids
GRADE LEVEL: Middle school
CONTENTS: N/A

734   HOLLIHAN, K. *Rightfully ours: how women won the vote: 21 activities*. 2012, Chicago Review Press (ISBN: 9781883052898). 144 p.
SERIES: For kids
GRADE LEVEL: Middle school
CONTENTS: Soap—play a game of blindman's bluff—disconnect and reconnect—
time for tea and talk—a memory—an oil lamp—practice your posture—finding
Polaris—the north star—picture yourself as a Victorian—stage a reader's theater for
suffrage—bake a cake with suffrage frosting—how comfortable is a corset—paint
your plate!—design a suffragist postcard—jump in time to a suffrage rhyme—water-
lily eggs—sing a song of suffragists—dress up for suffrage—a coat-hanger banner—a
five-pointed star with just one cut—you be the judge

735   HOLLOW, M. *Nifty thrifty sports crafts*. 2008, Enslow (ISBN: 9780766027824). 32 p.
SERIES: Nifty thrifty crafts for kids
GRADE LEVEL: Elementary
CONTENTS: Sports—baseball fans—pennants—business card holder—game of grace—
toss and catch—jump rope—personalized water bottle—scrapbook—frame—
bowling

736   HOLLOW, M. *Nifty thrifty math crafts*. 2008, Enslow (ISBN: 9780766027817). 32 p.
SERIES: Nifty thrifty crafts for kids
GRADE LEVEL: Elementary
CONTENTS: Piggy bank—age kite—hat—clock—picture frame—shadow puppet—secret
message—coin pouch—cube weight—butterfly

737   HOPWOOD, J. *Cool distance assistants: fun science projects to propel things*. 2008, ABDO (ISBN: 9781599289069). 32 p.
SERIES: Cool science
GRADE LEVEL: Upper elementary
CONTENTS: Sling—power stick—catapult—air power—air & water rockets

738   HOPWOOD, J. *Cool dry ice devices: fun science projects with dry ice*. 2008, ABDO (ISBN: 9781599289076). 32 p.
SERIES: Cool science
GRADE LEVEL: Upper elementary
CONTENTS: N/A

739   HOPWOOD, J. *Cool gravity activities: fun science projects about balance*. 2008, ABDO (ISBN: 9781599289083). 32 p.
SERIES: Cool science

GRADE LEVEL: Upper elementary

CONTENTS: Cane trick—tops—breakfast—balance—acrobatics—flying forks

740 HORSLEY, A. *How to improve at skateboarding*. 2009, Crabtree (ISBN: 9780778735755). 48 p.

SERIES: How to improve at

GRADE LEVEL: Elementary

CONTENTS: Equipment—terrain—getting started: warming up and padding up—pushing off—basic skills: moving—turning and carving—ollie—flip the board—grind—sliding a flatbar—on a ramp—rock and roll—rock fakie—backside 50-50 axle stalls—frontside and backside ollie—frontside and backside flips—pop shove-it and 360 kickflip—frontside boardslide and K-grind—slide 180 and the fakie kickflip—pumping a vert ramp

741 HOUGHTON, G. *Creating a budget*. 2009, PowerKids Press (ISBN: 9781435827745).

SERIES: Invest kids

GRADE LEVEL: Elementary

CONTENTS: The plan—your budget—know your goal—know your habits—get a job—earning money—write it down—keeping it safe—expenses—spending

742 HOUSEWRIGHT, E. *Winning track and field for girls*. 2010, Chelsea House (ISBN: 9780816077182). 194 p.

SERIES: Winning sports for girls

GRADE LEVEL: Middle school – high school

CONTENTS: N/A

743 HUMPHREY, P. *How to make a card*. 2008, Sea to Sea (ISBN: 9781597711005).

SERIES: Crafty kids

GRADE LEVEL: Lower Elementary

CONTENTS: Cutting out the snout—coloring in the snout—drawing the dragon—gluing the snout—opening up the card—adding the tongue—finishing the card—sending your card

744 HUNTER, N. *Fun magic tricks*. 2013, Heinemann-Raintree (ISBN: 9781410950055). 32 p.

SERIES: Try this at home; don't try this at home

GRADE LEVEL: Upper elementary – middle school

CONTENTS: That's knot magic—making money—into thin air—card sharp—mind reader—predict the card

745 HUNTER, N. *Silly circus tricks*. 2013, Heinemann-Raintree (ISBN: 9781410950031). 32 p.

SERIES: Try this at home; don't try this at home

GRADE LEVEL: Upper elementary – middle school

CONTENTS: Roll up! Roll up!—amazing acrobats—jazzing juggling—stilt crazy—walking a tightrope—clowning around—showtime

746 HUNTER, R. *Athletics*. 2009, Franklin Watts (ISBN: 9780749689438). 30 p.

SERIES: Starting sport

GRADE LEVEL: Lower elementary
CONTENTS: N/A

747   **HUNTER, R. *Basketball*.** 2009, Franklin Watts (ISBN: 9780749689445). 30 p.
SERIES: Starting sport
GRADE LEVEL: Lower elementary
CONTENTS: N/A

748   **HUNTER, R. *Gymnastics*.** 2008, Franklin Watts (ISBN: 9780749678340). 30 p.
SERIES: Starting sport
GRADE LEVEL: Lower elementary
CONTENTS: N/A

749   **HUNTER, R. *Rugby*.** 2008, Wayland (ISBN: 9780750253819). 32 p.
SERIES: Sporting skills
GRADE LEVEL: Elementary
CONTENTS: N/A

750   **HUNTER, R. *Swimming*.** 2008, Franklin Watts (ISBN: 9780749678357). 30 p.
SERIES: Starting sport
GRADE LEVEL: Lower elementary
CONTENTS: N/A

751   **HUNTER, R. *Tennis*.** 2008, Franklin Watts (ISBN: 9780749678326). 30 p.
SERIES: Starting sport
GRADE LEVEL: Lower elementary
CONTENTS: N/A

752   **HURDMAN, C. *Hands-on history! Stone Age: step back to the time of the earliest humans, with 15 step-by-step projects and 380 exciting pictures*.** 2013, Armadillo (ISBN: 9781843229742). 64 p.
SERIES: Hands-on history!
GRADE LEVEL: Upper elementary
CONTENTS: N/A

753   **HYNES, M. *Mountains*.** 2012, Kingfisher (ISBN: 9780753468357). 56 p.
SERIES: Discover science
GRADE LEVEL: Elementary
CONTENTS: N/A

754   **HYNES, M. *Polar lands*.** 2012, Kingfisher (ISBN: 9780753468333). 56 p.
SERIES: Discover science
GRADE LEVEL: Elementary
CONTENTS: N/A

755   **IGGULDEN, C. *The dangerous book for boys*.** 2007, Collins (ISBN: 9780061243585). 270 p.
GRADE LEVEL: Elementary
CONTENTS: N/A

756 IGGULDEN, C. *The pocket dangerous book for boys: things to do*. 2008, Collins (ISBN: 9780061656828). 203 p.
GRADE LEVEL: Elementary
CONTENTS: N/A

757 INMAN, R. *The judo handbook*. 2008, Rosen (ISBN: 9781404213937). 256 p.
SERIES: Martial arts
GRADE LEVEL: Middle school – high school
CONTENTS: Fundamentals—throwing techniques—combination and counter techniques—ground techniques—hold-downs—strangles/chokes—armlocks—combination and counter techniques

758 IPCIZADE, C. *How to make frightening Halloween decorations*. 2011, Capstone (ISBN: 9781429654234). 32 p.
SERIES: Halloween extreme
GRADE LEVEL: Elementary
CONTENTS: Knock knock—witch's brew—glow-in-the-dark aliens—floating eyeballs—buried alive—batty for blood—tabletop spiders—zombie witch—intestines in a jar—trash bag spiders

759 IRVINE, J. *How to make super pop-ups*. 2008, Dover (ISBN: 9780486465890). 96 p.
GRADE LEVEL: Elementary
CONTENTS: N/A

760 ISAAC, D. *Garden crafts for children: 35 fun projects for children to sow, grow, and make*. 2012, Cico Books (ISBN: 9781908170255). 48 p.
GRADE LEVEL: Upper elementary – middle school
CONTENTS: N/A

761 JACKSON, P. *Origami toys that tumble, fly, and spin*. 2012, Gibbs Smith (ISBN: 9781423605249).
GRADE LEVEL: Middle school – high school
CONTENTS: Pecking bird—feeding bird—woodpecker—squawking bird—flapping bird—snapping crocodile—nodding dog—puppet beak—croaking frog—scuttling mouse—barking dog—moving lips—kissing cousins—horse and rider—swimming fish—big beak—clacker—lip smacker—whip crack—dreidel—domino rally—pencil propeller—quasar—catapult—the cutter—T-glider

762 JACOBSON, R. *Step-by-step experiments with light and vision*. 2012, Child's World (ISBN: 9781609735884). 32 p.
SERIES: Step-by-step experiments
GRADE LEVEL: Lower elementary
CONTENTS: Light and vision—seven steps—money—eye—colored—black

763 JAKUBIAK, D. *A smart kid's guide to doing Internet research*. 2010, PowerKids Press (ISBN: 9781404281165). 24 p.
SERIES: Kids online
GRADE LEVEL: Elementary

CONTENTS: Research everything—World Wide Web—an engine for your search—other starting points—go to the source—whom to trust—learning or buying—keeping track

764   JANTNER, J. *Drawing fantasy monsters*. 2013, PowerKids Press (ISBN: 9781477703113). 32 p.

SERIES: How to draw monsters

GRADE LEVEL: Upper elementary – middle school

CONTENTS: Monsters—wicked giant—evil wizard—awesome ore—deadly dragon—sorceress—dark elf

765   JANTNER, J. *Drawing horror-movie monsters*. 2013, PowerKids Press (ISBN: 9781477703083). 32 p.

SERIES: How to draw monsters

GRADE LEVEL: Upper elementary – middle school

CONTENTS: Movie monsters—werewolf—King Kong—Godzilla—king of the ocean—zombie—alien—terror from space—mummy monster

766   JANTNER, J. *Drawing monsters from great books*. 2013, PowerKids Press (ISBN: 9781477703137). 32 p.

SERIES: How to draw monsters

GRADE LEVEL: Upper elementary – middle school

CONTENTS: N/A

767   JANTNER, J. *Drawing mythological monsters*. 2013, PowerKids Press (ISBN: 9781477703090). 32 p.

SERIES: How to draw monsters

GRADE LEVEL: Upper elementary – middle school

CONTENTS: N/A

768   JANTNER, J. *Drawing science-fiction monsters*. 2013, PowerKids Press (ISBN: 9781477703106). 32 p.

SERIES: How to draw monsters

GRADE LEVEL: Upper elementary – middle school

CONTENTS: N/A

769   JANTNER, J. *Drawing unexplained-mystery monsters*. 2013, PowerKids Press (ISBN: 9781477703120). 32 p.

SERIES: How to draw monsters

GRADE LEVEL: Upper elementary – middle school

CONTENTS: N/A

770   JEFFRIE, S. *The girls' book of glamour: a guide to being a goddess*. 2009, Scholastic (ISBN: 9780545085373).

GRADE LEVEL: Upper elementary – middle school

CONTENTS: N/A

771   JENKINS, S. *97 things to do before you finish high school*. 2007, Zest Books (ISBN: 9780979017308).

GRADE LEVEL: High school

CONTENTS: Redo your bedroom—start a collection—create a journal—assemble a photo album—listen to new music—give technology a break—look closely at a work of art—attend a theater performance—connect with a role model—develop the art of conversation—make a public speech—interpret a dream—join a club—host a film festival—throw a house party—read one another's palm—end an argument—correspond with a pen pal in another country—make a gift—start a book club—sing karaoke—dine high-end on a low budget—take a road trip—research your family tree—reach out to a long-lost relative—record an oral history—spend quality time with your grandparents—make peace with a sibling—plan a cool family outing—cook a three course dinner—prepare a presentation for a special event—learn a martial art—establish an exercise routine—enter a sports competition—determine your blood type—study food labels—detox your body—plant an herb garden—know your silhouette and colors—learn about safe sex—get a passport—visit a foreign country—participate in a new cultural tradition—visit your state capital—take a camping trip—hike to a mountaintop—learn the constellations—make a podcast—keep a scrapbook—make a video—learn to match beats—create a comic strip—take an art class—paint your room—learn to play an instrument—take a dance class—participate in a performance—write your manifesto—make your own Halloween costume—design a t-shirt—write a real letter—write a letter to your future self—create a tasty dessert—volunteer for a nonprofit organization—go green—contribute to community beautification—visit your local officials—join a political campaign—feed the needy—understand how a farm works—write an op-ed—donate to a homeless shelter—raise money for charity—get a job—write a resume—make and follow a budget—open a savings account—understand the stock market—take care of a pet—take care of a houseplant—get a driver's license—learn basic car maintenance—assemble a toolbox—learn basic clothes maintenance—learn CPR—be prepared for an emergency—try a new hairstyle—confess a crush—tell someone your darkest secret—go skinny-dipping—get an astrology reading—ride a horse—build a bonfire—watch the sunrise—spend a day in silence—bury a time capsule

772 JENNINGS, M. *Baseball step-by-step.* 2009, Rosen Central (ISBN: 9781435833616). 96 p.
SERIES: Skills in motion
GRADE LEVEL: Upper elementary – middle school
CONTENTS: The basics—pitching—catching—fielding—hitting—base running

773 JENNINGS, M. *Magic step-by-step.* 2010, Rosen Central (ISBN: 9781435833630). 96 p.
SERIES: Skills in motion
GRADE LEVEL: Upper elementary – middle school
CONTENTS: N/A

774 JENNINGS, M. *Soccer step-by-step.* 2010, Rosen Central (ISBN: 9781435833623). 96 p.
SERIES: Skills in motion
GRADE LEVEL: Upper elementary – middle school
CONTENTS: Passing—control—shooting—getting past opponents—turns—heading the ball—running with the ball—goalkeeping

775 JENNINGS, M. *Tai chi step-by-step*. 2011, Rosen Central (ISBN: 9781448815517). 96 p.
SERIES: Skills in motion
GRADE LEVEL: Upper elementary – middle school
CONTENTS: N/A

776 JENSON-ELLIOTT, C. *Camping*. 2012, Capstone (ISBN: 9781429648127). 32 p.
SERIES: Wild outdoors
GRADE LEVEL: Lower elementary
CONTENTS: Pack up—skills and techniques—safety—camping out

777 JENSON-ELLIOTT, C. *Fly fishing*. 2012, Rosen Central (ISBN: 9781448846016). 62 p.
SERIES: Fishing tips and techniques
GRADE LEVEL: Upper elementary
CONTENTS: N/A

778 JOHNSON, A. *Indie girl: from starting a band to launching a fashion company, nine ways to turn your creative talent into reality*. 2008, Zest Books (ISBN: 9780979017339).
GRADE LEVEL: Middle school – high school
CONTENTS: Start a band—publish a zine—put on a play—film a tv show—create an art exhibit—form a dance troupe—launch a fashion company—hold a poetry slam—make a parade

779 JOHNSON, J. *Animal tracks and signs*. 2008, National Geographic (ISBN: 9781426302534). 192 p.
GRADE LEVEL: Elementary
CONTENTS: Mammals—amphibians and reptiles—birds—insects and other invertebrates

780 JOHNSON, J. *Senses*. 2010, Kingfisher (ISBN: 9780753464526). 56 p.
SERIES: Discover science
GRADE LEVEL: Elementary
CONTENTS: N/A

781 JOHNSON, K. *Grilled pizza sandwich and other vegetarian recipes*. 2009, Capstone (ISBN: 9781429620185). 32 p.
SERIES: Fun food for cool cooks
GRADE LEVEL: Elementary
CONTENTS: Grilled pizza sandwich—fruity kebobs—spaghetti salad—tofu nuggets—pita pocket salad—easy cheesy potatoes—bean burrito bake—perfect pasta—raspberry cream pie—peanut butter and jelly muffins

782 JOHNSON, K. *Oodle doodles tuna noodle and other salad recipes*. 2008, Capstone (ISBN: 9781429613415). 32 p.
SERIES: Fun food for cool cooks
GRADE LEVEL: Elementary
CONTENTS: N/A

783   JOHNSON, K. *Peanut butter and jelly sushi and other party recipes*. 2008, Capstone (ISBN: 9781429613408). 32 p.
　　　　SERIES: Fun food for cool cooks
　　　　GRADE LEVEL: Elementary
　　　　CONTENTS: N/A

784   JOHNSON, K. *Reindeer crunch and other Christmas recipes*. 2009, Capstone (ISBN: 9781429620178). 32 p.
　　　　SERIES: Fun foods for cool cooks
　　　　GRADE LEVEL: Elementary
　　　　CONTENTS: Reindeer crunch—Christmas dip—spritz sticks—candy cane bark—cookie ornaments—triple chocolate fudge—peanut butter thumbprints—hot cocoa mix—marshmallow wreaths—gumdrop soda pop cupcakes

785   JOHNSON, S. *How to draw Nickelodeon Avatar: The Last Airbender*. 2007, Walter Foster (ISBN: 9781560107835). 31 p.
　　　　GRADE LEVEL: Upper elementary – middle school
　　　　CONTENTS: N/A

786   JOHNSON, T. *Girls' ice hockey: dominating the rink*. 2008, Capstone (ISBN: 9781429601337). 32 p.
　　　　SERIES: Girls got game
　　　　GRADE LEVEL: Elementary
　　　　CONTENTS: Burying the biscuit—sticking to the rules—joining the team—being the best

787   JONES, J. *Braiding hair: beyond the basics*. 2009, Capstone (ISBN: 9781429623124). 32 p.
　　　　SERIES: Crafts
　　　　GRADE LEVEL: Elementary
　　　　CONTENTS: N/A

788   JONES, J. *Cool crafts with cardboard and wrapping paper: green projects for resourceful kids*. 2011, Capstone (ISBN: 9781429647656). 32 p.
　　　　SERIES: Green crafts
　　　　GRADE LEVEL: Elementary
　　　　CONTENTS: Wrap it up—bag lady—stamp of approval—pressed paper—eco-chic frames—best bow—pinned up—check it out—off the cuff

789   JONES, J. *Cool crafts with flowers, leaves, and twigs: green projects for resourceful kids*. 2011, Capstone (ISBN: 9781429647663). 32 p.
　　　　SERIES: Green crafts
　　　　GRADE LEVEL: Upper elementary – middle school
　　　　CONTENTS: Petals—light—twigs—blooms—dream—coasters—sign language—memories—frame—green crafting

790   JONES, J. *Cool crafts with newspapers, magazines, and junk mail: green projects for resourceful kids*. 2011, Capstone (ISBN: 9781429647649). 32 p.
　　　　SERIES: Green crafts

GRADE LEVEL: Elementary

CONTENTS: Future dreamin'—it's a wrap—boho beads—artistic notions—pocket books—funny gifts—journal—flower power—bowl-tastic

791   **JONES, J.** *Cool crafts with old wrappers, cans, and bottles: green projects for resourceful kids.* 2011, Capstone (ISBN: 9781429640084). 32 p.

SERIES: Green crafts

GRADE LEVEL: Upper elementary – middle school

CONTENTS: Light—frames—cuffs—sundae—tidy—ring—beads—boxes—cranes—green crafting

792   **JONES, J.** *Updos: cool hairstyles for all occasions.* 2009, Capstone (ISBN: 9781429623131). 32 p.

SERIES: Crafts

GRADE LEVEL: Elementary

CONTENTS: N/A

793   **JONES, T.** *How to play chess and win!* 2007, Franklin Watts (ISBN: 9780749673543). 32 p.

GRADE LEVEL: Elementary

CONTENTS: N/A

794   **JOVINELLY, J.** *The crafts and culture of a Medieval cathedral.* 2007, Rosen (ISBN: 9781404207585). 48 p.

SERIES: Crafts of the middle ages

GRADE LEVEL: Elementary

CONTENTS: Cathedral model—stained glass—iconic cross—chalice—Eucharist dove—incense censer—reliquary casket—pilgrim badge

795   **JOVINELLY, J.** *The crafts and culture of a Medieval guild.* 2007, Rosen (ISBN: 9781404207578). 48 p.

SERIES: Crafts of the middle ages

GRADE LEVEL: Elementary

CONTENTS: Guild seal—jewelry—gargoyle—gingerbread men—peasant's hut—armor—shoes—clay jug

796   **JOVINELLY, J.** *The crafts and culture of a Medieval manor.* 2007, Rosen (ISBN: 9781404207561). 48 p.

SERIES: Crafts of the middle ages

GRADE LEVEL: Elementary

CONTENTS: Manor—peasant house—peasant sack—windmill—vegetable pottage—storage chest—Nine Man Morris—Magna Carta

797   **JOVINELLY, J.** *The crafts and culture of a Medieval monastery.* 2007, Rosen (ISBN: 9781404207592). 48 p.

SERIES: Crafts of the middle ages

GRADE LEVEL: Elementary

CONTENTS: Monastery model—prayer beads—illuminated manuscript—bookbinding—beehive—pretzels—herb garden—plague mask

798 JOVINELLY, J. *The crafts and culture of a Medieval town*. 2007, Rosen (ISBN: 9781404207615). 48 p.

SERIES: Crafts of the middle ages

GRADE LEVEL: Elementary

CONTENTS: Town house—inside the town house—hornbook—coins in a pouch—fortified gate—lantern—bread—psaltery

799 KALMAN, B. *I can write a book about butterflies*. 2012, Crabtree (ISBN: 9780778779964). 32 p.

SERIES: I can write a book

GRADE LEVEL: Upper elementary

CONTENTS: N/A

800 KALMAN, B. *I can write a book about countries*. 2012, Crabtree (ISBN: 9780778779889). 32 p.

SERIES: I can write a book

GRADE LEVEL: Upper elementary

CONTENTS: N/A

801 KALMAN, B. *I can write a book about culture*. 2012, Crabtree (ISBN: 9780778779896). 32 p.

SERIES: I can write a book

GRADE LEVEL: Upper elementary

CONTENTS: N/A

802 KALMAN, B. *I can write a book about history*. 2012, Crabtree (ISBN: 9780778779902). 32 p.

SERIES: I can write a book

GRADE LEVEL: Upper elementary

CONTENTS: N/A

803 KALMAN, B. *I can write a book about how to be healthy and happy*. 2012, Crabtree (ISBN: 9780778779919). 32 p.

SERIES: I can write a book

GRADE LEVEL: Upper elementary

CONTENTS: N/A

804 KALMAN, B. *I can write a book about landforms*. 2012, Crabtree (ISBN: 9780778779926). 32 p.

SERIES: I can write a book

GRADE LEVEL: Upper elementary

CONTENTS: Will you write a book—parts of a book—landform words—ideas about landforms—getting started—researching—body of the book—an ABC book—fonts and handwriting—revising and editing—designing—publishing—cover and title page

805 KALMAN, B. *I can write a book about my life*. 2012, Crabtree (ISBN: 9780778779933). 32 p.

SERIES: I can write a book

GRADE LEVEL: Upper elementary

CONTENTS: N/A

806 KALMAN, B. *I can write a book called "If I could talk to animals."* 2012, Crabtree (ISBN: 9780778779940). 32 p.

SERIES: I can write a book

GRADE LEVEL: Upper elementary

CONTENTS: N/A

807 KAMBERG, M. *Saltwater fishing*. 2012, Rosen Central (ISBN: 9781448845996). 62 p.

SERIES: Fishing tips and techniques

GRADE LEVEL: Upper elementary

CONTENTS: N/A

808 KARMEL, A. *You can cook*. 2010, DK (ISBN: 9780756658632). 128 p.

GRADE LEVEL: Elementary

CONTENTS: N/A

809 KAUFMAN, R. *Knack magic tricks: a step-by-step guide to illusions, sleight of hand, and amazing feats*. 2010, Knack (ISBN: 9781599217796). 244 p.

SERIES: Knack make it easy

GRADE LEVEL: Upper elementary – middle school

CONTENTS: Automatic card tricks—simple card tricks—intermediate card tricks—advanced card tricks—simple coin tricks—advanced coin tricks—anytime tricks—string tricks—simple mental magic—intermediate mental magic—advanced mental magic—rope tricks—bill tricks—handkerchief and napkin tricks—fruit tricks—glass and cup tricks

810 KELLER, K. *Camping*. 2008, Capstone (ISBN: 9781429608152). 32 p.

SERIES: Great outdoors

GRADE LEVEL: Upper elementary

CONTENTS: N/A

811 KELLER, K. *Hiking*. 2008, ABDO (ISBN: 9781599289595). 24 p.

SERIES: Outdoor adventure!

GRADE LEVEL: Elementary

CONTENTS: Hiking hopes—why hike?—the location—the plan—must-haves—longer treks—tasty treats—water—conservation—trail manners—wild animals—stay safe

812 KELLER, M. *Ancient Greece*. 2007, Edupress (ISBN: 9781564720221). 63 p.

SERIES: Hands-on heritage

GRADE LEVEL: Upper elementary

CONTENTS: N/A

813 KELLER, M. *Mexico*. 2007, Edupress (ISBN: 9781564720344). 63 p.

SERIES: Hands-on heritage

GRADE LEVEL: Upper elementary

CONTENTS: N/A

814 **KELSEY, J.** *Woodworking*. 2009, Fox Chapel (ISBN: 9781565233539). 99 p.
SERIES: Kid crafts
GRADE LEVEL: Upper elementary – middle school
CONTENTS: N/A

815 **KENNEDY, D.** *Pilates for beginners*. 2012, Rosen (ISBN: 9781448848157). 96 p.
SERIES: From couch to conditioned
GRADE LEVEL: Middle school – high school
CONTENTS: The six Pilates principles—physical fundamentals—the program

816 **KENNEY, K.** *Cool costumes: stage your very own show*. 2010, ABDO (ISBN: 9781604537147). 32 p.
SERIES: Cool performances
GRADE LEVEL: Elementary
CONTENTS: Performances—getting dressed—a pattern to follow—stage kit—robe—skirt—t-shirt transformers—pirate patch—scales—medallion—bracelets—heads—glasses—masks—animal ears

817 **KENNEY, K.** *Cool hip-hop music: create & appreciate what makes music great*. 2008, ABDO (ISBN: 9781599289717). 32 p.
SERIES: Cool music
GRADE LEVEL: Elementary
CONTENTS: Human beatbox—write a rap—do the robot—sneaker art—b-boy – b-girl dance off

818 **KENNEY, K.** *Cool holiday parties: perfect party planning for kids*. 2012, ABDO (ISBN: 9781617149740). 32 p.
SERIES: Cool parties
GRADE LEVEL: Elementary
CONTENTS: Valentine invitation—May pole mini pot—newspaper seedling pot—caramel nut apples—New Year's party hat—patriotic pinwheels—lucky Irish soap

819 **KENNEY, K.** *Cool international parties: perfect party planning for kids*. 2012, ABDO (ISBN: 9781617148757). 32 p.
SERIES: Cool parties
GRADE LEVEL: Elementary
CONTENTS: Italiano invitation—pretty Diwali lanterns—joey magnet—yakitori—mancala—castanets—pitch pipes

820 **KENNEY, K.** *Cool makeup: stage your very own show*. 2010, ABDO (ISBN: 9781604537154). 32 p.
SERIES: Cool performances
GRADE LEVEL: Elementary
CONTENTS: Performances—makeup—lowdown on makeup—stage kit—instant old age—glamour girl—beard—mustache—wound and bruise—cat—mouse—robot—alien—skeleton

821 **KENNEY, K.** *Cool productions: stage your very own show*. 2010, ABDO (ISBN: 9781604537161). 32 p.

SERIES: Cool performances

GRADE LEVEL: Elementary

CONTENTS: Performances—the big performance—behind the scenes—a look at a theater—timelines—stage kit—poster—flyers—banner—tickets—program—intermission treats—strike it—cast party

822 KENNEY, K. *Cool reggae music: create & appreciate what makes music great.* 2008, ABDO (ISBN: 9781599289731). 32 p.

SERIES: Cool music

GRADE LEVEL: Elementary

CONTENTS: Bongos—claves—bamboo scraper—dub song lyrics—cool reggae dance—sound-system party

823 KENNEY, K. *Cool rock music: create & appreciate what makes music great.* 2008, ABDO (ISBN: 9781599289748). 32 p.

SERIES: Cool music

GRADE LEVEL: Elementary

CONTENTS: Milk carton guitar—rock to the beat—write a rock song—cool rock dances—make a rock video

824 KENNEY, K. *Cool school clubs: fun ideas and activities to build school spirit.* 2011, ABDO (ISBN: 9781617146664). 32 p.

SERIES: Cool school spirit

GRADE LEVEL: Elementary

CONTENTS: N/A

825 KENNEY, K. *Cool school drama and theater: fun ideas and activities to build school spirit.* 2011, ABDO (ISBN: 9781617146688).

SERIES: Cool school spirit

GRADE LEVEL: Elementary

CONTENTS: Magnet mania—t-e-a-m-o—group identity—buy a star—theater tote

826 KENNEY, K. *Cool scripts and acting: stage your very own show.* 2010, ABDO (ISBN: 9781604537178). 32 p.

SERIES: Cool performances

GRADE LEVEL: Elementary

CONTENTS: Performances—scripts and acting—parts of a script—a look at a script—playing your part—whose left—adapt-a-story—write-a-script—picture script—zip zap zop—not my hands—it's how you say it—stage whisper—projecting your voice

827 KENNEY, K. *Cool sets and props: stage your very own show.* 2010, ABDO (ISBN: 9781604537185). 32 p.

SERIES: Cool performances

GRADE LEVEL: Elementary

CONTENTS: Performances—setting the stage—found and bought—stage kit—backdrops—bushes—mirror—boxes—goblet—magic wand—bouquet—sword

828 KENNEY, K. *Cool slumber parties: perfect party planning for kids.* 2012, ABDO (ISBN: 9781617149764). 32 p.

SERIES: Cool parties

GRADE LEVEL: Elementary

CONTENTS: Wrist twist invitation—beach ball banner—jewels—s'mores—arm warmers—face mask—friend trivia

829   **KENNEY, K.** *Cool special effects: stage your very own show*. 2010, ABDO (ISBN: 9781604537192). 32 p.

SERIES: Cool performances

GRADE LEVEL: Elementary

CONTENTS: Performances—light effects—sound effects—special effects—stage kit—prompt book—glowing gobos—gleaming gels—black light—sounds real—singing glasses—starry night—rolling waves

830   **KENNEY, K.** *Cool sports parties: perfect party planning for kids*. 2012, ABDO (ISBN: 9781617149771). 32 p.

SERIES: Cool parties

GRADE LEVEL: Elementary

CONTENTS: Soccer ball invitation—bowling ball & pin curtain—personalized water bottles—touchdown taters—gnarly board t-shirt—sporty race car frames—martial arts headband

831   **KENNEY, K.** *Cool theme parties: perfect party planning for kids*. 2012, ABDO (ISBN: 9781617149788). 32 p.

SERIES: Cool parties

GRADE LEVEL: Elementary

CONTENTS: Lei invitation—spooky wall decals—guitar pick chain—cupcakes—badge—bubble potion—Medieval shield

832   **KENNEY, K.** *Strength training for teen athletes: exercises to take your game to the next level*. 2012, Capstone (ISBN: 9781429680028).

SERIES: Sports Illustrated kids

GRADE LEVEL: High school

CONTENTS: Shoulder rotations—seated shoulder press—triceps press—hammer curl—the plank—ball crunch—the back bend—single-leg squat—bench press—push ups—medicine ball push—chest press—dumbbell squat—90-degree jumps—leg curls—power lunges

833   **KENNEY, K.** *Super simple art to wear: fun and easy-to-make crafts for kids*. 2010, ABDO (ISBN: 9781604536225). 32 p.

SERIES: Super simple crafts

GRADE LEVEL: Elementary

CONTENTS: Tools and supplies—painted shoelaces—clips and bands—custom cap—totally you tee—glitter bracelet—bandana-rama—circle purse—skinny braided belt—fuzzy fleece scarf

834   **KENNEY, K.** *Super simple clay projects: fun and easy-to-make crafts for kids*. 2010, ABDO (ISBN: 9781604536232). 32 p.

SERIES: Super simple crafts

GRADE LEVEL: Elementary

CONTENTS: Making the clay—foil is your friend—baking the clay—fixing cracks and breaks—painting and sealing—silly snakes—cute critters—fun frames—tasty treats—pencil holder—room signs

835 KENNEY, K. *Super simple jewelry: fun and easy-to-make crafts for kids*. 2010, ABDO (ISBN: 9781604536256). 32 p.
SERIES: Super simple crafts
GRADE LEVEL: Elementary
CONTENTS: Critter pins—button bracelets—safety pin jewelry—fuzzy felt pins—paper beads—washer wear—funky clay beads

836 KENNEY, K. *Super simple magnets: fun and easy-to-make crafts for kids*. 2010, ABDO (ISBN: 9781604536263). 32 p.
SERIES: Super simple crafts
GRADE LEVEL: Elementary
CONTENTS: Marbles—bottle caps—bugs—clothespins—fairies—butterflies—tiles—frames—flowers

837 KENNEY, K. *Super simple masks: fun and easy-to-make crafts for kids*. 2010, ABDO (ISBN: 9781604536270). 32 p.
SERIES: Super simple crafts
GRADE LEVEL: Elementary
CONTENTS: Jungle animals—monster—buzz buzz fly—fun masks—party mask—bags—faces

838 KERR, J. *How to improve at cricket*. 2007, Ticktock (ISBN: 9781846960093).
GRADE LEVEL: Elementary
CONTENTS: N/A

839 KERROD, R. *Exploring science: volcanoes & earthquakes—an amazing fact file and hands-on project book: with 19 easy-to-do experiments and 280 exciting pictures*. 2013, Armadillo (ISBN: 9781861473066). 64 p.
SERIES: Exploring science
GRADE LEVEL: Upper elementary
CONTENTS: N/A

840 KERROD, R. *Exploring science: weather—an amazing fact file and hands-on project book: with 16 easy-to-do experiments and 250 exciting pictures*. 2013, Armadillo (ISBN: 9781861473073). 64 p.
SERIES: Exploring science
GRADE LEVEL: Upper elementary
CONTENTS: N/A

841 KESSELRING, S. *5 steps to drawing crawlers and fliers*. 2012, Child's World (ISBN: 9781609731946). 32 p.
SERIES: 5 steps to drawing
GRADE LEVEL: Elementary
CONTENTS: N/A

842 **KESSELRING, S.** *5 steps to drawing faces*. 2012, Child's World (ISBN: 9781609731977). 32 p.
  SERIES: 5 steps to drawing
  GRADE LEVEL: Elementary
  CONTENTS: Eyes—nose—mouth—plain face—happy face—sad face—scared face—silly face

843 **KESSELRING, S.** *5 steps to drawing machines at work*. 2012, Child's World (ISBN: 9781609732011). 32 p.
  SERIES: 5 steps to drawing
  GRADE LEVEL: Elementary
  CONTENTS: Digger—concrete mixer—tractor—big rig with side dump—bulldozer—dump truck—crane—steamroller

844 **KESSELRING, S.** *5 steps to drawing zoo animals*. 2012, Child's World (ISBN: 9781609732004). 32 p.
  SERIES: 5 steps to drawing
  GRADE LEVEL: Elementary
  CONTENTS: Giraffe—elephant—alligator—lion—penguin—giant panda—kangaroo – chimpanzee

845 **KESSLER, C.** *A project guide to reptiles and birds*. 2011, Mitchell Lane (ISBN: 9781584158745). 48 p.
  SERIES: Life science projects for kids
  GRADE LEVEL: Upper elementary
  CONTENTS: N/A

846 **KESSLER, C.** *A project guide to sponges, worms, and mollusks*. 2011, Mitchell Lane (ISBN: 9781584158769). 48 p.
  SERIES: Life science projects for kids
  GRADE LEVEL: Upper elementary
  CONTENTS: N/A

847 **KESSLER, C.** *A project guide to the solar system*. 2010, Mitchell Lane (ISBN: 9781584158677). 48 p.
  SERIES: Earth science projects for kids
  GRADE LEVEL: Upper elementary – middle school
  CONTENTS: N/A

848 **KILGALLON, C.** *Tai chi for beginners*. 2012, Rosen (ISBN: 9781448848164). 96 p.
  SERIES: From couch to conditioned
  GRADE LEVEL: Middle school – high school
  CONTENTS: N/A

849 **KING, M.** *Mac King's campfire magic*. 2010, Black Dog and Leventhal (ISBN: 9781579128296). 176 p.
  GRADE LEVEL: Elementary
  CONTENTS: N/A

850 KISSOCK, H. *Military vehicles*. 2013, AV2 by Weigl (ISBN: 9781619132429). 32 p.
SERIES: Learn to draw
GRADE LEVEL: Upper elementary – middle school
CONTENTS: What is an aircraft carrier—fighter jet—helicopter—humvee—submarine—tank—test your knowledge—draw an environment

851 KJELLE, M. *Explore transportation! 25 great projects, activities, experiments*. 2009, Nomad Press (ISBN: 9781934670453). 96 p.
SERIES: Explore your world
GRADE LEVEL: Upper elementary
CONTENTS: N/A

852 KJELLE, M. *A project guide to wind, weather, and the atmosphere*. 2011, Mitchell Lane (ISBN: 9781584158691). 48 p.
SERIES: Earth science projects for kids
GRADE LEVEL: Upper elementary – middle school
CONTENTS: Sun—air—pressure—changing pressure—saturation and evaporation—highs and lows—front and center—the wind—spin—the sky—static electricity—weather

853 KLEIN, A. *Archery*. 2008, ABDO (ISBN: 9781599289557). 24 p.
SERIES: Outdoor adventure!
GRADE LEVEL: Elementary
CONTENTS: Beginner's luck—back in time—choosing the bow—the arrow—equipment—shooting steps—the target—competition—the range

854 KLEIN, A. *Hiking*. 2008, Capstone (ISBN: 9781429608213). 32 p.
SERIES: Great outdoors
GRADE LEVEL: Upper elementary
CONTENTS: N/A

855 KLOBUCHAR, L. *The history and activities of the Aztecs*. 2007, Heinemann (ISBN: 9781403479211). 32 p.
SERIES: Hands-on ancient history
GRADE LEVEL: Elementary
CONTENTS: Corn tortillas—feather headdress—codex—Patolli board

856 KNIGHT, E. *Chemistry around the house*. 2011, Crabtree (ISBN: 9780778752837). 32 p.
GRADE LEVEL: Upper elementary – middle school
CONTENTS: Science accidents—matter—scientific method—chemistry—house—testing—a penny—windows—found—chemists—want to learn more?

857 KNOWLES, H. *Learn to draw Disney Tangled: learn to draw Rapunzel, Flynn Rider, and other characters from Disney's Tangled step by step!* 2010, Walter Foster (ISBN: 9781600581908). 32 p.
GRADE LEVEL: Upper elementary – middle school
CONTENTS: N/A

858   KOHLER, C. *Music performance: vocals and band*. 2012, Rosen (ISBN: 9781448868759). 64 p.

 SERIES: Glee club

 GRADE LEVEL: Upper elementary – middle school

 CONTENTS: N/A

859   KOONTZ, R. *Jewelry making for fun!* 2008, Compass Point (ISBN: 97807565327345). 48 p.

 SERIES: For fun!

 GRADE LEVEL: Elementary

 CONTENTS: Looking good—hidden treasures—found items—pretty and useful—tools for the job—tips—tricks—and safety—basic techniques—doing it—your space—bracelet—necklace—brooch—bracelet from paper—wire wrapping—bead necklace—make and bake jewelry—people, places, and fun—famous wearers—strange but beautiful—jewelry jobs—fab four

860   KOOSMANN, M. *Recipe and craft guide to South Africa*. 2012, Mitchell Lane (ISBN: 9781612280806). 63 p.

 SERIES: World crafts and recipes

 GRADE LEVEL: Upper elementary – middle school

 CONTENTS: Rock art—mud brick house—millet porridge—message bracelet—sextant—pap and veg—bobotie—koeksisters—Cape Minstrel festival face paint—chili bites—imitation biltong—chicken curry—bunny chow—bead flower—recycled paper baskets—African animal embroidery—lamb braai—homemade soccer ball—fish and chips—vuvuzela

861   KOVACS, L. *Inca: discover the culture and geography of a lost civilization*. 2013, Nomad Press (ISBN: 9781619301412). 128 p.

 SERIES: Build it yourself

 GRADE LEVEL: Upper elementary – middle school

 CONTENTS: Andes landscape—cloud forest terrarium—navigate using the stars—quipa—battle club—rope bridge—language—Sapa Inca—herbal tea—Zampona—ch'unu—charki—chicha morada—plumb bob—erosion—terraces—sundial—army tunic—spindle—t-shirt—Atahualpa's ransom—Spanish Conquest—devil mask—learn to braid

862   KRAMER, L. *Great ancient China projects you can build yourself*. 2008, Nomad Press (ISBN: 9781934670026). 128 p.

 SERIES: Build it yourself

 GRADE LEVEL: Upper elementary – middle school

 CONTENTS: Yurts—feng shui house—paper—moveable type—ink—terracotta army—kite—jade bi jewelry—suspension bridge—relief map—compass—Chinese junk—t'ai ch'i—bronze foundry—moon cakes—Chinese egg noodles—tea ceremony—ice cream—string instruments—puppets—seismograph—abacus—tangrams—snowflakes

863   KUNICZAK, E. *Start to felt*. 2008, Search Press (ISBN: 9781844482627). 48 p.

 SERIES: Start to

GRADE LEVEL: Upper elementary – middle school

CONTENTS: Secret garden—book bag—felted jewelry—charms

864 KUNTZ, J. *Celebrate the USA: hands-on history activities for kids*. 2007, Gibbs Smith (ISBN: 9781586858469). 80 p.

GRADE LEVEL: Elementary

CONTENTS: Map of your world—find the north star—cave drawings—a compass—family tree—spearmint tea—secret messages—your list of rights—Franklin's glass harmonica—colonial clothes—five-pointed star—berry flag cake—club seal—cookies—match money to mugs—kitchen fireworks—dictionary detective—beach-towel banner—patriotic flip-flops—watermelon bowl fruit salad—create patriotic wreath—penny necklace—support our troops—"thankful" list

865 KURZWEIL, A. *Potato chip science: 29 incredible experiments*. 2010, Workman (ISBN: 9780761148258). 96 p.

GRADE LEVEL: Upper elementary – middle school

CONTENTS: Blaster—compass—challenge—wave—kite—hydrofoil—analyzer—detective kit—chips—composter—$E=mc^2$—chipmobile—tosser—mirror—fipper—spinner—"color" wheel—battery—bender—buddy—pipe—shrunken head—crud—bird feeder—gobbler—cannon—tubes—walkie-talkie—windmill

866 KUSKOWSKI, A. *Cool body basics: healthy and fun ways to get your body moving*. 2013, ABDO (ISBN: 9781617834257). 32 p.

SERIES: Cool health and fitness

GRADE LEVEL: Elementary

CONTENTS: Clean center—fresh toothpaste—mirror—body wash—travel toiletries—food for thought—clean science—mint

867 KUSKOWSKI, A. *Cool eating: healthy and fun ways to get your body moving*. 2013, ABDO (ISBN: 9781617834264). 32 p.

SERIES: Cool health and fitness

GRADE LEVEL: Elementary

CONTENTS: N/A

868 KUSKOWSKI, A. *Cool relaxing: healthy and fun ways to get your body moving*. 2013, ABDO (ISBN: 9781617834288). 32 p.

SERIES: Cool health and fitness

GRADE LEVEL: Elementary

CONTENTS: N/A

869 KUSKOWSKI, A. *Cool sleeping: healthy and fun ways to get your body moving*. 2013, ABDO (ISBN: 9781617834295). 32 p.

SERIES: Cool health and fitness

GRADE LEVEL: Elementary

CONTENTS: N/A

870 KUSKOWSKI, A. *Cool thinking: healthy and fun ways to get your body moving*. 2013, ABDO (ISBN: 9781617834301). 32 p.

SERIES: Cool health and fitness

GRADE LEVEL: Elementary

CONTENTS: N/A

871   **KUSKOWSKI, A.** *Science experiments with food*. 2014, ABDO (ISBN: 9781617838491). 32 p.

SERIES: More super simple science

GRADE LEVEL: Upper elementary

CONTENTS: N/A

872   **KUSKOWSKI, A.** *Science experiments with light*. 2014, ABDO (ISBN: 9781617838514). 32 p.

SERIES: More super simple science

GRADE LEVEL: Upper elementary

CONTENTS: N/A

873   **KUSKOWSKI, A.** *Science experiments with liquid*. 2014, ABDO (ISBN: 9781617838521). 32 p.

SERIES: More super simple science

GRADE LEVEL: Upper elementary

CONTENTS: N/A

874   **KUSKOWSKI, A.** *Science experiments with magnets*. 2014, ABDO (ISBN: 9781617838538). 32 p.

SERIES: More super simple science

GRADE LEVEL: Upper elementary

CONTENTS: N/A

875   **KUSKOWSKI, A.** *Science experiments with sight & sound*. 2014, ABDO (ISBN: 9781617838545). 32 p.

SERIES: More super simple science

GRADE LEVEL: Upper elementary

CONTENTS: N/A

876   **KUSKOWSKI, A.** *Super simple African art: fun and easy art from around the world*. 2012, Abdo (ISBN: 9781617832109). 32 p.

SERIES: Super simple cultural art

GRADE LEVEL: Elementary

CONTENTS: Mkeke—cook kufi cap—African drum—adinkra t-shirt—tribal mask—warrior's shield—Masai collar necklace—hamsa key chain

877   **KUSKOWSKI, A.** *Super simple American art: fun and easy art from around the world*. 2012, Abdo (ISBN: 9781617832147). 32 p.

SERIES: Super simple cultural art

GRADE LEVEL: Elementary

CONTENTS: World art—art in America—log cabin—magnets—box—rocket—headband & torch—turkey—poppy

878   **KUSKOWSKI, A.** *Super simple Chinese art: fun and easy art from around the world*. 2012, Abdo (ISBN: 9781617832123). 32 p.

SERIES: Super simple cultural art

GRADE LEVEL: Elementary

CONTENTS: World art—Chinese art—plum tree—rattle-drum—firework fan—lantern—mask—kite—lucky envelope—dragon puppet

879 KUSKOWSKI, A. *Super simple Mexican art: fun and easy art from around the world*. 2012, Abdo (ISBN: 9781617832130). 32 p.

SERIES: Super simple cultural art

GRADE LEVEL: Elementary

CONTENTS: World art—Mexican art—materials—god's eye—paper flowers—Aztec sun—hojalata—banner—poncho—pinata

880 KUSKOWSKI, A. *Super simple Native American art: fun and easy art from around the world*. 2012, Abdo (ISBN: 9781617832147). 32 p.

SERIES: Super simple cultural art

GRADE LEVEL: Elementary

CONTENTS: World art—Native American art—headdress—rainstick—dream catcher—coil pot—medicine bag—totem pole—kachina doll—sand painting

881 KUSKOWSKI, A. *Super simple South and Central American art: fun and easy art from around the world*. 2012, Abdo (ISBN: 9781617832154). 32 p.

SERIES: Super simple cultural art

GRADE LEVEL: Elementary

CONTENTS: Quetzal—mola tote—maracas—Mayan tunic—jewelry—worry dolls—codex

882 LABAFF, S. *Draw aliens and space objects in 4 easy steps: then write a story*. 2012, Enslow (ISBN: 9781464400148). 48 p.

SERIES: Drawing in 4 easy steps

GRADE LEVEL: Upper elementary – middle school

CONTENTS: Getting started—follow the 4 steps—astronauts—aliens—spaceships—robots—planetary objects—write a story in 5 easy steps—our story

883 LABAFF, S. *Draw animals in 4 easy steps: then write a story*. 2012, Enslow (ISBN: 9780766038400). 48 p.

SERIES: Drawing in 4 easy steps

GRADE LEVEL: Upper elementary – middle school

CONTENTS: Getting started—the 4 steps—pets—wild animals—farm animals—marine animals—backyard animals—write a story in 5 steps—our story

884 LABAFF, S. *Draw cartoon people in 4 easy steps: then write a story*. 2012, Enslow (ISBN: 9780766038431). 48 p.

SERIES: Drawing in 4 easy steps

GRADE LEVEL: Upper elementary – middle school

CONTENTS: Follow the 4 steps—cartoon people—objects—faces—write a story in 5 easy steps—our story

885 LABAFF, S. *Draw pirates in 4 easy steps: then write a story*. 2012, Enslow (ISBN: 9780766038394). 48 p.

SERIES: Drawing in 4 easy steps

GRADE LEVEL: Upper elementary – middle school

CONTENTS: Introduction—how to draw—characters—creatures—props—how to write a story—pirate story

886   **LABAFF, S. *Draw princesses in 4 easy steps: then write a story*.** 2012, Enslow (ISBN: 9780766038387). 48 p.

SERIES: Drawing in 4 easy steps

GRADE LEVEL: Upper elementary – middle school

CONTENTS: Getting started—the 4 steps—princesses—prince—fairy godmother—woodsman—witch—animals—dragon—jewelry—crowns—shoes—magic wand—pot of gold—furniture—tree—carriage—castle—write a story—our story

887   **LABAFF, S. *Draw superheroes in 4 easy steps: then write a story*.** 2012, Enslow (ISBN: 9780766038424). 48 p.

SERIES: Drawing in 4 easy steps

GRADE LEVEL: Upper elementary – middle school

CONTENTS: Getting started—superheroes—armor—write a story—disappearing supers

888   **LABIGNAN, I. *Hook, line, and sinker: everything kids want to know about fishing*.** 2007, Key Porter Books (ISBN: 9781552635490). 64 p.

GRADE LEVEL: Elementary

CONTENTS: N/A

889   **LABRECQUE, E. *Amazing bike tricks*.** 2013, Capstone (ISBN: 9781410950017). 32 p.

SERIES: Try this at home; don't try this at home

GRADE LEVEL: Upper elementary – middle school

CONTENTS: What are bike tricks?—be safe!—strike a pose—endo—front hop—manual—ride a fakie—bunny hop—bar spin—drop in—can can—be stylish!

890   **LABRECQUE, E. *Cool board tricks*.** 2013, Capstone (ISBN: 9781410950024). 32 p.

SERIES: Try this at home; don't try this at home

GRADE LEVEL: Upper elementary – middle school

CONTENTS: The ollie—boardslide—drop in—manual—frontside air—let's snowboard!—nail a jump—indy grab—lookin' cool

891   **LABRECQUE, E. *Coordination: catch, shoot, and throw better*.** 2012, Heinemann-Raintree (ISBN: 9781406242034). 32 p.

SERIES: Exercise

GRADE LEVEL: Elementary

CONTENTS: The weave—moving backward—stork stand—walk the line—catching on your back—wall ball

892   **LABRECQUE, E. *Flexibility: stretch and move farther*.** 2012, Heinemann-Raintree (ISBN: 9781432967307). 32 p.

SERIES: Exercise

GRADE LEVEL: Elementary

CONTENTS: Body circles—leg lifts—butterfly—triceps stretch—yoga time—downward dog

893   **LABRECQUE, E.** *Impressive dance moves*. 2013, Capstone (ISBN: 9781410950048). 32 p.
   SERIES: Try this at home; don't try this at home
   GRADE LEVEL: Upper elementary – middle school
   CONTENTS: Let's dance—be safe—the spin—moonwalk—robot—crisscross—worm—arm wave—clow—Tut—everyday moves—melting—look smooth

894   **LABRECQUE, E.** *Speed: get quicker!* 2012, Heinemann-Raintree (ISBN: 9781432967321). 32 p.
   SERIES: Exercise
   GRADE LEVEL: Elementary
   CONTENTS: Running right—Frankenstein walk—backside kick—basketball slides

895   **LABRECQUE, E.** *Stamina: get stronger and play longer*. 2012, Heinemann-Raintree (ISBN: 9781432967338). 32 p.
   SERIES: Exercise
   GRADE LEVEL: Elementary
   CONTENTS: Jumping jacks—jumping rope—jump rope rhythms—make an obstacle course—hit the hills—ready—set—run!

896   **LABRECQUE, E.** *Strength: build muscles and climb higher*. 2012, Heinemann-Raintree (ISBN: 9781432967352). 32 p.
   SERIES: Exercise
   GRADE LEVEL: Elementary
   CONTENTS: The inchworm—bear crawl—crab walk—duck walk—airplane ride—circuits

897   **LANE, M.** *Coin magic*. 2012, Windmill Books (ISBN: 9781615335107).
   SERIES: Miraculous magic tricks
   GRADE LEVEL: Elementary
   CONTENTS: N/A

898   **LANE, M.** *Paper magic*. 2012, Windmill Books (ISBN: 9781615335114).
   SERIES: Miraculous magic tricks
   GRADE LEVEL: Elementary
   CONTENTS: The magician's pledge—stepping through paper—magical mend—floating cup—paper jump—a tree from paper—overhead—money morph—tic tac toe—rip it—restore it—psychic paper

899   **LAPENTA, M.** *Artful snacks*. 2011, Bearport (ISBN: 9781617723070). 24 p.
   SERIES: Yummy tummy recipes
   GRADE LEVEL: Elementary
   CONTENTS: Cheese and fruit kabobs—peanut butter bars—snack mix—lemon hummus—fruit pops—cheese tortilla with salsa—pretzels—bug parade—chocolate-dipped fruit—apple puzzle—guacamole dip—deviled egg delights—pizza bites—yogurt—granola—and fruit creations

900   **LAPENTA, M.** *Cool cookies*. 2011, Bearport (ISBN: 9781617723087). 24 p.
   SERIES: Yummy tummy recipes

GRADE LEVEL: Elementary

CONTENTS: Oatmeal delights—granola crisps—bran drops—thumbprint jammies—chewy granola bars—pumpkin raisin cookies—banana apple cookies—peanut butter treats—chocolate nests—layered squares—chocolate chip classic—butter cookies

901 LAPENTA, M. *Fall shakes to harvest bakes*. 2013, Bearport (ISBN: 9781617727429). 24 p.

SERIES: Yummy tummy recipes: seasons

GRADE LEVEL: Elementary

CONTENTS: Pumpkin spice smoothie—apple shake—grape surprise fizzle—mulled apple cider—popcorn trail mix—pumpkin mousse—apple rings—cranberry nut bars—kale chips—pumpkin seeds—sweet potatoes with black bean topping—pumpkin muffins—baked stuffed apples

902 LAPENTA, M. *Spring spreads to "nutty" breads*. 2013, Bearport (ISBN: 9781617727443). 24 p.

SERIES: Yummy tummy recipes: seasons

GRADE LEVEL: Elementary

CONTENTS: Artichoke spread—baked tortilla chips—asparagus spread—tuna spread—peanut butter banana nut bread—yogurt pancakes—berry sauce—chocolate fruit smoothie—fruit frosty—carrot vegetable soup—apricot oatmeal cookies—chocolate pieces—carrot muffins—orange pecan mini breads

903 LAPENTA, M. *Summer sips to "chill" dips*. 2013, Bearport (ISBN: 9781617727412). 24 p.

SERIES: Yummy tummy recipes: seasons

GRADE LEVEL: Elementary

CONTENTS: Peach raspberry shake—mango berry creamsicle—cool green smoothie—watermelon lemonade—strawberry sensation—berry melon mint pops—rainbow kebabs—Fourth of July red, white, and blue chips—seven-layer dip—spinach hummus dip—salsa—cucumber dip—zucchini chips—black bean and corn dip

904 LAPENTA, M. *Super 'wiches*. 2012, Bearport (ISBN: 9781617723063). 24 p.

SERIES: Yummy tummy recipes

GRADE LEVEL: Elementary

CONTENTS: Thanksgiving treat—pumpernickel veggie delight—cucumber garden sandwich—turkey and apple stack—peanut butter creations—sandwich monsters—grilled cheese surprise—chicken orange wrap—tuna avocado roll-up—breakfast egg wrap—black-bean spread with salsa—salad medley—chicken and grapes with yogurt dressing

905 LAPENTA, M. *Way cool drinks*. 2012, Bearport (ISBN: 9781617721632). 24 p.

SERIES: Yummy tummy recipes

GRADE LEVEL: Elementary

CONTENTS: Melon medley—volcano—fruit punch—mango tango—fruit fusion—kiwi concoction—winter punch—slushy—blueberry smoothie—banana bonanza—peachango paradise—berry fling—apple cinnamon swirl—chocolate peanut butter shake

906   LAPENTA, M. *Winter punches to nut crunches*. 2013, Bearport (ISBN: 9781617727436). 24 p.

SERIES: Yummy tummy recipes: seasons

GRADE LEVEL: Elementary

CONTENTS: Cranberry punch—pumpkin nog—peppermint hot chocolate—wassailing punch—Valentine hot chocolate—St. Patrick's day smoothie—milk tea—apple nut oatmeal—corn chowder—butternut squash soup—ginger cookies—coconut balls—nut-and-honey bars—crunchy granola

907   LAROCHE, A. *Recipe and craft guide to France*. 2011, Mitchell Lane (ISBN: 9781584159360). 63 p.

SERIES: World crafts and recipes

GRADE LEVEL: Upper elementary – middle school

CONTENTS: French crafts: cave painting—tablet gift box—mask—rose window—pomander—model chateau—frame—Versailles style—Christmas santon—Napoleon's hat—sachet or pouch—recipes: pain perdu—crepes—celery with Roquefort—sausage en croute—Croques Monsieur—quiche—pot au feu—pommes frites—French apple pie—king's cake

908   LARREW, B. *Apple pie calzones and other cookie recipes*. 2008, Capstone (ISBN: 9781429613361). 32 p.

SERIES: Fun food for cool cooks

GRADE LEVEL: Elementary

CONTENTS: Apple pie calzone cookies—cookies—peanut butter sandwich cookies—banana split cookies—yin and yang cookies—peanut butter s'mores—rainbow braids—brownie bursts—lollipop cookies—peppermint drops

909   LARREW, B. *Banana-berry smoothies and other breakfast recipes*. 2009, Capstone (ISBN: 9781429620154). 32 p.

SERIES: Fun food for cool cooks

GRADE LEVEL: Elementary

CONTENTS: N/A

910   LARREW, B. *Cheesecake cupcakes and other cake recipes*. 2009, Capstone (ISBN: 9781429620161). 32 p.

SERIES: Fun food for cool cooks

GRADE LEVEL: Elementary

CONTENTS: N/A

911   LARREW, B. *Wormy apple croissants and other Halloween recipes*. 2008, Capstone (ISBN: 9781429613385). 32 p.

SERIES: Fun food for cool cooks

GRADE LEVEL: Elementary

CONTENTS: N/A

912   LATHAM, D. *Amazing biome projects you can build yourself*. 2009, Nomad Press (ISBN: 9781934670392). 128 p.

SERIES: Build it yourself

GRADE LEVEL: Upper elementary – middle school

CONTENTS: Globe—paper—turf—flipbook—birdfeeder—acid rain—totem pole—
hummingbird garden—crunch 'n' munch—pictographs—rainstick—desertarium—
tornado—doll – pretzels—snakes—bread—lightning—air quality—glacier—speed
race—volcano—water erosion—mitt—walkabout

913 LATHAM, D. *Bridges and tunnels: investigate feats of engineering with 25
projects*. 2012, Nomad Press (ISBN: 9781936749515). 128 p.
SERIES: Build it yourself
GRADE LEVEL: Upper elementary – middle school
CONTENTS: N/A

914 LATHAM, D. *Canals and dams: investigate feats of engineering with 25 projects*.
2013, Nomad Press (ISBN: 9781619301658). 128 p.
SERIES: Build it yourself
GRADE LEVEL: Upper elementary – middle school
CONTENTS: Watershed—zipping—forcebuster—boat—move it—barge—raisins—
cartesian diver—locked—waterproof or waterlogged?—spinning bucket—hover
craft—polluted waters—piling foundations—ice jam—water flow—beaver dam—
arch dam—velocity—tsunami—marshmallow arch—timber jam—water flow!—raw
water—engineer

915 LATHAM, D. *Garbage: investigate what happens when you throw it out with 25
projects*. 2011, Nomad Press (ISBN: 9781936313464). 128 p.
SERIES: Build it yourself
GRADE LEVEL: Upper elementary – middle school
CONTENTS: Trash—midden—artifacts—dye—pomander—biodegradation—air-
pollution—water pollution—landfill—oil spill—cleaners—detergents—compost
heap—worm farmer—avocado plant—picture frame—locker pocket—necklace—
milk jug—wind chimes—crayons—fuel—herb garden—shampoo—lunch

916 LATHAM, D. *Music: investigate the evolution of American sound*. 2013, Nomad
Press (ISBN: 9781619301993). 128 p.
SERIES: Inquire and investigate
GRADE LEVEL: Middle school – high school
CONTENTS: N/A

917 LATHAM, D. *Skyscrapers: investigate feats of engineering with 25 projects*. 2013,
Nomad Press (ISBN: 9781619301894). 128 p.
SERIES: Build it yourself
GRADE LEVEL: Upper elementary – middle school
CONTENTS: N/A

918 LATNO, M. *Backyard biology: investigate habitats outside your door, with 25
projects*. 2013, Nomad Press (ISBN: 9781619301511). 128 p.
SERIES: Build it yourself
GRADE LEVEL: Upper elementary – middle school
CONTENTS: Cell model—mold—balloon—see it—microbes—pond samples—
microorganisms—salad—greenhouse garden—t-shirt—chromatography—
sunshine—eggheads—phototropism—geotropism—habitat observation—animal

tracker—fantanimal—roly-poly habitat—fine-feathered friends—metamorpho-plate—clean up—coral reef—wetland plant pollution—butterfly feeders

919   LATNO, M. *The paper boomerang book: build them, throw them, and get them to return every time*. 2010, Chicago Review Press (ISBN: 9781569762820). 145 p.
  GRADE LEVEL: Upper elementary – middle school
  CONTENTS: Quick construction—making—throwing—common problems and experimentation—long-distance paper boomerangs—the art of tuning boomerangs—boomerang theory—tricks and throws—artwork—paper boomerangs of different sizes

920   LAUGHLIN, K. *Beautiful bags for the crafty fashionista*. 2012, Capstone (ISBN: 9781429665506). 32 p.
  SERIES: FashionCraft studio
  GRADE LEVEL: Elementary
  CONTENTS: N/A

921   LAUGHLIN, K. *Hip hair accessories for the crafty fashionista*. 2012, Capstone (ISBN: 9781429665513). 32 p.
  SERIES: FashionCraft studio
  GRADE LEVEL: Elementary
  CONTENTS: N/A

922   LAUGHLIN, K. *Marvelous memories: paper keepsake creations*. 2013, Capstone (ISBN: 9781620650448). 32 p.
  SERIES: Paper creations
  GRADE LEVEL: Middle school – high school
  CONTENTS: Hanging notes—captivating container—timeline journal—locket—photo ornament—party scrapbook—keepsake box—photo frame—time capsule—quilled—flowering friends—idea book

923   LAWRENCE, E. *Color*. 2013, Bearport (ISBN: 9781617727382). 24 p.
  SERIES: Fundamental experiments
  GRADE LEVEL: Lower elementary
  CONTENTS: Rainbow—colors make things warmer—new colors—different color?—lighter or darker colors—new colors—animals and color

924   LAWRENCE, E. *Dirt*. 2013, Bearport (ISBN: 9781617727375). 24 p.
  SERIES: Fundamental experiments
  GRADE LEVEL: Lower elementary
  CONTENTS: Soil—rocks become soil—dead plants—what is in soil—soil that holds water best—soil that is best for growing plants—worms help plants

925   LAWRENCE, E. *Motion*. 2013, Bearport (ISBN: 9781617727399). 24 p.
  SERIES: Fundamental experiments
  GRADE LEVEL: Lower elementary
  CONTENTS: Pushes—a pull—force and objects—force and heavy objects?—friction—force and rockets—falling objects

926 **LAWRENCE, E.** *Water*. 2013, Bearport (ISBN: 9781617727368). 24 p.

SERIES: Fundamental experiments

GRADE LEVEL: Lower elementary

CONTENTS: Frozen water—heating water—water vapor—dissolving in water—is water sticky?—water and its shape—what makes water sticky?

927 **LAY, R.** *A green kid's guide to composting*. 2013, Magic Wagon (ISBN: 9781616419431). 24 p.

SERIES: A green kid's guide to gardening!

GRADE LEVEL: Elementary

CONTENTS: Trash—poop—recycle—getting started—your pile—keep your pile alive—fertilizer—you're ready!

928 **LAY, R.** *A green kid's guide to garden pest removal*. 2013, Magic Wagon (ISBN: 9781616419448). 24 p.

SERIES: A green kid's guide to gardening!

GRADE LEVEL: Elementary

CONTENTS: Poison—good bugs—bad bugs—hands—secrets—enemies—mint—keep the good ones—frog house

929 **LAY, R.** *A green kid's guide to organic fertilizers*. 2013, Magic Wagon (ISBN: 9781616419455). 24 p.

SERIES: A green kid's guide to gardening!

GRADE LEVEL: Elementary

CONTENTS: Ice cream—worms—feeding—hungry plants—green gardener—counting worms

930 **LAY, R.** *A green kid's guide to preventing plant diseases*. 2013, Magic Wagon (ISBN: 9781616419462). 24 p.

SERIES: A green kid's guide to gardening!

GRADE LEVEL: Elementary

CONTENTS: Plant doctor—feeding—thirst—cover—germs—the best—walk the plants—cleanliness—around the house—healthy plant—sick plant

931 **LAY, R.** *A green kid's guide to soil preparation*. 2013, Magic Wagon (ISBN: 9781616419479). 24 p.

SERIES: A green kid's guide to gardening!

GRADE LEVEL: Elementary

CONTENTS: Gardeners—beds—a site—the size of a bed—measure—frame—soil—blanket—container garden

932 **LAY, R.** *A green kid's guide to watering plants*. 2013, Magic Wagon (ISBN: 9781616419486). 24 p.

SERIES: A green kid's guide to gardening!

GRADE LEVEL: Elementary

CONTENTS: Planting—where to plant?—it's time to plant—thirst—showers—when plants should drink—no more lost water—rain—seedlings

933   **LEAVITT, L.** *Candy science*. 2013, Andrews McMeel (ISBN: 9781449418366). 160 p.
GRADE LEVEL: Upper elementary
CONTENTS: N/A

934   **LEBOUTILLIER, N.** *Play basketball like a pro: key skills and tips*. 2011, Capstone (ISBN: 9781429648264). 32 p.
SERIES: Play like the pros
GRADE LEVEL: Upper elementary – middle school
CONTENTS: Get in condition—dribbling—layups—free throws—three-pointers—interior moves—perimeter moves—rebound—pass—fast breaks—playing defense— teamwork

935   **LEE, F.** *Creating the cover for your graphic novel*. 2012, PowerKids Press (ISBN: 9781448864577). 32 p.
SERIES: How to draw your own graphic novel
GRADE LEVEL: Middle school
CONTENTS: Classic hero cover—the story cover—the teaser cover—horror and manga covers

936   **LEE, F.** *Drawing action in your graphic novel*. 2012, PowerKids Press (ISBN: 9781448864775). 32 p.
SERIES: How to draw your own graphic novel
GRADE LEVEL: Middle school
CONTENTS: Dynamic poses—run for it—fighting poses—fighting hero—action poses— flying heroine

937   **LEE, F.** *Drawing the heroes in your graphic novel*. 2012, PowerKids Press (ISBN: 9781448864478). 32 p.
SERIES: How to draw your own graphic novel
GRADE LEVEL: Middle school
CONTENTS: N/A

938   **LEE, F.** *Drawing the villains in your graphic novel*. 2012, PowerKids Press (ISBN: 9781448864492). 32 p.
SERIES: How to draw your own graphic novel
GRADE LEVEL: Middle school
CONTENTS: N/A

939   **LEE, F.** *Fun with Chinese cooking*. 2010, PowerKids Press (ISBN: 9781435834538). 32 p.
SERIES: Let's get cooking!
GRADE LEVEL: Upper elementary – middle school
CONTENTS: Spring rolls—shrimp and pork dim sum—sweet corn soup with crabmeat— four-color soup—sweet and sour prawns—tofu with pork—braised mushrooms— Chinese New Year—vegetables with oyster sauce—Chinese omelet—fried rice— long-life noodles—red bean soup—egg custard tarts

940 LEE, F. *Penciling, inking, and coloring your graphic novel*. 2012, PowerKids Press (ISBN: 9781448864355). 32 p.
SERIES: How to draw your own graphic novel
GRADE LEVEL: Middle school
CONTENTS: N/A

941 LEE, F. *Telling the story in your graphic novel*. 2012, PowerKids Press (ISBN: 9781448864539). 32 p.
SERIES: How to draw your own graphic novel
GRADE LEVEL: Middle school
CONTENTS: N/A

942 LEET, K. *Gross pranks*. 2013, Capstone (ISBN: 9781429699228).
SERIES: Gross guides
GRADE LEVEL: Upper elementary
CONTENTS: N/A

943 LEVETE, S. *Make an animation*. 2013, Arcturus (ISBN: 9781848585744). 32 p.
SERIES: Find your talent
GRADE LEVEL: Middle school – high school
CONTENTS: Find your talent—moving pictures—the basics—classical style—junkyard—make your own—cut it out—story time—shoot and load—picture perfect—computer magic—sound it out—step up a gear

944 LEW, K. *Cool biology activities for girls*. 2012, Capstone (ISBN: 9781429676762). 32 p.
SERIES: Girls science club
GRADE LEVEL: Middle school
CONTENTS: Dolphins—daffodils—color—blow me up—the eyes—mini garden—remember me?—enzyme—cell—beady DNA—banana DNA

945 LEW, K. *Science experiments that fly and move*. 2011, Capstone (ISBN: 9781429654265). 32 p.
SERIES: Fun projects for curious kids
GRADE LEVEL: Elementary
CONTENTS: Air ball—air—shooter—balloons—lifter—whirlybird—roller—wind walker

946 LILLEY, K. *Eco-friendly crafting with kids: 35 step-by-step projects for preschool kids and adults to create together*. 2012, Ryland Peters & Small (ISBN: 9781849752046).
GRADE LEVEL: Elementary
CONTENTS: Playdough—watercolor paints—homemade chalk—rainbow crayons—cardboard box guitar—bongo—shaker & guiro—ankle bells—rainstick—xylophone—ribbon rings—seed bombs—nature stones—bug house—walnut shell boats—birdfeeder—kaleidoscope—marble maze—paper cup popper—magnetic fishing game—bubble discovery bottle—discovery bottles—cardboard castle—shadow makers—jar of love—catapult planet—Pac Man mobile—paper jumping beans—bead necklace—box loom—sock hobby horse—paper garland—sewing cards—magic potion—colored flowers—invisible ink—Oobleck—boredom busters

947 LINDEEN, C. *Freshwater fishing*. 2011, Capstone (ISBN: 9781429648103). 32 p.
SERIES: Wild outdoors
GRADE LEVEL: Lower elementary
CONTENTS: Rods—tackle—and more—cast your line—safety first—reel in some fun—
equipment diagram

948 LINDEEN, M. *Cool classical music: create & appreciate what makes music great*.
2008, ABDO (ISBN: 9781599289694). 32 p.
SERIES: Cool music
GRADE LEVEL: Elementary
CONTENTS: Make your own trombone—classical music rhythm—write a classical
song—dance the waltz—stage your own opera

949 LINDEEN, M. *Cool country music: create & appreciate what makes music great*.
2008, ABDO (ISBN: 9781599289700). 32 p.
SERIES: Cool music
GRADE LEVEL: Elementary
CONTENTS: Make your own banjo—country music rhythm—write a country song—
dance the Texas two-step—have a barn dance

950 LINDEEN, M. *Cool Latin music: create & appreciate what makes music great*.
2008, ABDO (ISBN: 9781599289724). 32 p.
SERIES: Cool music
GRADE LEVEL: Elementary
CONTENTS: Make your own cuíca—Latin music rhythm—write a salsa song—dance the
samba—make a Latin music video

951 LIPSEY, J. *I love to collage!* 2007, Lewes (ISBN: 9781579907709). 48 p.
SERIES: My very favorite art book
GRADE LEVEL: Elementary
CONTENTS: N/A

952 LIPSEY, J. *I love to draw cartoons!* 2007, Lark Books (ISBN: 9781579908195). 48 p.
SERIES: My very favorite art book
GRADE LEVEL: Elementary
CONTENTS: Cartooning—letter faces—eyes—noses—mouths—simple people—poseable
people—circle animals—cats—dogs—farm animals—jungle animals—desert
critters—pond animals—dinosaurs—monsters—funny folks—cars—buildings—
comic strips—cartoon words

953 LIPSEY, J. *I love to draw dogs!* 2008, Lark Books (ISBN: 9781600591532). 48 p.
SERIES: My very favorite art book
GRADE LEVEL: Elementary
CONTENTS: Mutts—collie—sheepdog—Doberman—German shepherd—St. Bernard—
Siberian husky—cocker spaniel—Labrador retriever—basset hound—bloodhound—
beagle—dachshund—chihuahua—Boston terrier—bulldog—Lhasa Apso—poodle—
schnauzer—Shar-Pei—cartoon dogs

954 **LIPSEY, J.** *I love to draw horses!* 2008, Lark Books (ISBN: 9781600591525). 48 p.

    SERIES: My very favorite art book

    GRADE LEVEL: Elementary

    CONTENTS: Horse parts—horse colors—grazing horse—galloping horse—horse lying down—foals—Shetland pony—face markings—horse portraits—Arabian—Appaloosa—jumping horse—bucking horse—rearing horse—tack—racing horse—work horse—draft horse—rodeo horse—unicorn – Pegasus

955 **LITTLEFIELD, C.** *Crafts across America: more than 40 crafts that immigrated to America.* 2009, Williamson (ISBN: 9780824968090). 160 p.

    SERIES: Kids can

    GRADE LEVEL: Elementary

    CONTENTS: Apple dolls—juggling—ink prints—radish art—doughcraft—tree of life—animalitos—rainmakers—ornaments—sand art—pinch pots—stacked stones—paper cutting—leis—paper craft—quilting—mosaic—origami—paper-mache—collage—reed baskets—masks—sunglasses—macrame—friendship bracelets—worry dolls—string-snap stamps—come-back toy—banjo—woolen toys—Navajo weaving—cowboy braids—yarn painting—felt fashions—applique—jigsaw—frilly flowers—tie-dye t-shirt—wall art

956 **LLANAS, S.** *Easy breakfasts from around the world.* 2012, Enslow (ISBN: 9780766037076). 48 p.

    SERIES: Easy cookbooks for kids

    GRADE LEVEL: Elementary

    CONTENTS: Brown bread with honey-molasses butter—chorizo con huevos—ful medames—khichadi—pannukakku—kielbasa and toast—fresh fruit—googs and soldiers—la bouillie—coconut syrup—anijsmelk and hagelslag

957 **LLANAS, S.** *Easy lunches from around the world.* 2012, Enslow (ISBN: 9780766037083). 48 p.

    SERIES: Easy cookbooks for kids

    GRADE LEVEL: Elementary

    CONTENTS: Sushi—quesadillas—daal—tabouli—bánh mì—fried zucchini with yogurt sauce—pyttipanna—sauerkraut soup—couscous—arepas—corn and shrimp soup—smørrebrød—mousetraps

958 **LLANAS, S.** *Easy vegetarian foods from around the world.* 2012, Enslow (ISBN: 9780766037649). 48 p.

    SERIES: Easy cookbooks for kids

    GRADE LEVEL: Elementary

    CONTENTS: Sabji—tofu—chiles rellenos—cabbage pie—spinach peanut stew—barley soup—tomatoes rougaille and rice—asparagus frittata—pea soup and doughboys—gado gado—falafel

959 **LLIMÓS PLOMER, A.** *Earth-friendly Christmas crafts in 5 easy steps.* 2014, Enslow (ISBN: 9780766041882). 31 p.

    SERIES: Earth-friendly crafts in 5 easy steps

    GRADE LEVEL: Elementary

CONTENTS: Place card clips—angel—ornaments—greeting cards—wrapping paper—reindeer and sleigh—decorations—Santa card holder—Christmas tree—garland—flowerpot stake—winter scene—little bells—shooting star

960 LLIMÓS PLOMER, A. *Earth-friendly clay crafts in 5 easy steps*. 2013, Enslow (ISBN: 978066041899). 31 p.
SERIES: Easy crafts in 5 steps
GRADE LEVEL: Elementary
CONTENTS: N/A

961 LLIMÓS PLOMER, A. *Earth-friendly crafts from recycled stuff in 5 easy steps*. 2014, Enslow (ISBN: 9780766041905). 31 p.
SERIES: Earth-friendly crafts in 5 easy steps
GRADE LEVEL: Elementary
CONTENTS: Gift bag—paper dragon—hair roller doll—ladybugs—worms—plane—bird—straw box—funnel puppet—necklaces—octopus—flying saucer—hairy insect—puppet theater

962 LLIMÓS PLOMER, A. *Earth-friendly crafts with nuts and veggies in 5 easy steps*. 2014, Enslow (ISBN: 9780766041912). 31 p.
SERIES: Earth-friendly crafts in 5 easy steps
GRADE LEVEL: Elementary
CONTENTS: Caterpillar—gourd art—maraca—sheep—raffia doll—eagle—little monster—poppy pod puppet—snake—mandala—bird—boat—cabin—tic-tac-toe

963 LLIMÓS PLOMER, A. *Earth-friendly papier-mache crafts in 5 easy steps*. 2013, Enslow (ISBN: 9780766041929). 31 p.
SERIES: Easy crafts in 5 steps
GRADE LEVEL: Elementary
CONTENTS: N/A

964 LLIMÓS PLOMER, A. *Earth-friendly wood crafts in 5 easy steps*. 2013, Enslow (ISBN: 9780766041936). 31 p.
SERIES: Easy crafts in 5 steps
GRADE LEVEL: Elementary
CONTENTS: N/A

965 LLIMÓS PLOMER, A. *Easy bead crafts in 5 steps*. 2008, Enslow (ISBN: 9780766030824). 31 p.
SERIES: Easy crafts in 5 steps
GRADE LEVEL: Lower elementary
CONTENTS: Kite—bracelet and ring—worm—bookmark—wire house—clay necklace—ballerina—peacock—star necklace—flowers—necklace and earrings—snake—belt—napkin ring

966 LLIMÓS PLOMER, A. *Easy cardboard crafts in 5 steps*. 2008, Enslow (ISBN: 9780766030831). 31 p.
SERIES: Easy crafts in 5 steps
GRADE LEVEL: Lower elementary

CONTENTS: Bee—flowers—folder—mushroom—cards—watch—house box—lion—drum—hand puppet—notebook—hang-glider—serpent—cart and donkey

967 **LLIMÓS PLOMER, A.** *Easy clay crafts in 5 steps*. 2008, Enslow (ISBN: 9780766030855). 31 p.
SERIES: Easy crafts in 5 steps
GRADE LEVEL: Lower elementary
CONTENTS: Croissant—martian—cat—pear-shaped box—letter holder—igloo and Eskimo—snake—flower vase—cow—fish platter—cord doll—jewels—hanging house—paperweight

968 **LLIMÓS PLOMER, A.** *Easy cloth crafts in 5 steps*. 2008, Enslow (ISBN: 9780766030848). 31 p.
SERIES: Easy crafts in 5 steps
GRADE LEVEL: Lower elementary
CONTENTS: Little fish—tray—turtle—clown—flower—purse—necklace and bracelet—dog—puppet—owl—doll—key ring—seagull—fabric collage

969 **LLIMÓS PLOMER, A.** *Easy earth-friendly crafts in 5 steps*. 2008, Enslow (ISBN: 9780766030862). 31 p.
SERIES: Easy crafts in 5 steps
GRADE LEVEL: Lower elementary
CONTENTS: King—piggy—coin purse—camel—worm—ladybug—doll—hippopotamus—spinning top—fireman—box cake—penguin—helicopter—clock

970 **LLIMÓS PLOMER, A.** *Easy paper crafts in 5 steps*. 2008, Enslow (ISBN: 9780766030879). 31 p.
SERIES: Easy crafts in 5 steps
GRADE LEVEL: Lower elementary
CONTENTS: Dragon—classroom—bowl—apple—bag puppet—elephant—basket—bus—bird—jungle—trumpet—daytime and nighttime—butterfly—surprise card

971 **LLIMÓS PLOMER, A.** *Fairy tale adventure crafts*. 2011, Enslow (ISBN: 9780766037366). 32 p.
SERIES: Fun adventure crafts
GRADE LEVEL: Elementary
CONTENTS: N/A

972 **LLIMÓS PLOMER, A.** *Haunted house adventure crafts*. 2011, Enslow (ISBN: 9780766037304). 32 p.
SERIES: Fun adventure crafts
GRADE LEVEL: Elementary
CONTENTS: Coffin—vampire—candles—scary spider—mummy—haunted house—ghost—Frankenstein—scary rat—skeleton—bat and tombstone—create your own story

973 **LLIMÓS PLOMER, A.** *Medieval castle adventure crafts*. 2011, Enslow Elementary (ISBN: 9780766037342). 32 p.
SERIES: Fun adventure crafts

GRADE LEVEL: Elementary

CONTENTS: King—queen—castle—minstrel—princess—dragon—catapult—horse—knight—shield and lance—court jester—create story

974 **LLIMÓS PLOMER, A.** *Pirate ship adventure crafts*. 2011, Enslow Elementary (ISBN: 9780766037281). 32 p.
SERIES: Fun adventure crafts
GRADE LEVEL: Elementary
CONTENTS: Parrot—Captain Redbeard—pirate girl and her troop—cannon—pirate ship—mast—cabin boy—shark—prisoner—Caribbean island—treasure chest—create story

975 **LLIMÓS PLOMER, A.** *Space adventure crafts*. 2011, Enslow (ISBN: 9780766037328). 32 p.
SERIES: Fun adventure crafts
GRADE LEVEL: Middle school
CONTENTS: N/A

976 **LOCKWOOD, S.** *Junior scientists: experiment with heat*. 2011, Cherry Lake (ISBN: 9781602798434). 32 p.
SERIES: Science explorer junior
GRADE LEVEL: Lower elementary
CONTENTS: Temperature—warmth—heat—do it yourself

977 **LOCKWOOD, S.** *Junior scientists: experiment with rocks*. 2011, Cherry Lake (ISBN: 9781602798366). 32 p.
SERIES: Science explorer junior
GRADE LEVEL: Lower elementary
CONTENTS: Rocks—dinosaurs—scratch it

978 **LOCKWOOD, S.** *Super cool science experiments: electricity*. 2010, Cherry Lake (ISBN: 9781602795334). 32 p.
SERIES: Science explorer
GRADE LEVEL: Elementary
CONTENTS: Lightning—first things first—shocking—charge—battery—conductors—circuits—do it yourself

979 **LOCKWOOD, S.** *Super cool science experiments: minerals*. 2010, Cherry Lake (ISBN: 9781602795242). 32 p.
SERIES: Science explorer
GRADE LEVEL: Elementary
CONTENTS: Mineral—first things first—hardness—cleaner—sparks—crystals—gravity—do it yourself

980 **LOCKWOOD, S.** *Super cool science experiments: rocks*. 2010, Cherry Lake (ISBN: 9781602795235). 32 p.
SERIES: Science explorer
GRADE LEVEL: Elementary

CONTENTS: Long ago—first things first—island—rocks—twist—dinosaurs—scratch—do it yourself

981 **LOCRICCHIO, M.** *Teen cuisine*. 2010, Marshall Cavendish (ISBN: 9780761457152). 207 p.
GRADE LEVEL: High school
CONTENTS: Breakfasts—snacks—soups—salads and dressings—sandwiches and burgers—pizza—side shows—entrees—desserts

982 **LOEWEN, N.** *Action! Writing your own play*. 2010, Picture Window Books (ISBN: 9781404863927). 32 p.
SERIES: Writer's toolbox
GRADE LEVEL: Elementary
CONTENTS: N/A

983 **LOEWEN, N.** *It's all about you: writing your own journal*. 2009, Picture Window Books (ISBN: 9781404856981). 32 p.
SERIES: Writer's toolbox
GRADE LEVEL: Elementary
CONTENTS: N/A

984 **LOEWEN, N.** *Just the facts: writing your own research report*. 2009, Picture Window Books (ISBN: 9781404855199). 32 p.
SERIES: Writer's toolbox
GRADE LEVEL: Elementary
CONTENTS: N/A

985 **LOEWEN, N.** *Make me giggle: writing your own silly story*. 2009, Picture Window Books (ISBN: 9781404855182). 32 p.
SERIES: Writer's toolbox
GRADE LEVEL: Elementary
CONTENTS: N/A

986 **LOEWEN, N.** *Once upon a time: writing your own fairy tales*. 2009, Picture Window Books (ISBN: 9781404853362). 32 p.
SERIES: Writer's toolbox
GRADE LEVEL: Elementary
CONTENTS: N/A

987 **LOEWEN, N.** *Share a scare: writing your own scary story*. 2009, Picture Window Books (ISBN: 9781404855175). 32 p.
SERIES: Writer's toolbox
GRADE LEVEL: Elementary
CONTENTS: N/A

988 **LOEWEN, N.** *Show me a story: writing your own picture book*. 2009, Picture Window Books (ISBN: 9781404853416). 32 p.
SERIES: Writer's toolbox

GRADE LEVEL: Elementary

CONTENTS: N/A

989 **LOEWEN, N.** *Sincerely yours: writing your own letter*. 2009, Picture Window Books (ISBN: 9781404853393). 32 p.

SERIES: Writer's toolbox

GRADE LEVEL: Elementary

CONTENTS: N/A

990 **LOEWEN, N.** *Words, wit, and wonder: writing your own poem*. 2009, Picture Window Books (ISBN: 9781404853454). 32 p.

SERIES: Writer's toolbox

GRADE LEVEL: Elementary

CONTENTS: N/A

991 **LOPEZ, D.** *Amazing solar system projects you can build yourself*. 2008, Nomad Press (ISBN: 9780979226816). 128 p.

SERIES: Build it Yourself

GRADE LEVEL: Upper elementary – middle school

CONTENTS: Astronomical unit—greenhouse experiment—planetary rings—phases of the moon—orbit of the moon around the earth—geocentric and heliocentric—solar wind—craters—asteroid belt—jigsaw puzzle—tectonic plates & volcanism—Galileo ramp—Galilean telescope—Newtonian telescope—rockets—Sputnik satellite—aerostat balloon—eagle lander—magnetic rail launcher—space elevator—spacecraft—ion drive ship—seismometer—dynamo—communications center—Mars exploration rovers—big bang balloon—nebula picture—pulsar—solar system—light-year

992 **LOTER, J.** *Learn to draw Walt Disney's Mickey Mouse*. 2011, Walter Foster (ISBN: 9781936309023). 31 p.

SERIES: Learn to draw

GRADE LEVEL: Upper elementary – middle school

CONTENTS: N/A

993 **LOWRY, B.** *Juicy writing: inspiration and techniques for young writers*. 2008, Allen and Unwin (ISBN: 9781741750485). 201 p.

GRADE LEVEL: High school

CONTENTS: Starting out—transforming your world—juicy stuff—writing essentials—writing and life

994 **LUNDGREN, J.** *Camping*. 2010, Rourke (ISBN: 9781606943670). 24 p.

SERIES: Outdoor adventures

GRADE LEVEL: Elementary

CONTENTS: Get ready—set up camp—camp kitchen—safety

995 **LUNDGREN, J.** *Hiking*. 2010, Rourke (ISBN: 9781606943663). 24 p.

SERIES: Outdoor adventures

GRADE LEVEL: Elementary

CONTENTS: Footwork—equipment basics—trails and adventures—safety—caring for trails

996 LUNDQUIST, J. *Recycling, step by step*. 2012, Capstone (ISBN: 9781429660266). 32 p.
SERIES: Step-by-step stories
GRADE LEVEL: Lower elementary
CONTENTS: N/A

997 LUXBACHER, I. *1-2-3 I can make prints!* 2008, Kids Can Press (ISBN: 9781554530403). 23 p.
SERIES: Starting art
GRADE LEVEL: Lower Elementary
CONTENTS: N/A

998 LUXBACHER, I. *1-2-3 I can build!* 2009, Kids Can Press (ISBN: 9781554533169). 23 p.
SERIES: Starting art
GRADE LEVEL: Lower elementary
CONTENTS: N/A

999 LUXBACHER, I. *1-2-3 I can collage!* 2009, Kids Can Press (ISBN: 9781554533138). 23 p.
SERIES: Starting art
GRADE LEVEL: Lower elementary
CONTENTS: N/A

1000 LUXBACHER, I. *1-2-3 I can draw!* 2008, Kids Can Press (ISBN: 9781554530397). 23 p.
SERIES: Starting art
GRADE LEVEL: Lower elementary
CONTENTS: N/A

1001 LUXBACHER, I. *1-2-3 I can paint!* 2007, Kids Can Press (ISBN: 9781554530373). 23 p.
SERIES: Starting art
GRADE LEVEL: Lower elementary
CONTENTS: N/A

1002 LUXBACHER, I. *1-2-3 I can sculpt!* 2007, Kids Can Press (ISBN: 9781554530380). 23 p.
SERIES: Starting art
GRADE LEVEL: Lower elementary
CONTENTS: N/A

1003 LYNETTE, R. *Let's throw a Halloween party!* 2012, PowerKids Press (ISBN: 9781448825691).
SERIES: Holiday parties
GRADE LEVEL: Elementary

CONTENTS: Party planning—invitation time—decorate—egg-carton bat—spooky table—games—snacks—goody bags

1004 MACDONALD, F. *The amazing world of mummies*. 2008, Southwater (ISBN: 9781844766086). 64 p.
GRADE LEVEL: Elementary
CONTENTS: N/A

1005 MACDONALD, F. *The Ancient Egyptians: eat, write, and play just like the Egyptians*. 2012, QEB (ISBN: 9781595663528). 32 p.
SERIES: Hands-on history
GRADE LEVEL: Elementary
CONTENTS: N/A

1006 MACDONALD, F. *Aztecs: eat, write, and play just like the Aztecs*. 2007, QEB (ISBN: 9781595663542). 32 p.
SERIES: Hands-on history
GRADE LEVEL: Elementary
CONTENTS: N/A

1007 MACDONALD, F. *Hands-on history! Ancient Japan: step back to the time of Shoguns and Samurai, with 15 step-by-step projects and over 330 exciting pictures*. 2013, Armadillo (ISBN: 9781843228240). 64 p.
SERIES: Hands-on history!
GRADE LEVEL: Upper elementary
CONTENTS: N/A

1008 MACDONALD, F. *Hands-on history! Aztec & Maya: rediscover the lost world of Ancient Central America, with 450 exciting pictures and 15 step-by-step projects*. 2013, Armadillo (ISBN: 9781843227304). 64 p.
SERIES: Hands-on history!
GRADE LEVEL: Upper elementary
CONTENTS: N/A

1009 MACDONALD, F. *Hands-on history! The Celts: step into the world of the Celtic peoples, with 15 step-by-step projects and over 400 exciting pictures*. 2013, Armadillo (ISBN: 9781843229933). 64 p.
SERIES: Hands-on history!
GRADE LEVEL: Upper elementary
CONTENTS: N/A

1010 MACDONALD, F. *Romans: dress, eat, write and play just like the Romans*. 2008, Crabtree (ISBN: 9780778740711). 32 p.
SERIES: Hands-on history
GRADE LEVEL: Elementary
CONTENTS: N/A

1011 MACDONALD, F. *Vikings: eat, write, and play just like the Vikings*. 2007, QEB (ISBN: 9781595663542). 32 p.
SERIES: Hands-on history

GRADE LEVEL: Elementary

CONTENTS: N/A

1012 MACK, G. *Kickboxing*. 2012, Marshall Cavendish Benchmark (ISBN: 9780761449362). 47 p.

SERIES: Martial arts in action

GRADE LEVEL: Upper elementary – middle school

CONTENTS: N/A

1013 MACNEAL, N. *10-minute puppets*. 2010, Workman (ISBN: 9780761157144). 173 p.

GRADE LEVEL: Elementary

CONTENTS: N/A

1014 MADER, J. *Let's go camping!* 2007, Pebble Plus Books (ISBN: 9780736863605). 24 p.

SERIES: Sports and activities

GRADE LEVEL: Lower elementary

CONTENTS: N/A

1015 MAGLOFF, L. *Experiments with heat and energy*. 2010, Gareth Stevens (ISBN: 9781433934506). 32 p.

SERIES: Cool science

GRADE LEVEL: Upper elementary

CONTENTS: Temperature—conduction—heat—thermos—convection—calories—ice—oven of the sun—geysers—make a cloud—ice cream

1016 MANNING, M. *Drama school*. 2008, Frances Lincoln (ISBN: 9781845078454).

GRADE LEVEL: Elementary

CONTENTS: N/A

1017 MANTELL, P. *Chess in action: from first attack to checkmate*. 2010, Sterling (ISBN: 9781402760464). 118 p.

GRADE LEVEL: Elementary

CONTENTS: N/A

1018 MARGLES, S. *Mythbusters science fair book*. 2011, Scholastic (ISBN: 9780545237451). 128 p.

SERIES: Mythbusters science fair

GRADE LEVEL: Upper elementary – middle school

CONTENTS: Mentos and diet cola—other ways to make a geyser—shine a penny—remove stains with cola—dissolve a steak with cola—loosen a rusty bolt with cola—polish chrome with aluminum foil and cola—dissolve a human tooth with cola—keeping a beverage bubbly—cola and pop rocks—a cereal box or cereal?—clothes for a snowman—running in the rain—rain gauge—how to cool a beverage—how to keep a beverage cold—make snowflakes—make icicles—peppers and milk—burning wood to cool your house—popcorn?—talking to plants—keep needles from falling off your Christmas tree—transpiration—plants and evaporation—pigments in plant leaves—make a battery with an onion and a sports drink—dirtier than a toilet—bacteria on your toothbrush—double-dipping food—food and the five-second rule—mold and washing your hands—make bananas ripen faster—how quickly does milk go bad—lift a sunken ship with ping-pong balls—electroscope—duct tape wallet—

erase credit cards with magnets—galvanometer—make a battery from a lemon—lemon battery and a light bulb—water rocket—phone book friction—contagious yawns—gravity and buttered toast—eye-black and glare from the sun—make a volcano—test for acid with a cabbage—fish memory

1019 MARGLES, S. *Mythbusters: confirm or bust! Science fair book #2*. 2012, Scholastic (ISBN: 9780545433976). 128 p.
SERIES: Mythbusters science fair
GRADE LEVEL: Upper elementary – middle school
CONTENTS: Rat pee and soda cans—black light—gassy foods—cold feet—cookbook—jawbreaker—McGyver—compass—candle—paint—paper folding—make paper—lights on or off?—energy and home appliances—refrigerated batteries—solar cell—biogas digester—pirate eye patches—sneezing—how to stop a sneeze—runny nose—catching a cold by shaking hands—sanitizers—latent fingerprints—fingerprint data—walking in a straight line—baseball bat's sweet spot—hammock—salsa—toilet paper strength—bed sheets strength—use antacids to launch a rocket—falling into water—catapult—paper armor protection—paper armor—boat—tornado—lightning—tsunami—seismometer—helium balloons—metal detector

1020 MARIAFFI, D. *Eat it up! Lip-smacking recipes for kids*. 2009, Owlkids (ISBN: 9781897349564). 93 p.
GRADE LEVEL: Elementary
CONTENTS: N/A

1021 MARKS, J. *How to make a bouncing egg*. 2011, Capstone (ISBN: 9781429652919). 24 p.
SERIES: Hands-on science fun
GRADE LEVEL: Lower elementary
CONTENTS: Get started—bouncing egg—how does it work

1022 MARROQUIN-BURR, K. *Learn to draw Angry Birds*. 2012, Walter Foster (ISBN: 9781600583063). 32 p.
SERIES: Learn to draw
GRADE LEVEL: Upper elementary – middle school
CONTENTS: N/A

1023 MARSICO, K. *Step-by-step experiments with insects*. 2012, Child's World (ISBN: 9781609733391). 32 p.
SERIES: Step-by-step experiments
GRADE LEVEL: Lower elementary
CONTENTS: Insects—seven steps—critters—bug—a group—nighttime noisemakers

1024 MARSICO, K. *Step-by-step experiments with life cycles*. 2012, Child's World (ISBN: 9781609735876). 32 p.
SERIES: Step-by-step experiments
GRADE LEVEL: Lower elementary
CONTENTS: Life cycles—seven steps—the bean—the worm—make a move—seed search

1025 MARSICO, K. *Step-by-step experiments with taste and digestion*. 2012, Child's World (ISBN: 9781609736149). 32 p.

SERIES: Step-by-step experiments

GRADE LEVEL: Lower elementary

CONTENTS: Taste and digestion—seven steps—nose—spit—tongue—chewing

1026 **MARTIN, A.** *How to improve at judo*. 2009, Crabtree (ISBN: 9780778735960). 48 p.

SERIES: How to improve at

GRADE LEVEL: Elementary

CONTENTS: Judo belt—judo dojo—competition area—prepare to play—breakfalls—front breakfalls—tapping out—gripping—hip throws—hand throws—leg throws—sacrifice throws—pinning—choke holds—joint locks—tournament rules—diet and mental attitude

1027 **MARTIN, A.** *How to improve at karate*. 2008, Crabtree (ISBN: 9780778735687). 48 p.

SERIES: How to improve at

GRADE LEVEL: Elementary

CONTENTS: Warming up and stretching—karate techniques—skills and drills—karate tournaments—diet and mental attitude

1028 **MARTINEAU, S.** *Astonishing art*. 2012, Windmill Books (ISBN: 9781615333691).

SERIES: Awesome activities

GRADE LEVEL: Upper elementary

CONTENTS: Before you begin—two of you—wacky weaving—onion fish—big box croc—masks—cuttings—Jurassock park—on guard—eggy mosiacs—fit for a pharaoh

1029 **MARTINEAU, S.** *Bubbles in the bathroom*. 2012, Windmill Books (ISBN: 9781615333714). 24 p.

SERIES: Everyday science experiments

GRADE LEVEL: Elementary

CONTENTS: Bubbles—mirrors—beakers—float a boat—water—siphon—toothbrush—squeezers—plughole—skin

1030 **MARTINEAU, S.** *Cool circuits*. 2011, Windmill Books (ISBN: 9781615334049). 24 p.

SERIES: Awesome activities

GRADE LEVEL: Upper elementary

CONTENTS: N/A

1031 **MARTINEAU, S.** *Crazy contraptions*. 2011, Windmill Books (ISBN: 9781615334056). 24 p.

SERIES: Awesome activities

GRADE LEVEL: Upper elementary

CONTENTS: N/A

1032 **MASIELLO, R.** *Ralph Masiello's ancient Egypt drawing book*. 2008, Charlesbridge (ISBN: 9781570915338).

GRADE LEVEL: Elementary

CONTENTS: Great Pyramid of Khafre—Udjat—Eye of Horus—symbols and emblems—winged solar disk—Anubis, god of the dead—Sphinx—Kriosphinx head—Hieracosphinx head—Androsphinx head—Osiris, god of the dead—ancient Egyptian gods—body of a god—Isis, queen of the gods—Queen Nefertiti—Tutankhamun

1033 MASIELLO, R. *Ralph Masiello's dragon drawing book*. 2007, Charlesbridge (ISBN: 9781570915314).

GRADE LEVEL: Upper elementary

CONTENTS: Aboriginal rainbow serpent—Ouroboros—mushussu—Maya celestial dragon—Lambton wyrm—wyvern—Fafnir—cockatrice—Makara and Naga—Chinese imperial dragon—Draco Quabbininus Americanus

1034 MASIELLO, R. *Ralph Masiello's fairy drawing book*. 2013, Charlesbridge (ISBN: 9781570915390).

GRADE LEVEL: Elementary

CONTENTS: N/A

1035 MASIELLO, R. *Ralph Masiello's farm drawing book*. 2012, Charlesbridge (ISBN: 978157091538).

GRADE LEVEL: Elementary

CONTENTS: Baby chicks—hen—rooster—pig—billy goat—dairy cow—horses—farmer and tractor—barn

1036 MASIELLO, R. *Ralph Masiello's Halloween drawing book*. 2012, Charlesbridge (ISBN: 9781670915413).

GRADE LEVEL: Elementary

CONTENTS: Pumpkins—bat—ghosts—black cat—gravestones—graveyard fence—witch—owl—raven—scary tree—skeleton—haunted mansion

1037 MASIELLO, R. *Ralph Masiello's robot drawing book*. 2011, Charlesbridge (ISBN: 9781570915352).

GRADE LEVEL: Elementary

CONTENTS: N/A

1038 MASON, A. *Motion, magnets and more: the big book of primary physical science*. 2010, Kids Can Press (ISBN: 9781554537075). 128 p.

GRADE LEVEL: Lower elementary

CONTENTS: N/A

1039 MASON, P. *Bike mechanic: how to be an ace bike mechanic*. 2012, Capstone (ISBN: 9781429668828). 48 p.

SERIES: Instant expert

GRADE LEVEL: Upper elementary – middle school

CONTENTS: Cleaning—sitting comfortably—adjust brakes—brake pads—adjusting gears and chains—cleaning chains and gears—new chain—fixed wheels and single speeds—cranks—bottom brackets—tires—tubes and punctures—bicycle tourist—headset—handlebars—pro mechanic—troubleshooting

1040 MASON, P. *Biking*. 2008, Smart Apple Media (ISBN: 9781599201306). 32 p.

SERIES: Recreational sports

GRADE LEVEL: Upper elementary

CONTENTS: Setting up your bike—bike maintenance—biking equipment—basic skills—riding uphill—downhill riding—cornering safety—bike tricks and BMX

1041 **MASON, P.** *Cycling*. 2010, Sea to Sea (ISBN: 9781597712187). 30 p.

SERIES: Know your sport

GRADE LEVEL: Upper elementary

CONTENTS: The best bike for you—clothing and safety—fitness and training—cadence and gears—uphill riding skills—downhill riding skills—ollies—road racing—track racing—off-road racing

1042 **MASON, P.** *Fishing*. 2008, Smart Apple Media (ISBN: 9781599201313). 32 p.

SERIES: Recreational sports

GRADE LEVEL: Upper elementary

CONTENTS: Fishing gear—setting up your gear—casting—finding fish—hooking a fish—landing a fish—releasing a fish

1043 **MASON, P.** *Gymnastics*. 2010, Sea to Sea (ISBN: 9781597712132). 30 p.

SERIES: Know your sport

GRADE LEVEL: Upper elementary

CONTENTS: Gymnastics basics—the floor—vaulting—the balance beam—the bars—the parallel bars—the pommel horse and rings—rhythmic gymnastics—trampolining

1044 **MASON, P.** *Hiking and camping*. 2008, Smart Apple Media (ISBN: 9781599201290). 32 p.

SERIES: Recreational sports

GRADE LEVEL: Upper elementary

CONTENTS: Hiking equipment—planning your route—finding your way—overnight trips—pitching your tent—eating and cooking—survival skills—fit to hike

1045 **MASON, P.** *How to improve at swimming*. 2008, Crabtree (ISBN: 9780778735700). 48 p.

SERIES: How to improve at

GRADE LEVEL: Elementary

CONTENTS: Swimming pools—equipment—the strokes—warming up—freestyle—backstroke—breaststroke—basic butterfly—advanced butterfly—starts and turns—learning to dive—racing starts—racing turns—backstroke starts and turns—diet and fitness—race tactics and events—triathlon and water polo—safety: water safety—lifesaving

1046 **MASON, P.** *Judo*. 2009, Sea to Sea (ISBN: 9781597711517). 30 p.

SERIES: Know your sport

GRADE LEVEL: Upper elementary

CONTENTS: Judo basics—training—falling—first skills—breaking balance—hip throws—shoulder throws—reaping throws—groundwork

1047 **MASON, P.** *Mountain biking*. 2011, PowerKids Press (ISBN: 9781448832965). 32 p.

SERIES: Get outdoors

GRADE LEVEL: Upper elementary

CONTENTS: N/A

1048 MASON, P. *Rock climbing and rappeling*. 2008, Smart Apple Media (ISBN: 9781599201320). 32 p.

SERIES: Recreational sports

GRADE LEVEL: Upper elementary

CONTENTS: Top rope climbing and belaying—climbing equipment—basic technique—natural rock—bouldering—leading climbs—climbing signals—rappeling—climbing knots—fit to climb

1049 MASON, P. *Self-defense: be a master at self-defense*. 2012, Capstone (ISBN: 9781429668859). 48 p.

SERIES: Velocity

GRADE LEVEL: Upper elementary – middle school

CONTENTS: Avoid—escape—defend—confidence and body language—safe places—public transportation—the three Ds—bullying—run—shout—ignore your ego—the A to H of escape—defending yourself physically—the upward block—combined up-down block—sideways block—slip—slap—slop—attacks from behind—martial arts—what to do if . . .

1050 MASON, P. *Snorkeling and diving*. 2008, Smart Apple Media (ISBN: 9781599201283). 32 p.

SERIES: Recreational sports

GRADE LEVEL: Upper elementary

CONTENTS: Snorkeling equipment—where to snorkel—getting into the water—saving energy—clearing your snorkel and mask—snorkeling safely—scuba diving—underwater science—fit for the ocean

1051 MASON, P. *Swimming*. 2010, Sea to Sea (ISBN: 9781597712163). 30 p.

SERIES: Know your sport

GRADE LEVEL: Upper elementary

CONTENTS: N/A

1052 MASON, P. *Trampolining*. 2010, Sea to Sea (ISBN: 9781597712194). 30 p.

SERIES: Know your sport

GRADE LEVEL: Upper elementary

CONTENTS: N/A

1053 MASURA, S. *Record it! Shooting and editing digital video*. 2013, Cherry Lake (ISBN: 9781610804844).

SERIES: Information explorer junior

GRADE LEVEL: Elementary

CONTENTS: Plan—shoot—edit—share

1054 MATTERN, J. *Recipe and craft guide to China*. 2011, Mitchell Lane (ISBN: 9781584159377). 63 p.

SERIES: World crafts and recipes

GRADE LEVEL: Upper elementary – middle school

CONTENTS: White rice—chicken and pineapple fried rice—pork lo mein—cold sesame noodles—steamed dumplings—wonton soup—egg rolls—almond cookies—tea—sweet rice balls—moon cakes—tangrams—paper cutouts—fireworks—kites—

dragon boats—scented bag—dough clay figures—red lanterns—dragon toy—paper firecracker

1055 MATTOX, W. *Babysitting skills: traits and training for success*. 2007, Capstone (ISBN: 9780736864664).

SERIES: Babysitting

GRADE LEVEL: Middle school

CONTENTS: Super sitter—training and experience—honesty and more—diapering and feeding babies—staying alert—thoughtful and creative—responsible and encouraging—problem-solving skills—calm and quick—handling misbehavior

1056 MAURER, T. *Fabulous fashion crafts*. 2010, Rourke (ISBN: 9781606943410). 32 p.

SERIES: Creative crafts for kids

GRADE LEVEL: Elementary

CONTENTS: Bobby pin—angel necklace—ribbon belt—denim purse—signed t-shirt—splashy socks—sporty shoelaces—fluffy flip-flops—to wear or to share

1057 MAURER, T. *Scrapbook starters*. 2010, Rourke (ISBN: 9781606943434).

GRADE LEVEL: Lower elementary

CONTENTS: N/A

1058 MAXWELL, S. *I can cook: recipes for kids shown step by step*. 2013, Armadillo (ISBN: 9781843227557).

SERIES: Show me how

GRADE LEVEL: Elementary

CONTENTS: N/A

1059 MAYES, A. *Netball*. 2009, A. and C. Black (ISBN: 9781408114087). 32 p.

SERIES: Know the game skills

GRADE LEVEL: Elementary

CONTENTS: N/A

1060 MAYHEW, M. *How to cook: delicious dishes perfect for teen cooks*. 2011, DK (ISBN: 9780756672140). 127 p.

GRADE LEVEL: Middle school – high school

CONTENTS: Fast food—big food—something sweet—bake-off

1061 MCCAFFERTY, C. *Learn to draw princesses*. 2011, Walter Foster (ISBN: 9781936309238). 32 p.

SERIES: Learn to draw

GRADE LEVEL: Upper elementary – middle school

CONTENTS: N/A

1062 MCCALLUM, A. *Eat your math: recipes for inquiring minds*. 2014, Charlesbridge (ISBN: 9781570917806). 46 p.

GRADE LEVEL: Elementary

CONTENTS: N/A

1063 MCCALLUM, A. *Eat your science homework: recipes for inquiring minds*. 2014, Charlesbridge (ISBN: 9781570912986). 46 p.

GRADE LEVEL: Upper elementary

CONTENTS: Popcorn balls—dressing and veggie sticks—roll-over snacks—cookies—pizza lasagna—lava cakes—breakfast swallow-ups

1064 MCCARTHY, P. *Friends of the Earth: a history of American environmentalism with 21 activities*. 2013, Chicago Review Press (ISBN: 9781569767184). 144 p.

GRADE LEVEL: Upper elementary

CONTENTS: N/A

1065 MCCURRY, K. *How to draw amazing airplanes and spacecraft*. 2013, Capstone (ISBN: 9781429687492). 64 p.

SERIES: Smithsonian drawing books

GRADE LEVEL: Elementary

CONTENTS: 1903 Wright flyer—Apollo command module—Arlington 515U 1A—Bell AH-1 Super Cobra—Bell X-1—Boeing B-17 Flying Fortress—Boeing B-52 Stratofortress—Boeing C-17 Globemaster—Boeing F-15 Eagle—Boeing F/A-1b Hornet—Concorder—Explorer I—General Atomics MQ-1 Predator—Grumman EA-6b Prowler—Grumman G-14 tTomcat—Lockheed F-117 Nighthawk—Lockheed F-22 Raptor—Lockheed 5R-71 Blackbird—North American P-51 Mustang—North American X-15—Northrop B-2—Phoenix Mars Lander—Piper J-3 Cub—Rutan Voyager—Ryan NYP Spirit of St. Louis—Saturn V rocket—space shuttle with rocket launcher—Spaceshipone

1066 MCCURRY, K. *How to draw amazing animals*. 2013, Capstone (ISBN: 9781429699396). 64 p.

SERIES: Smithsonian drawing books

GRADE LEVEL: Elementary

CONTENTS: African elephant—alligator—Arabian horse—bald eagle—barn owl—basilisk lizard—black rhinoceros—cheetah—chimpanzee—eastern diamondback rattlesnake—emperor penguin—Galapagos tortoise—giant panda—giraffe—grizzly bear

1067 MCCURRY, K. *How to draw incredible dinosaurs*. 2013, Capstone (ISBN: 9781429687508). 64 p.

SERIES: Smithsonian drawing books

GRADE LEVEL: Elementary

CONTENTS: Albertosaurus—Allosaurus—Ankylosaurus—Brachiosaurus—Chungkingosaurus—Coelophysis—Corythosaurus—Deinonychus—Diplodocus—Edmontania—Edmontosaurus—Falcarius—Gasparinisaura—Gastonia—GigantSpinosaurus—Kentrosaurus—Leaellynasaura—Maisaura—microaptor—Omeisaurus—Ouranosaurus—Pachycephalosaurus—Plateosaurus—Rugops—Stegosaurus—Styracosaurus—Thescelosaurus—Triceratops—Tyrannosaurus—Velociraptor

1068 MCCURRY, K. *How to draw incredible ocean animals*. 2013, Capstone (ISBN: 9781429699402). 64 p.

SERIES: Smithsonian drawing books

GRADE LEVEL: Elementary

CONTENTS: Anemonefish—Atlantic blue marlin—Atlantic bluefin tuna—blue whale—bottlenose dolphin—box jellyfish—coelacanth—deep sea anglerfish—giant moray eel—giant octopus—great white shark—green sea turtle—hammerhead shark—hermit crab—horseshoe crab—leafy sea dragon—lionfish—manatee—manta ray—marine iguana—narwhal—orca—porcupinefish—purple sea star—sailfish—sea otter—walrus—wandering albatross—whale shark—yeti crab

1069 MCFEE, S. *Let's learn martial arts*. 2008, PowerKids Press (ISBN: 9781404241961). 24 p.

SERIES: Let's get active

GRADE LEVEL: Lower elementary

CONTENTS: Martial arts—what are martial arts—karate—tae kwon do—judo—learning martial arts—martial arts on the job—honor

1070 MCFEE, S. *Let's play baseball*. 2008, PowerKids Press (ISBN: 9781404241947). 24 p.

SERIES: Let's get active

GRADE LEVEL: Lower elementary

CONTENTS: National pastime—bat-and-ball—where to play—play ball—strike three! You are out!—the players—the lineup—teamwork

1071 MCFEE, S. *Let's play basketball*. 2008, PowerKids Press (ISBN: 9781404241930). 24 p.

SERIES: Let's get active

GRADE LEVEL: Lower elementary

CONTENTS: Basketball—peach baskets—what you need—rules—referee—players—coach—teamwork and sportsmanship

1072 MCFEE, S. *Let's play football*. 2008, PowerKids Press (ISBN: 9781404241923). 24 p.

SERIES: Let's get active

GRADE LEVEL: Lower elementary

CONTENTS: Soccer + rugby + time = football—ouch!—100 yards and 11 people—the rules of the game—offense and defense—the coach—teamwork

1073 MCFEE, S. *Let's play ice hockey*. 2008, PowerKids Press (ISBN: 9781404241954). 24 p.

SERIES: Let's get active

GRADE LEVEL: Lower elementary

CONTENTS: Ice hockey—grass to ice—skates and sticks—the rink—the team—penalty box—the coach—teamwork

1074 MCFEE, S. *Let's play soccer*. 2008, PowerKids Press (ISBN: 9781404241916). 24 p.

SERIES: Let's get active

GRADE LEVEL: Lower elementary

CONTENTS: Two thousand years of soccer—soccer gear—the team—gooooaaaal!—kickers—practice makes perfect—teamwork

1075 MCGEE, R. *Paper crafts for Chinese New Year*. 2008, Enslow (ISBN: 9780766029507). 48 p.

SERIES: Paper craft fun for holidays

GRADE LEVEL: Lower elementary

CONTENTS: Dragon puppet—tangrams—lion dancer mask—lai see—red gift envelope—shadow puppets—Chinese lantern—fire cracker decorations—Chinese symbols banners

1076 MCGEE, R. *Paper crafts for Christmas*. 2009, Enslow (ISBN: 9780766029521). 48 p.

    SERIES: Paper craft fun for holidays

    GRADE LEVEL: Lower elementary

    CONTENTS: O Christmas tree—holly wreath—little Santa—pop-up chimney card—Santa reindeer—ornament—falling snowflakes—paper plate angel

1077 MCGEE, R. *Paper crafts for Day of the Dead*. 2008, Enslow (ISBN: 9780766029514). 48 p.

    SERIES: Paper craft fun for holidays

    GRADE LEVEL: Lower elementary

    CONTENTS: Paper marigolds—skeleton candy basket—skeleton figures—skeleton pets—clothes for the skeletons—skull mask—window dressings—Aztec animal decorations

1078 MCGEE, R. *Paper crafts for Easter*. 2012, Enslow (ISBN: 9780766037236). 48 p.

    SERIES: Paper craft fun for holidays

    GRADE LEVEL: Lower elementary

    CONTENTS: Tissue paper "pysanky" eggs—Easter egg stands—Easter lily pop-up card—bunny ears—bunnies and chicks—hatching chick—Easter place mats—paper stained glass windows

1079 MCGEE, R. *Paper crafts for Halloween*. 2009, Enslow (ISBN: 9780766029477). 48 p.

    SERIES: Paper craft fun for holidays

    GRADE LEVEL: Lower elementary

    CONTENTS: Scarecrow jumping jack—flying bat—haunted house with ghosts—bat and ghost chains—standing little witchie—sitting black cat—skull headdress—goofy goggles

1080 MCGEE, R. *Paper crafts for Kwanzaa*. 2008, Enslow (ISBN: 9780766029491). 48 p.

    SERIES: Paper craft fun for holidays

    GRADE LEVEL: Lower elementary

    CONTENTS: Kinara pop-up card—Mkeka—ear of corn—Vibunzi or Muhindi—Kwanzaa figures—fruit tree—standing words—lion—African style hat

1081 MCGEE, R. *Paper crafts for Mardi Gras*. 2012, Enslow (ISBN: 9780766037243). 48 p.

    SERIES: Paper craft fun for holidays

    GRADE LEVEL: Lower elementary

    CONTENTS: Columbina mask—paper bead throw necklace—Mardi Gras rhythm maker—gold doubloon necklace—full face mask—jester's cap—krewe king or queen (or royalty) crown—Mardi Gras mask card

1082 MCGEE, R. *Paper crafts for Thanksgiving*. 2012, Enslow (ISBN: 9780766037229). 48 p.

    SERIES: Paper craft fun for holidays

    GRADE LEVEL: Lower elementary

    CONTENTS: Turkey pop-up card—pilgrim boy and girl—American Indian boy and girl—table greeting—turkey stencil—Indian corn and gourd paper chain—tree sculpture—mobile

1083 MCGEE, R. *Paper crafts for the 4th of July*. 2012, Enslow (ISBN: 9780766037274). 48 p.

SERIES: Paper craft fun for holidays

GRADE LEVEL: Lower elementary

CONTENTS: American flag pennant—paper firework fountain—"the bombs bursting in air"—liberty crown—stars and stripes paper chain—America's Uncle Sam—American spectacle—patriotic placemats

1084 MCGEE, R. *Paper crafts for Valentine's Day*. 2009, Enslow (ISBN: 9780766029484). 48 p.

SERIES: Paper craft fun for holidays

GRADE LEVEL: Lower elementary

CONTENTS: Cupid figure—heart sculpture—lacy heart card—pop-up heart card—Valentine heart crown—heart flowers—Valentine heart pop-up puppet—woven heart basket

1085 MCGUIRE, K. *The all-new woodworking for kids*. 2008, Lark Books (ISBN: 9781600590351).

GRADE LEVEL: Middle school – high school

CONTENTS: Miter box—tool box—compass tool—bench hook—weekend workbench—look-inside birdhouse—pooch palace—squirrel lounger—bird buffet—cat tail cat toy—observation station—quintuple bike stand—paddle racers—rope ladder—speed board—baseball hold-all—favorite things shelf—jewelry tree—desktop organizer—study partner—tabletop easel—heart box—place-card holders—key condo—round and round media tower—travel checkers—high flyer—slit drum—tessellation puzzle

1086 MCKINNEY, J. *Let's go geocaching*. 2008, DK (ISBN: 9780756637170). 48 p.

SERIES: Boys' life series

GRADE LEVEL: Lower elementary

CONTENTS: N/A

1087 MCKINNEY, J. *Let's go hiking*. 2011, DK (ISBN: 9780756650384). 48 p.

SERIES: Boys' life series

GRADE LEVEL: Lower elementary

CONTENTS: N/A

1088 MCMAHON, D. *Baseball skills*. 2009, Enslow (ISBN: 9780766032040). 48 p.

SERIES: How to play like a pro

GRADE LEVEL: Upper elementary

CONTENTS: Hitting—pitching—fielding—base running

1089 MCMILLAN, S. *How to improve at drawing*. 2010, Crabtree (ISBN: 9780778735984). 48 p.

SERIES: How to improve at

GRADE LEVEL: Elementary

CONTENTS: Equipment—perspective and observation—tone, texture and color—composition—water and sky—flowers—birds—cats—dogs—horses—leprechauns—fairies—dragons

1090 MCMILLAN, S. *How to improve at making jewelry*. 2010, Crabtree (ISBN: 9780778735779). 48 p.

    SERIES: How to improve at

    GRADE LEVEL: Elementary

    CONTENTS: Beads—equipment and tools—needles—thread—findings—stringing and prep—links and wirework—necklaces—bugle necklace—glass pendants—pendants—other necklaces—bracelets—safety pin bracelet—knotted bracelets—charm bracelets—felt bead bracelets—chunky bead bracelets—other jewelry—rings—earrings—hair adornments—decorative items

1091 MCNAB, C. *The boy's book of outdoor survival: 101 courageous skills for exploring the dangerous wild*. 2008, Ulysses Press (ISBN: 9781569756850). 128 p.

    GRADE LEVEL: Upper elementary – middle school

    CONTENTS: N/A

1092 MEBANE, J. *Ice fishing*. 2012, Capstone (ISBN: 9781429660068). 32 p.

    SERIES: Wild outdoors

    GRADE LEVEL: Lower elementary

    CONTENTS: N/A

1093 MEBANE, J. *Pheasant hunting*. 2012, Capstone (ISBN: 9781429660051). 32 p.

    SERIES: Wild outdoors

    GRADE LEVEL: Lower elementary

    CONTENTS: N/A

1094 MEDINA, S. *Having fun with collage*. 2008, PowerKids Press (ISBN: 9781404237216). 24 p.

    SERIES: Fun art projects

    GRADE LEVEL: Elementary

    CONTENTS: Feathered friend—modern art picture—food—treasure

1095 MEDINA, S. *Having fun with paint*. 2008, PowerKids Press (ISBN: 9781404237186). 24 p.

    SERIES: Fun art projects

    GRADE LEVEL: Elementary

    CONTENTS: N/A

1096 MEDINA, S. *Having fun with paper*. 2008, PowerKids Press (ISBN: 9781404237162). 24 p.

    SERIES: Fun art projects

    GRADE LEVEL: Elementary

    CONTENTS: Picture of me—concertina bracelet—flower shapes—colorful mat—whiteboard—flower garland—day and night clock—scary monster

1097 MEDINA, S. *Having fun with printing*. 2008, PowerKids Press (ISBN: 9781404237193). 24 p.

    SERIES: Fun art projects

    GRADE LEVEL: Elementary

CONTENTS: Printing fun—poppy field—street scene—money tube—person print—on the moon—come to my party—tic-tac-toe—happy-sad clown chest—spotted bag—under the sea—lush green trees—stained-glass window

1098 MEDINA, S. *Having fun with sculpture*. 2007, Wayland (ISBN: (9780750248921). 24 p.
SERIES: Let's do art
GRADE LEVEL: Elementary
CONTENTS: N/A

1099 MEDINA, S. *Having fun with textiles*. 2007, Wayland (ISBN: 9780750248884). 24 p.
SERIES: Let's do art
GRADE LEVEL: Elementary
CONTENTS: N/A

1100 MEINKING, M. *Creative nail art for the crafty fashionista*. 2012, Capstone (ISBN: 9781429665520). 32 p.
SERIES: FashionCraft studio
GRADE LEVEL: Elementary
CONTENTS: N/A

1101 MEINKING, M. *Easy origami: a step-by-step guide for kids*. 2010, Capstone (ISBN: 9781429650342). 112 p.
SERIES: Origami
GRADE LEVEL: Elementary
CONTENTS: N/A

1102 MEINKING, M. *Not-quite-so-easy origami*. 2009, Capstone (ISBN: 9781429620215). 112 p.
SERIES: Origami
GRADE LEVEL: Elementary
CONTENTS: Trapdoor envelope—bookmark—gliding airplane—somersault square—coaster—pine tree—cicada—hopping frog—pinwheel—flapping crane

1103 MEINKING, M. *Stylish shoes for the crafty fashionista*. 2012, Capstone (ISBN: 9781429665544). 32 p.
SERIES: FashionCraft studio
GRADE LEVEL: Elementary
CONTENTS: N/A

1104 MEISSNER, S. *Learn to draw American landmarks & historical heroes*. 2012, Walter Foster (ISBN: 9781600583070). 32 p.
SERIES: Learn to draw
GRADE LEVEL: Upper elementary – middle school
CONTENTS: N/A

1105 MELLETT, P. *Matter and materials*. 2013, Kingfisher (ISBN: 9780753469736). 32 p.
SERIES: Hands-on science
GRADE LEVEL: Upper elementary

CONTENTS: Denting and squeezing—stretching and snapping—soil—heat—solids—liquids—gases—materials—expanding and contracting—heating substances—changing state—permanent changes—burning—sieving solids—solutions and suspensions—mixtures—evaporating solutions—saturated solutions

1106 MERCER, B. *The flying machine book: build and launch 35 rockets, gliders, helicopters, boomerangs, and more*. 2012, Chicago Review Press (ISBN: 9781613740866). 240 p.
SERIES: Science in motion
GRADE LEVEL: Middle school – high school
CONTENTS: N/A

1107 MICHAELS, A. *The kids' multicultural art book: art & craft experiences from around the world*. 2007, Williamson (ISBN: 9780824968076). 160 p.
SERIES: Kids can
GRADE LEVEL: Elementary
CONTENTS: Vest—magic shield—charm bag—sun dance skull—finger mask—animal totem pole—storyteller animated mask—kachina cradle doll—hand mask—sponge painting—dream catcher—sun god—codex—yarn art—tin rooster—tree of life—paper flowers—loom weaving—worry doll—cart—paper pollo—wildcat—animalitos—plate designs—green toad bank—paper beads—mirror pouch—kufi—foil mask—mini-masks—animal nose mask—papier-mâché calabash—akuaba doll—paper weaving—sponge stamps—mud cloth—palm puppet—peacock—egg figurine—kokeshi soll—uchiwa—folding screen—Korean dragon puppet—good-luck dragon—egg painting—traditional papercuts—hanging owl—Vietnamese dancing dragon

1108 MIHALTCHEV, A. *Kid-agami sea life: easy-to-make paper toys*. 2013, Dover (ISBN: 9780486497440).
GRADE LEVEL: Elementary
CONTENTS: N/A

1109 MILLER, B. *Thomas Jefferson for kids: his life and times with 21 activities*. 2011, Chicago Review Press (ISBN: 9781569763483). 160 p.
SERIES: Kids can
GRADE LEVEL: Elementary
CONTENTS: Plot a map—dance a reel—palladian window—a plant from cutting—grape juice—Declaration of Independence word search—model solar system—ivory notebook—organize your library—microscope—Doric, Ionic, or Corinthian?—classical column—macaroni and cheese pie—weaving—floor plan and elevation—buffalo robe—compass rose—observe the weather—leaf collection—peace medal—word game—theorem painting

1110 MILLER, F. *Winning basketball for girls*. 2009, Chelsea House (ISBN: 9780816077595). 170 p.
SERIES: Winning sports for girls
GRADE LEVEL: Middle school – high school
CONTENTS: N/A

1111 MILLER, H. *Nifty thrifty art crafts*. 2008, Enslow (ISBN: 9780766027800). 32 p.

SERIES: Nifty thrifty crafts for kids

GRADE LEVEL: Elementary

CONTENTS: Cave painting placemats—hieroglyphic symbols—pyramid paperweight—Chinese window decorations—Japanese journal cover—American Indian pouch—pointillism portraits—pop art stamp—Jackson Pollock pencil holder—Calder's CD mobile—what it really looks like—patterns

1112 MILLS, J. *The everything kids' easy science experiments book: explore the world of science through quick and fun experiments*. 2010, Adams Media (ISBN: 9781440501586). 144 p.

GRADE LEVEL: Elementary

CONTENTS: Biology—chemistry—physics—the human body—planet Earth

1113 MINDEN, C. *How to write a biography*. 2012, Cherry Lake (ISBN: 9781610804912). 24 p.

SERIES: Language arts explorer junior

GRADE LEVEL: Elementary

CONTENTS: What a life!—write about anyone—what do you want to know—questions and answers—organize your information—presentation

1114 MINDEN, C. *How to write a book report*. 2011, Cherry Lake (ISBN: 9781602799929). 24 p.

SERIES: Language arts explorer junior

GRADE LEVEL: Elementary

CONTENTS: Parts of a book report—what do you think—nonfiction—writing your book report—editing

1115 MINDEN, C. *How to write a business letter*. 2012, Cherry Lake (ISBN: 9781610806671). 24 p.

SERIES: Language arts explorer junior

GRADE LEVEL: Elementary

CONTENTS: N/A

1116 MINDEN, C. *How to write a fairy tale*. 2012, Cherry Lake (ISBN: 9781610803090). 24 p.

SERIES: Language arts explorer junior

GRADE LEVEL: Elementary

CONTENTS: N/A

1117 MINDEN, C. *How to write a how-to*. 2012, Cherry Lake (ISBN: 9781610803175). 24 p.

SERIES: Language arts explorer junior

GRADE LEVEL: Elementary

CONTENTS: N/A

1118 MINDEN, C. *How to write a journal*. 2011, Cherry Lake (ISBN: 9781610802727). 24 p.

SERIES: Language arts explorer junior

GRADE LEVEL: Elementary

CONTENTS: About you—write about place—write about an event—write about your feelings—write about your opinion—write about your wishes and dreams—keep writing

1119 **MINDEN, C.** *How to write a letter*. 2011, Cherry Lake (ISBN: 9781610802734). 24 p.
SERIES: Language arts explorer junior
GRADE LEVEL: Elementary
CONTENTS: Friendly letter—greetings—read all about it—P.S. sign your name—the envelope—please—ready to mail

1120 **MINDEN, C.** *How to write a mystery*. 2012, Cherry Lake (ISBN: 9781610806626). 24 p.
SERIES: Language arts explorer junior
GRADE LEVEL: Elementary
CONTENTS: What's a whodunit—plot—clues—setting—solve it—case closed

1121 **MINDEN, C.** *How to write a news article*. 2012, Cherry Lake (ISBN: 9781610803182). 24 p.
SERIES: Language arts explorer junior
GRADE LEVEL: Elementary
CONTENTS: Read all about it!—get the facts—building your article—here's the story—making headlines—your own byline

1122 **MINDEN, C.** *How to write a play*. 2012, Cherry Lake (ISBN: 9781610804905). 24 p.
SERIES: Language arts explorer junior
GRADE LEVEL: Elementary
CONTENTS: N/A

1123 **MINDEN, C.** *How to write a poem*. 2011, Cherry Lake (ISBN: 9781610802741). 24 p.
SERIES: Language arts explorer junior
GRADE LEVEL: Elementary
CONTENTS: Poetry—rhymes—taking shape—making sense—poem on the side—poems that count

1124 **MINDEN, C.** *How to write a report*. 2012, Cherry Lake (ISBN: 9781610801058). 24 p.
SERIES: Language arts explorer junior
GRADE LEVEL: Elementary
CONTENTS: Sharing information—keep it simple—ready to research—the facts—final report—reread your writing

1125 **MINDEN, C.** *How to write a review*. 2012, Cherry Lake (ISBN: 9781610803205). 24 p.
SERIES: Language arts explorer junior
GRADE LEVEL: Elementary
CONTENTS: What do you think—what is it—does it work—how does it compare—do you like it—share your ideas

1126 **MINDEN, C.** *How to write a thank-you letter*. 2012, Cherry Lake (ISBN: 9781610804899). 24 p.

SERIES: Language arts explorer junior

GRADE LEVEL: Elementary

CONTENTS: N/A

1127 MINDEN, C. *How to write about your adventure*. 2012, Cherry Lake (ISBN: 9781610801065). 24 p.

SERIES: Language arts explorer junior

GRADE LEVEL: Elementary

CONTENTS: N/A

1128 MINDEN, C. *How to write an ad*. 2011, Cherry Lake (ISBN: 9781610802796). 24 p.

SERIES: Language arts explorer junior

GRADE LEVEL: Elementary

CONTENTS: Be persuasive—the way ads work—attention please—made you look—bringing everything together—final check

1129 MINDEN, C. *How to write an e-mail*. 2011, Cherry Lake (ISBN: 9781602799936). 24 p.

SERIES: Language arts explorer junior

GRADE LEVEL: Elementary

CONTENTS: You've got mail—from me to you—keep it friendly—extras—another thing—that was easy

1130 MINDEN, C. *How to write an essay*. 2012, Cherry Lake (ISBN: 9781610804929). 24 p.

SERIES: Language arts explorer junior

GRADE LEVEL: Elementary

CONTENTS: N/A

1131 MINDEN, C. *How to write an interview*. 2011, Cherry Lake (ISBN: 9781602799967). 24 p.

SERIES: Language arts explorer junior

GRADE LEVEL: Elementary

CONTENTS: N/A

1132 MINDEN, C. *How to write and give a speech*. 2012, Cherry Lake (ISBN: 9781610801089). 24 p.

SERIES: Language arts explorer junior

GRADE LEVEL: Elementary

CONTENTS: Speak about what you know—get their attention—the body of your speech—wrapping everything up—practice

1133 MINDEN, C. *Starting your own business*. 2009, Cherry Lake (ISBN: 9781602793132). 32 p.

SERIES: Real world math, personal finance

GRADE LEVEL: Upper elementary

CONTENTS: A great idea—writing a business plan—do the math—investors—marketing—managing a successful business

1134 MITCHEM, J. *The big book of things to make*. 2013, DK (ISBN: 9781465402554).
GRADE LEVEL: Elementary
CONTENTS: Sink 'em ships—urban periscope—balloon drag racer—paper planes—recycled robots—alien masks—secret book safe—monster mirror—knight puppet—musical instruments—milk planets—pizza dough—pizza party—cookies—milk shake mayhem—glow-in-the-dark Jello—erupting volcano—soap monsters—soda fountain—make your own slime—launch a bottle rocket—pinhole camera—cactus garden—fingerprint doodles—miniature golf—trick your taste buds—make a board game—become a detective—magic tricks—balloon shapes—balloon dog—juggling—super spy gear—prank patrol—spot the difference—flipbook animation—write a scary story—unusual ball games—let's have a water fight—outdoor games—making camp—playing pirates—Olympics outdoors—throw a party—a world of robots—prehistoric trivia—castles and forts—survive in the wilderness—spotting snakes—animal quiz—cook up a storm—play like a pro—cowboy capers—that's impossible—explore the Seven Wonders of the Ancient World

1135 MOFFORD, J. *Recipe and craft guide to Japan*. 2011, Mitchell Lane (ISBN: 9781584159339). 63 p.
SERIES: World crafts and recipes
GRADE LEVEL: Upper elementary – middle school
CONTENTS: N/A

1136 MOFFORD, J. *Recipe and craft guide to the Caribbean*. 2011, Mitchell Lane (ISBN: 9781584159353). 64 p.
SERIES: World crafts and recipes
GRADE LEVEL: Upper elementary – middle school
CONTENTS: Tropical fruit salad—coconut rice—calabash bowl—callaloo—treasure chest—griot—seed beads—arroz con pollo—trembleque—Christmas pudding—maracas—guiro—steel drums—gingerbread with lemon sauce—spice bag – carnival mask—stamp and go—fritters—mobile—flying fish—Valentines—mosaics—banana bread—Jolly Roger—jerk chicken—tropical flowers—curried lamb

1137 MONAGHAN, K. *Organic crafts: 75 Earth-friendly art activities*. 2007, Chicago Review Press (ISBN: 9781556526404).
GRADE LEVEL: Lower elementary
CONTENTS: N/A

1138 MONTANO, M. *CosmoGirl! Cool Room: 35 make-it-yourself projects*. 2009, Hearst Books (ISBN: 9781588167422).
GRADE LEVEL: Middle school – high school
CONTENTS: N/A

1139 MONTGOMERIE, C. *Knitting for children: 35 simple knits kids will love to make*. 2010, Cico Books (ISBN: 9781907563218). 128 p.
GRADE LEVEL: Elementary
CONTENTS: N/A

1140 MOONEY, C. *Amazing Africa projects you can build yourself*. 2010, Nomad Press (ISBN: 9781934670415). 128 p.
SERIES: Build it yourself

GRADE LEVEL: Upper elementary – middle school

CONTENTS: Rainforest vine—golden amulet—African savanna—leopard mask—Adinkra stamping—hunters—horned staff—antelope mask—mud painting—rock paintings—beaded necklace—house painting—family compound—banana fritters—basket—mancala game—soccer ball—strip weaving—beaded bracelet—African drum—rain stick—initiation shield—mask—fable—story banner

1141 **MOONEY, C.** *Explore rivers and ponds! With 25 great projects*. 2012, Nomad Press (ISBN: 9781451773897). 96 p.

SERIES: Explore your world

GRADE LEVEL: Upper elementary

CONTENTS: Food chain game—freshwater—water cycle experiment—dipping net—ecologist's field kit—a puddle—pond life—tadpoles become frogs—fishless aquarium—bug card—name the bug—freshwater scientist—bark rubbing—water layers—river rocks—stream speed—animal track molds—wetland—erosion—wetlands absorbing water—cattails—dripping faucet—clean water naturally—freshwater species—watershed replica

1142 **MOONEY, C.** *Explorers of the new world: discover the golden age of exploration with 22 projects*. 2011, Nomad Press (ISBN: 9781936313433). 128 p.

SERIES: Build it yourself

GRADE LEVEL: Upper elementary – middle school

CONTENTS: Cross staff—spice mixes—log book—clay padraos—compass—latitude and longitude—quadrant—mapquest—sailor's dice game—ocean in a bottle—sand hourglass—sea biscuits—sailor's lanyard—papier-mâché globe—coconut milk—Spanish galleon—balsa raft—sailor's knot—Aztec art—corn bread—dream catcher—felt beaver hat

1143 **MOONEY, C.** *Forensics: uncover the science and technology of crime investigation*. 2013, Nomad Press (ISBN: 9781619301887). 128 p.

SERIES: Inquire and investigate

GRADE LEVEL: Middle school – high school

CONTENTS: Crime scene—eyewitness—fingerprint patterns—lifting fingerprints—match the print—lifting prints – chemical method—blood or not—blood splatter—bones to predict height—extract DNA—match the bite mark—shoe print—tire tracks—tools—footprint clues—refraction—analyzing soil—fiber burn analysis—mystery powder—chemical analysis flame test—find the density of glass—study hairs—ink chromatography—find the forgery—handwriting analysis

1144 **MOONEY, C.** *Genetics: breaking the code of your DNA*. 2014, Nomad Press (ISBN: 9781619302082). 128 p.

SERIES: Inquire and investigate

GRADE LEVEL: Middle school – high school

CONTENTS: N/A

1145 **MOONEY, C.** *George Washington: 25 great projects you can build yourself*. 2010, Nomad Press (ISBN: 9781934670637). 128 p.

SERIES: Build it yourself

GRADE LEVEL: Upper elementary – middle school

CONTENTS: Silver plate—cup & ball—hornbook—book of manners—compass—quill pen—surveyor's map—George Washington sword—spyglass—George Washington hat—pomander—weather vane—colonial apron—hoecakes—revolutionary soldiers—battle map—cipher wheel—invisible ink—purple heart medal—letter seal—wig—colonial flag—silhouette art—clay bust—Washington monument

1146 MOONEY, C. *Get all tied up: tying knots*. 2010, Norwood House (ISBN: 9781599533841). 48 p.

SERIES: Creative adventure guides

GRADE LEVEL: Elementary

CONTENTS: The right knot for the job—learning knots: ten knots to tie—putting it together—building with knots

1147 MOONEY, C. *The Industrial Revolution: investigate how technology changed the world with 25 projects*. 2011, Nomad Press (ISBN: 9781936313808). 128 p.

SERIES: Build it yourself

GRADE LEVEL: Upper elementary – middle school

CONTENTS: Knitting spool—hand loom—soap—water-powered wheel—cotton—assembly car—inventor—picket sign—working song—today's workplace—paddlewheel steamship—canal lock—origami steamship—electronic telegraph—Morse code message—tin can telephones—lightbulb—homemade battery—electromagnet—zoetrope—flipbook—pinhole camera—radio program—new industrial revolution—balloon-powered car

1148 MOONEY, C. *Light your way: make a candle*. 2011, Norwood House (ISBN: 9781599533872). 48 p.

SERIES: Creative adventure guides

GRADE LEVEL: Elementary

CONTENTS: Lighting—how it works—beeswax candle—milk carton candle

1149 MOONEY, C. *Starting a business: have fun and make money*. 2011, Norwood House Press (ISBN: 9781599533865). 48 p.

SERIES: Creative adventure guides

GRADE LEVEL: Elementary

CONTENTS: Getting started: your idea—business basics—writing your business plan

1150 MOORE, W. *All about Japan*. 2011, Tuttle (ISBN: 9784805310779). 64 p.

GRADE LEVEL: Lower elementary

CONTENTS: N/A

1151 MORRIS, N. *Knights*. 2008, Franklin Watts (ISBN: 9780749678517). 32 p.

SERIES: Making history

GRADE LEVEL: Elementary

CONTENTS: N/A

1152 MORRIS, T. *Arts and crafts of ancient China*. 2007, Mitchell Lane (ISBN: 9781583409145). 32 p.

SERIES: Arts and crafts of the ancient world

GRADE LEVEL: Elementary

CONTENTS: Monster face—lantern—kite—lacquered bowl

1153 MORRIS, T. *Arts and crafts of ancient Egypt*. 2007, Smart Apple Media (ISBN: 9781583409114). 32 p.

SERIES: Arts and crafts of the ancient world

GRADE LEVEL: Elementary

CONTENTS: Paint a temple wall—amulet—mummy case—hieroglyphics—scarab seal

1154 MORRIS, T. *Arts and crafts of ancient Greece*. 2007, Smart Apple Media (ISBN: 9781583409121). 32 p.

SERIES: Arts and crafts of the ancient world

GRADE LEVEL: Elementary

CONTENTS: Paint a mural—amphora—actor's mask—scroll

1155 MORRIS, T. *Arts and crafts of ancient Rome*. 2007, Smart Apple Media (ISBN: 9781583409138). 32 p.

SERIES: Arts and crafts of the ancient world

GRADE LEVEL: Elementary

CONTENTS: Relief—mosaic—Roman vase—jewelry

1156 MORRIS, T. *Arts and crafts of the Aztecs and Maya*. 2007, Smart Apple Media (ISBN: 9781583409152). 32 p.

SERIES: Arts and crafts of the ancient world

GRADE LEVEL: Elementary

CONTENTS: Ball game—mosaic mask—paper cutout—feather headdress

1157 MORRIS, T. *Arts and crafts of the Native Americans*. 2007, Smart Apple Media (ISBN: 9781583409169). 32 p.

SERIES: Arts and crafts of the ancient world

GRADE LEVEL: Elementary

CONTENTS: Kachina doll—feather headdress—totem pole—false-face mask

1158 MOSS, S. *The bumper book of nature: a user's guide to the outdoors*. 2010, Harmony (ISBN: 9780307589996). 272 p.

GRADE LEVEL: Elementary

CONTENTS: N/A

1159 MUEHLENHARDT, A. *Thanksgiving crafts*. 2011, Picture Window Books (ISBN: 9781404862821). 24 p.

SERIES: Thanksgiving

GRADE LEVEL: Elementary

CONTENTS: Indian corn sculpture—pilgrim hats—Thanksgiving placemats—turkey snack cups—thankful family—turkey pop-up card—fall wreath—seed mosaic—turkey tambourine

1160 MUELLER, P. *Learn to draw pets: learn to draw and color 23 favorite animals, step by easy step, shape by simple shape!* 2011, Walter Foster (ISBN: 9781936309177). 40 p.

SERIES: Learn to draw
GRADE LEVEL: Upper elementary – middle school
CONTENTS: N/A

1161 MULLINS, M. *Junior scientists: experiment with liquids*. 2011, Cherry Lake (ISBN: 9781602798465). 32 p.
SERIES: Science explorer junior
GRADE LEVEL: Lower elementary
CONTENTS: Changes—density and weight—drops

1162 MULLINS, M. *Super cool science experiments: cells*. 2010, Cherry Lake (ISBN: 9781602795174). 32 p.
SERIES: Science explorer
GRADE LEVEL: Elementary
CONTENTS: Cells—first things first—cells are small—not huge—in and out-part one—in and out-part two—replace—do it yourself

1163 MULLINS, M. *Super cool science experiments: ecosystems*. 2010, Cherry Lake (ISBN: 9781602795167). 32 p.
SERIES: Science explorer
GRADE LEVEL: Elementary
CONTENTS: Community—first things first—borders—the temperature—preventing erosion—pollution—do it yourself

1164 MULLINS, M. *Super cool science experiments: planet Earth*. 2010, Cherry Lake (ISBN: 9781602795150). 32 p.
SERIES: Science explorer
GRADE LEVEL: Elementary
CONTENTS: House—first things first—sphere—earth—water—changes to Earth—atmosphere—do it yourself

1165 MULLINS, M. *Super cool science experiments: states of matter*. 2010, Cherry Lake (ISBN: 9781602795358). 32 p.
SERIES: Science explorer
GRADE LEVEL: Elementary
CONTENTS: Matter—first things first—matter bonds—solids—liquids—gases—density and weight—do it yourself

1166 MUSSARI, M. *Poetry*. 2012, Marshall Cavendish (ISBN: 9781608705009). 95 p.
SERIES: Craft of writing
GRADE LEVEL: Middle school
CONTENTS: Types of poetry—techniques—from first idea to finish—anyone can write

1167 NASH, M. *How to draw the coolest, most creative tattoo art*. 2012, Capstone (ISBN: 9781429675390). 48 p.
SERIES: Velocity
GRADE LEVEL: Middle school – high school
CONTENTS: Skull ribbon—American Indian eagle—Chinese dragon—Celtic dragon head—terrifying turtle—fire-breathing dragon—Egyptian tattoo—Chinese fish—

shark attack—monster wave—Celtic dragon—snake and skull—butterfly—Celtic wolf—Japanese fish—steam-punk robotic arm—mermaid—Aztec tattoo—flaming skull—angry tiger—sinister skull

1168 NASH, M. *How to draw the meanest, most terrifying monsters*. 2012, Capstone (ISBN: 9781429675383). 48 p.

SERIES: Velocity

GRADE LEVEL: Middle school – high school

CONTENTS: Gargoyle—swamp beast—gruesome gorgon—banshee—Arachne—centaur—evil octopus—minotaur—alien slug—monster dragon—rapmaging reptilian—raging warrior—scorpio—snakasaur—boggit—troglodyte—Frankenstein's monster—bloodthirsty bird—wraith—harpy—Cerberus

1169 NAVARRA, N. *How to draw Teenage Mutant Ninja Turtles: learn to draw Leonardo, Raphael, Donatello, and Michelangelo step by step!* 2013, Walter Foster (ISBN: 9781600582967). 32 p.

SERIES: Learn to draw

GRADE LEVEL: Upper elementary – middle school

CONTENTS: Leonardo—Leonardo in action—Raphael—Raphael in action—Michelangelo—Michelangelo in action—Donatello—Donatello in action—Splinter—Shredder—Kraang—April O'Neil—Foot Clan

1170 NICHOLSON, N. *Start to applique*. 2008, Search Press (ISBN: 9781844482610). 64 p.

SERIES: Start to

GRADE LEVEL: Upper elementary – middle school

CONTENTS: Brilliant brooch—skirt trim—perfect picture—beady bird—throw cushion—pretty pocket—felt bag

1171 NICHOLSON, N. *Start to patchwork*. 2009, Search Press (ISBN: 9781844482641). 48 p.

SERIES: Start to

GRADE LEVEL: Upper elementary – middle school

CONTENTS: Pet's quilt—pin cushion—belt—patchwork pillow—heart decoration—bird—zigzag bag

1172 NISHIDA, M. *Drawing manga animals*. 2008, PowerKids Press (ISBN: 9781404238466). 24 p.

SERIES: How to draw manga

GRADE LEVEL: Elementary

CONTENTS: Cat—dog—mouse—horse—marlin—rabbit—tiger—lion

1173 NISHIDA, M. *Drawing manga dinosaurs*. 2008, PowerKids Press (ISBN: 9781404238459). 24 p.

SERIES: How to draw manga

GRADE LEVEL: Elementary

CONTENTS: Tyrannosaur—Velociraptor—Oviraptor—Diplodocus—Stegasaurus—Triceratops—Pterosaur—Elamosaurus

1174 NISHIDA, M. *Drawing manga insects*. 2008, PowerKids Press (ISBN: 9781404238473). 24 p.

SERIES: How to draw manga

GRADE LEVEL: Elementary

CONTENTS: Ant—butterfly—caterpillar—scorpion—ladybug—spider—dragonfly—
bumblebee

1175 NISHIDA, M. *Drawing manga martial arts figures*. 2008, PowerKids Press (ISBN:
9781404238503). 24 p.

SERIES: How to draw manga

GRADE LEVEL: Elementary

CONTENTS: Aikido figure—jujitsu figure—judo figure—karate figure—kung fu figure—tae
kwon do figure—tai chi figure—hapkido figure

1176 NISHIDA, M. *Drawing manga Medieval castles and knights*. 2008, PowerKids Press
(ISBN: 9781404238497). 24 p.

SERIES: How to draw manga

GRADE LEVEL: Elementary

CONTENTS: Castle exterior—armored knight—armor—jousting knight—a castle under
attack—princess—Medieval women's clothing—Medieval jester

1177 NISHIDA, M. *Drawing manga vehicles*. 2008, PowerKids Press (ISBN:
9781404238480). 24 p.

SERIES: How to draw manga

GRADE LEVEL: Elementary

CONTENTS: Fighter plane—bicycle—bullet train—fire engine—helicopter—monster
truck—motorboat—sports car

1178 NITTA, H. *The manga guide to physics*. 2010, No Starch Press (ISBN:
9781593271961). 272 p.

SERIES: EduManga

GRADE LEVEL: High school

CONTENTS: N/A

1179 NIVEN, F. *Nifty thrifty music crafts*. 2008, Enslow (ISBN: 9780766027848). 32 p.

SERIES: Nifty thrifty crafts for kids

GRADE LEVEL: Elementary

CONTENTS: Xylophone—rhythm blocks—panpipes—finger cymbals—colonial drum—
American Indian clapper—tambourine—rain stick—maracas—ukulele

1180 OAKES, L. *Hands-on history! Mesopotamia: all about ancient Assyria and
Babylonia, with 15 step-by-step projects and more than 300 exciting pictures*.
2013, Armadillo (ISBN: 9781843229704). 64 p.

SERIES: Hands-on history!

GRADE LEVEL: Upper elementary

CONTENTS: N/A

1181 OLDHAM, T. *All about collage*. 2012, Ammo Books (ISBN: 9781934429891). 32 p.

SERIES: Kids made modern

GRADE LEVEL: Elementary

CONTENTS: Post card—decoupage—paper—paper pattern—collage—guitar—family portraits—boom deck—iron-on graffiti—tissue paper planets

1182 OLDHAM, T. *All about dye*. 2012, Ammo Books (ISBN: 9781934429907). 32 p.

SERIES: Kids made modern

GRADE LEVEL: Elementary

CONTENTS: Snow cone dip dye—fold up button down—fan fold frenzy—dry dye diffusion—mix effect remix—freeze style—ice sheets—swimming pool stripes—old school wrap—technicolor dream tote

1183 OLDHAM, T. *All about embroidery*. 2012, Ammo Books (ISBN: 9781934429914). 32 p.

SERIES: Kids made modern

GRADE LEVEL: Elementary

CONTENTS: Web address—you're a star—embroider-bee—embroidery invasion—night owl—plaid—sweater mash-up—spider spun stitch—pegboard

1184 OLDHAM, T. *All about fabric painting*. 2012, Ammo Books (ISBN: 9781934429921). 32 p.

SERIES: Kids made modern

GRADE LEVEL: Elementary

CONTENTS: Happy stamper—shoestring theory—pattern over print—word-up button down—hot potato—sweater press—kitchen sink zip-up—hands on printing—felt prints—masking tape mosaic

1185 OLIVER, M. *The how-to handbook: shortcuts and solutions for the problems of everyday life*. 2013, Zest Books (ISBN: 9781936976348).

GRADE LEVEL: High school

CONTENTS: Address an audience—avoid motion sickness—banish hiccups—be safe in a city—catch a spider—live a hacker-free life online—look after a plant—manage your money—pack a suitcase—prepare for a test—remove a ring—take great photos—wrap a gift—write a thank-you note—looking and smelling better: brush better—get a good night's sleep—iron a pair of pants—pop a pimple—prevent shoe odor—shine your shoes—tie a bowtie—tie a tie—wash your hands like a surgeon—get to know your kitchen: eat a balanced meal—kitchen essentials—set a table—unjam a jar—load the dishwasher—peel potatoes—chop garlic—chop an onion—crack an egg—cook superlative pasta—create an omelet—make your own trail mix—make a smoothie—prepare perfect pancakes—serve transcendent tea—clean up like a pro: clean windows—clean your room in five minutes—do the laundry—fold a fitted sheet—put on a duvet cover—put your clothes away—rake the leaves—remove a stain—unstick chewing gum—wash a car—do it yourself: fix a flat—inflate your bike tires—mend a seam—pitch a tent—sew on a button—test a smoke alarm—thread a needle—tie a bowline—tie a reef knot—tighten a screw—emergency skills 101: deal with muscle cramps—dress a cut—extract a splinter—help a choking victim—stop a nosebleed—take a pulse—treat a bee sting—treat a burn

1186 OLSON, K. *Beginning knitting: stitches with style*. 2007, Capstone (ISBN: 9780736864732). 32 p.

SERIES: Crafts

GRADE LEVEL: Elementary

CONTENTS: N/A

1187 O'NEAL, C. *Exploring Earth's biomes*. 2010, Mitchell Lane (ISBN: 9781584158783). 48 p.

SERIES: Life science projects for kids

GRADE LEVEL: Upper elementary

CONTENTS: N/A

1188 O'NEAL, C. *A project guide to earthquakes*. 2010, Mitchell Lane (ISBN: 9781584158707). 48 p.

SERIES: Earth science projects for kids

GRADE LEVEL: Upper elementary – middle school

CONTENTS: N/A

1189 O'NEAL, C. *A project guide to volcanoes*. 2011, Mitchell Lane (ISBN: 9781584158684). 48 p.

SERIES: Earth science projects for kids

GRADE LEVEL: Upper elementary – middle school

CONTENTS: Volcanoes—Paricutin—cinder cone—Kilauea—shelf volcano—Mt. Krispies—stratovolcano—hot spots—eruption—lava viscosity and flow—lava bombs—volcanic ash—big effects—fudge—geothermal power—measuring eruptions

1190 O'NEAL, C. *Projects in genetics*. 2010, Mitchell Lane (ISBN: 9781584158776). 48 p.

SERIES: Life science projects for kids

GRADE LEVEL: Upper elementary

CONTENTS: N/A

1191 ORR, T. *Junior scientists: experiment with weather*. 2011, Cherry Lake (ISBN: 9781602798410). 32 p.

SERIES: Science explorer junior

GRADE LEVEL: Lower elementary

CONTENTS: Breeze—rain—nasty weather

1192 ORR, T. *A kid's guide to earning money*. 2009, Mitchell Lane (ISBN: 9781584156437). 48 p.

SERIES: Money matters: a kid's guide to money

GRADE LEVEL: Upper elementary

CONTENTS: To work or not to work—the work for work begins—why wait—legal matters

1193 ORR, T. *Super cool science experiments: circulation*. 2010, Cherry Lake (ISBN: 9781602795204). 32 p.

SERIES: Science explorer

GRADE LEVEL: Elementary

CONTENTS: Muscle—beat—a trip—trouble—tricks—do it yourself

1194 ORR, T. *Super cool science experiments: digestion.* 2010, Cherry Lake (ISBN: 9781602795181). 32 p.

SERIES: Science explorer

GRADE LEVEL: Elementary

CONTENTS: Chew—first things first—open—down it goes—mixer—a digestion—journey's end—do it yourself

1195 ORR, T. *Super cool science experiments: respiration.* 2010, Cherry Lake (ISBN: 9781602795198). 32 p.

SERIES: Science explorer

GRADE LEVEL: Elementary

CONTENTS: Breathe—first things first—nose—windpipe—bronchi—lungs—muscles—do it yourself

1196 ORR, T. *Super cool science experiments: weather.* 2010, Cherry Lake (ISBN: 9781602795280). 32 p.

SERIES: Science explorer

GRADE LEVEL: Elementary

CONTENTS: No lab coat—first things first—breeze—rain—under pressure—nasty weather—do it yourself

1197 O'SHEI, T. *How to survive in the wilderness.* 2009, Capstone (ISBN: 9781429622813). 32 p.

SERIES: Prepare to survive

GRADE LEVEL: Elementary

CONTENTS: Shelter—fire—water—food—crossing water—toilet—rescue signals—navigation—wash clothes—escape a bear—escape a cougar—treat a snake bite

1198 O'SHEI, T. *How to survive on a deserted island.* 2009, Capstone (ISBN: 9781429622820). 32 p.

SERIES: Prepare to survive

GRADE LEVEL: Elementary

CONTENTS: N/A

1199 OWEN, R. *Christmas and Hanukkah origami.* 2013, Rosen (ISBN: 9781448878604). 32 p.

SERIES: Holiday origami

GRADE LEVEL: Elementary

CONTENTS: N/A

1200 OWEN, R. *Easter origami.* 2013, Rosen (ISBN: 9781448878611). 32 p.

SERIES: Holiday origami

GRADE LEVEL: Elementary

CONTENTS: Origami in action—folding—Easter egg—Easter chick—Easter egg stand—Easter bunny—mini baskets—tulips

1201 OWEN, R. *Easter sweets and treats.* 2013, Windmill Books (ISBN: 9781448880843). 32 p.

SERIES: Holiday cooking for kids

GRADE LEVEL: Upper elementary

CONTENTS: Brunch eggs—bunny cookies—carrot cake—nest cupcakes—Easter eggs—deviled eggs

1202 OWEN, R. *Halloween origami*. 2013, Rosen (ISBN: 9781448878628). 32 p.
SERIES: Holiday origami
GRADE LEVEL: Elementary
CONTENTS: Jack o' lanterns—Halloween claws—witchcraft—witch's cat—bats

1203 OWEN, R. *Halloween sweets and treats*. 2013, Windmill Books (ISBN: 9781448880799). 32 p.
SERIES: Holiday cooking for kids
GRADE LEVEL: Upper elementary
CONTENTS: Monster caramel apples—roasted jack-o'-lantern pumpkin seeds—Halloween cookies—witch's fingers—pumpkin soup—eyeball cupcakes—black bean and corn dip

1204 OWEN, R. *Independence Day origami*. 2013, Rosen (ISBN: 9781448878635). 32 p.
SERIES: Holiday origami
GRADE LEVEL: Elementary
CONTENTS: N/A

1205 OWEN, R. *Science and craft projects with insects, spiders, and other minibeasts*. 2013, PowerKids Press (ISBN: 9781477702451). 32 p.
SERIES: Get crafty outdoors
GRADE LEVEL: Elementary
CONTENTS: Minibeasts—ladybugs—dominoes—butterflies—make a butterfly—butterfly babies—caterpillar sculpture—spider webs—catch a spider's web—garden snail—race track—earthworms—worm farm

1206 OWEN, R. *Science and craft projects with plants and seeds*. 2013, PowerKids Press (ISBN: 9781477702475). 32 p.
SERIES: Get crafty outdoors
GRADE LEVEL: Elementary
CONTENTS: Plants—plant parts—pressed flowers—seeds—clips—sunflower—new plant—mosaics—a good place to grow—picture—food from plants—t-shirt

1207 OWEN, R. *Science and craft projects with rocks and soil*. 2013, PowerKids Press (ISBN: 9781477702468). 32 p.
SERIES: Get crafty outdoors
GRADE LEVEL: Elementary
CONTENTS: Rocky planet—igneous rocks—rock sculpture—sediment—sand—paperweights—sedimentary rocks—pebble pictures—metamorphic rocks—display case—minerals—crystals—fossils—make a fossil

1208 OWEN, R. *Science and craft projects with trees and leaves*. 2013, PowerKids Press (ISBN: 9781477702482). 32 p.
SERIES: Get crafty outdoors
GRADE LEVEL: Elementary

CONTENTS: Trees—trunks—twigs—tree parts—bark castings—plants can cook—raft—fall leaves—wreath—evergreen trees—snowy evergreen trees—tree house—mask—forests—collage

1209 OWEN, R. *Science and craft projects with weather*. 2013, PowerKids Press (ISBN: 9781477702444). 32 p.

SERIES: Get crafty outdoors

GRADE LEVEL: Elementary

CONTENTS: Weather watching—weather—sun catcher—water cycle—friendship bracelets—wet weather—collage—snowy weather—snowflakes—hailstone—garden stones—thunder and lightning—weather wheel

1210 OWEN, R. *Science and craft projects with wildlife*. 2013, PowerKids Press (ISBN: 9781477702437). 32 p.

SERIES: Get crafty outdoors

GRADE LEVEL: Elementary

CONTENTS: Neighbors—birds—nests—trees—bird's nest—raccoons—mask—tadpoles to frogs—collage—bird feeder—storing food for winter—storage jars—tracking wildlife—animal track models

1211 OWEN, R. *Thanksgiving origami*. 2013, Rosen (ISBN: 9781448878642). 32 p.

SERIES: Holiday origami

GRADE LEVEL: Elementary

CONTENTS: Origami in action—folding—pilgrim—turkey—pumpkins—ears of corn—apple harvest—autumn leaves

1212 OWEN, R. *Valentine's Day origami*. 2013, Rosen (ISBN: 9781448878659). 32 p.

SERIES: Holiday origami

GRADE LEVEL: Elementary

CONTENTS: Two color hearts—I love you message—red rose greeting—swan heart boat—friendship bracelets

1213 OXLADE, C. *Cricket*. 2010, Franklin Watts (ISBN: 9781445101361). 30 p.

SERIES: Know your sport

GRADE LEVEL: Upper elementary

CONTENTS: N/A

1214 OXLADE, C. *Simple experiments with inclined planes*. 2014, Windmill Books (ISBN: 9781615337521). 32 p.

SERIES: Science experiments with simple machines

GRADE LEVEL: Upper elementary

CONTENTS: Simple machines—inclined plane—ramps—lifting—steep or shallow?—steep and shallow inclined planes—going down—steep and shallow—inclined planes in the past—transport—more transport planes—zig-zags

1215 OXLADE, C. *Simple experiments with pulleys*. 2014, Windmill Books (ISBN: 9781615337514). 32 p.

SERIES: Science experiments with simple machines

GRADE LEVEL: Upper elementary

CONTENTS: Simple machines—pulley parts—pulleys—lifting—bigger forces—
compound pulleys—pulleys afloat—pulley system—pulleys in the past—pulley
belts—changing forces—bicycle pulleys

1216 OXLADE, C. *Simple experiments with wheels and axles*. 2014, Windmill Books
(ISBN: 9781615337545). 32 p.

SERIES: Science experiments with simple machines

GRADE LEVEL: Upper elementary

CONTENTS: Simple machines—wheel and axle—rolling on wheels—dragging and
rolling—wheels—axles—and forces—gear wheels—and gears at work—wheel
and axle system—inventing the wheel—wheels and axles in the past—rolling and
slowing—rough and smooth—amazing machines

1217 PALIKA, L. *Dog obedience: getting your pooch off the couch and other dog training
tips*. 2012, Capstone (ISBN: 9781429665254).

SERIES: Dog ownership

GRADE LEVEL: Elementary

CONTENTS: Easy—give—sit—all done—down—stay—come—wait—leave it—walk—
heel—stand—off

1218 PALIKA, L. *Dog tricks: teaching your doggie to shake hands and other tricks*. 2012,
Capstone (ISBN: 9781429665261).

SERIES: Dog ownership

GRADE LEVEL: Elementary

CONTENTS: Shake hands—high five—crawl—the weave—roll over—go to sleep—spin—
take a bow!—jump—teaching your dog to read—wait for it—yes—please

1219 PANCHYK, R. *Charting the world: geography and maps from cave paintings to
GPS with 21 activities*. 2011, Chicago Review Press (ISBN: 9781569763445). 144 p.

SERIES: For kids

GRADE LEVEL: Middle school

CONTENTS: Elevation—four-color challenge—navigation game—reading maps—
population density—map experiment—draw a map to scale—contour map come
to life—engrave a map—geographical profile—be a surveyor—place name origins—
altering the environment—zoning map—nautical chart—photo-auto map—state
shapes—war strategy game—treasure search—satellite photo to street map—moon
observation

1220 PANCHYK, R. *New York City history for kids: from New Amsterdam to the Big
Apple with 21 activities*. 2012, Chicago Review Press (ISBN: 9781883052935). 144 p.

SERIES: For kids

GRADE LEVEL: Middle school

CONTENTS: Samp porridge—replica fort—Fort George—Dutch fireplace tile—backyard
archeology—landfill game—mock trial—liberty pole—park walking tour—
neighborhood walking tour—Randal plan game—be a journalist—political cartoon—
Fifth Avenue walking tour—your ancestors—Broadway show—then and now
game—Gibson girl—be a songwriter—stickball—skyscraper walking tour—bagels

1221 PARENT, N. *Learn to draw Disney/Pixar Finding Nemo: draw your favorite
characters, step by simple step*. 2012, Walter Foster (ISBN: 9781936309344). 31 p.

SERIES: Learn to draw

GRADE LEVEL: Upper elementary – middle school

CONTENTS: N/A

1222 **PARKS, P.** *How to improve at golf*. 2008, Crabtree (ISBN: 9780778735670). 48 p.

SERIES: How to improve at

GRADE LEVEL: Elementary

CONTENTS: Know the game—basics—swings and shots—advice from the pros—rules and scoring

1223 **PARRATORE, P.** *101 hands-on experiments*. 2008, Prufrock Press (ISBN: 9781593633172). 136 p.

GRADE LEVEL: Upper elementary – middle school

CONTENTS: Candle—peel—pop du-wops—ashes to ashes—banana—fanna' foe—cup—light—balancing candles—pie—money—fountains—oxygen—chalk—haunted bottle—popcorn—secret message—ol'rusty—moth balls—volcano—smoke rings—breath—have a ball—ice cube—an action reaction—dueling balloons—indy 500—water—air balloon—attraction—jet engine balloon—space shuttle—fly-wheel—but it won't fill up—fly away—hutt 'n'puff—without spilling a drop—ding-dong diver—waterworks—genie—the clean machine—blast off—fountain—no joking matter—water—cool it—bouncing ball—sweaty palms—how big is water?—mothball frost—plop—a cut above—collapsing bottle—polar bear—the iceberg—dew process—sweetie pie—snowflakes—gobbully-gukk—rainbow bright—colors—seeing red—color creations—black—rainbow—color disk—crystal garden—acids and bases—celery stalker—math . . . for trees—orange you glad—popcorn push-ups—sour apple juice—water lilies—you're all wet—gimme' some air—pinecone pixies—don't cry for these cells—down they go—I'm crackin' up—chlorophyll—heads or tails?—noisy bugs—spider tension—eyes—candy bugs—flies—spider art—snails—worms move in—worms move out—ants—butter beaters—potato power—brown cow—battery—invisible ink—marshmallow glacier—egg power—instant mousse—ice cream—yeast beasts

1224 **PATCHETT, F.** *Children's book of baking*. 2007, EDC (ISBN: 9780794514389). 95 p.

GRADE LEVEL: Upper elementary

CONTENTS: N/A

1225 **PAWLETT, M.** *The tae kwon do handbook*. 2008, Rosen (ISBN: 9781404213968). 256 p.

SERIES: Martial arts

GRADE LEVEL: Middle school – high school

CONTENTS: Fitness for tae kwon do—stepping and stances—techniques—poomsae—kyorugi or sparring

1226 **PAWLETT, R.** *The karate handbook*. 2008, Rosen (ISBN: 9781404213944). 256 p.

SERIES: Martial arts

GRADE LEVEL: Middle school – high school

CONTENTS: Fitness for karate—stances and stepping—basic techniques—kata—sparring

1227 **PAWLETT, R.** *The tai chi handbook*. 2010, Rosen (ISBN: 9781435853607). 246 p.

SERIES: A young woman's guide to health and well-being

GRADE LEVEL: Middle school – high school

CONTENTS: Tai chi practice: getting started—the essence of tai chi—tai chi styles—martial applications

1228 PEOT, M. *Inkblot: drip, splat, and squish your way to creativity*. 2011, Boyds Mills (ISBN: 9781590787205). 56 p.

GRADE LEVEL: Elementary

CONTENTS: Inkblots—drawing into inkblots—how to look—how to see—the inkblot sketchbook—the final fold

1229 PETERS, R. *Midnight feast magic: sleepover fun and food*. 2009, Frances Lincoln (ISBN: 9781845077839).

GRADE LEVEL: Elementary

CONTENTS: Drinks—dips—snacks—suppers—cupboard's bare—treats—freezy frenzy

1230 PETERSEN, C. *A project guide to Earth's waters*. 2010, Mitchell Lane (ISBN: 9781584158714). 48 p.

SERIES: Earth science projects for kids

GRADE LEVEL: Upper elementary – middle school

CONTENTS: N/A

1231 PETERSEN, C. *A project guide to mammals*. 2011, Mitchell Lane (ISBN: 9781584158752). 48 p.

SERIES: Life science projects for kids

GRADE LEVEL: Upper elementary

CONTENTS: N/A

1232 PETERSON, J. *Fishing in lakes and ponds*. 2012, Rosen Central (ISBN: 9781448845972). 62 p.

SERIES: Fishing tips and techniques

GRADE LEVEL: Upper elementary

CONTENTS: N/A

1233 PETERSON, M. *How to build hair-raising haunted houses*. 2011, Capstone (ISBN: 9781429654210). 32 p.

SERIES: Halloween extreme

GRADE LEVEL: Upper elementary

CONTENTS: Lawn of the dead—man in the window—Dracula's coffin—hairy hallway—dying room—faces in the fog—witch's kitchen—zombieland

1234 PETRILLO, V. *A kid's guide to Asian American history: more than 70 activities*. 2007, Chicago Review Press (ISBN: 9781556526343). 256 p.

SERIES: A kid's guide

GRADE LEVEL: Upper elementary – middle school

CONTENTS: Immigrant trunk—folding fan—bubble tea—tiger hat—evil spirit apron—opera face painting—shoulder yoke—Chinese characters—Mandarin—brush painting—lacquer box—paper cutting—feng shui—nian gao—jiaozi—lai see—sweet tray—lion—gong—calligraphy banner—dragon lantern—moon festival picnic—shadow puppet show—double happiness signature cloth—tai chi—dragon's tail—

abacus—use an abacus—ribbon dance—bento lunch—beanbag game—Daruma doll—miso soup—furoshiki—rice balls—say it in Japanese—origami dog and cat—haiku—taiko drumming—Japanese fish printing—kabuki face painting—kadomatsu—Bon Odori dance—carp streamer—Japanese tea ceremony—rock garden—Japanese cut flower arrangement—jan—ken—pon—milk-cap game—say it in Korean—Korean flag—arrow throwing—tassel kicking—a fortune-telling birthday party—tae kwon do front kick—Korean wrapping cloths—ttok-kuk soup—good luck bag—yet: a game played with sticks—Korean kite—Filipino shell crafts—say it in Filipino—halo-halo—tumbang preso—sungka—balikbayan box—star lantern—bibingka—pandando sa llaw—jeepney—sari—say it in Hindi—Asian Indian dancing bells—yoga—banana lassi—snakes and ladders—diya for Diwali—chalk rangoli—Asian Indian hand painting—sponsor box—Vietnamese beef noodle soup—foam dragon for Tet—pov pob—Hmong flower cloth—storytelling cloth—Cambodian court dances—Khmer theater mask—say it in Khmer—Cambodian spring rolls

1235 **PETRONIS, L. *47 things you can do for the environment*.** 2012, Zest Books (ISBN: 9780982732212). 128 p.

GRADE LEVEL: Middle school – high school

CONTENTS: Clean shave—shower—natural beauty—green Christmas—a green house—eat your greens—put down the bottle—carbon footprint—cans—bottles—paper—what?—waste—the right stuff—paper chase—paint—take it to the top—technology—save your cell—compute the difference—rewind and unplug—bring your own bag to shop—vintage clothes—give green—keep it local—organic—traveling—the pool—an eco-adventure—green guest—have a "stuff" sale—swap—film festival—date—green plate special—green-style party—the community—free time into green time—trees—get growing—bins—do that—politics—spread the word

1236 **PHILLIPS, J. *Adorable accessories: paper creations to wear*.** 2013, Capstone (ISBN: 9781620650431). 32 p.

SERIES: Paper creations

GRADE LEVEL: Middle school – high school

CONTENTS: N/A

1237 **PHILLIPS, J. *Snappy style: paper decoration creations*.** 2013, Capstone (ISBN: 9781620650424). 32 p.

SERIES: Paper creations

GRADE LEVEL: Middle school – high school

CONTENTS: Newspaper basket—silhouette tree—bookshelf zoo—lanterns—coverlet—sachet—creatures—letter lineup—dot art—picture lamp—jewelry box tree—wind chime—candle sleeve

1238 **PIETROMARCHI, S. *The book book: a journey into bookmaking*.** 2007, Tara (ISBN: 9788186211243). 131 p.

GRADE LEVEL: Upper elementary – middle school

CONTENTS: N/A

1239 **PIPE, J. *Make a movie!*** 2013, Arcturus (ISBN: 9781848585737). 32 p.

SERIES: Find your talent

GRADE LEVEL: Middle school – high school

CONTENTS: Find your talent—what sort of film?—create a script—make a shot list—casting actors—location!—the right look—action!—sound and lighting—the shoot—all in the edit—find an audience—step up a gear

1240 POHLEN, J. *Albert Einstein and relativity for kids: his life and ideas with 21 activities and thought experiments*. 2012, Chicago Review Press (ISBN: 9781613740286). 144 p.

SERIES: For kids

GRADE LEVEL: Middle school

CONTENTS: Compass and magnet—cards—Munich to Mulan—capillaries—photoelectricity—light—$E=mc^2$—H space—relative motion—simultaneity—time dilation—time dilation part II—twin paradox—Zozon—blue skies and red sunsets—accelerating elevator—bending light—solar eclipse—galaxies—expanding universe—chain reaction—sailboat challenge—toying with the principle of equivalence

1241 PORTER, S. *Sailing*. 2011, PowerKids Press (ISBN: 9781448832972). 32 p.

SERIES: Get outdoors

GRADE LEVEL: Upper elementary

CONTENTS: Get started—equipment—the wind—getting afloat—changing direction—making a turn—deep water—next step—open water—competition

1242 POSKITT, K. *Codes — how to make them and break them*. 2007, Scholastic (ISBN: 9780439943284). 157 p.

SERIES: Murderous maths

GRADE LEVEL: Upper elementary

CONTENTS: N/A

1243 POWELL, B. *Skateboarding skills: the rider's guide*. 2008, Firefly Books (ISBN: 9781554073603). 128 p.

GRADE LEVEL: Middle school – high school

CONTENTS: Get on your board—beginning—concrete skateparks—wooden parks—plazas—events—sponsorship—equipment—skateboard anatomy—decks—skateboard trucks—wheels—footwear—stances—safety equipment—beginner tricks—intermediate tricks—advanced tricks

1244 POWELL, M. *Crafty activities: over 50 fun and easy things to make*. 2007, Search (ISBN: 9781844482504). 159 p.

GRADE LEVEL: Elementary

CONTENTS: N/A

1245 POWER, T. *The ABCs of yoga for kids*. 2009, Stafford House (ISBN: 9780982258705). 32 p.

GRADE LEVEL: Elementary

CONTENTS: N/A

1246 PRICE, P. *Cool cakes and cupcakes: easy recipes for kids to bake*. 2010, ABDO (ISBN: 9781604537741). 32 p.

SERIES: Cool baking

GRADE LEVEL: Elementary

CONTENTS: Cat in the Hat cupcakes—lemon pound cake—angel food cake—fudge cake—flourless cake—cupcakes—wraps

1247 PRICE, P. *Cool cookies and bars: easy recipes for kids to bake*. 2010, ABDO (ISBN: 9781604537758). 32 p.
SERIES: Cool baking
GRADE LEVEL: Elementary
CONTENTS: Classic chocolate chip cookies—choco-wakka cookies—meringues—oatmeal raisin cookies—sand tarts—brownies—turtle bars—wrap it up

1248 PRICE, P. *Cool pet treats: easy recipes for kids to bake*. 2010, ABDO (ISBN: 9781604537772). 32 p.
SERIES: Cool baking
GRADE LEVEL: Upper elementary
CONTENTS: Cheddar cornbread—turkey treats—peanut butter pooches—bacon bites—kitty catnip cookies—kitty chews—tuna tidbits

1249 PRICE, P. *Cool quick breads: easy recipes for kids to bake*. 2010, ABDO (ISBN: 9781604537795). 32 p.
SERIES: Cool baking
GRADE LEVEL: Upper elementary
CONTENTS: Cornbread—banana bread—zucchini bread—pumpkin bread—muffins—monkey bread—pull-aparts

1250 PRIDDY, R. *Activity*. 2010, Priddy Books (ISBN: 9780312508593). 64 p.
SERIES: Smart kids
GRADE LEVEL: Lower elementary
CONTENTS: Animal masks—tissue pom-poms—paper roses—scented pillow—scanner art—rainbow crayons—friendship tree—desk organizer—book covers—paper people—cupcake creations—friendship necklaces—pasta jewelry—Valentine heart bag—bird feeders—pebble caterpillar—mini dessert—herb garden—marbled eggs—pressed flowers—east pictures—creepy candies—Halloween pumpkins—pumpkin lanterns—jelly jar lantern—Halloween pictures—pom-pom wreath—potato print gift wrap—cookie stars—candy tree—celebration cookies—snowflakes—Christmas pictures—wizard hat—wizard wand

1251 PRIDDY, R. *Smart kids activity*. 2010, Priddy Books (ISBN: 9780312508593). 64 p.
SERIES: Smart kids
GRADE LEVEL: Lower elementary
CONTENTS: N/A

1252 PURNELL, G. *How to go fishing and catch fish!* 2009, Franklin Watts (ISBN: 9780749693442).
GRADE LEVEL: Elementary
CONTENTS: N/A

1253 PURPERHART, H. *Yoga exercises for teens: developing a calmer mind and a stronger body*. 2009, Hunter House (ISBN: 9780897935036).
SERIES: Smartfun activity books
GRADE LEVEL: Middle school – high school

CONTENTS: Exercises and postures—breathing exercises—getting to know the body—stretching exercises—movement exercises—visualizations and waking up

1254 **RABBAT, S.** *Citing sources: learning to use the copyright page*. 2013, Cherry Lake (ISBN: 9781624310232). 24 p.
SERIES: Information explorer junior
GRADE LEVEL: Elementary
CONTENTS: All kinds of property—what is copyright?—smart steps to using information—giving credit

1255 **RABBAT, S.** *Post it! Sharing photos with friends and family*. 2013, Cherry Lake (ISBN: 9781610804851). 24 p.
SERIES: Information explorer junior
GRADE LEVEL: Elementary
CONTENTS: Know your camera—photo-taking tips—tool for taking pictures—photo projects

1256 **RANDALL, R.** *Thanksgiving sweets and treats*. 2013, Windmill Books (ISBN: 9781448880829). 32 p.
SERIES: Holiday cooking for kids
GRADE LEVEL: Upper elementary
CONTENTS: Apple-honey cranberry sauce—super simple succotash—pumpkin pie—gobblin' good cookies—turkey salad mini rolls—turkey noodle soup—thick and tasty pumpkin smoothies

1257 **RANSOM, C.** *Scrapbooking just for you! How to make fun, personal, save-them-forever keepsakes*. 2010, Sterling (ISBN: 9781402740961).
GRADE LEVEL: Upper elementary
CONTENTS: N/A

1258 **RAU, D.** *Ace your creative writing project*. 2009, Enslow (ISBN: 9780766033955). 48 p.
SERIES: Ace it! Information literacy series
GRADE LEVEL: Elementary
CONTENTS: Unpacking your ideas—characters and setting—what's the story?—revision—time to share

1259 **RAU, D.** *Ace your writing assignment*. 2009, Enslow (ISBN: 9780766033948). 48 p.
SERIES: Ace it! Information literacy series
GRADE LEVEL: Elementary
CONTENTS: Building with words—prewriting—drafting—revision—peer review—publishing

1260 **RAU, D.** *Become an explorer: make and use a compass*. 2011, Norwood House Press (ISBN: 9781599533834). 48 p.
SERIES: Creative adventure guides
GRADE LEVEL: Elementary
CONTENTS: The compass—how a compass works—making and using your own compass—the sport of orienteering

1261 **RAU, D.** *Braiding hair*. 2012, Cherry Lake (ISBN: 9781610804714). 32 p.
SERIES: How-to library
GRADE LEVEL: Upper elementary
CONTENTS: Three-strand basic braiding—two-strand fishtail braiding—French braiding—braided rose bun—hidden fairy braids—glitter crown—wavy seashore braid—tropical paradise braid

1262 **RAU, D.** *Building birdhouses*. 2013, Cherry Lake (ISBN: 9781610804783). 32 p.
SERIES: How-to library
GRADE LEVEL: Upper elementary
CONTENTS: Wren house—big top birdhouse—camouflage cabin—robin platform—sky box—up on the farm

1263 **RAU, D.** *Building sandcastles*. 2013, Cherry Lake (ISBN: 9781610804684). 32 p.
SERIES: How-to library
GRADE LEVEL: Upper elementary
CONTENTS: Haunted hill—classical temple—mini modern city—castle tower—sand sentry—sand maze

1264 **RAU, D.** *Candle making for fun!* 2008, Compass Point (ISBN: 9780756532765). 48 p.
SERIES: For fun!
GRADE LEVEL: Elementary
CONTENTS: N/A

1265 **RAU, D.** *Carving pumpkins*. 2013, Cherry Lake (ISBN: 9781610804707). 32 p.
SERIES: How-to library
GRADE LEVEL: Upper elementary
CONTENTS: Picking our pumpkin—making a plan—pumpkin personalities—scooping the goop—carving tips—adding details—hanging lantern—alien encounter—haunted house display

1266 **RAU, D.** *Crafting with duct tape*. 2013, Cherry Lake (ISBN: 9781624311475). 32 p.
SERIES: How-to library
GRADE LEVEL: Upper elementary
CONTENTS: Fringe flowers—a colorful meal—jars—reversible belt—pencil case—tissue box—stadium seat—cover it

1267 **RAU, D.** *Crafting with recyclables*. 2013, Cherry Lake (ISBN: 9781624311468). 32 p.
SERIES: How-to library
GRADE LEVEL: Upper elementary
CONTENTS: Sun catcher—t-shirt makeover—scrap paper bowl—paint sample stool—mittens—book box—gift card chandelier—do your part

1268 **RAU, D.** *Creating Thanksgiving crafts*. 2013, Cherry Lake (ISBN: 9781624311482). 32 p.
SERIES: How-to library
GRADE LEVEL: Upper elementary
CONTENTS: Painting and sewing tips—turkey puppet—cornucopia—banner—place cards—bean bag toss—feast for the birds—corn husk doll

1269 RAU, D. *Creating winter crafts*. 2013, Cherry Lake (ISBN: 9781624311505). 32 p.

SERIES: How-to library

GRADE LEVEL: Upper elementary

CONTENTS: Ribbon wreath—oversized dreidel—Kwanzaa garland—magazine trees—frosted snowflake mirror—light-up lantern—foil wrapping paper—noisemakers and confetti cannons

1270 RAU, D. *Eye candy: crafting cool candy creations*. 2013, Capstone (ISBN: 9781429686204). 32 p.

SERIES: Dessert designers

GRADE LEVEL: Elementary

CONTENTS: Roses—icicles—stars—flower party favors—licorice butterflies—candy shake—mix-and-match monsters—sushi—bead bracelet—turtles—lollipop disco ball

1271 RAU, D. *Fitness for fun!* 2009, Compass Point (ISBN: 9780756540319). 48 p.

SERIES: For fun!

GRADE LEVEL: Elementary

CONTENTS: N/A

1272 RAU, D. *Folding origami*. 2013, Cherry Lake (ISBN: 9781624311451). 32 p.

SERIES: How-to library

GRADE LEVEL: Upper elementary

CONTENTS: Rainbow wheel—robot nesting boxes—yawning cats—fruit bowl—flapping bird

1273 RAU, D. *Handmade cards for fun!* 2008, Compass Point (ISBN: 9780756532796). 48 p.

SERIES: For fun!

GRADE LEVEL: Elementary

CONTENTS: Papyrus to computers—ways to fold—choices—cut it out—stick to it—write on—decorate—planning first—fancy Valentine—party invitation—birthday pop up—snowman card—nature in an envelope—making a statement—people, places, and fun—in any style—celebrate with cards—designing on the computer

1274 RAU, D. *Learning to knit*. 2013, Cherry Lake (ISBN: 9781610804776). 32 p.

SERIES: How-to library

GRADE LEVEL: Upper elementary

CONTENTS: Hand warmers—binder cover—t-shirt rug

1275 RAU, D. *Making a paper airplane and other paper toys*. 2013, Cherry Lake (ISBN: 9781610804738). 32 p.

SERIES: How-to library

GRADE LEVEL: Upper elementary

CONTENTS: N/A

1276 RAU, D. *Making books for fun!* 2009, Compass Point (ISBN: 9780756538590). 48 p.

SERIES: For fun!

GRADE LEVEL: Elementary

CONTENTS: Types of books—parts of a book—binding techniques—supplies—tools—measuring and cutting—folding—doing it

1277 RAU, D. *Making jewelry*. 2013, Cherry Lake (ISBN: 9781610804752). 32 p.
SERIES: How-to library
GRADE LEVEL: Upper elementary
CONTENTS: Cuff bracelet—ribbon barrette—earrings—anklet—forever necklaces

1278 RAU, D. *Painting rocks*. 2013, Cherry Lake (ISBN: 9781610804790). 32 p.
SERIES: How-to library
GRADE LEVEL: Upper elementary
CONTENTS: Bouquet rock—gnome stones—shoes—pebble pins—speaking stones—give a gift

1279 RAU, D. *Piece of cake! Decorating awesome cakes*. 2013, Capstone (ISBN: 9781429686181). 32 p.
SERIES: Dessert designers
GRADE LEVEL: Upper elementary
CONTENTS: Coaster cake—PB&J—pool party—box of chocolates—t-shirt—guitar—mini mice—peacock—mani-pedi dresser—zebra-striped purse

1280 RAU, D. *Quilting for fun!* 2009, Compass Point (ISBN: 756538602). 48 p.
SERIES: For fun!
GRADE LEVEL: Elementary
CONTENTS: Basics—types of quilts—what you need—simple stitches—planning your design—measuring—putting it together—project 1—quilt top—putting it together—triangle sachet—free-form quilted wall hanging—quilted purse—happy cat face—quilts as art—memory quilts

1281 RAU, D. *Recipes from China*. 2014, Capstone Raintree (ISBN: 9781410959713). 48 p.
SERIES: Cooking around the world
GRADE LEVEL: Elementary
CONTENTS: Zaoshang hao—small bites—ancient wok—fan and mein—Chinese sweets

1282 RAU, D. *Recipes from India*. 2014, Capstone Raintree (ISBN: 9781410959720). 48 p.
SERIES: Cooking around the world
GRADE LEVEL: Elementary
CONTENTS: Masala meals—vegetarian dishes—Thali tradition—desserts and drinks

1283 RAU, D. *Recipes from Italy*. 2014, Capstone Raintree (ISBN: 9781410959737). 48 p.
SERIES: Cooking around the world
GRADE LEVEL: Elementary
CONTENTS: Buongiorno—fresco e delizioso—basta pasta—quant'e buono—la dolce vita

1284 RAU, D. *Recipes from Mexico*. 2014, Capstone Raintree (ISBN: 9781410959744). 48 p.
SERIES: Cooking around the world
GRADE LEVEL: Elementary
CONTENTS: Por la manana—cocinar con carne—con la comida—dulces Mexicanos

1285 RAU, D. *Rock climbing for fun!* 2008, Compass Point (ISBN: 9780756533960). 48 p.
SERIES: For fun!
GRADE LEVEL: Elementary
CONTENTS: N/A

1286 RAU, D. *Smart cookie: designing creative cookies.* 2013, Capstone (ISBN: 9781429686198). 32 p.
SERIES: Dessert designers
GRADE LEVEL: Elementary
CONTENTS: Clear sky rainbows—wise old owl—fancy topper—witch—doghouse—bugging out—fairy ring—spacey treats—curled cat—place card—monkey around

1287 RAU, D. *Super cool science experiments: light.* 2010, Cherry Lake (ISBN: 9781602795310). 32 p.
SERIES: Science explorer
GRADE LEVEL: Elementary
CONTENTS: Science—first things first—the sun—shadows—bouncing off the wall—bent out of shape—colors—do it yourself

1288 RAU, D. *What's up cupcake? Creating amazing cupcakes.* 2013, Capstone (ISBN: 9781429686174). 32 p.
SERIES: Dessert designers
GRADE LEVEL: Upper elementary
CONTENTS: Cupcakes—berry basket—bunny—gifts from the sea—popcorn treat—gorilla—snowman—sweet tweet—flower tower—armadillo—burger

1289 REGAN, L. *Bugs.* 2011, Windmill Books (ISBN: 9781615332656). 32 p.
SERIES: Let's draw
GRADE LEVEL: Upper elementary
CONTENTS: Snail—ladybug—caterpillar—centipede—butterfly—crane fly—earwig—shield bug—dragonfly—scarab beetle—tarantula—ant—bluebottle—grasshopper—bee

1290 REGAN, L. *Indoor games!* 2010, QEB (ISBN: 9781595669315). 32 p.
SERIES: Games handbook
GRADE LEVEL: Elementary
CONTENTS: Dinosaur hunt—works of art—pennies in the pot—matching pairs—blowout—jack of the pack—dressing up—picture puzzle—sockey—card wars—singing star—treasure hunt—sardines—snap!—beetledice—mountain climbing—totally—on your marks—runny noses—dice golf—pea brains—basketball—card lottery—where in the world?—hide and snap—jacks—coin catcher

1291 REGAN, L. *Outdoor games!* 2010, QEB (ISBN: 9781595669346). 32 p.
SERIES: Games handbook
GRADE LEVEL: Elementary
CONTENTS: N/A

1292 REID, S. *Art & craft: discover the things people made and the games they played around the world.* 2008, Southwater (ISBN: 9781844766185). 64 p.

SERIES: Hands-on history

GRADE LEVEL: Elementary

CONTENTS: N/A

1293 REILLY, K. *Energy: 25 projects to investigate why we need power & how we get it*. 2009, Nomad Press (ISBN: 9781934670347). 128 p.

SERIES: Build it yourself

GRADE LEVEL: Upper elementary – middle school

CONTENTS: Newton's cradle—energy car—energy converter—jumping frogs—lemon battery—electromagnet—hydrogen—oil spill experiment—natural gas—coal candy—coal layers—coal mining experiments—bowling set—hovercraft—anemometer—instrument—turbine—water wheel—solar laser—s'mores—water heater—cupcakes—steamboat—fumarole—fire starters—cow pies—photosynthesis experiment—home energy audit

1294 REILLY, K. *Explore life cycles! 25 great projects, activities, experiments*. 2011, Nomad Press (ISBN: 9781934670804). 96 p.

SERIES: Explore your world

GRADE LEVEL: Upper elementary

CONTENTS: Mobius strip—viewing strips—nature quest—snack mix—nursery—classification system—plant seedling—yeast experiment—seeds experiment—plant—egg—spore print—underwater viewer—pizza—mold growth experiments—it's crowded in here experiment—tree measuring stick—baked bear Alaska—jellyfish—rotting log—parachute—compost bin—habitat survival challenge—acid rain experiment—oil spill experiment

1295 REILLY, K. *Explore weather and climate! 25 great projects, activities, experiments*. 2012, Nomad Press (ISBN: 9781936313846). 96 p.

SERIES: Explore your world

GRADE LEVEL: Upper elementary

CONTENTS: N/A

1296 REILLY, K. *Food: 25 amazing projects*. 2010, Nomad Press (ISBN: 9781934670590). 128 p.

SERIES: Build it yourself

GRADE LEVEL: Upper elementary – middle school

CONTENTS: Hot chocolate—marshmallows—dehydrated food—Nile—harvest experiment—maze—cake—Gali akpono—price sheet—spice mix—pot—food packaging—catchy package—home food safety—food additive experiment—Doodh pak—cake—hardtack—pemmican—plate—cards—home-grown vegetable sampler—bug fest—blossoms—bean gravity experiment—salt flat experiment

1297 REILLY, K. *The human body: 25 fantastic projects that illuminate how the body works*. 2008, Nomad Press (ISBN: 9781934670248). 128 p.

SERIES: Build it yourself

GRADE LEVEL: Upper elementary – middle school

CONTENTS: Heart squirter—blood—dissection lab—lung—air ball—tooth—nutrition balance—muscle—model hand—decalcifying bone experiment—joints—spine—cell—skin care products—fingerprint kit—reaction tester—"seeing is believing"

experiment—indoor sensory garden—3-D images—inheritance model—optical illusions—ear—sniffer tester—DNA extraction—ball soap—immunity slush drink

1298 REILLY, K. *Natural disasters: investigate Earth's most destructive forces*. 2012, Nomad Press (ISBN: 9781619301474). 128 p.

SERIES: Build it yourself

GRADE LEVEL: Upper elementary – middle school

CONTENTS: Tsunami simulator—shake table—seismograph—volcano—volcano models—lava flow—balloon battle—convection currents—convection in color— hurricane—barometer—wind tunnel—flood plain—water-powered wheel— absorbency project—rain barrel—drought landscape—fire line—fire escape plan— insulation project—avalanche experiment—lake eruption—crater experiment—home emergency kit—pet emergency kit

1299 REILLY, K. *Planet Earth: 25 environmental projects you can build yourself*. 2008, Nomad Press (ISBN: 9781934670040). 128 p.

SERIES: Build it yourself

GRADE LEVEL: Upper elementary – middle school

CONTENTS: Granola—funnel—plant-oxygen experiment—air blaster—bubble machine—water-testing experiment—pond—miniature water cycle—terrarium— oven—sundial—sunflower house—pond exploration kit—food chain—butterfly feeder—dog collar—ladybug house—garbage picker-upper—global warming— ozone hole trick—hydroponic planter—t-shirt—food supply experiment—shopping tote—castle—recycled paper—chain bracelet—bring the earth back into balance game

1300 REUSSER, K. *Recipe and craft guide to Indonesia*. 2011, Mitchell Lane (ISBN: 9781584159346). 63 p.

SERIES: World crafts and recipes

GRADE LEVEL: Upper elementary – middle school

CONTENTS: Spicy peanut sauce—coconut rice—yellow rice—fried rice—fried noodles— chicken in soy sauce—cooked vegetable salad—pepper salad with sesame seeds— rice rolls—meat satay—paper placemat—yarn weaving—rain stick—shadow puppet—kenong musical instrument—music drum—flower—mask—Komodo dragon—batik t-shirt

1301 RITSCHEL, J. *The kickboxing handbook*. 2008, Rosen (ISBN: 9781404213951). 256 p.

SERIES: Martial arts

GRADE LEVEL: Middle school – high school

CONTENTS: Warm-up exercises—stretching—strength-training—training—stances and footwork—punches—kicks—strikes—blocking—combinations—kickboxing as self-defense

1302 ROBBINS, K. *Shoe print art: step into drawing*. 2013, Gibbs Smith (ISBN: 9780971144118).

GRADE LEVEL: Elementary

CONTENTS: N/A

1303 ROBINSON, R. *Start to batik*. 2009, Search Press (ISBN: 9781844483532). 48 p.
GRADE LEVEL: Upper elementary – middle school
CONTENTS: Pink and orange scarf—Aboriginal art—sunflower bag—dotty book cover

1304 ROBINSON, T. *Basketball skills*. 2009, Enslow (ISBN: 9780766032057). 48 p.
SERIES: How to play like a pro
GRADE LEVEL: Upper elementary
CONTENTS: Pregame—advanced dribbling—stops and starts—creating space—chest pass—bounce pass—ball fake—receiving a pass—set shot—jump shot—foul shots—scoring on the inside—scoring in transition—defensive position—defending players—defending the ball—rebounding

1305 ROCHE, A. *Cartooning: the only cartooning book you'll ever need to be the artist you've always wanted to be*. 2010, Lewes (ISBN: 9781402775154). 111 p.
SERIES: Art for kids
GRADE LEVEL: Elementary
CONTENTS: Making faces—drawing bodies—drawing stuff—drawing animals—writing jokes—putting it all together—publishing your cartoons

1306 ROCK, L. *Canoeing and kayaking*. 2010, PowerKids Press (ISBN: 9781435830417). 32 p.
SERIES: Get outdoors
GRADE LEVEL: Upper elementary
CONTENTS: Equipment—launch and land—feel the water—get right in—full speed ahead—trips and expeditions—moving on—whitewater

1307 RODERICK, S. *Centsibility*. 2008, Kids Can Press (ISBN: 9781554532087). 80 p.
SERIES: Planet girl
GRADE LEVEL: Middle school – high school
CONTENTS: It really doesn't grow on trees—herstory of money—making your own money—at-home earner—working girl—mizz bizz—keeping track—safety—paper beads—save it—what's your money purse-onality?—savings = choices—goals—bank on it—picture frame wall safe

1308 ROSIER, M. *Aliens*. 2013, Bellwether Media (ISBN: 9781600148989). 24 p.
SERIES: You can draw it
GRADE LEVEL: Upper elementary – middle school
CONTENTS: N/A

1309 ROSIER, M. *Dinosaurs*. 2013, Bellwether Media (ISBN: 9781600148996). 24 p.
SERIES: You can draw it
GRADE LEVEL: Upper elementary – middle school
CONTENTS: Ankylosaurus—Brachiosaurus—Quetzalcoatlus—Spinosaurus—Stegosaurus—Triceratops—Tyrannosaurus—Velociraptor

1310 ROSIER, M. *Robots*. 2013, Bellwether Media (ISBN: 9781600149009). 24 p.
SERIES: You can draw it

GRADE LEVEL: Upper elementary – middle school

CONTENTS: Crush—Raze—D-Buggr—Point—AR-lift—Athletixx—Spike—Bit

1311 **ROSIER, M.** *Sharks*. 2013, Bellwether Media (ISBN: 9781600149016). 24 p.

SERIES: You can draw it

GRADE LEVEL: Upper elementary – middle school

CONTENTS: Goblin shark—great white shark—hammerhead shark—mako shark—sand tiger shark—saw shark—thresher shark—whale shark

1312 **ROSINSKY, N.** *Write your own biography*. 2008, Compass Point (ISBN: 9780756533663). 64 p.

SERIES: Write your own

GRADE LEVEL: Upper elementary – middle school

CONTENTS: Setting the scene—characters—viewpoint—synopses and plots—winning words—scintillating speech

1313 **ROSINSKY, N.** *Write your own fable*. 2009, Compass Point (ISBN: 9780756541286). 64 p.

SERIES: Write your own

GRADE LEVEL: Upper elementary – middle school

CONTENTS: N/A

1314 **ROSINSKY, N.** *Write your own fairy tale*. 2008, Compass Point (ISBN: 9780756533694). 64 p.

SERIES: Write your own

GRADE LEVEL: Upper elementary – middle school

CONTENTS: Setting the scene—characters—viewpoint—synopses and plots—winning words—scintillating speech

1315 **ROSINSKY, N.** *Write your own folktale*. 2008, Compass Point (ISBN: 9780756535162). 64 p.

SERIES: Write your own

GRADE LEVEL: Upper elementary – middle school

CONTENTS: Setting the scene—characters—viewpoint—synopses and plots – winning words

1316 **ROSINSKY, N.** *Write your own graphic novel*. 2009, Compass Point (ISBN: 9780756538569). 64 p.

SERIES: Write your own

GRADE LEVEL: Upper elementary – middle school

CONTENTS: Setting the scene—characters—viewpoint—synopses and plots—winning words—scintillating speech

1317 **ROSINSKY, N.** *Write your own legend*. 2008, Compass Point (ISBN: 9780756535698). 64 p.

SERIES: Write your own

GRADE LEVEL: Upper elementary – middle school

CONTENTS: Setting the scene—characters—viewpoint—synopses and plots—winning words—scintillating speech

1318 ROSINSKY, N. *Write your own myth*. 2008, Compass Point (ISBN: 9780756533724). 64 p.

SERIES: Write your own

GRADE LEVEL: Upper elementary – middle school

CONTENTS: Setting the scene—characters—viewpoint—synopses and plots—winning words—scintillating speech

1319 ROSINSKY, N. *Write your own nonfiction*. 2009, Compass Point (ISBN: 9780756541309). 64 p.

SERIES: Write your own

GRADE LEVEL: Upper elementary – middle school

CONTENTS: Setting the scene—characters—viewpoint—synopses and plots—winning words—scintillating speech

1320 ROSINSKY, N. *Write your own tall tale*. 2008, Compass Point (ISBN: 9780756533755). 64 p.

SERIES: Write your own

GRADE LEVEL: Upper elementary – middle school

CONTENTS: Setting the scene—characters—viewpoint—synopses and plots—winning words—scintillating speech

1321 ROSS, K. *All new crafts for Kwanzaa*. 2007, Millbrook Press (ISBN: 9780761334019).

SERIES: All new holiday crafts for kids

GRADE LEVEL: Elementary

CONTENTS: N/A

1322 ROSS, K. *All new holiday crafts for Mother's Day and Father's Day*. 2007, Millbrook Press (ISBN: 9780822563679).

SERIES: All new holiday crafts for kids

GRADE LEVEL: Elementary

CONTENTS: N/A

1323 ROSS, K. *Beautiful beads*. 2010, Millbrook Press (ISBN: 9780822592143). 48 p.

SERIES: Girl crafts

GRADE LEVEL: Upper elementary

CONTENTS: Fabric beads—textured beads—thread beads—ribbon beads—sparkle stem beads—beads skill game—beads design game—felt bead bracelet—cluster pin—seed bead flower magnet—beaded dog—spaghetti doll—beaded envelope—changing beads desk diva—beaded doll sandals—beaded picture board—buttons and beads garland—beady bookmark—beaded tissue box—flower jar bead storage—bead storage stabile

1324 ROSS, K. *Bedroom makeover crafts*. 2009, Millbrook Press (ISBN: 9780822575931). 48 p.

SERIES: Girl crafts

GRADE LEVEL: Upper elementary

CONTENTS: Web holder—treasure shelf—letter holder—earring doll—doorknob posy—doll bubble—dresser boxes—pocket board—perpetual calendar—flowers pillow—dresser knob flowers—pj bag—jewelry pouch—days of the week hangers—photo garland—gems message can—sock stasher—flower letters—caterpillar bank—earring basket—can and bottle covers—floor table

1325 **ROSS, K.** *Crafts for kids who are learning about dinosaurs*. 2008, Millbrook Press (ISBN: 9780822568094). 48 p.

SERIES: Crafts for kids who are learning about

GRADE LEVEL: Lower elementary

CONTENTS: Necklace—Seismosaurus—Compsognathus—Brachiosaurus—bow tree—bathtub toy—dinosaur puppet—clip—dinosaur puppet—pencil topper—magnet—hat—Parasaurolophus puppet—Spinosaurus magnet—scrap box—hatching dinosaur—bookmark—lapel pin—ball—dinosaur pet—quick cup—tape dispenser

1326 **ROSS, K.** *Crafts for kids who are learning about farm animals*. 2007, Millbrook Press (ISBN: 9780822563662). 48 p.

SERIES: Crafts for kids who are learning about

GRADE LEVEL: Lower elementary

CONTENTS: Farmer puppet—barn—finger puppet—hat—tractor—field mouse—cat—duck—ducklings—chicken

1327 **ROSS, K.** *Crafts for kids who are learning about insects*. 2009, Millbrook Press (ISBN: 9780822575917). 48 p.

SERIES: Crafts for kids who are learning about

GRADE LEVEL: Lower elementary

CONTENTS: Change keeper—puppet—finger puppet—mosquito—ladybug—magnet—firefly—pin—walking stick—shaker—caterpillar—caterpillar pin—butterfly—hairclip—fluttery butterfly—butterfly wings—message center—game—container—bike bopper—termite game

1328 **ROSS, K.** *Crafts for kids who are learning about transportation*. 2007, Millbrook Press (ISBN: 9780761394648). 48 p.

SERIES: Crafts for kids who are learning about

GRADE LEVEL: Elementary

CONTENTS: Baby carriage photo frame—wagon puzzle—bike bobber—doll friend saucer—horse and rider—honking car—race car photo holder—police car/getaway car—bulldozer—tow-truck—dump truck—garbage truck—fire truck—snowplow attachment—tissue box bus—train necklace—bath boat—balloon motorboat—airplane—helicopter puppet—rocket ships—vehicle tin

1329 **ROSS, K.** *Creative kitchen crafts*. 2011, Millbrook Press (ISBN: 9780822592174). 48 p.

SERIES: Girl crafts

GRADE LEVEL: Upper elementary

CONTENTS: N/A

1330 **ROSS, K.** *Earth-friendly crafts: clever ways to reuse everyday items*. 2009, Millbrook Press (ISBN: 9780822590996).

GRADE LEVEL: Elementary

CONTENTS: Tiny toy bookmark—picture board—designer car clip—marker caps pencil holder—changing faces necklace—box board links—beaded picture boxes—necktie clown pin—coloring book collage—glove octopus puppet—puzzle pieces alligator—balloon bird magnet—stand-up frame—changing faces pin—slinky CD holder—

royal jewelry—game board art folder—hairbrush hair clip holder—fashionable note card and envelope—display bird—art cards

1331 ROSS, K. *Fairy world crafts*. 2008, Millbrook Press (ISBN: 9780822590248). 48 p.

SERIES: Girl crafts

GRADE LEVEL: Upper elementary

CONTENTS: Fairy skirt and headpiece—starry wand—fairy outfit—fairy wings—flower fairy wand—fairy necklace—flower fairy wand—fairy necklace—leaf fairy pin—jingle bell fairy fob—fairy magnet—tooth fairy tooth holder—toadstools—fairy in flight—snail friend—cupcake fairy—fairy log house—butterfly wings fairy—leaf table and bed—dragonfly friend

1332 ROSS, K. *Jazzy jewelry, pretty purses, and more!* 2009, Millbrook Press (ISBN: 9780822592129). 48 p.

SERIES: Girl crafts

GRADE LEVEL: Upper elementary

CONTENTS: Flower belt—pet pin—cuff bracelet—broach—charm—wrist purse—hat—shoe necklace—headband—key cover—key fob—pocket purse—jewelry—id tag—art pin—sneaker clips—charm bracelet—pet gloves—autograph hound—dresser dish — sunglasses

1333 ROSS, K. *One-of-a-kind stamps and crafts*. 2010, Millbrook Press (ISBN: 9780822592167). 48 p.

SERIES: Girl crafts

GRADE LEVEL: Upper elementary

CONTENTS: N/A

1334 ROSS, K. *Step-by-step crafts for gifts*. 2007, Boyds Mills (ISBN: 9781590783610). 48 p.

SERIES: Step-by-step crafts

GRADE LEVEL: Elementary

CONTENTS: Message man—bookworm bookmark—casserole cover—lap desk—hat stand—gift wrap sleeve—frog pin—pet-collar cover—pincushion—baby picture—nail and screw tender—cat toy—cell phone case—mobile—sand-and-shower shoes—yarn dispenser—accessory notepad—cup holder—message center—desk clips

1335 ROSS, K. *Step-by-step crafts for summer*. 2007, Boyds Mills (ISBN: 9781590783603). 48 p.

SERIES: Step-by-step crafts

GRADE LEVEL: Elementary

CONTENTS: Water-bottle holder—quarter keeper—message can—plant marker—picture frame—bird pin—autograph hound—Fourth of July noisemaker—toss game—pennants—tablecloth weights—desk birds—fish puppet—pin—flower jar—stick letters—button snake—coaster—moving-target game—handlebar tassels

1336 ROSS, N. *Fishing*. 2010, PowerKids Press (ISBN: 9781435830424). 32 p.

SERIES: Get outdoors

GRADE LEVEL: Upper elementary

CONTENTS: World of fishing—get started—fishing equipment—types of fish—bait—using the equipment—basic techniques—unhooking and releasing a fish—location—location—location—types of fishing—fly fishing and sea fishing—clubs and competitions—fish from around the world

1337 ROY, J. *Sharpen your business letter writing skills*. 2012, Enslow (ISBN: 9780766039728). 64 p.
SERIES: Sharpen your writing skills
GRADE LEVEL: Middle school – high school
CONTENTS: N/A

1338 ROY, J. *Sharpen your debate and speech writing skills*. 2012, Enslow (ISBN: 766039048). 64 p.
SERIES: Sharpen your writing skills
GRADE LEVEL: Middle school – high school
CONTENTS: Prepare—about—before you write—ready to write—revising—editing—proofreading—presenting

1339 ROY, J. *Sharpen your essay writing skills*. 2012, Enslow (ISBN: 9780766039032). 64 p.
SERIES: Sharpen your writing skills
GRADE LEVEL: Middle school – high school
CONTENTS: Write an essay—about essays—before you write—time to write—making it even better—presenting

1340 ROY, J. *Sharpen your good grammar skills*. 2012, Enslow (ISBN: 9780766039025). 64 p.
SERIES: Sharpen your writing skills
GRADE LEVEL: Middle school – high school
CONTENTS: N/A

1341 ROY, J. *Sharpen your report writing skills*. 2012, Enslow (ISBN: 9780766039056). 64 p.
SERIES: Sharpen your writing skills
GRADE LEVEL: Middle school – high school
CONTENTS: Write a report—what's in them—getting started—getting the stuff in order—time to write

1342 ROY, J. *Sharpen your story or narrative writing skills*. 2012, Enslow (ISBN: 9780766039018). 64 p.
SERIES: Sharpen your writing skills
GRADE LEVEL: Middle school – high school
CONTENTS: Write a narrative—inside the narrative—making it more interesting—prewriting—time to write—share it and publish it

1343 ROYLE, T. *Gymnastics*. 2009, Wayland (ISBN: 9780750258357). 32 p.
SERIES: Master this!
GRADE LEVEL: Upper elementary – middle school
CONTENTS: N/A

1344 ROZA, G. *Frequently asked questions about emergency lifesaving techniques.* 2010, Rosen Central (ISBN: 9781435853270). 64 p.

SERIES: FAQ: Teen life

GRADE LEVEL: Middle school – high school

CONTENTS: Basics techniques—airway management and CPR—wounds—bleeding—broken bones—poisoning—burns—heat and cold emergencies

1345 RUNYAN, E. *Watch me draw Disney's Mickey Mouse clubhouse.* 2012, Walter Foster (ISBN: 9781936309740). 24 p.

SERIES: Watch me draw

GRADE LEVEL: Upper elementary

CONTENTS: N/A

1346 RUSCH, E. *Girls' tennis: conquering the court.* 2007, Capstone (ISBN: 9780736868259). 32 p.

SERIES: Girls got game

GRADE LEVEL: Elementary

CONTENTS: N/A

1347 RYALL, J. *Clay art.* 2013, Windmill Books (ISBN: 9781448880850).

SERIES: Awesome art

GRADE LEVEL: Elementary

CONTENTS: Curly pots—dinosaur dish—3-D picture frame—cute pencil tops—door plate—ocean mobile—pinch pots—three little pigs—make a medal—money box—Christmas decorations

1348 RYALL, J. *Junk art.* 2013, Windmill Books (ISBN: 9781448881406).

SERIES: Awesome art

GRADE LEVEL: Elementary

CONTENTS: Beautiful buttonfly—mirror—foil fish—spoon puppet—junk trunk—egg box robot—hanging monkey—in the frame—super rocket—fairy-take castle

1349 RYBOLT, T. *Environmental science fair projects: revised and expanded using the scientific method.* 2010, Enslow (ISBN: 9780766034266). 160 p.

GRADE LEVEL: Upper elementary – middle school

CONTENTS: N/A

1350 SABBETH, C. *Van Gogh and the Post-Impressionists for kids: their lives and ideas, 21 activities.* 2011, Chicago Review Press (ISBN: 9781448794249).

SERIES: For kids

GRADE LEVEL: Middle school

CONTENTS: Pannekoeken—a picture in words—shades of gray—lights, camera, action—portrait a la Tanguy—Japanese fold-out album—birdfeeder—Vincent's sunflowers—self-portrait of your room—Vincent's mixed-up soup—draw a mirror image—starry night peep box—a self-portrait—dreamscape—the (you) school—the poster—Paris shadow theater—pointillist sailboat—stained glass alphabet—acrostic poem—woven styles

1351 SADLER, J. *The new jumbo book of easy crafts*. 2009, Kids Can Press (ISBN: 9781554532391). 176 p.
GRADE LEVEL: Elementary
CONTENTS: N/A

1352 SALAS, L. *Canoeing*. 2008, Capstone (ISBN: 9781429608169). 32 p.
SERIES: Great outdoors
GRADE LEVEL: Upper elementary
CONTENTS: N/A

1353 SALAS, L. *Picture yourself writing poetry: using photos to inspire writing*. 2012, Capstone (ISBN: 9781429661249). 32 p.
SERIES: Fact finders. See it, write it
GRADE LEVEL: Middle school – high school
CONTENTS: A magical world—ideas—images—and metaphor—word choices—characters—arranging words on a page

1354 SALAS, L. *Scrapbooking for fun!* 2008, Compass Point (ISBN: 9780756532703). 48 p.
SERIES: For fun!
GRADE LEVEL: Elementary
CONTENTS: Basics—what matters most—start with a book—picture this—right tools for the job—cut and trim—plan your page—frame—pizzazz—natural scrapbook—make pages pop—stick to it—journaling—make your mark—what's inside—people, places, and fun: local flair—where to learn—two voices

1355 SALAS, L. *Write your own poetry*. 2008, Compass Point (ISBN: 9780756535193). 64 p.
SERIES: Write your own
GRADE LEVEL: Upper elementary – middle school
CONTENTS: Poetic forms—language of poetry—imagery—point of view—meter and rhyme—poems on the page

1356 SANDERS, N. *Frederick Douglass for kids: his life and times with 21 activities*. 2012, Chicago Review Press (ISBN: 9781569767177). 144 p.
SERIES: For kids
GRADE LEVEL: Middle school
CONTENTS: Help a child read—debate club—stepping into freedom—take off spots of any sort—keep flies away—tarpaulin hat and cravat—slave market—clothespin dolls—sugar water—carpetbag—black abolitionists—boiled dinner—oratorical contest—a voice for the nation—Civil War haversack—John Brown song—Civil War timeline—create a memory—cane—microfinancing—sculpt a statue—beaten biscuits—banana leaf card

1357 SAUTTER, A. *The boy's guide to drawing aliens, warriors, robots and other cool stuff*. 2009, Capstone (ISBN: 9781429629171). 144 p.
GRADE LEVEL: Elementary
CONTENTS: N/A

1358 SAUTTER, A. *How to draw amazing motorcycles*. 2008, Capstone (ISBN: 9781429600736). 32 p.

SERIES: Drawing cool stuff

GRADE LEVEL: Elementary

CONTENTS: N/A

1359 SAUTTER, A. *How to draw comic heroes*. 2008, Capstone (ISBN: 9781429600743). 32 p.

SERIES: Drawing cool stuff

GRADE LEVEL: Elementary

CONTENTS: N/A

1360 SAUTTER, A. *How to draw crazy fighter planes*. 2008, Capstone (ISBN: 9781429612982). 32 p.

SERIES: Drawing cool stuff

GRADE LEVEL: Elementary

CONTENTS: P-51 Mustang—P-38 Lightning—P-80 Shooting Star—Russian Mig-15—SR-71 Blackbird—B-2 Spirit—F-4 Phantom II—AV-8B Harrier—A-10 "Warthog"—K-17 Hornet—dogfight

1361 SAUTTER, A. *How to draw disgusting aliens*. 2008, Capstone (ISBN: 1429600756). 32 p.

SERIES: Drawing cool stuff

GRADE LEVEL: Elementary

CONTENTS: N/A

1362 SAUTTER, A. *How to draw ferocious animals*. 2008, Capstone (ISBN: 9781429612999). 32 p.

SERIES: Drawing cool stuff

GRADE LEVEL: Elementary

CONTENTS: Great white shark—hippopotamus—mountain lion—grizzly bear—Komodo dragon—timber wolf—Bengal tiger—silverback gorilla—African elephant—saltwater crocodile

1363 SAUTTER, A. *How to draw ferocious dinosaurs*. 2008, Capstone (ISBN: 9781429600767). 32 p.

SERIES: Drawing cool stuff

GRADE LEVEL: Elementary

CONTENTS: Apatosaurus—lunch time—Plesiosaur—Pteranodon—Tyrannosaurus Rex—T-Rex action—Spinosaurus—Stegosaurus—Triceratops—Velociraptor

1364 SAUTTER, A. *How to draw grotesque monsters*. 2008, Capstone (ISBN: 9781429613002). 32 p.

SERIES: Drawing cool stuff

GRADE LEVEL: Elementary

CONTENTS: One-eyed cyclops—Count Vlad—Kracked Karl—Medusa—skeletal soldier—Frank Stein—sinister scarecrow—King Hotep—Fishy Phil—Ugh the Thug—monster mash

1365 SAUTTER, A. *How to draw incredible cars*. 2008, Capstone (ISBN: 1429600772). 32 p.

SERIES: Drawing cool stuff

GRADE LEVEL: Elementary

CONTENTS: N/A

1366 SAUTTER, A. *How to draw indestructible tanks*. 2008, Capstone (ISBN: 9781429613019). 32 p.

SERIES: Drawing cool stuff

GRADE LEVEL: Elementary

CONTENTS: M4 Sherman—M109 Paladin—BLT bridge layer—MK2 flame thrower—S7 drift buster—AMX mine sweeper—ST2 ocean crawler—martian-MB3—Skorp-7—Annihilator—B60 barricade buster

1367 SAUTTER, A. *How to draw manga warriors*. 2008, Capstone (ISBN: 1429600780). 32 p.

SERIES: Drawing cool stuff

GRADE LEVEL: Elementary

CONTENTS: N/A

1368 SAUTTER, A. *How to draw monster trucks*. 2008, Capstone (ISBN: 1429600799). 32 p.

SERIES: Drawing cool stuff

GRADE LEVEL: Elementary

CONTENTS: N/A

1369 SAUTTER, A. *How to draw terrifying robots*. 2008, Capstone (ISBN: 9781429600804). 32 p.

SERIES: Drawing cool stuff

GRADE LEVEL: Elementary

CONTENTS: Bob-V2.5—Mech-troopers—FXR-UPR—Echo-4000—Tentacle Terror X-22—Bio-scout MKS—Padifier P-17s—Jet Defender-7—Rampage-XT3—Buzz-bot 6—robot rumble

1370 SAUTTER, A. *How to draw unreal spaceships*. 2008, Capstone (ISBN: 9781429613026). 32 p.

SERIES: Drawing cool stuff

GRADE LEVEL: Elementary

CONTENTS: Martian missile—Slyth saucer—Fontana racer—Belko boomerang—H-wing raptor—Vespan stinger—Darklyte saber—Starlite freighter—SS-8 planet jumper—Ares battle cruiser—battle stations

1371 SAVAGE, J. *Top 25 gymnastics skills, tips, and tricks*. 2012, Enslow (ISBN: 9780766038684). 48 p.

SERIES: Top 25 sports skills, tips, and tricks

GRADE LEVEL: Elementary

CONTENTS: N/A

1372 SAVAGE, J. *Top 25 hockey skills, tips, and tricks*. 2012, Enslow (ISBN: 9780766038691). 48 p.

SERIES: Top 25 sports skills, tips, and tricks

GRADE LEVEL: Elementary

CONTENTS: N/A

1373 SAVAGE, J. *Top 25 soccer skills, tips, and tricks*. 2012, Enslow (ISBN: 9780766038608). 48 p.

SERIES: Top 25 sports skills, tips, and tricks

GRADE LEVEL: Elementary

CONTENTS: N/A

1374 SCHEUNEMANN, P. *Cool fabric projects: creative ways to upcycle your trash into treasure*. 2013, ABDO (ISBN: 9781617834325). 32 p.

SERIES: Cool trash to treasure

GRADE LEVEL: Upper elementary – middle school

CONTENTS: N/A

1375 SCHEUNEMANN, P. *Cool glass and ceramic projects: creative ways to upcycle your trash into treasure*. 2013, ABDO (ISBN: 9781617834332). 32 p.

SERIES: Cool trash to treasure

GRADE LEVEL: Upper elementary – middle school

CONTENTS: N/A

1376 SCHEUNEMANN, P. *Cool metal projects: creative ways to upcycle your trash into treasure*. 2013, ABDO (ISBN: 9781617834349). 32 p.

SERIES: Cool trash to treasure

GRADE LEVEL: Upper elementary – middle school

CONTENTS: N/A

1377 SCHEUNEMANN, P. *Cool odds and ends projects: creative ways to upcycle your trash into treasure*. 2013, ABDO (ISBN: 9781617834356). 32 p.

SERIES: Cool trash to treasure

GRADE LEVEL: Upper elementary – middle school

CONTENTS: N/A

1378 SCHEUNEMANN, P. *Cool paper projects: creative ways to upcycle your trash into treasure*. 2013, ABDO (ISBN: 9781617834363). 32 p.

SERIES: Cool trash to treasure

GRADE LEVEL: Upper elementary – middle school

CONTENTS: N/A

1379 SCHEUNEMANN, P. *Cool plastic projects: creative ways to upcycle your trash into treasure*. 2013, ABDO (ISBN: 9781617834370). 32 p.

SERIES: Cool trash to treasure

GRADE LEVEL: Upper elementary – middle school

CONTENTS: N/A

1380 SCHEUNEMANN, P. *Cool stuff for bath & beauty: creative handmade projects for kids*. 2012, ABDO (ISBN: 9781617149801). 32 p.

SERIES: Cool stuff

GRADE LEVEL: Elementary

CONTENTS: Lip gloss—salt scrub—bath salts—bath bubblers—bath melts—hand lotion—makeup box—headband—button ponytail ties—flower hairpins

1381 SCHEUNEMANN, P. *Cool stuff for family & friends: creative handmade projects for kids*. 2012, ABDO (ISBN: 9781617149818). 32 p.

SERIES: Cool stuff

GRADE LEVEL: Elementary

CONTENTS: Mouse pad—draft dodger—hammer time—cool coasters—necklace—stroke counter golf gift—candles

1382 SCHEUNEMANN, P. *Cool stuff for reading & writing: creative handmade projects for kids*. 2012, ABDO (ISBN: 9781617149825). 32 p.

SERIES: Cool stuff

GRADE LEVEL: Elementary

CONTENTS: Posh pens—notepads—bookmarks—bookplates—book cover—bookends

1383 SCHEUNEMANN, P. *Cool stuff for school: creative handmade projects for kids*. 2012, ABDO (ISBN: 9781617149832). 32 p.

SERIES: Cool stuff

GRADE LEVEL: Elementary

CONTENTS: Locker accessories—lunch bag—book covers—photo album—pencil box—message board and tacks

1384 SCHEUNEMANN, P. *Cool stuff for your garden: creative handmade projects for kids*. 2012, ABDO (ISBN: 9781617149849). 32 p.

SERIES: Cool stuff

GRADE LEVEL: Elementary

CONTENTS: N/A

1385 SCHEUNEMANN, P. *Cool stuff for your room: creative handmade projects for kids*. 2012, ABDO (ISBN: 9781617149856). 32 p.

SERIES: Cool stuff

GRADE LEVEL: Elementary

CONTENTS: Switch plates—lampshades—throw pillows—curtain tiebacks—drawer knobs—canvas art—necklace holder

1386 SCHUETTE, S. *An astronaut cookbook: simple recipes for kids*. 2011, Capstone (ISBN: 9781429653763). 24 p.

SERIES: First cookbooks

GRADE LEVEL: Elementary

CONTENTS: Shooting stars—flying saucers—moon rock salad—comet crunch—the big dipper—astronaut ice cream—Saturn's rings

1387 SCHUETTE, S. *A ballerina cookbook: simple recipes for kids*. 2012, Capstone (ISBN: 9781429676229). 24 p.

SERIES: First cookbooks

GRADE LEVEL: Elementary

CONTENTS: Tutu toppers—plié poppers—stage bites—breakfast—refreshers—snacker—prima ballerinas

1388 **SCHUETTE, S.** *A Christmas cookbook: simple recipes for kids*. 2012, Capstone (ISBN: 9781429659994). 24 p.
  SERIES: First cookbooks
  GRADE LEVEL: Elementary
  CONTENTS: N/A

1389 **SCHUETTE, S.** *A dinosaur cookbook: simple recipes for kids*. 2012, Capstone (ISBN: 9781429676212). 24 p.
  SERIES: First cookbooks
  GRADE LEVEL: Elementary
  CONTENTS: N/A

1390 **SCHUETTE, S.** *A football cookbook: simple recipes for kids*. 2012, Capstone (ISBN: 9781429676205). 24 p.
  SERIES: First cookbooks
  GRADE LEVEL: Elementary
  CONTENTS: Pizza—quarterback snack—chili—guacamole—tacos—dippers—freeze

1391 **SCHUETTE, S.** *How to carve freakishly cool pumpkins*. 2011, Capstone (ISBN: 9781429654203). 32 p.
  SERIES: Halloween extreme
  GRADE LEVEL: Upper elementary
  CONTENTS: Carving basics—spider bite—wicked witch—spooky skeleton—attack of the killer pumpkin—under the sea—get inked—witch's cauldron—mummy pumpkin—creepy critter—hoot hoot—puking pumpkin

1392 **SCHUETTE, S.** *A monster cookbook: simple recipes for kids*. 2011, Capstone (ISBN: 9781429653770). 24 p.
  SERIES: First cookbooks
  GRADE LEVEL: Elementary
  CONTENTS: N/A

1393 **SCHUETTE, S.** *A pirate cookbook: simple recipes for kids*. 2011, Capstone (ISBN: 9781429653756). 24 p.
  SERIES: First cookbooks
  GRADE LEVEL: Elementary
  CONTENTS: Gangplank dippers—chocolate gunpowder—scurvy soup—Peg-Leg pickles—Blackbeard's breakfast—sea swords—parrot punch

1394 **SCHUETTE, S.** *A princess cookbook: simple recipes for kids*. 2011, Capstone (ISBN: 9781429653749). 24 p.
  SERIES: First cookbooks
  GRADE LEVEL: Elementary
  CONTENTS: Magic wands—royal jewels—fairy-tale floats—princess and the pea salad—slipper sandwiches—castle crunch—princess parfait

1395 **SCHUETTE, S.** *A superhero cookbook: simple recipes for kids*. 2012, Capstone (ISBN: 9781429659987). 24 p.
  SERIES: First cookbooks

GRADE LEVEL: Elementary

CONTENTS: N/A

1396 SCHWARTZ, H. *Banana split pizza and other snack recipes*. 2008, Capstone (ISBN: 9781429613392). 32 p.

SERIES: Fun food for cool cooks

GRADE LEVEL: Elementary

CONTENTS: N/A

1397 SCHWARTZ, H. *Cool engineering activities for girls*. 2012, Capstone (ISBN: 9781429676779). 32 p.

SERIES: Girls science club

GRADE LEVEL: Middle school

CONTENTS: Engineering—litter grabber—fruit—table—carnival secrets—world—water filter—quiet spot—jewelry—tie-dyes—s'mores—fun

1398 SCHWARTZ, H. *Girls' figure skating: ruling the rink*. 2007, Capstone (ISBN: 9780736868228). 32 p.

SERIES: Girls got game

GRADE LEVEL: Elementary

CONTENTS: Skating by the rules—getting started—becoming the best

1399 SCHWARTZ, H. *Girls' golf: teeing it up*. 2008, Capstone (ISBN: 9781429601320). 32 p.

SERIES: Girls got game

GRADE LEVEL: Elementary

CONTENTS: On the green—playing by the rules—hitting the course—becoming the best

1400 SCHWARTZ, H. *Girls' snowboarding: showing off your style*. 2008, Capstone (ISBN: 9781429601351). 32 p.

SERIES: Girls got game

GRADE LEVEL: Elementary

CONTENTS: Ready to ride—staying on the board—beyond the basics—becoming the best

1401 SCHWARTZ, H. *Girls' softball: winning on the diamond*. 2007, Capstone (ISBN: 736868240). 32 p.

SERIES: Girls got game

GRADE LEVEL: Elementary

CONTENTS: Play ball—taking the field—get in the game—becoming the best

1402 SCHWARTZ, H. *Girls' volleyball: setting up success*. 2007, Capstone (ISBN: 9780736868266). 32 p.

SERIES: Girls got game

GRADE LEVEL: Elementary

CONTENTS: Get set—hitting the court—get in the game—becoming the best

1403 SCHWARZ, R. *Wind chimes and whirligigs*. 2007, Kids Can Press (ISBN: 9781553378686).

GRADE LEVEL: Upper elementary – middle school

CONTENTS: Crazy kitten—ring-a-ding bug—clothespin fly—caterpillar—flutterfly—crested key bird—whili-bug—racing snails—spiderweb—big fish—little fish—wind dragon—whirli-bird

1404 SCOTT, J. *Painting more animal friends*. 2008, North Light Books (ISBN: 9781600610349).

GRADE LEVEL: Middle school – high school

CONTENTS: N/A

1405 SEGARRA, M. *Pizza and pasta: little chef recipes*. 2013, Enslow (ISBN: 9780766042636).

GRADE LEVEL: Lower elementary

CONTENTS: N/A

1406 SELLERS, L. *Batting*. 2008, A. and C. Black (ISBN: 9780713687033). 32 p.

SERIES: Know the game skills

GRADE LEVEL: Elementary

CONTENTS: N/A

1407 SELLERS, L. *Bowling*. 2008, A. and C. Black (ISBN: 9780713687026). 32 p.

SERIES: Know the game skills

GRADE LEVEL: Elementary

CONTENTS: N/A

1408 SELLERS, L. *Cricket: fielding*. 2008, A. and C. Black (ISBN: 9780713686944). 32 p.

SERIES: Know the game skills

GRADE LEVEL: Elementary

CONTENTS: N/A

1409 SESKIN, S. *Sing my song: a kid's guide to songwriting*. 2008, Tricycle Press (ISBN: 9781582462660).

GRADE LEVEL: Elementary

CONTENTS: Music terms—songs—good morning—you are what you eat—if I had a million dollars—my pets—my chicken—my dog—a world without family—four Rs—read about it—we're all different—dreams and nightmares—school spirit—write a song

1410 SEXTON, B. *You can draw fairies and princesses*. 2012, Picture Window Books (ISBN: 9781404868083). 24 p.

SERIES: You can draw

GRADE LEVEL: Lower elementary

CONTENTS: N/A

1411 SEXTON, B. *You can draw pets*. 2011, Picture Window Books (ISBN: 9781404862777). 24 p.

SERIES: You can draw

GRADE LEVEL: Lower elementary

CONTENTS: N/A

1412 SEXTON, B. *You can draw planes, trains, and other vehicles*. 2011, Picture Window Books (ISBN: 9781404862784). 24 p.
SERIES: You can draw
GRADE LEVEL: Lower elementary
CONTENTS: N/A

1413 SHASKAN, T. *Art panels, BAM! Speech bubbles, POW! Writing your own graphic novel*. 2010, Picture Window Books (ISBN: 9781404863934). 32 p.
SERIES: Writer's toolbox
GRADE LEVEL: Elementary
CONTENTS: N/A

1414 SHEEN, B. *Foods of Afghanistan*. 2011, KidHaven Press (ISBN: 9780737754209). 64 p.
SERIES: Taste of culture
GRADE LEVEL: Upper elementary – middle school
CONTENTS: Cultural connection—honored tradition—tea and snacks—special foods for special days

1415 SHEEN, B. *Foods of Australia*. 2010, KidHaven Press (ISBN: 9780737748123). 64 p.
SERIES: Taste of culture
GRADE LEVEL: Upper elementary – middle school
CONTENTS: Nature's bounty—casual living—delicious snacks—foods for holidays and celebrations

1416 SHEEN, B. *Foods of Brazil*. 2008, KidHaven Press (ISBN: 9780737737738). 64 p.
SERIES: Taste of culture
GRADE LEVEL: Upper elementary – middle school
CONTENTS: Food rooted in the past—different regions—different dishes—tasty snacks and healthy drinks—food for fiestas

1417 SHEEN, B. *Foods of Chile*. 2011, KidHaven Press (ISBN: 9780737754216). 64 p.
SERIES: Taste of culture
GRADE LEVEL: Upper elementary – middle school
CONTENTS: N/A

1418 SHEEN, B. *Foods of Cuba*. 2011, KidHaven Press (ISBN: 9780737751130). 64 p.
SERIES: Taste of culture
GRADE LEVEL: Upper elementary – middle school
CONTENTS: Beautiful land—cultural stew—snacks and treats—time to celebrate

1419 SHEEN, B. *Foods of Egypt*. 2010, KidHaven Press (ISBN: 9780737748437). 64 p.
SERIES: Taste of culture
GRADE LEVEL: Upper elementary – middle school
CONTENTS: Ancient ingredients—healthy and satisfying meals—irresistible street food—time for sharing

1420 SHEEN, B. *Foods of Ethiopia*. 2008, KidHaven Press (ISBN: 9780737737752). 64 p.
SERIES: Taste of culture
GRADE LEVEL: Upper elementary – middle school

CONTENTS: Ethiopian cooking—favorite foods—coffee and snacks—special occasions

1421 SHEEN, B. *Foods of Germany*. 2007, KidHaven Press (ISBN: 737735546). 64 p.
SERIES: Taste of culture
GRADE LEVEL: Upper elementary – middle school
CONTENTS: Three important ingredients—satisfying hearty appetites—sandwiches and sweets—holiday treats

1422 SHEEN, B. *Foods of India*. 2007, KidHaven Press (ISBN: 9780737735536). 64 p.
SERIES: Taste of culture
GRADE LEVEL: Upper elementary – middle school
CONTENTS: Colorful, fragrant, and delicious—common threads—tasty snacks—honored guests

1423 SHEEN, B. *Foods of Ireland*. 2011, KidHaven Press (ISBN: 9780737751147). 64 p.
SERIES: Taste of culture
GRADE LEVEL: Upper elementary – middle school
CONTENTS: Basic ingredients—simple—filling—and flavorful—it is tea time—let's celebrate

1424 SHEEN, B. *Foods of Kenya*. 2010, KidHaven Press (ISBN: 9780737748130). 64 p.
SERIES: Taste of culture
GRADE LEVEL: Upper elementary – middle school
CONTENTS: Land of contrast—many influences—all kinds of snacks—welcome

1425 SHEEN, B. *Foods of Korea*. 2011, KidHaven Press (ISBN: 9780737751154). 64 p.
SERIES: Taste of culture
GRADE LEVEL: Upper elementary – middle school
CONTENTS: The heart of Korean cooking—a delicious balance—a snacker's paradise—meaningful foods

1426 SHEEN, B. *Foods of Peru*. 2011, KidHaven Press (ISBN: 9780737753462). 64 p.
SERIES: Taste of culture
GRADE LEVEL: Upper elementary – middle school
CONTENTS: N/A

1427 SHEEN, B. *Foods of Scandinavia*. 2010, KidHaven Press (ISBN: 9780737748147). 64 p.
SERIES: Taste of culture
GRADE LEVEL: Upper elementary – middle school
CONTENTS: Days of darkness, days of light—favorite foods—coffee—celebrating with food

1428 SHEEN, B. *Foods of Spain*. 2008, KidHaven Press (ISBN: 9780737735390). 64 p.
SERIES: Taste of culture
GRADE LEVEL: Upper elementary – middle school
CONTENTS: Healthy ingredients—geography and history—round-the-clock treats—special foods for special days

1429 SHEEN, B. *Foods of the Caribbean*. 2008, KidHaven Press (ISBN: 9780737737745). 64 p.
SERIES: Taste of culture
GRADE LEVEL: Upper elementary – middle school
CONTENTS: N/A

1430 SHIRLEY, R. *I want to be a fairy*. 2012, Windmill Books (ISBN: 9781615333585). 24 p.
SERIES: Let's play dress up
GRADE LEVEL: Lower elementary
CONTENTS: Dress—wings—feet—flowers—wand—headband—jewelry—fluttering friend—fairy dust—a fairy's best friend

1431 SHIRLEY, R. *I want to be a knight*. 2012, Windmill Books (ISBN: 9781615333547). 24 p.
SERIES: Let's play dress up
GRADE LEVEL: Lower elementary
CONTENTS: N/A

1432 SHIRLEY, R. *I want to be a pirate*. 2012, Windmill Books (ISBN: 9781615333554). 24 p.
SERIES: Let's play dress up
GRADE LEVEL: Lower elementary
CONTENTS: Tattered togs—vest—bandana—eye—hats—by hook or by crook—a feathered friend—land ahoy!—a trusty cutlass—X marks the spot

1433 SHIRLEY, R. *I want to be a princess*. 2012, Windmill Books (ISBN: 9781615333561). 24 p.
SERIES: Let's play dress up
GRADE LEVEL: Lower elementary
CONTENTS: Gown—sash—toes—gloves—cloak—crown—all that glitters—brooch— hat—along came a prince

1434 SHIRLEY, R. *I want to be a robot*. 2012, Windmill Books (ISBN: 9781615333578). 24 p.
SERIES: Let's play dress up
GRADE LEVEL: Lower elementary
CONTENTS: N/A

1435 SHIRLEY, R. *I want to be an astronaut*. 2012, Windmill Books (ISBN: 9781615333592). 24 p.
SERIES: Let's play dress up
GRADE LEVEL: Lower elementary
CONTENTS: Suit—a helmet—boots and equipment belt—moon dust—astro pack—space speak—alien detector—do you believe in aliens?—snapping in space—the flag

1436 SHORES, L. *How to build a fizzy rocket*. 2011, Capstone (ISBN: 9781429644938). 24 p.
SERIES: Hands-on science fun

GRADE LEVEL: Lower elementary

CONTENTS: Get started—fizzy rocket—how does it work

1437 SHORES, L. *How to build a tornado in a bottle*. 2011, Capstone (ISBN: 9781429644938). 24 p.

SERIES: Hands-on science fun

GRADE LEVEL: Lower elementary

CONTENTS: Get started—tornado in a bottle—how does it work

1438 SHORES, L. *How to build flipsticks*. 2011, Capstone (ISBN: 9781429652926). 24 p.

SERIES: Hands-on science fun

GRADE LEVEL: Lower elementary

CONTENTS: Get started—flipstick—how does it work

1439 SHORES, L. *How to make a liquid rainbow*. 2011, Capstone (ISBN: 9781429652940). 24 p.

SERIES: Hands-on science fun

GRADE LEVEL: Lower elementary

CONTENTS: Rainbow—liquid rainbow—how does it work

1440 SHORES, L. *How to make a mystery smell balloon*. 2011, Capstone (ISBN: 9781429644945). 24 p.

SERIES: Hands-on science fun

GRADE LEVEL: Lower elementary

CONTENTS: Get started—secret smell—how does it work

1441 SHORES, L. *How to make bubbles*. 2011, Capstone (ISBN: 9781429652933). 24 p.

SERIES: Hands-on science fun

GRADE LEVEL: Lower elementary

CONTENTS: Get started—bubbles—how does it work

1442 SHORES, L. *How to make slime*. 2010, Capstone (ISBN: 9781429655750). 24 p.

SERIES: Hands-on science fun

GRADE LEVEL: Lower elementary

CONTENTS: Get started—slime—how does it work

1443 SIMON, C. *Junior scientists: experiment with water*. 2011, Cherry Lake (ISBN: 9781602798380). 32 p.

SERIES: Science explorer junior

GRADE LEVEL: Lower elementary

CONTENTS: Skin—moving water—water—water everywhere

1444 SIMON, C. *Super cool science experiments: compounds and mixtures*. 2010, Cherry Lake (ISBN: 9781602795365). 32 p.

SERIES: Science explorer

GRADE LEVEL: Elementary

CONTENTS: Mixtures—first things first—mix it up—solution—suspension—substances—compound—do it yourself

1445 SIMON, C. *Super cool science experiments: erosion*. 2010, Cherry Lake (ISBN: 9781602795259). 32 p.

SERIES: Science explorer

GRADE LEVEL: Elementary

CONTENTS: Scientist—first things first—rust—freeze and thaw—erosion—blown bare—pushed ahead—left behind—eaten by erosion—slopes—do it yourself

1446 SIMON, C. *Super cool science experiments: water*. 2010, Cherry Lake (ISBN: 9781602795297). 32 p.

SERIES: Science explorer

GRADE LEVEL: Elementary

CONTENTS: Scientist—first things first—skin—sink or float—water—water everywhere!—water on the move—water power—do it yourself

1447 SIMS, S. *Drawing dungeon creatures*. 2011, Gareth Stevens (ISBN: 9781433940583). 32 p.

SERIES: You can draw fantasy figures

GRADE LEVEL: Upper elementary – middle school

CONTENTS: Orc warrior—goblin assassin—evil wizard

1448 SIMS, S. *Drawing heroic warriors*. 2011, Gareth Stevens (ISBN: 9781433940521). 32 p.

SERIES: You can draw fantasy figures

GRADE LEVEL: Upper elementary – middle school

CONTENTS: Male warrior—female warrior—dwarf warrior

1449 SINGH, A. *How to draw the darkest, baddest graphic novel*. 2012, Capstone (ISBN: 9781429665940). 48 p.

SERIES: Velocity

GRADE LEVEL: Middle school – high school

CONTENTS: About face—body basics—style file—superheros—power women—supervillains—setting the scene—making a story

1450 SINGH, A. *How to draw the most exciting, awesome manga*. 2012, Capstone (ISBN: 9781429665933). 48 p.

SERIES: Velocity

GRADE LEVEL: Middle school

CONTENTS: Pieces and parts—body basics—details—heroes and heroines—special characters

1451 SIRRINE, C. *Cool crafts with old CDs: green projects for resourceful kids*. 2011, Capstone (ISBN: 9781429640077). 32 p.

SERIES: Green crafts

GRADE LEVEL: Upper elementary – middle school

CONTENTS: N/A

1452 SIRRINE, C. *Cool crafts with old jeans: green projects for resourceful kids*. 2010, Capstone (ISBN: 9781429640060). 32 p.

SERIES: Green crafts

GRADE LEVEL: Elementary

CONTENTS: Pocket magnet—dreaming of denim—braided belt—wrist wrap—jean scene—pocket purse—hey good looking—denim dining—jean jacket—booty bag

1453 SIRRINE, C. *Cool crafts with old t-shirts: green projects for resourceful kids*. 2010, Capstone (ISBN: 9781429640091). 32 p.

SERIES: Green crafts

GRADE LEVEL: Elementary

CONTENTS: Picture perfect—T-bone—on the go—pillow—fast and fabulous—T-yarn scarf—kozies—undercover—a unique twist

1454 SIRRINE, C. *Cool crafts with old wrappers, cans, and bottles: green projects for resourceful kids*. 2010, Capstone (ISBN: 9781429640084). 32 p.

SERIES: Green crafts

GRADE LEVEL: Elementary

CONTENTS: Lighten up—itty bitty frames—cuff 'em—sundae special—tool tidy—candy lover's ring—hot beads—sweet boxes—origami cranes

1455 SKILLICORN, H. *Friendship crafts*. 2010, Gareth Stevens (ISBN: 9781433935589). 32 p.

SERIES: Creative crafts for kids

GRADE LEVEL: Elementary

CONTENTS: Linking lockets—hand in hand—bubble book—fortune cookies—woven bracelet—message decoder—tropical drink tray—green grub frame—pirate portrait—smile card—sunshine badge—claddagh box

1456 SKILLICORN, H. *Spooky crafts*. 2010, Gareth Stevens (ISBN: 9781433935640). 32 p.

SERIES: Creative crafts for kids

GRADE LEVEL: Elementary

CONTENTS: Creepy claws—flashlight lantern—count costume—owl puppet—mystery box—trick finger—witch piñata—bat mobile—monster mask—ghostly whirrer—flaming cauldron—bonehead cookie

1457 SLADE, S. *Cool physics activities for girls*. 2012, Capstone (ISBN: 9781429676755). 32 p.

SERIES: Girls science club

GRADE LEVEL: Middle school

CONTENTS: Magnets—floating needle—water trick—party punch trick—party drinks—sticks—divers—balancing can—gravity—ping-pong ball—slime

1458 SLADE, S. *Fencing for fun!* 2009, Compass Point (ISBN: 9780756538668). 48 p.

SERIES: For fun!

GRADE LEVEL: Elementary

CONTENTS: The basics—introduction: the art of sword fighting—the strip—types of fencing: foil—épée—saber—equipment—physical chess—offense—defense—doing it—the salute—on guard!—advance and retreat: fancy footwork—lunge—attack—parry—electric fencing—a bout—etiquette

1459 SLADE, S. *Let's go camping*. 2007, PowerKids Press (ISBN: 9781404236509). 32 p.

SERIES: Adventures outdoors

GRADE LEVEL: Elementary

CONTENTS: Camping—planning—choosing a site—gear—pitching a tent—weather—cooking—the campfire—critters—camping and nature

1460   SLADE, S. *Let's go canoeing and kayaking*. 2007, PowerKids Press (ISBN: 9781404236493). 32 p.

SERIES: Adventures outdoors

GRADE LEVEL: Elementary

CONTENTS: Canoeing and kayaking—where to go—gear—learning to canoe—white-water canoeing—canoeing and camping—early canoes—kayaking—the first kayaks—sea kayaking—canoeing—kayaking and nature

1461   SLADE, S. *Let's go fishing*. 2007, PowerKids Press (ISBN: 9781404236479). 32 p.

SERIES: Adventures outdoors

GRADE LEVEL: Elementary

CONTENTS: Where to fish—fishing gear—bait—casting a line—freshwater fishing—fishing in the ocean—fly-fishing—ice fishing—kinds of fish—fishing and nature

1462   SLADE, S. *Let's go hiking*. 2007, PowerKids Press (ISBN: 9781404236516). 32 p.

SERIES: Adventures outdoors

GRADE LEVEL: Elementary

CONTENTS: Hiking—preparing for your hiking trip—hiking gear—hitting the trail—day hikes—overnight hikes—hiking in all kinds of weather—orienteering—mountaineering—popular hiking trails—hiking and nature

1463   SMALLEY, C. *A project guide to fish and amphibians*. 2011, Mitchell Lane (ISBN: 9781584158738). 48 p.

SERIES: Life science projects for kids

GRADE LEVEL: Upper elementary

CONTENTS: N/A

1464   SMART, D. *The children's baking book*. 2009, DK (ISBN: 9780756657888). 128 p.

GRADE LEVEL: Upper elementary – middle school

CONTENTS: Cookies and baked goods—doughs—cakes—pastry—decoration

1465   SNYDER, B. *Everything butt art at the zoo*. 2011, Madbrook (ISBN: 9780983065708). 48 p.

SERIES: Everything butt art

GRADE LEVEL: Elementary

CONTENTS: Baboon—anaconda—chameleon—alligator—hippo—gorilla—snow monkey—panda—tiger—kangaroo—bird—ostrich—giraffe—lion—zebra—elephant

1466   SNYDER, B. *Everything butt art on the farm*. 2011, Madbrook (ISBN: 9780983065715). 48 p.

SERIES: Everything butt art

GRADE LEVEL: Elementary

CONTENTS: Horse—chicken—rooster—goat—llama—pig—cat—mouse—sheep—sheepdog—goose—cow—tractor—rabbit—gopher—scarecrow

1467 **SOBEY, E.** *Electric motor experiments*. 2011, Enslow (ISBN: 9780766033061). 128 p.

SERIES: Cool science projects with technology

GRADE LEVEL: Upper elementary – middle school

CONTENTS: Motors at home—transistor battery—measure a battery's voltage—measure common materials' voltage—DC motor—take a motor apart—make a motor—direct drive—belt drive—pulley set—cam—crank—gear set—connect motor—measure voltages—add resistance to circuit—switch—model car—propeller dive—three-wheel car with direct drive—belt drive—gear drive—shake drive—test a battery—swamp boat—propellers—side-wheel electrical boat—hydraulic drive—waterproofing motors—build an electric sculpture

1468 **SOBEY, E.** *The motorboat book: build and launch 20 jet boats, paddle-wheelers, electric submarines & more*. 2013, Chicago Review Press (ISBN: 9781613744475). 224 p.

SERIES: Science in motion

GRADE LEVEL: Middle school – high school

CONTENTS: Large ocean—smaller oceans—seas—hulls—aluminum hulls—two-minute boats—aluminum boat hulls—sails—gravity-powered boat—gravity-powered boat with electric pump—balloon-powered boat—nose hook boat—stern wheeler or paddle-wheeler—side wheeler or side paddle-wheeler—swamp boat—easier swamp boat—motor duck—motorboat—belt drive boat—gear drive boat—water jet boat—solar-powered boat—rainy-day solar-powered boat—steamboat—jet boat—plop—skiff—semisubmersible—water pistol—hand pump—electric pump—baster pump—diaphragm pump—electric pump—siphon pump—medusa submarine—organic submarine—waterproof a motor—electric submarine—waterproof a battery case—submersible rov—holdup—submarine—foghorn—steel float—waves—more waves

1469 **SOBEY, E.** *Radio-controlled car experiments*. 2011, Enslow (ISBN: 9780766033047). 128 p.

SERIES: Cool science projects with technology

GRADE LEVEL: Upper elementary – middle school

CONTENTS: R/C car—motor—measuring speed—top speed—radar gun—deceleration—radio range—radio waves through buildings—radio waves through other materials—antenna lengths—lengthening the antennas—compare antenna lengths—receiving antenna—dragging a bag—stopping distance—dragging a rope—towing capacity—dragging materials—increasing the load—weight—increase size of wheels—increase size of front wheels—model car—electric car—reversing the leads—measure voltage—measuring voltages while the motor is running—measuring current—battery—direct drive car—belt-drive car—remote-controlled car—convert remote-controlled car to radio-controlled car

1470 **SOBEY, E.** *Robot experiments*. 2011, Enslow (ISBN: 9780766033030). 128 p.

SERIES: Cool science projects with technology

GRADE LEVEL: Upper elementary – middle school

CONTENTS: Motorized appliance—battery voltage—sensors—servo motor—wheel clock—write a program—operate the servo—double the distance—zero value—test another servo motor—standard servos—continuous rotation servos—make sounds—cascading sounds—a tune—lay out the robot—test the robot—control motion—make left turn—run the square—led—variable pulse length—light up—miscoswitch—switch circuit—touch sensor—maze—switch—light sensor

1471 SOBEY, E. *Solar cell and renewable energy experiments*. 2011, Enslow (ISBN: 9780766033054). 128 p.
SERIES: Cool science projects with technology
GRADE LEVEL: Upper elementary – middle school
CONTENTS: N/A

1472 SOMERVILL, B. *Oral reports*. 2009, Heinemann (ISBN: 9781432911720). 32 p.
SERIES: School projects survival guides
GRADE LEVEL: Upper elementary – middle school
CONTENTS: What is an oral report—topic—research—organizing—knowing the audience—writing and revising—visual aids—practice—presenting the report—graphic organizers

1473 SOMERVILL, B. *Studying and tests*. 2009, Heinemann (ISBN: 9781432911737). 32 p.
SERIES: School projects survival guides
GRADE LEVEL: Upper elementary – middle school
CONTENTS: How you learn—planning for studying—getting the best from books—learning from other sources—different types of tests—studying and preparing for a test—test day—study aids

1474 SOMERVILL, B. *Team projects*. 2009, Heinemann (ISBN: 9781432911744). 32 p.
SERIES: School projects survival guides
GRADE LEVEL: Upper elementary – middle school
CONTENTS: What is a team project—choosing a project—working with a team—making choices—researching—team troubles—putting it all together—finishing up—ideas—research resources

1475 SOMERVILL, B. *Written reports*. 2009, Heinemann (ISBN: 9781432911751). 32 p.
SERIES: School projects survival guides
GRADE LEVEL: Upper elementary – middle school
CONTENTS: What is a written report—topic—research—notes and organizing—the rough draft—editing and revising—publishing—graphic organizers

1476 SOO-WARR, L. *Self-defense for women*. 2010, Rosen (ISBN: 9781435853584). 256 p.
SERIES: A young woman's guide to health and well-being
GRADE LEVEL: Middle school – high school
CONTENTS: What is self-defense—A.P.A.P.—awareness—evasions—protecting yourself—in the car—everyday situations—sexual interference—knife attacks—at home—in the office

1477 SOUTHGATE, A. *Drawing manga boys*. 2012, Rosen Central (ISBN: 9781448847990). 80 p.
SERIES: Manga magic
GRADE LEVEL: Middle school – high school
CONTENTS: Male faces—male hairstyles—basic hand poses—action hand and arm poses—feet and legs—male footwear—clothes and costuming

1478 SOUTHGATE, A. *Drawing manga expressions and poses*. 2012, Rosen Central (ISBN: 9781448848003). 80 p.

   SERIES: Teen guide to drawing manga

   GRADE LEVEL: Middle school – high school

   CONTENTS: Female figures—male figures—female faces—male faces—expressions—emotions—and character types

1479 SOUTHGATE, A. *Drawing manga faces and bodies*. 2012, Rosen Central (ISBN: 9781448892631). 80 p.

   SERIES: Teen guide to drawing manga

   GRADE LEVEL: Middle school – high school

   CONTENTS: N/A

1480 SOUTHGATE, A. *Drawing manga mecha, weapons, and wheels*. 2013, Rosen Central (ISBN: 9781448892426). 80 p.

   SERIES: Teen guide to drawing manga

   GRADE LEVEL: Middle school – high school

   CONTENTS: Manga machines and robots—fighting manga—moving manga—dressing up manga

1481 SOUTHGATE, A. *Drawing manga men*. 2013, Rosen Central (ISBN: 9781448892402). 80 p.

   SERIES: Teen guide to drawing manga

   GRADE LEVEL: Middle school – high school

   CONTENTS: Male faces and features—men's manga hairstyles—male bodies—men's manga clothing

1482 SOUTHGATE, A. *Drawing manga weapons, vehicles, and accessories*. 2012, Rosen Central (ISBN: 9781448848010). 80 p.

   SERIES: Teen guide to drawing manga

   GRADE LEVEL: Middle school – high school

   CONTENTS: Accessories—weapons—vehicles

1483 SOUTHGATE, A. *Drawing manga women*. 2013, Rosen Central (ISBN: 9781448892396). 80 p.

   SERIES: Teen guide to drawing manga

   GRADE LEVEL: Middle school – high school

   CONTENTS: N/A

1484 SPANGLER, S. *Fire bubbles and exploding toothpaste: more unforgettable experiments that make science fun*. 2011, Greenleaf Book Group (ISBN: 9781608321896). 160 p.

   SERIES: Steve Spangler science

   GRADE LEVEL: Upper elementary – middle school

   CONTENTS: Windbag—soda bottle race—water suspension—rocket straws—bottle music—blender-smoothie—top—smoke bubbles—convection currents—eggshells—rocket car—nails—puzzle—seesaw—color mixing—pendulum catch—balloon—smile—skewer through balloon—bowling balls—bubbles—tornado—peanuts—exploding toothpaste—kid-friendly exploding toothpaste

1485 SPANGLER, S. *Naked eggs and flying potatoes: unforgettable experiments that make science fun*. 2010, Greenleaf Book Group (ISBN: 9781608320608). 160 p.
SERIES: Steve Spangler science
GRADE LEVEL: Upper elementary – middle school
CONTENTS: Ping pong balls and toilet paper—straw through potato—potatoes—bottle—can crusher—smoke rings—lava bottle—milk—CO_2 sandwich—soap souffle—cabbage chemistry—nails for breakfast—penny cleaner—sinking soda—density column—egg in the bottle—eggs—folding egg—subzero science – dry ice—dry ice crystal ball bubble—goo—glacier gak—baby diaper—floating water—leakproof bag—egg drop—screaming balloon—burning money—geyser experiment

1486 SPEECHLEY, G. *Arts and crafts for myths and tales*. 2010, Gareth Stevens (ISBN: 9781433935671). 32 p.
SERIES: Creative crafts for kids
GRADE LEVEL: Upper elementary
CONTENTS: Magic amulet—snake demon—little lyre—sand painting—glinting dagger—pixie pen tops—pot of gold—phoenix clip—cyclops eye—totem pole—Trojan horse—flying fairies

1487 SPEECHLEY, G. *Birthday crafts*. 2010, Gareth Stevens (ISBN: 9781433935527). 32 p.
SERIES: Creative crafts for kids
GRADE LEVEL: Elementary
CONTENTS: Candy chain—snack stand—glitter balloons—cake slice box—tumbler—memory book—crazy cats—splat invites—bug muncher—door knocker—magic dollar—birthday card

1488 SPEECHLEY, G. *Valentine crafts*. 2010, Gareth Stevens (ISBN: 9781433936005). 32 p.
SERIES: Creative crafts for kids
GRADE LEVEL: Elementary
CONTENTS: Spinning Valentine—kiss seal—fortuneteller—love bugs—lip smackers—lovebird—red rose—heart jigsaw—lavender heart—heart cookies—keepsakes—chocolate lollipops

1489 SPEECHLEY, G. *World crafts*. 2010, Gareth Stevens (ISBN: 9781433935619). 32 p.
SERIES: Creative crafts for kids
GRADE LEVEL: Elementary
CONTENTS: Mardi Gras tambourine—Celtic window—mask—mirror—bracelets—dream catcher—didgeridoo—armadillo—dragon—dancing bear—treasure box—fan

1490 SPILLING, M. *Yoga step-by-step*. 2011, Rosen Central (ISBN: 9781448815500). 96 p.
SERIES: Skills in motion
GRADE LEVEL: Upper elementary – middle school
CONTENTS: N/A

1491 ST. JOHN, A. *5 steps to drawing dogs and cats*. 2012, Child's World (ISBN: 9781609731960). 32 p.
SERIES: 5 steps to drawing
GRADE LEVEL: Elementary

CONTENTS: Puppies and kittens—dogs—cats—drawing tips—long-haired Himalayan—short-haired tabby—Manx cat—Calico kitten—boxer—border collie—Saint Bernard—Scottish terrier

1492 **ST. JOHN, A.** *5 steps to drawing magical creatures*. 2012, Child's World (ISBN: 9781609731984). 32 p.
SERIES: 5 steps to drawing
GRADE LEVEL: Elementary
CONTENTS: Elf—wizard—mermaid—gnome—fairy—dragon—unicorn—leprechaun

1493 **ST. JOHN, A.** *5 steps to drawing monsters*. 2012, Child's World (ISBN: 9781609732028). 32 p.
SERIES: 5 steps to drawing
GRADE LEVEL: Elementary
CONTENTS: N/A

1494 **ST. JOHN, A.** *5 steps to drawing sea creatures*. 2012, Child's World (ISBN: 9781609732042). 32 p.
SERIES: 5 steps to drawing
GRADE LEVEL: Elementary
CONTENTS: N/A

1495 **ST. JOHN, C.** *Wrestling*. 2012, PowerKids Press (ISBN: 9781448852864). 32 p.
SERIES: Master this!
GRADE LEVEL: Upper elementary – middle school
CONTENTS: N/A

1496 **STAMPS, C.** *Horse riding: a step-by-step guide to the secrets of horse riding*. 2012, DK (ISBN: 9781405391498). 64 p.
GRADE LEVEL: Upper elementary
CONTENTS: N/A

1497 **STEELE, P.** *The amazing world of pirates*. 2008, Anness (ISBN: 9781844766000). 64 p.
SERIES: The Amazing World of
GRADE LEVEL: Elementary
CONTENTS: N/A

1498 **STEELE, P.** *Ancient Egypt*. 2009, Rosen (ISBN: 9781435851733). 64 p.
SERIES: Passport to the past
GRADE LEVEL: Upper elementary – middle school
CONTENTS: Crown—Egyptian house—lotus tile—pyramid—canopic jars—Udjat eye—shaduf—cake—mirror—water clock—rattle—Mehen board—lion that roars—golden fly—boat

1499 **STEELE, P.** *Hands-on history! Ancient China: step into the time of the Chinese Empire, with 15 step-by-step projects and over 300 exciting pictures*. 2013, Armadillo (ISBN: 9781843229698). 64 p.
SERIES: Hands-on history!

GRADE LEVEL: Upper elementary

CONTENTS: N/A

1500 STEELE, P. *Hands-on history! Ancient Egypt: find out about the land of the pharaohs, with 15 step-by-step projects and over 400 exciting pictures.* 2013, Armadillo (ISBN: 9781843229636). 64 p.
SERIES: Hands-on history!
GRADE LEVEL: Upper elementary
CONTENTS: N/A

1501 STEELE, P. *Hands-on history! Ancient Rome: step into the time of the Roman Empire, with 15 step-by-step projects and over 370 exciting pictures.* 2013, Armadillo (ISBN: 9781843226925). 64 p.
SERIES: Hands-on history!
GRADE LEVEL: Upper elementary
CONTENTS: N/A

1502 STEELE, P. *Hands-on history! Incas: step into the spectacular world of Ancient South America, with 340 exciting pictures and 15 step-by-step projects.* 2013, Armadillo (ISBN: 9781843227311). 64 p.
SERIES: Hands-on history!
GRADE LEVEL: Upper elementary
CONTENTS: N/A

1503 STEELE, P. *Hands-on history! Viking world: learn about the legendary Norse raiders, with 15 step-by-step projects and more than 350 exciting pictures.* 2013, Armadillo (ISBN: 9781843226949). 64 p.
SERIES: Hands-on history!
GRADE LEVEL: Upper elementary
CONTENTS: N/A

1504 STEPHENS, S. *Show off: how to do absolutely everything one step at a time.* 2009, Candlewick Press (ISBN: 9780763645991). 224 p.
GRADE LEVEL: Elementary
CONTENTS: N/A

1505 STOCK, C. *Skateboarding: step-by-step.* 2010, Rosen Central (ISBN: 9781435833654). 96 p.
SERIES: Skills in motion
GRADE LEVEL: Upper elementary – middle school
CONTENTS: Beginner—intermediate—advanced

1506 STOREY, R. *Animals.* 2014, Smart Apple Media (ISBN: 9781599208961). 32 p.
SERIES: Have fun with arts & crafts
GRADE LEVEL: Elementary
CONTENTS: Big cat masks—bendy monkeys—Japanese fish kites—horse puppet—cartoon animals—flippy frogs—egg box bugs—furry hamster—pom-pom animals—snappy croc—dancing dragon—cake-pop piglets—crazy penguin cards

1507 STOREY, R. *Cycling*. 2008, Franklin Watts (ISBN: 9780749683405). 30 p.
SERIES: Know your sport
GRADE LEVEL: Upper elementary
CONTENTS: N/A

1508 STOREY, R. *Dinghy sailing*. 2009, Franklin Watts (ISBN: 9780749688592). 30 p.
SERIES: Know your sport
GRADE LEVEL: Upper elementary
CONTENTS: N/A

1509 STOREY, R. *Fairies*. 2014, Smart Apple Media (ISBN: 9781599208985). 32 p.
SERIES: Have fun with arts & crafts
GRADE LEVEL: Elementary
CONTENTS: Fairy wand—fairy tutu—gossamer wings—snowflakes—fairy crown—dream catcher—tea party—collage picture—fairy homes—sleeping beauty bed—flying fairies—flower garden—frame

1510 STOREY, R. *Fishing*. 2009, Franklin Watts (ISBN: 9780749688615). 30 p.
SERIES: Know your sport
GRADE LEVEL: Upper elementary
CONTENTS: N/A

1511 STOREY, R. *Irish dancing: and other national dances*. 2007, Sea to Sea (ISBN: 9781597710503). 32 p.
SERIES: Get dancing
GRADE LEVEL: Elementary
CONTENTS: Irish dancing—feet of flames—Spanish flamenco—Indian dancing—other national dances

1512 STOREY, R. *Jive and street dance*. 2010, Franklin Watts (ISBN: 9780749693657). 32 p.
SERIES: Simply dance
GRADE LEVEL: Upper elementary
CONTENTS: N/A

1513 STOREY, R. *Knights and castles*. 2013, Franklin Watts (ISBN: 9781445110677). 32 p.
SERIES: Have fun with arts & crafts
GRADE LEVEL: Elementary
CONTENTS: N/A

1514 STOREY, R. *Line dancing: and other folk dances*. 2007, Sea to Sea (ISBN: 9781597710527). 32 p.
SERIES: Get dancing
GRADE LEVEL: Elementary
CONTENTS: Line dancing—boot scootin' steps—electric slide—Ceilidh dancing—Hungarian folk dance—special folk dances

1515 STOREY, R. *Make your own creative cards*. 2011, PowerKids Press (ISBN: 9781615325917). 24 p.
SERIES: Do it yourself projects!

GRADE LEVEL: Upper elementary

CONTENTS: Printed card—surprise card—pop-up card—pull-tab card—padded card—photo card—origami card—glowing card

1516 STOREY, R. *Make your own toys*. 2010, PowerKids Press (ISBN: 9781615325924). 24 p.
    SERIES: Do it yourself projects!
    GRADE LEVEL: Upper elementary
    CONTENTS: Yo-yo—racing bug—jumping jack—beanbag frog—racing car—penguin family—kaleidoscope—carousel

1517 STOREY, R. *Rock 'n' roll: and other dance crazes*. 2007, Sea to Sea (ISBN: 9781597710510). 32 p.
    SERIES: Get dancing
    GRADE LEVEL: Elementary
    CONTENTS: Rock and roll dancing—do the hand jive—the twist—disco dancing—the salsa—other dance crazes

1518 STOREY, R. *Samba and salsa*. 2010, Franklin Watts (ISBN: 9780749693640). 32 p.
    SERIES: Simply dance
    GRADE LEVEL: Upper elementary
    CONTENTS: N/A

1519 STOREY, R. *Tango and paso doble*. 2010, Franklin Watts (ISBN: 9780749693633). 32 p.
    SERIES: Simply dance
    GRADE LEVEL: Upper elementary
    CONTENTS: N/A

1520 STOREY, R. *Toys*. 2013, Wayland (ISBN: 9780750271899). 24 p.
    SERIES: Make and use
    GRADE LEVEL: Upper elementary
    CONTENTS: N/A

1521 STOREY, R. *Tractors and trucks*. 2014, Smart Apple Media (ISBN: 9781599209012). 32 p.
    SERIES: Have fun with arts & crafts
    GRADE LEVEL: Elementary
    CONTENTS: N/A

1522 STOREY, R. *Waltz and quick step*. 2010, Franklin Watts (ISBN: 9780749693664). 32 p.
    SERIES: Simply dance
    GRADE LEVEL: Upper elementary
    CONTENTS: N/A

1523 STOTTER, M. *Hands-on history! Native Americans: find out about the world of North American Indians, with 400 exciting pictures and 15 step-by-step projects*. 2013, Armadillo (ISBN: 9781843229759). 64 p.
    SERIES: Hands-on history!

GRADE LEVEL: Upper elementary

CONTENTS: N/A

1524 STRAND, J. *Holiday crafting and baking with kids: gifts, sweets, and treats for the whole family*. 2011, Chronicle (ISBN: 9781452101095).

GRADE LEVEL: Elementary

CONTENTS: N/A

1525 STUDELSKA, J. *Archery for fun!* 2008, Compass Point (ISBN: 9780756533908). 48 p.

SERIES: For fun!

GRADE LEVEL: Elementary

CONTENTS: Native American archery—basic tackle and targets—types of bows—varieties of arrows—extras and accessories—doing it—play it safe—strength—endurance—and flexibility—measuring up—what to wear—mimicking: practice without shooting—shooting the arrow—improving your shot

1526 STUDELSKA, J. *Camping for fun!* 2008, Compass Point (ISBN: 9780756533991). 48 p.

SERIES: For fun!

GRADE LEVEL: Elementary

CONTENTS: Shelter—equipment—wildlife—camping clean-up—weather—doing it—picking a campsite—making a fire—first—camp food—camping at home—no tent needed—other places to camp—canoe camping—winter camping

1527 STUDELSKA, J. *Skateboarding for fun!* 2008, Compass Point (ISBN: 756532914). 48 p.

SERIES: For fun!

GRADE LEVEL: Elementary

CONTENTS: On the roll—catch a wave—no limits—on a deck—gear—parks and camps—the first few rides—doing it—ollie—flow and kick turn—dropping in—50-50—manualing—kick flip—shuvit—grinding

1528 STUDELSKA, J. *Yoga for fun!* 2008, Compass Point (ISBN: 9780756532826). 48 p.

SERIES: For fun!

GRADE LEVEL: Elementary

CONTENTS: Why yoga—spiritual side—kinds of yoga—sneak peak—keep moving—doing it—getting started—sit or easy position: sukhasana—cat dog: bidalasana and svanasana—mountain: tadasana—standing forward bend: uttanasana—cobra: bhujangasana—sun salutation: surya namaskar—corpse: shavasana

1529 STUTT, R. *The skateboarding field manual*. 2009, Firefly Books (ISBN: 9781554073627). 143 p.

GRADE LEVEL: Middle school – high school

CONTENTS: Skateboarding 101—flat ground basics—transition basics—flip tricks—grinds—slides

1530 SUEN, A. *Developing and designing your glee club performance*. 2012, Rosen (ISBN: 9781448868773). 64 p.

SERIES: Glee club

GRADE LEVEL: Upper elementary – middle school

CONTENTS: N/A

1531 SUNDSTEN, B. *My first book of knots*. 2009, Skyhorse (ISBN: 9781602396234). 44 p.

GRADE LEVEL: Upper elementary

CONTENTS: Some basic knots—other useful knots—different ways to splice two lines—shortening and reinforcing ropes—heaving-line knot—protect the rope end—fishing knots—everyday knots—decorative knots—knots for games and outdoor activities

1532 SUTHERLAND, A. *Take great photos*! 2013, Arcturus (ISBN: 9781848585768). 32 p.

SERIES: Find your talent

GRADE LEVEL: Middle school – high school

CONTENTS: Find your talent—pick the moment—great photos—sharp and clear—light it up—still got it—say cheese—fine-tuning portraits—action shots—playing with animals—downloading—software

1533 SUTTON, A. *Motocross: how to be an awesome motocross rider*. 2012, Capstone (ISBN: 9781429668866). 48 p.

SERIES: Velocity

GRADE LEVEL: Upper elementary – middle school

CONTENTS: Buying a used bike—riding equipment—where to ride—fitness and training—accelerating—braking—cornering—advanced cornering—starts—supercross—basic jumping—advanced jumping—extreme conditions—be a pro mechanic—cleaning your bike—pre-ride preparations—troubleshooting

1534 SWISSLER, B. *Winning lacrosse for girls*. 2009, Chelsea House (ISBN: 9780816077120). 212 p.

SERIES: Winning sports for girls

GRADE LEVEL: Middle school – high school

CONTENTS: N/A

1535 TAKEMURA, M. *The manga guide to biochemistry*. 2010, No Starch Press (ISBN: 9781593272760). 272 p.

SERIES: EduManga

GRADE LEVEL: High school

CONTENTS: N/A

1536 TAKEMURA, M. *The manga guide to molecular biology*. 2009, No Starch Press (ISBN: 9781593272029). 272 p.

SERIES: EduManga

GRADE LEVEL: High school

CONTENTS: N/A

1537 TAMES, R. *Hands-on history! Ancient Greece: step into the world of the classical Greeks, with 15 step-by-step projects and 350 exciting pictures*. 2013, Armadillo (ISBN: 9781843229643). 64 p.

SERIES: Hands-on history!

GRADE LEVEL: Upper elementary

CONTENTS: N/A

1538 TAYLOR, B. *Apes and monkeys*. 2011, Kingfisher (ISBN: 9780753466032). 56 p.
   SERIES: Discover science
   GRADE LEVEL: Elementary
   CONTENTS: N/A

1539 TAYLOR, B. *Insects*. 2010, Kingfisher (ISBN: 9780753464496). 56 p.
   SERIES: Discover science
   GRADE LEVEL: Elementary
   CONTENTS: N/A

1540 TAYLOR, D. *Cartoons and manga*. 2012, PowerKids Press (ISBN: 9781448852833). 32 p.
   SERIES: Master this!
   GRADE LEVEL: Upper elementary – middle school
   CONTENTS: Body basics—heads and faces—hands—poses—objects—inking and coloring—animation

1541 TAYLOR-BUTLER, C. *Junior scientists: experiment with magnets*. 2011, Cherry Lake (ISBN: 9781602798441). 32 p.
   SERIES: Science explorer junior
   GRADE LEVEL: Lower elementary
   CONTENTS: Force—opposites—power

1542 TAYLOR-BUTLER, C. *Junior scientists: experiment with solar energy*. 2011, Cherry Lake (ISBN: 9781602798403). 32 p.
   SERIES: Science explorer junior
   GRADE LEVEL: Lower elementary
   CONTENTS: Up—clean water—garden

1543 TAYLOR-BUTLER, C. *Super cool science experiments: magnets*. 2010, Cherry Lake (ISBN: 9781602795303). 32 p.
   SERIES: Science explorer
   GRADE LEVEL: Elementary
   CONTENTS: Magnets—first things first—force—opposites—power—North—the body—do it yourself

1544 TAYLOR-BUTLER, C. *Super cool science experiments: solar energy*. 2010, Cherry Lake (ISBN: 9781602795273). 32 p.
   SERIES: Science explorer
   GRADE LEVEL: Elementary
   CONTENTS: Sun—first things first—up—the sun—clean water—garden—hot dog—do it yourself

1545 TAYLOR-BUTLER, C. *Super cool science experiments: sound*. 2010, Cherry Lake (ISBN: 9781602795327:). 32 p.
   SERIES: Science explorer
   GRADE LEVEL: Elementary
   CONTENTS: Listen—first things first—ear drum—waves—music—pitch—sound barrier—do it yourself

1546 TELLER, J. *Skateboarding: an awesome skateboarder*. 2012, Capstone (ISBN: 9781429668835). 48 p.

  SERIES: Velocity

  GRADE LEVEL: Upper elementary – middle school

  CONTENTS: Types of skateboards—basic equipment—from sidewalk surfer to skater—designing your own board—changing truck bushings—truck removal and installation—changing wheels—bearing removal and replacement—installing grip tape—skate greats—basic stance and moving the board—turning and stopping—learning to ollie—identifying basic tricks—ramp riding: dropping in—simple and advanced transitions—skateboard etiquette—longboarding and slalom—skateboarding faqs

1547 TEMPLE, K. *Drawing in color*. 2009, Lark Books (ISBN: 9781579908218). 112 p.

  SERIES: Art for kids

  GRADE LEVEL: Upper elementary

  CONTENTS: N/A

1548 THALACKER, K. *Knitting with Gigi: includes step-by-step instructions and 8 patterns*. 2007, Martingale and Co. (ISBN: 9781564777584).

  GRADE LEVEL: Upper elementary

  CONTENTS: Learning to knit—what you need—yarn ball—make a slipknot and cast on—knit stitch—decrease—start a new yarn ball or color—bind off—sew a seam—weave in ends—fix mistakes—patterns—pot holder—belt—baby blanket—scarves—wrist warmers—bag—hat

1549 THOMAS, J. *Start to bead*. 2008, Search Press (ISBN: 9781844483914). 48 p.

  SERIES: Start to

  GRADE LEVEL: Upper elementary – middle school

  CONTENTS: Ethnic pendant—safety pin bracelet—daisy ring—charm bracelet—trinket pot—bugle necklace—mini bag—friendship bracelet

1550 THOMAS, L. *100% pure fake: gross out your friends and family with 25 great special effects!* 2009, Kids Can Press (ISBN: 9781554532902).

  GRADE LEVEL: Upper elementary – middle school

  CONTENTS: Fake blood—scars and blisters—scar face—rotting skin—hair mole—s'not snot—eyeballs—brain pie—shrunken heads—severed finger—broken glass—chocolate milk spill—slimy worms—road kill guts—veggie vomit—edible barf—cat and dog doo-doos—edible doo-doos—puddle of pee

1551 THOMSON, R. *Masks: craft ideas from around the world*. 2011, Sea to Sea (ISBN: 9781445101576). 32 p.

  SERIES: World of design

  GRADE LEVEL: Elementary

  CONTENTS: Carnival masks—eye mask—wolf mask—monster mask—bird mask—dramatic mask

1552 THOMSON, R. *Musical instruments: craft ideas from around the world*. 2011, Sea to Sea (ISBN: 9781597712125). 32 p.

SERIES: World of design

GRADE LEVEL: Elementary

CONTENTS: Guiro—maracas—sistrum—monkey drum—ocarina—one-string violin

1553 THOMSON, R. *Toys and models: craft ideas from around the world*. 2011, Sea to Sea (ISBN: 9781597712095). 32 p.

SERIES: World of design

GRADE LEVEL: Elementary

CONTENTS: Robot—animal—truck—acrobat—nodding tiger—puppet

1554 THORPE, Y. *Canoeing and kayaking*. 2011, Sea to Sea (ISBN: 9781597712859). 30 p.

SERIES: Know your sport

GRADE LEVEL: Upper elementary

CONTENTS: Types of boat—clothing and equipment—launching—paddling and steering—safety—white-water paddling—reading the river—slalom and wildwater—sprint racing—surf kayaking

1555 TILLI, L. *My cookbook of baking*. 2012, QEB (ISBN: 9781609922788). 64 p.

SERIES: My cookbook

GRADE LEVEL: Upper elementary – middle school

CONTENTS: N/A

1556 TILLI, L. *My cookbook of cakes*. 2012, QEB (ISBN: 9781609922795). 64 p.

SERIES: My cookbook

GRADE LEVEL: Upper elementary – middle school

CONTENTS: N/A

1557 TJERNAGEL, K. *Gross recipes*. 2013, Capstone (ISBN: 9781429699259).

SERIES: Gross Guides

GRADE LEVEL: Upper elementary – middle school

CONTENTS: N/A

1558 TORRES, J. *Top 25 basketball skills, tips, and tricks*. 2012, Enslow (ISBN: 9780766038578). 48 p.

SERIES: Top 25 sports skills, tips, and tricks

GRADE LEVEL: Elementary

CONTENTS: N/A

1559 TORRES, J. *Top 25 football skills, tips, and tricks*. 2012, Enslow (ISBN: 9780766038585). 48 p.

SERIES: Top 25 sports skills, tips, and tricks

GRADE LEVEL: Elementary

CONTENTS: Passing and receiving—rushing—line play—defense and special teams—fun tricks and training

1560 TORRES, L. *Rock your party*. 2010, QEB (ISBN: 9781595669353). 32 p.

SERIES: QEB rock your . . .

GRADE LEVEL: Upper elementary

CONTENTS: Paper punch art invitations—newspaper party hats—name tags—fingerprint cards—sock friend—favor bags—piñata—yarn pals—ball toss—tissue paper puffs—wreath—birthday garland

1561 TORRES, L. *Rock your room*. 2011, QEB (ISBN: 9781595669384). 32 p.
  SERIES: QEB rock your . . .
  GRADE LEVEL: Upper elementary
  CONTENTS: Picture frame—photo holder—starry night box—sun catchers—bulletin board—art tacks—switch-it—clips—mini dresser—stained glass—pencil holder—banner

1562 TORRES, L. *Rock your school stuff*. 2010, QEB (ISBN: 9781595669360). 32 p.
  SERIES: QEB rock your . . .
  GRADE LEVEL: Upper elementary
  CONTENTS: Pencil toppers—stickers—zipper pulls—notebook—beaded pens—people pencil toppers—candy tin trinket box—bookmark—book covers—pocket book cover—mini-notepads—pencil holder—rock a recycled style

1563 TORRES, L. *Rock your wardrobe*. 2010, QEB (ISBN: 9781595669377). 32 p.
  SERIES: QEB rock your . . .
  GRADE LEVEL: Upper elementary
  CONTENTS: Socks—friendship bracelet—rubber band belt—bead bracelet—shoelaces—scarf—t-shirt—cotton bag—pendant—snazzy sneakers—stencil style—picture pendant

1564 TORRINGTON, E. *Street dance*. 2012, PowerKids Press (ISBN: 9781448852857). 32 p.
  SERIES: Master this!
  GRADE LEVEL: Upper elementary – middle school
  CONTENTS: N/A

1565 TRAIL, S. *Sew with Sara: PJs, pillows, bags and more: fun stuff to keep, give, sell!* 2009, C. and T. (ISBN: 9781571206039). 112 p.
  GRADE LEVEL: Upper elementary – middle school
  CONTENTS: Sewing vocabulary—makin' money—projects—cell phone or MP3 player cover—child's apron—envelope pillow—pj bottoms—scrunchy—drawstring bag—tote bag—rip-n-strip top—school folder

1566 TREMAINE, J. *Magical illusions*. 2010, QEB (ISBN: 9781595669445). 32 p.
  SERIES: Magic handbook
  GRADE LEVEL: Elementary
  CONTENTS: Amazing illusions—simple thimble—sense of direction—upside-down card—safety first—one-way street—crazy shoelaces—jumpin' joker—last straw—bangle wangle—double your money—mind reading—magical clock—coin in pocket—elastic arm

1567 TREMAINE, J. *Paper tricks*. 2010, QEB (ISBN: 9781595668523). 32 p.
  SERIES: Magic handbook
  GRADE LEVEL: Elementary

CONTENTS: Torn and restored paper—walking through a postcard—smarty pants—who would you like to be?—newspaper clippings—the hindoo papers—the magic tree—climb the ladder—cornucopia cone—the magic rabbits—boy meets girl—topsy turvy money—monopoly money—it was an accident

1568 TREMAINE, J. *Pocket tricks*. 2010, QEB (ISBN: 9781595668530). 32 p.

SERIES: Magic handbook

GRADE LEVEL: Elementary

CONTENTS: Magic in your pocket—vanishing pencil—magic paper clips—cash in hand—the penny drops—money know-how—ghostly banknote—magic matchstick—pencil and paper—ring of mystery—coining it—on your head—breaking bread—up your sleeve—tiny grooves

1569 TRIANO, J. *Basketball basics: play like the pros*. 2009, Greystone Books (ISBN: 9781553654513). 80 p.

GRADE LEVEL: Middle school – high school

CONTENTS: N/A

1570 TRUDEL, R. *Easy carving projects for kids*. 2010, Linden (ISBN: 9781933502304). 128 p.

SERIES: Kid crafts

GRADE LEVEL: Upper elementary – middle school

CONTENTS: Coasters—napkin rings—trivets—bread board—serving platter—salad hands—place card holder—wine glass holders—chopsticks and rest—walking stick—puzzle—spoon and fork—toy fishing rod and fish—watermelon knife—geocache trade item—clapper—xylophone—noisemaker—whistle—double whistle—Quebecois spoons—box drum—pan flute—baseball award—football plaque—kitchen sign—desk set—ornament—name stamp—tic tac toe game stamps—gift tag stamp—chip-carved woodcut—Chinese character woodcut—bookplate—making a chop—a woodcut scene

1571 TRUESDELL, A. *Fire away: asking great interview questions*. 2013, Cherry Lake (ISBN: 9781610804813). 32 p.

SERIES: Explorer library: information explorer

GRADE LEVEL: Upper elementary

CONTENTS: N/A

1572 TRUESDELL, A. *Make your point: creating PowerPoint presentations*. 2013, Cherry Lake (ISBN: 9781624310195). 32 p.

SERIES: Explorer library: information explorer

GRADE LEVEL: Upper elementary

CONTENTS: Know your stuff—showing off—looking good—be prepared

1573 TRUESDELL, A. *Super smart information strategies: wonderful wikis*. 2013, Cherry Lake (ISBN: 9781610804806). 32 p.

SERIES: Explorer library: information explorer

GRADE LEVEL: Upper elementary

CONTENTS: What is a wiki—why use a wiki—working on wikis—following the rules

1574 TRUSTY, B. *The kids' guide to balloon twisting*. 2011, Capstone (ISBN: 9781429654449). 32 p.

  SERIES: Kids' guides

  GRADE LEVEL: Elementary

  CONTENTS: Buzzing bee—walk the dog—hats off—the flying mouse—sword fight—slithery snake—ray gun—terrific tentacles—gone fishing—one cool penguin

1575 TUMINELLY, N. *Cool cake & cupcake food art: easy recipes that make food fun to eat!* 2011, ABDO (ISBN: 9781616133627). 32 p.

  SERIES: Cool food art

  GRADE LEVEL: Elementary

  CONTENTS: Cupcakes—flower cake—monarch—bug cupcakes—panda—snow cupcakes—hole in one cupcakes—cupcake crew

1576 TUMINELLY, N. *Cool creepy food art: easy recipes that make food fun to eat!* 2011, ABDO (ISBN: 9781616133634). 32 p.

  SERIES: Cool food art

  GRADE LEVEL: Elementary

  CONTENTS: Severed finger pizza—floating head cider—to die for dip—eyeball spaghetti—gross-out pita—garbage goop—bloody hand punch—snot stick pretzels

1577 TUMINELLY, N. *Cool dairy-free recipes: delicious & fun foods without dairy*. 2013, ABDO (ISBN: 9781617835810). 32 p.

  SERIES: Cool recipes for your health

  GRADE LEVEL: Elementary

  CONTENTS: Pastry pockets—chocolate shake—tofu scramble—broccoli salad—peanut noodles—baked quinoa—play ball—mini corn dogs—brownie-wowies

1578 TUMINELLY, N. *Cool fruit and veggie food art: easy recipes that make food fun to eat!* 2011, ABDO (ISBN: 9781616133641). 32 p.

  SERIES: Cool food art

  GRADE LEVEL: Elementary

  CONTENTS: Fabulous froggy—mice mouthfuls—funny face salad—apple flutterfly—catnip and dip—watermelon mobile—veg head party pleaser—flying cucumber

1579 TUMINELLY, N. *Cool holiday food art: easy recipes that make food fun to eat!* 2011, ABDO (ISBN: 9781616133658). 32 p.

  SERIES: Cool food art

  GRADE LEVEL: Elementary

  CONTENTS: Sushi—dreidel pretzel snacks—little peepers—July Fourth cones—creepy popcorn balls—shadow cupcakes—fruit gobble gobble—reindeer cookies

1580 TUMINELLY, N. *Cool meat-free recipes: delicious & fun foods without meat*. 2013, ABDO (ISBN: 9781617835827). 32 p.

  SERIES: Cool recipes for your health

  GRADE LEVEL: Elementary

  CONTENTS: Breakfast bars—pizza pinwheels—tofu stir-fry—veggie burger—no-meat sloppy Joes—veggie side dish—tofu pudding surprise—chili mac

1581 TUMINELLY, N. *Cool nut-free recipes: delicious & fun foods without nuts.* 2013, ABDO (ISBN: 9781617835834). 32 p.

 SERIES: Cool recipes for your health

 GRADE LEVEL: Elementary

 CONTENTS: Cheese & apple dip—bean goulash—snack mixers—cranberry chicken—party pinwheels—pretzel chocolate bark—mixed fruit pie—oatmeal cookies

1582 TUMINELLY, N. *Cool raw food recipes: delicious & fun foods without cooking.* 2013, ABDO (ISBN: 9781617835841). 32 p.

 SERIES: Cool recipes for your health

 GRADE LEVEL: Elementary

 CONTENTS: Breakfast blend—carob shake—hummus dip—vegetable salad—watermelon soup—lettuce wrap—orange ice pop—fridge cookies

1583 TUMINELLY, N. *Cool sandwich food art: easy recipes that make food fun to eat!* 2011, ABDO (ISBN: 9781616133665). 32 p.

 SERIES: Cool food art

 GRADE LEVEL: Elementary

 CONTENTS: PB&J flower—tuna boat—cat's meowich—bugwich—sammie—hoagie—racer—wrap

1584 TUMINELLY, N. *Cool snack food art: easy recipes that make food fun to eat!* 2011, ABDO (ISBN: 9781616133672). 32 p.

 SERIES: Cool food art

 GRADE LEVEL: Elementary

 CONTENTS: Snacks—beach ball cheese ball—bug bites—chili snake dogs—peanut butter and candy pizza—sunflower surprise—kookie katerpillar—sweet treat flowerpots

1585 TUMINELLY, N. *Cool sugar- free recipes: delicious & fun foods without refined sugar.* 2013, ABDO (ISBN: 9781617835858). 32 p.

 SERIES: Cool recipes for your health

 GRADE LEVEL: Elementary

 CONTENTS: Rice pudding—cake—muffins—smoothie—chocolate fudge—fruity bread—chocolate fondue—apricot cookie

1586 TUMINELLY, N. *Cool wheat-free recipes: delicious & fun foods without gluten.* 2013, ABDO (ISBN: 9781617835865). 32 p.

 SERIES: Cool recipes for your health

 GRADE LEVEL: Elementary

 CONTENTS: Gluten-free flour mixture—blueberry pancakes—avocado tacos—cheesy lasagna—spinach salad—chicken fingers—fancy cupcakes—pineapple muffins

1587 TUMINELLY, N. *Let's cook with apples! Delicious & fun apple dishes kids can make.* 2013, ABDO (ISBN: 9781617834189). 32 p.

 SERIES: Super simple recipes

 GRADE LEVEL: Elementary

 CONTENTS: Apple-wich—apple sundaes—apple pickles—apple chips—apple salsa—hot candy apples—baked apples—apple tartlets

1588 TUMINELLY, N. *Let's cook with cereal! Delicious & fun cereal dishes kids can make*. 2013, ABDO (ISBN: 9781617834196). 32 p.

    SERIES: Super simple recipes

    GRADE LEVEL: Elementary

    CONTENTS: Corn flake balls—sunrise surprise—crispy cheese puffies—scrumptious squares—coconut kisses—ice cream snack-wich—cocoa & fruit parfait—lemon delight bars

1589 TUMINELLY, N. *Let's cook with cheese! Delicious & fun cheese dishes kids can make*. 2013, ABDO (ISBN: 9781617834202). 32 p.

    SERIES: Super simple recipes

    GRADE LEVEL: Elementary

    CONTENTS: Cheesy mac—cheese dip—cheese bites—cheese nibbler—grilled cheese—cheese fritters—cheese chowder—cheddar crispies

1590 TUMINELLY, N. *Let's cook with eggs! Delicious & fun egg dishes kids can make*. 2013, ABDO (ISBN: 9781617834219). 32 p.

    SERIES: Super simple recipes

    GRADE LEVEL: Elementary

    CONTENTS: Omelet—egg boats—egg tacos—egg pizza pie—muffin melts—egg bowl—egg 'n stuff casserole—meringues

1591 TUMINELLY, N. *Let's cook with noodles! Delicious & fun noodle dishes kids can make*. 2013, ABDO (ISBN: 9781617834226). 32 p.

    SERIES: Super simple recipes

    GRADE LEVEL: Elementary

    CONTENTS: Fruit noodle salad—fusilli lasagna—cheese shells—chili macaroni—apple noodle kugel—peanut Asian noodles—noodle soup—pasta supreme

1592 TUMINELLY, N. *Let's cook with popcorn! Delicious & fun apple dishes kids can make*. 2013, ABDO (ISBN: 9781617834233). 32 p.

    SERIES: Super simple recipes

    GRADE LEVEL: Elementary

    CONTENTS: Popcorn mix—kettle corn—Mexican popcorn—cocoa-latta popcorn—caramel popcorn—popcorn balls—pop-corny cookies—popcorn muffins

1593 TUMINELLY, N. *Super simple bend and stretch: healthy and fun activities to move your body*. 2012, ABDO (ISBN: 9781617149597). 32 p.

    SERIES: Super simple exercise

    GRADE LEVEL: Elementary

    CONTENTS: N/A

1594 TUMINELLY, N. *Super simple breakfasts: easy no-bake recipes for kids*. 2011, ABDO (ISBN: 9781616133832). 32 p.

    SERIES: Super simple cooking

    GRADE LEVEL: Elementary

    CONTENTS: Breakfast in a cone—peanutty banana split—waffle sandwich—rollup—shakes—ham & cheese bagel—buenos días burrito—sunny o's—applesauce

1595 **TUMINELLY, N.** *Super simple desserts: easy no-bake recipes for kids*. 2011, ABDO (ISBN: 9781616133849). 32 p.

SERIES: Super simple cooking

GRADE LEVEL: Elementary

CONTENTS: Cheesecake tarts—peanut butter bites—banana split pie—maple cranberry drops—candy apple treats—cherry surprise—chocolate éclair cake—truffles—popcorn cake

1596 **TUMINELLY, N.** *Super simple dinners: easy no-bake recipes for kids*. 2011, ABDO (ISBN: 9781616133870). 32 p.

SERIES: Super simple cooking

GRADE LEVEL: Elementary

CONTENTS: Wrap—veggie pockets—chicken salad pitas—bean salad—salad burro—tuna salad—aso tuna burritos—ham & cheese pinwheels—carrot-apple rollups

1597 **TUMINELLY, N.** *Super simple holiday treats: easy no-bake recipes for kids*. 2011, ABDO (ISBN: 9781616133863). 32 p.

SERIES: Super simple cooking

GRADE LEVEL: Elementary

CONTENTS: Chinese New Year munch—Valentine crispies—leprechaun lollipops—Mazel Tov matzo cakes—Cinco de Mayo fizzies—red, white & blue trifle—Halloween pumpkin pie—horn of veggies—Christmas gumdrop bars

1598 **TUMINELLY, N.** *Super simple hop and jump: healthy and fun activities to move your body*. 2012, ABDO (ISBN: 9781617149603). 32 p.

SERIES: Super simple exercise

GRADE LEVEL: Elementary

CONTENTS: N/A

1599 **TUMINELLY, N.** *Super simple move and shake: healthy and fun activities to move your body*. 2012, ABDO (ISBN: 9781617149610). 32 p.

SERIES: Super simple exercise

GRADE LEVEL: Elementary

CONTENTS: N/A

1600 **TUMINELLY, N.** *Super simple punch and kick: healthy and fun activities to move your body*. 2012, ABDO (ISBN: 9781617149627). 32 p.

SERIES: Super simple exercise

GRADE LEVEL: Elementary

CONTENTS: N/A

1601 **TUMINELLY, N.** *Super simple snacks: easy no-bake recipes for kids*. 2011, ABDO (ISBN: 9781616133887). 32 p.

SERIES: Super simple cooking

GRADE LEVEL: Elementary

CONTENTS: Fruit slurp slushy—cranberry nut crunch—guacamole—peanut butter sticks—Tex-Mex salsa—carrot top canapés—peanutty power balls—coconut delight—grahamy-bananny popsicles

1602 TUMINELLY, N. *Super simple throw and catch: healthy and fun activities to move your body*. 2012, ABDO (ISBN: 9781617149634). 32 p.
SERIES: Super simple exercise
GRADE LEVEL: Elementary
CONTENTS: N/A

1603 TUMINELLY, N. *Super simple walk and run: healthy and fun activities to move your body*. 2012, ABDO (ISBN: 9781617149641). 32 p.
SERIES: Super simple exercise
GRADE LEVEL: Elementary
CONTENTS: Time to walk and run—muscle mania—healthy eating—move it chart—tools and supplies—total body walk—neat neighborhood—stairs everywhere—whistle play—scavenger walk—spy hunt—rag tag—bag skate—obstacle run—keep moving

1604 TURNBULL, S. *Accessories: style secrets for girls*. 2014, Smart Apple Media (ISBN: 9781599209432). 32 p.
SERIES: Girl talk
GRADE LEVEL: Middle school – high school
CONTENTS: N/A

1605 TURNBULL, S. *Card tricks*. 2012, Smart Apple Media (ISBN: 9781599204956). 32 p.
SERIES: Secrets of magic
GRADE LEVEL: Elementary
CONTENTS: N/A

1606 TURNBULL, S. *Cards and gifts: style secrets for girls*. 2014, Smart Apple Media (ISBN: 9781599209449). 32 p.
SERIES: Girl talk
GRADE LEVEL: Middle school – high school
CONTENTS: N/A

1607 TURNBULL, S. *Circus skills*. 2013, Smart Apple Media (ISBN: 9781599207995).
SERIES: Super skills
GRADE LEVEL: Elementary
CONTENTS: Starting to juggle—mastering juggling—clever juggling tricks—perfect plate spinning—taking a tumble—hula hooping—balancing skills—becoming a clown—clowning around—clown props—daredevil stunts, what next?

1608 TURNBULL, S. *Close-up tricks*. 2012, Smart Apple Media (ISBN: 9781599204963). 32 p.
SERIES: Secrets of magic
GRADE LEVEL: Elementary
CONTENTS: Tricks of the trade—card magic—coin magic—clever coin moves—big money tricks—dice magic—cups and balls—rubber bands—amazing matches—mealtime magic—fun with food

1609 TURNBULL, S. *Cooking skills*. 2014, Usborne (ISBN: 9781770921467). 32 p.
SERIES: Super skills

GRADE LEVEL: Elementary

CONTENTS: N/A

1610 TURNBULL, S. *Craft skills*. 2013, Smart Apple Media (ISBN: 9781599207964). 32 p.
   SERIES: Super skills
   GRADE LEVEL: Elementary
   CONTENTS: N/A

1611 TURNBULL, S. *Magic skills*. 2014, Usborne (ISBN: 9781770921481).
   SERIES: Super skills
   GRADE LEVEL: Elementary
   CONTENTS: N/A

1612 TURNBULL, S. *Mind-reading tricks*. 2012, Smart Apple Media (ISBN: 978599204987). 32 p.
   SERIES: Secrets of magic
   GRADE LEVEL: Elementary
   CONTENTS: Tricks of the trade—math magic—taking risks—memory magic—fakery— book tests—forcing a choice—one step ahead—secret helpers—telepathy—surprise endings—show time

1613 TURNBULL, S. *Prop tricks*. 2012, Smart Apple Media (ISBN: 9781599204994). 32 p.
   SERIES: Secrets of magic
   GRADE LEVEL: Elementary
   CONTENTS: Perfect prop magic—tricks of the trade—magic wands—silks—scarves—and hankies—brilliant balloons—paper props—cool tube tricks—matchbox magic—rope magic—hoops and rings—great escapes—show time!

1614 TURNBULL, S. *Vanishing tricks*. 2012, Smart Apple Media (ISBN: 9781599205007). 32 p.
   SERIES: Secrets of magic
   GRADE LEVEL: Elementary
   CONTENTS: Tricks of the trade—silly stuff—animal magic—hand moves—palming— hiding places—a knot . . . or not?—paper pranks—the paddle move—mealtime magic—gimmicks

1615 TYLER, B. *Picture yourself writing drama: using photos to inspire writing*. 2012, Capstone (ISBN: 9781429661263). 32 p.
   SERIES: Fact finders. See it, write it
   GRADE LEVEL: Middle school – high school
   CONTENTS: Acting on ideas—set it up—who did it?—telling the story—scene it

1616 UTTLEY, C. *Experiments with force and motion*. 2010, Gareth Stevens (ISBN: 9781433934599). 32 p.
   SERIES: Cool science
   GRADE LEVEL: Upper elementary
   CONTENTS: N/A

1617 VAN VLEET, C. *Amazing Arctic & Antarctic projects you can build yourself*. 2008, Nomad Press (ISBN: 9781934670088). 128 p.

SERIES: Build it yourself

GRADE LEVEL: Upper elementary – middle school

CONTENTS: Compass—electromagnet—light—picture—ice—ice core—popsicles—model—scarf—snowy owl—coin collector—toboggan—cup—tusk—goggles—dogloo—games—carving—Inuksuk—South Pole market—neck gator—terrarium—warmer temperature—ice—pin

1618 VAN VLEET, C. *Amazing Ben Franklin inventions you can build yourself*. 2007, Nomad Press (ISBN: 9780979226885). 128 p.

SERIES: Build it yourself

GRADE LEVEL: Upper elementary – middle school

CONTENTS: Swim paddles—solar-powered oven—baked apple—music stand—spectacle receptacle—hornbook long arm—paper mold—paper—letterpress—watermarked bill—invisible ink—piggy bank—"frugal" frame—thermometer—wave bottle—potato battery—kite—fire bucket—fire mark—feel-better bubble bath—paving brick—street lamp—personal mailbox—mail bag—parchment paper—feather pen—Liberty Bell—fur hat—travel log

1619 VAN VLEET, C. *Explore ancient Egypt! 25 great projects, activities, experiments*. 2008, Nomad Press (ISBN: 9780979226830). 128 p.

SERIES: Build it yourself

GRADE LEVEL: Upper elementary – middle school

CONTENTS: Papyrus plant—lotus flower—reed boat—hot and cool colors—Egyptian headrest—stool—dried apple—animal-shaped bread—bartering—home remedy book—rag doll—board game—tug-a-war—ostraca—collar necklace—Egyptian wig—cuff bracelet—tunic—false beard—King Tut sandals—Valley of the Kings—hieroglyph tablet—edible pyramid—sistrum—mummification

1620 VAN VLEET, C. *Explore ancient Greece! 25 great projects, activities, experiments*. 2008, Nomad Press (ISBN: 9781934670118). 96 p.

SERIES: Explore your world!

GRADE LEVEL: Elementary

CONTENTS: Sailboat—play pirates—oil lamp—column—basket—kylix—a symposium—Greek salad—chiton—brooch—foot scrub—Archimedes pie—scroll—morra—laurel wreath—long jump hand weights—mask—jury tokens—clock—greaves—hoplite shield—Medusa freeze tag—Trojan horse—Midas meal

1621 VAN VLEET, C. *Explore ancient Rome! 25 great projects, activities, experiments*. 2008, Nomad Press (ISBN: 9780979226847). 96 p.

SERIES: Explore your world!

GRADE LEVEL: Elementary

CONTENTS: Puzzle—aqueduct—plumb bob—roam like a Roman—mosaic—oscilla—bottled garden—strigil—dormice dish—amphora—loaf of bread—frieze—Roman dinner party—marbles—scroll—theater mask—charades—tunic—palla—toga—bulla—roman coin—write rules—votive

1622 VAN VLEET, C. *Explore electricity! With 25 great projects*. 2013, Nomad Press (ISBN: 9781619301801). 96 p.

SERIES: Explore your world

GRADE LEVEL: Upper elementary

CONTENTS: N/A

1623 VAN VLEET, C. *Seven wonders of the world: discover amazing monuments to civilization*. 2011, Nomad Press (ISBN: 9781934570828). 128 p.

SERIES: Build it yourself

GRADE LEVEL: Upper elementary – middle school

CONTENTS: Ship puzzle—Babylonian bricks—hanging garden—Ionic column bank—marbleized paper—trick photo—frieze—etching—"sail into Alexandria"—Petra façade—the Colosseum—chac mool—cloud in a bottle—millet porridge—inlaid design plaque—hand sculpture

1624 VANCLEAVE, J. *Janice VanCleave's big book of play and find out science projects: easy activities for young children*. 2007, Jossey-Bass (ISBN: 9780787989286). 224 p.

GRADE LEVEL: Elementary

CONTENTS: Catching air—parachute—bouncing balls—play clay—magnets—compass—boats—seat belt—shadow—rainbow—telephone—chewing—hair—flashlight—cats—plants—hard to see animals—cat eyes glowing in the dark—dogs—staying warm in the winter—can squirrels fly—fish moving in water—kitchen seeds—plants moving toward the sun—cacti in the desert—peeled bananas—flowers—catching insects—cricket—butterflies—grasshoppers—caterpillars—fleas—bees—fireflies—insect teeth—butterflies—walkingsticks—butterfly's wings—spiders—elbows—puckered skin—body hair—curly hair—the back—bones—scabs—the heart—the chest—breath—teeth—food—red eyes—food

1625 VANCLEAVE, J. *Step-by-step science experiments in astronomy*. 2013, Rosen (ISBN: 9781448869787). 80 p.

SERIES: Janice Vancleave's first-place science fair projects

GRADE LEVEL: Middle school

CONTENTS: Bent—sky—back up—see through—curves—speedy—on the move—spinner—how far?—balancing—satellite—in and out—camera—face forward—heavy—stars—planetarium—chart—twinkling star—up or down?—simple—bouncer

1626 VANCLEAVE, J. *Step-by-step science experiments in biology*. 2013, Rosen (ISBN: 9781448869824). 80 p.

SERIES: Janice Vancleave's first-place science fair projects

GRADE LEVEL: Middle school

CONTENTS: Spuds—stand up—freeze—breathing—colors—bean—maze—algae—waterlogged—mini-organisms—fuzz balls—decomposers—pressure—farm—temperature—feathers—in but not out—egg—onion—afterimage—small intestine—size change

1627 VANCLEAVE, J. *Step-by-step science experiments in chemistry*. 2013, Rosen (ISBN: 9781448869817). 80 p.

SERIES: Janice Vancleave's first-place science fair projects

GRADE LEVEL: Middle school

CONTENTS: Chain—how much—heat—tug of war—anti-gravity—mind of its own—dunk—paper—oil—fungus—how long—rust—blob—iron—ice—chill—needles—tyndall effect—puff signals—acid-base testing—strong-stronger—baking with acid

1628 VANCLEAVE, J. *Step-by-step science experiments in Earth science*. 2013, Rosen (ISBN: 9781448869831). 80 p.
SERIES: Janice Vancleave's first-place science fair projects
GRADE LEVEL: Middle school
CONTENTS: Ball—tilt—mega-weight—deposits—dripper—wash away—prints—rub-a-dub—pop top—spreader—swingers—detector—run off—speedy—fly away—up and down—cold and hot—breezes—more or less—water—tornado—currents

1629 VANCLEAVE, J. *Step-by-step science experiments in ecology*. 2013, Rosen (ISBN: 9781448869800). 80 p.
SERIES: Janice Vancleave's first-place science fair projects
GRADE LEVEL: Middle school
CONTENTS: Spreader—movers—small portion—partners—around—soaker—home alone—dripper—digger—brrr—nibblers—skin—shock absorbers—forest—pollution—bounce back—foamy—misty—sunblock—fill it up—wind power—fast

1630 VANCLEAVE, J. *Step-by-step science experiments in energy*. 2013, Rosen (ISBN: 9781448869794). 80 p.
SERIES: Janice Vancleave's first-place science fair projects
GRADE LEVEL: Middle school
CONTENTS: Uphill—equal—hopper—higher—swinger—can—standing—sounds—brighter—painting—loser—streamers—straight through—separator—attractive—stronger—cooler—half time—collectors—all alone—top to bottom—bouncing

1631 VIVION, N. *Easy biology Step-by-step: master high-frequency concepts and skills for biology proficiency—fast!* 2012, McGraw Hill (ISBN: 9780071767798). 216 p.
GRADE LEVEL: High school
CONTENTS: N/A

1632 WAGNER, L. *Cool African cooking: fun and tasty recipes for kids*. 2011, ABDO (ISBN: 9781617146589). 32 p.
SERIES: Cool world cooking
GRADE LEVEL: Elementary
CONTENTS: Chickpeas—groundnut stew—Jollof rice—Moroccan carrot salad—alecha—tropical fruit salad

1633 WAGNER, L. *Cool Chinese and Japanese cooking: fun and tasty recipes for kids*. 2011, ABDO (ISBN: 9781617146596). 32 p.
SERIES: Cool world cooking
GRADE LEVEL: Elementary
CONTENTS: Sesame noodles—chicken meatball yakitori—sukiyaki—chicken stir fry—fried rice—almond cookies

1634 WAGNER, L. *Cool French cooking: fun and tasty recipes for kids*. 2011, ABDO (ISBN: 9781617146602). 32 p.
SERIES: Cool world cooking

GRADE LEVEL: Elementary

CONTENTS: Salad nicoise—French onion soup—Croque Monsieur—quiche Lorraine—roast chicken—berry clafoutis

1635 WAGNER, L. *Cool Italian cooking: fun and tasty recipes for kids*. 2011, ABDO (ISBN: 9781617146619). 32 p.

SERIES: Cool world cooking

GRADE LEVEL: Elementary

CONTENTS: Fettuccine Alfredo—green beans parmigiana—legendary lasagna—marvelous meatballs—insalata mista—lemon granita

1636 WAGNER, L. *Cool Mexican cooking: fun and tasty recipes for kids*. 2011, ABDO (ISBN: 9781617146626). 32 p.

SERIES: Cool world cooking

GRADE LEVEL: Elementary

CONTENTS: Tostadas—mixed salad—Mexican rice—taquitos—tortilla soup—enchilada casserole

1637 WAGNER, L. *Cool Middle Eastern cooking: fun and tasty recipes for kids*. 2011, ABDO (ISBN: 9781617146633). 32 p.

SERIES: Cool world cooking

GRADE LEVEL: Elementary

CONTENTS: Harriet's tabbouleh—crunchy veggie salad—Turkish Kofta creations—potato latke—herbed chicken—nut wedges

1638 WALKER, A. *How to improve at fishing*. 2009, Crabtree (ISBN: 9780778735946). 48 p.

SERIES: How to improve at

GRADE LEVEL: Elementary

CONTENTS: Location and clothing—equipment—watercraft—rods and reels—bait—hooks and knots—floats and weights—river floats and troutting—casting—landing a fish—legering—indicators—fly fishing—casting—dry fly fishing—nymph fishing—sea fishing—shore fishing and pier fishing—casting—pollution—licenses and rules

1639 WALKER, P. *Computer science experiments*. 2009, Facts On File (ISBN: 9780816078066). 153 p.

GRADE LEVEL: High school

CONTENTS: Video production—conservation—carbon footprint—pig dissection—mass—trading cards—simple machines—hydrolysis and dehydration synthesis—cloud patterns—climatogram—lightning strikes—parasites—rocks and minerals—breathing—nanoscale—caves—sunspots—chemical bond—DDT—tsunami—chart—grade level—setting—findings

1640 WALKER, P. *Ecosystem science fair projects: revised and expanded using the scientific method*. 2010, Enslow (ISBN: 9780766034198). 160 p.

GRADE LEVEL: Upper elementary – middle school

CONTENTS: Ecosystems—the edge—the climate—the dark—plot—soil—nonliving factors and ecosystems—sprouts—drop in the bag—fermentation—fish—right light—living factors and ecosystems—space – plants—out of sight—too close for comfort—gas—humans and ecosystems—pollution—salt—acid—shrimp

1641 WALKER, W. *Draw it!* 2012, QEB (ISBN: 9781609922764).
SERIES: Smart art
GRADE LEVEL: Lower elementary
CONTENTS: N/A

1642 WALTON, S. *I can grow things: gardening projects for kids shown step by step*. 2013, Armadillo (ISBN: 9781843227564). 48 p.
SERIES: Show me how
GRADE LEVEL: Elementary
CONTENTS: N/A

1643 WARD, J. *Let's go outside! Outdoor activities and projects to get you and your kids closer to nature*. 2009, Roost Books (ISBN: 9781590306987). 175 p.
GRADE LEVEL: Elementary
CONTENTS: Kick the Can—Capture the Flag—flyin' frisbees—A Hunting We Will Go!—Twenty Questions—with a natural twist!—crazy for kites—scavengers are us—hop to it with hopscotch—five fine forts—ten types of tag—buried treasure—spy games—up with the birds—outdoor diner—make a tree swing—moonlight walk—cloud spotters—sun fun: shadow prints—paper makers—flower preservation—picture this—playground for poets—flower fashion—bubbles—rockin' nature—tree of my very own—peek and seek from underneath—begging for bike time—happy campers—Go Fish!—bugliest scavenger hunt—snow stepping—play with clay—wonders beneath the water—pan it—we're going on a hole hunt—toil with the soil—garden and nature journal—toad's castle—counting on ladybugs—backyard field guide—going wild—magnificent migrations—trash to treasure—for wildlife—rain catcher—bath time is for the birds—create a nature nut club—nectar nice—bird count—fall leaves—pollinator's palace

1644 WARD, K. *Fun with Mexican cooking*. 2010, PowerKids Press (ISBN: 9781435834521). 32 p.
SERIES: Let's get cooking!
GRADE LEVEL: Upper elementary – middle school
CONTENTS: Tortillas and eggs—hot chocolate—tortilla soup—beef and potato soup—guacamole—salsa—the Day of the Dead—wheat flour tortillas—Mexican rice—pinto beans with tomato—and bacon—tacos—churritos—flan—rice pudding

1645 WARD, L. *Jumping for kids*. 2007, Storey (ISBN: 1580176720).
GRADE LEVEL: Upper elementary
CONTENTS: Flying start—your first jump—exercises—solving problems—building and designing courses—shows—cross-country—teaching your horse

1646 WARR, P. *The kung fu handbook*. 2008, Rosen Central (ISBN: 9781404213920). 256 p.
SERIES: Martial arts
GRADE LEVEL: Middle school – high school
CONTENTS: Warm-up exercises—kung fu stances—stance—fist and foot training—hand and foot techniques—northern style—hand and foot techniques—southern style—tan tui forms—tan tui for self-protection—xingyiquan mind and will kung fu—the xingyiquan forms—xingyiquan for self-protection

1647 **WARWICK, E.** *Everywear*. 2008, Kids Can Press (ISBN: 9781553377993). 80 p.
SERIES: Planet girl
GRADE LEVEL: Elementary
CONTENTS: N/A

1648 **WARWICK, E.** *Fully woolly*. 2007, Kids Can Press (ISBN: 9781553377986). 80 p.
SERIES: Planet girl
GRADE LEVEL: Elementary
CONTENTS: Before you get the sticks clicking—gumball necklace—pouch—woven scarf—necklace—bangles—ruched scarf—cheeky choker—beaded bracelet—skullcap—pixie hat—messenger bag—circle bag—wall art—cushion—felted journal—project bag—needle roll—needles—wooly ways: knitty gritty—crochet play-by-play—felting

1649 **WATT, F.** *The Usborne big book of science things to make and do*. 2008, EDC (ISBN: 9780794519230). 96 p.
GRADE LEVEL: Elementary
CONTENTS: Wizard's brew—zoomer—fingerprint—detective—cars—shadow puppets—map—raisins—liquids—space picture—bags - ball game—head to head—painting—monkeys—chocolate circles—patterns—robot—leaf prints—spinner—flipbook—snake—mirror—ice cubes—boat—windsock—crocodile—ghost—balloon rocket—eggs—whale painting—flowers—lizard—spinner—monster heads—game - fingers—the eye—whale—skyline—tower—roll—dragon painting—bottles—straws—ink spots and stripes—bugs—monster drawing—helicopter—balancers—light catcher—water beastie—fish—plane—monster—slime

1650 **WEBER, B.** *Animal disguises*. 2010, Kingfisher (ISBN: 9780753464519). 56 p.
SERIES: Discover science
GRADE LEVEL: Elementary
CONTENTS: Homes—tigers—picture

1651 **WEBER, B.** *Reptiles*. 2011, Kingfisher (ISBN: 9780753466056). 56 p.
SERIES: Discover science
GRADE LEVEL: Elementary
CONTENTS: Cape—croc—stick—tongues

1652 **WESSON, S.** *Guitar*. 2011, PowerKids Press (ISBN: 9781615325993). 32 p.
SERIES: Master this!
GRADE LEVEL: Upper elementary – middle school
CONTENTS: Playing the guitar—types of guitar—other equipment—holding the guitar—chords and strumming—scales and picking—staves and rhythms—the musical alphabet—special effects—rhythm and chord skills—advanced techniques

1653 **WHEELER-TOPPEN, J.** *Cool chemistry activities for girls*. 2012, Capstone (ISBN: 9781429676748). 32 p.
SERIES: Girls science club
GRADE LEVEL: Middle school
CONTENTS: Fountain—bubbles—lip balm—shampoo—putty—air freshener—candle holders—muffin puff—jewels

1654 WHEELER-TOPPEN, J. *Gross science projects*. 2013, Capstone (ISBN: 9781429699242). 32 p.
SERIES: Gross guides
GRADE LEVEL: Upper elementary
CONTENTS: Cracker—the plunge—goo—slime—snot—sweat—mummy—ball—worm poop

1655 WHEELER-TOPPEN, J. *Science experiments that explode and implode*. 2011, Capstone (ISBN: 9781429654272). 32 p.
SERIES: Fun projects for curious kids
GRADE LEVEL: Elementary
CONTENTS: Powder—explosion—unpoppable balloon—bomb—blast off—gusher—egg trap—stink bombs—big squeeze—crushed—inside-out balloon

1656 WHEELER-TOPPEN, J. *Science experiments that fizz and bubble*. 2011, Capstone (ISBN: 9781429654258). 32 p.
SERIES: Fun projects for curious kids
GRADE LEVEL: Elementary
CONTENTS: Soda—juice—bubbles—fizzle out—puffer—blobs—fountain—Midas touch—inflation—shooter

1657 WHITEHEAD, E. *A girl's guide to fitting in fitness*. 2013, Zest Books (ISBN: 9781936976300).
GRADE LEVEL: High school
CONTENTS: N/A

1658 WILKES, A. *Animal homes*. 2012, Kingfisher (ISBN: 9780753467756). 56 p.
SERIES: Discover science
GRADE LEVEL: Elementary
CONTENTS: Homes—animals—making homes—hamster box

1659 WILLIAMS, A. *Learn to speak dance: a guide to creating, performing, and promoting your moves*. 2011, Owlkids Books (ISBN: 9781926818887). 96 p.
GRADE LEVEL: Upper elementary – middle school
CONTENTS: N/A

1660 WILLIAMS, C. *24 games you can play on a checkerboard*. 2007, Gibbs Smith (ISBN: 1423600118).
GRADE LEVEL: Elementary
CONTENTS: Traditional checkers—the coyote and the chickens—Albuquerque—achi—pyramid checkers—box the fox—giveaway checkers—diagonal checkers—dama checkers Turkish—French checkers—checkers Go-moku—Four Field Kono—Five Field Kono—Three Men's Morris—Seega—wolf and goats—Lasca—fox and geese—wildebeast—horseshoe—catching the pigs—hey! Get outta my line—leap frog—solitaire pyramid checkers

1661 WILLIAMS, Z. *Little monster's cookbook*. 2010, Gibbs Smith (ISBN: 9781423606000).
GRADE LEVEL: Upper elementary
CONTENTS: N/A

1662 WINTERBERG, J. *Watch me draw a boy's adventure*. 2012, Walter Foster (ISBN: 9781936309795). 24 p.

    SERIES: Watch me draw

    GRADE LEVEL: Upper elementary

    CONTENTS: N/A

1663 WINTERBERG, J. *Watch me draw favorite pets*. 2012, Walter Foster (ISBN: 9781936309771). 24 p.

    SERIES: Watch me draw

    GRADE LEVEL: Upper elementary

    CONTENTS: N/A

1664 WINTERBERG, J. *Watch me draw things girls love*. 2012, Walter Foster (ISBN: 9781936309788). 24 p.

    SERIES: Watch me draw

    GRADE LEVEL: Upper elementary

    CONTENTS: N/A

1665 WINTERS, E. *Calligraphy for kids*. 2007, Sterling (ISBN: 9781402739125). 128 p.

    GRADE LEVEL: Upper elementary – middle school

    CONTENTS: Vocabulary—tools and materials—ready to write—know your pen—italics: lowercase—italics: capitals—gothic: lowercase—gothic: capitals—uncial—Roman: lowercase—Roman: capitals—numbers and punctuation—writing smaller—borders—cards—invitations

1666 WINTERS, L. *Buzz about bees*. 2013, Fitzhenry & Whiteside (ISBN: 9781554552023). 32 p.

    GRADE LEVEL: Elementary

    CONTENTS: N/A

1667 WOELFLE, G. *The wind at work: an activity guide to windmills*. 2013, Chicago Review Press (ISBN: 9781613741009). 160 p.

    GRADE LEVEL: Upper elementary – middle school

    CONTENTS: Temperature—airflow—wind sock and wind vane—the wind—grain—writing about the wind—art—rolls—cobbler—collage—pot holder—pillow cover—corn dodgers—beans—a song—electricity—life before electricity—day without electricity—reading electric bills and meter—conserving electricity—energy sources—action—wind day—wind farm

1668 WOLF, L. *Recyclo-gami: 40 crafts to make your friends green with envy!* 2010, RP Teens (ISBN: 9780762440528). 112 p.

    GRADE LEVEL: Upper elementary

    CONTENTS: N/A

1669 WOLFE, B. *Fun face painting ideas for kids: 40 step-by-step demos*. 2013, Impact (ISBN: 9781440327063).

    GRADE LEVEL: Middle school – high school

    CONTENTS: Super hero—duck—roses—crocodile—cheetah mask—prehistoric lizard—ele-fly—white widow spider—wyvern ninja—airplane—koi fish—camouflage skull—Mardi Gras mask—Jeep—cyber-diva—fire fairy—bulldog—rainbow unicorn—swirl mask—T-Rex

1670 **WOOD, A.** *Akido*. 2013, PowerKids Press (ISBN: 9781477703526). 32 p.
   SERIES: Martial arts for kids
   GRADE LEVEL: Elementary
   CONTENTS: N/A

1671 **WOOD, A.** *Judo*. 2013, PowerKids Press (ISBN: 9781477703588). 32 p.
   SERIES: Martial arts for kids
   GRADE LEVEL: Elementary
   CONTENTS: N/A

1672 **WOOD, A.** *Jujitsu*. 2013, PowerKids Press (ISBN: 9781477703564). 32 p.
   SERIES: Martial arts for kids
   GRADE LEVEL: Elementary
   CONTENTS: N/A

1673 **WOOD, A.** *Karate*. 2013, PowerKids Press (ISBN: 9781477703144). 32 p.
   SERIES: Martial arts for kids
   GRADE LEVEL: Elementary
   CONTENTS: N/A

1674 **WOOD, A.** *Kung fu*. 2013, PowerKids Press (ISBN: 9781477703601). 32 p.
   SERIES: Martial arts for kids
   GRADE LEVEL: Elementary
   CONTENTS: N/A

1675 **WOOD, A.** *Tae kwon do*. 2013, PowerKids Press (ISBN: 9781477703540). 32 p.
   SERIES: Martial arts for kids
   GRADE LEVEL: Elementary
   CONTENTS: N/A

1676 **WOODFORD, C.** *Experiments with electricity and magnetism*. 2010, Gareth Stevens (ISBN: 9781433934445). 32 p.
   SERIES: Cool science
   GRADE LEVEL: Upper elementary
   CONTENTS: Battery—voltaic pile—electroscope—leyden jar—f fuse—curie point—motor—magnetic field—electromagnet—currents—metals

1677 **WOODFORD, C.** *Experiments with sound and hearing*. 2010, Gareth Stevens (ISBN: 9781433934568). 32 p.
   SERIES: Cool science
   GRADE LEVEL: Upper elementary
   CONTENTS: Waves—spotting sound—measuring sound—fork—a balloon—string instrument—pipes—toot—muffling sound—bullroarer—thunder

1678 WOODWARD, J. *This book made me do it*. 2010, DK (ISBN: 9780756668815). 192 p.

GRADE LEVEL: Elementary

CONTENTS: Amaze your friends—food—get creative—explore—survive—be a hero

1679 WOUK, H. *Kung fu*. 2011, Marshall Cavendish Benchmark (ISBN: 9780761449379). 47 p.

SERIES: Martial arts in action

GRADE LEVEL: Upper elementary – middle school

CONTENTS: N/A

1680 WRIGLEY, A. *We love to sew: 28 pretty things to make: jewelry, headbands, softies, t-shirts, pillows, bags & more*. 2013, Funstitch Studio (ISBN: 9781607056324).

GRADE LEVEL: Upper elementary – middle school

CONTENTS: Headbands—rings and jewels—necklace—pin—pom-poms—button rings—felt barrette—pom-pom earrings—doily tank—handy pouch—flower power tree—skirt—fabric design—MP3 player case—pouch—journal cover—storage trays—purse—pillow—hoop treats—silhouette pillow—name banner—artwork—flag quilt—bookends—owl—mushroom mansion—basil and midge

1681 YASUDA, A. *Explore flight! With 25 great projects*. 2013, Nomad Press (ISBN: 9781619301764). 96 p.

SERIES: Explore your world

GRADE LEVEL: Upper elementary

CONTENTS: N/A

1682 YASUDA, A. *Explore Native American cultures! With 25 great projects*. 2013, Nomad Press (ISBN: 9781619301603). 96 p.

SERIES: Explore your world!

GRADE LEVEL: Elementary

CONTENTS: Relief map of Native American regions—turtle shell rattle—longhouse—wampum belt—birchbark canoe—booger mask—beaded necklace—woven basket—dry painting—katsina doll—Mayan glyphs—plains tipi—sign language—parfleche—shield—decorative cuffs—totem pole—button blanket—basketry hat—bear claw necklace—soft twine bag—inuksuk display—tug-o-war—sculpture—cultures Madlib

1683 YASUDA, A. *Explore simple machines! With 25 great projects*. 2011, Nomad Press (ISBN: 9781936313822). 96 p.

SERIES: Explore your world

GRADE LEVEL: Upper elementary

CONTENTS: Straw—journal—mobile—lever—jumping jack—lifting with levers—chopstick—ice cream—golf challenge—ski slope—rollers—working together—dough rolling—spinning top—fruit top—jack—the twist—helicopter—wedges—boats—sewing—carving fruit—pulley—pulley relay—pulley system—inventions—scavenger hunt

1684 YASUDA, A. *Explore the solar system! 25 great projects, activities, experiments*. 2009, Nomad Press (ISBN: 9781934670361). 96 p.

> **SERIES:** Explore your world
>
> **GRADE LEVEL:** Upper elementary
>
> **CONTENTS:** Solar system—Earth—star—sun—liftoff—space—neighboring planets—asteroids—meteors & comets—light and bright stars

1685 YASUDA, A. *Explore the wild west! With 25 great projects*. 2012, Nomad Press (ISBN: 9781936740713). 96 p.

> **SERIES:** Explore your world!
>
> **GRADE LEVEL:** Elementary
>
> **CONTENTS:** Lewis and Clark's route—peace medal—panning for gold—clipper ship—lion dance mask—balance scale—wagon train board game—covered wagon—hardtack—thaumatrope—mini quilt—soddie—butter—sheriff's office—kinetoscope—newspaper—horseshoes—bandolier bag—the pattern game—horse dance stick—sculpture—spotted pup—cowboy hat—cowboy chaps—cattle brand

1686 YASUDA, A. *Explore water! 25 great projects, activities, experiments*. 2011, Nomad Press (ISBN: 9781936313426). 96 p.

> **SERIES:** Explore your world
>
> **GRADE LEVEL:** Upper elementary
>
> **CONTENTS:** Water—salt water—glacier—state of water—who is faster—capillary action—terrarium—transpiration—wrist band—journal—hygrometer—slides—nilometer—screw—make a shaduf—water wheel—Rome—oil spill—watershed—off I go—rain harvester—xeriscape—a mimic—sculpture—symphony

1687 YOMTOV, N. *How to write a comic book*. 2013, Cherry Lake (ISBN: 9781624313196). 24 p.

> **SERIES:** Language arts explorer junior
>
> **GRADE LEVEL:** Elementary
>
> **CONTENTS:** N/A

1688 YOMTOV, N. *How to write a fractured fairy tale*. 2013, Cherry Lake (ISBN: 9781624313189). 24 p.

> **SERIES:** Language arts explorer junior
>
> **GRADE LEVEL:** Elementary
>
> **CONTENTS:** N/A

1689 YOMTOV, N. *How to write a lab report*. 2013, Cherry Lake (ISBN: 9781624313172). 24 p.

> **SERIES:** Language arts explorer junior
>
> **GRADE LEVEL:** Elementary
>
> **CONTENTS:** N/A

1690 YOMTOV, N. *How to write a memoir*. 2013, Cherry Lake (ISBN: 9781624313202). 24 p.

> **SERIES:** Language arts explorer junior
>
> **GRADE LEVEL:** Elementary
>
> **CONTENTS:** N/A

1691 YOUNG, J. *Lazy days of summer*. 2007, Sleeping Bear Press (ISBN: 9781585362417).
GRADE LEVEL: Elementary
CONTENTS: N/A

1692 YOUNG, K. *Bug science: 20 projects and experiments about arthropods: insects, arachnids, algae, worms, and other small creatures*. 2009, National Geographic (ISBN: 9781426305191). 80 p.
SERIES: Science fair winners
GRADE LEVEL: Upper elementary – middle school
CONTENTS: Flies—bugs—ants—honey—hayfever—spiders—butterfly—inside an insect's head—flea's leg—arachnophobia—pillbugs—composting—compost worms—food—ant tunnels—bug eating habits—water striders—insect calls—silk—airplane—smell

1693 YOUNG, K. *Science fair winners: crime scene science: 20 projects and experiments about clues, crimes, criminals, and other mysterious things*. 2009, National Geographic (ISBN: 9781426305214). 80 p.
SERIES: Science fair winners
GRADE LEVEL: Upper elementary – middle school
CONTENTS: Fingerprints—crime scene prints—suspect's height—map the crime scene—cloak of invisibility—dude—bloodhound techniques—observational memories—improve visual memory—recognize faces—the liar—facial expressions—hair—blood analysis—sleight of hand—handwriting and paper fibers—postal bar codes—anthraxlike substances—DNA—who died—decomposition—observation and memory

1694 ZALME, R. *How to draw Goosebumps*. 2010, Scholastic (ISBN: 9780545248952).
GRADE LEVEL: Elementary
CONTENTS: N/A

1695 ZALME, R. *How to draw Sinnoh superstars*. 2010, Scholastic (ISBN: 9780545248273). 32 p.
GRADE LEVEL: Elementary
CONTENTS: N/A

1696 ZENON, P. *Cool card tricks: techniques for the advanced magician*. 2008, Rosen Central (ISBN: 9781404210851). 64 p.
SERIES: Amazing magic
GRADE LEVEL: Upper elementary
CONTENTS: N/A

1697 ZENON, P. *Gimmicks and card tricks: illusions for the intermediate magician*. 2008, Rosen Central (ISBN: 9781404210714). 64 p.
SERIES: Amazing magic
GRADE LEVEL: Upper elementary
CONTENTS: N/A

1698 ZENON, P. *Magic of the mind: tricks for the master magician*. 2008, Rosen Central (ISBN: 9781404210721). 64 p.
SERIES: Amazing magic

GRADE LEVEL: Upper elementary
CONTENTS: N/A

1699 ZENON, P. *Simple sleight-of-hand: card and coin tricks for the beginning magician*. 2008, Rosen Central (ISBN: 9781404210707). 64 p.
SERIES: Amazing magic
GRADE LEVEL: Upper elementary
CONTENTS: N/A

Titles by Series

Adventures outdoors (PowerKids Press)
Let's go camping, 1459
Let's go canoeing and kayaking, 1460
Let's go fishing, 1461
Let's go hiking, 1462

All new holiday crafts for kids (Millbrook Press)
All new crafts for Kwanzaa, 1321
All new holiday crafts for Mother's Day and Father's Day, 1322

Amazing magic (Rosen Central)
Cool card tricks: techniques for the advanced magician, 1696
Gimmicks and card tricks: illusions for the intermediate magician, 1697
Magic of the mind: tricks for the master magician, 1698
Simple sleight-of-hand: card and coin tricks for the beginning magician, 1699

The amazing world of (Anness)
The amazing world of pirates, 1497

American Girl do-it yourself (American Girl)
Craft sale: earn money making and selling fun easy crafts, 3

Art for kids (Lark Books)
Drawing in color, 1547
Cartooning: the only cartooning book you'll ever need to be the artist you've always wanted to be, 1305

Art smart (QEB)
Paint it! 410
Print it! 230

Arts and crafts of the ancient world (Mitchell Lane)
Arts and crafts of ancient China, 1152
Arts and crafts of ancient Egypt, 1153
Arts and crafts of ancient Greece, 1154
Arts and crafts of ancient Rome, 1155
Arts and crafts of the Aztecs and Maya, 1156
Arts and crafts of the Native Americans, 1157

ASPCA kids (Wiley)
Amazing pet tricks, 428

Awesome activities (Windmill Books)
Astonishing art, 1028
Cool circuits, 1030
Crazy contraptions, 1031

Awesome art (Windmill Books)

    Clay art, 1347

    Junk art, 1348

Babysitting (Capstone)

    Babysitting basics: caring for kids, 215

    Babysitting skills: traits and training for success, 1055

Be creative (Smart Apple Media)

    Accessories for all, 293

    Bedroom makeover, 294

    Cards, wraps, and tags, 295

    Customize your clothes, 296

Big bang science experiments (Windmill Books)

    Bright ideas: the science of light, 694

    Hot stuff: the science of heat and cold, 695

    It's alive! The science of plants and living things, 696

    Material world: the science of matter, 697

    Super sonic: the science of sound, 699

    Push and pull: the science of forces, 698

Boys' life series (DK)

    Let's go geocaching, 1086

    Let's go hiking, 1087

Build it yourself (Capstone)

    Build your own car, rocket, and other things that go, 443

    Build your own fort, igloo, and other hangouts, 444

    Build your own mini golf course, lemonade stand, and other things to do, 445

    Build your own periscope, flashlight, and other useful stuff, 446

    Amazing Africa projects you can build yourself, 1140

    Amazing Arctic & Antarctic projects you can build yourself, 1617

    Amazing Ben Franklin inventions you can build yourself, 1618

    Amazing biome projects you can build yourself, 912

    Amazing kitchen chemistry projects you can build yourself, 202

    Amazing math projects you can build yourself, 62

    Amazing solar system projects you can build yourself, 991

    Backyard biology: investigate habitats outside your door, with 25 projects, 918

    Bridges and tunnels: investigate feats of engineering with 25 projects, 913

    Canals and dams: investigate feats of engineering with 25 projects, 914

    Energy: 25 projects to investigate why we need power & how we get it, 1293

    Explore ancient Egypt! 25 great projects, activities, experiments, 1619

    Explorers of the new world: discover the golden age of exploration with 22 projects, 1142

    Food: 25 amazing projects, 1296

    Garbage: investigate what happens when you throw it out with 25 projects, 915

Recipes from Mexico, 1284

Cool art (ABDO)

Cool calligraphy: the art of creativity for kids!, 662
Cool collage: the art of creativity for kids!, 663
Cool drawing: the art of creativity for kids!, 664
Cool painting: the art of creativity for kids!, 665
Cool printmaking: the art of creativity for kids!, 667
Cool sculpture: the art of creativity for kids!, 668

Cool art with math & science (Checkerboard Books)

Cool paper folding: creative activities that make math and science fun for kids!, 666

Cool baking (ABDO)

Cool cakes and cupcakes: easy recipes for kids to bake, 1246
Cool cookies and bars: easy recipes for kids to bake, 1247
Cool pet treats: easy recipes for kids to bake, 1248
Cool quick breads: easy recipes for kids to bake, 1249

Cool CSI (ABDO)

Cool crime scene basics: securing the scene, 97
Cool eyewitness encounters: how's your memory?, 98

Cool food art (ABDO)

Cool cake & cupcake food art: easy recipes that make food fun to eat!, 1575
Cool creepy food art: easy recipes that make food fun to eat!, 1576
Cool fruit and veggie food art: easy recipes that make food fun to eat!, 1578
Cool holiday food art: easy recipes that make food fun to eat!, 1579
Cool sandwich food art: easy recipes that make food fun to eat!, 1583
Cool snack food art: easy recipes that make food fun to eat!, 1584

Cool garden to table (ABDO)

Cool basil from garden to table: how to plant, grow, and prepare basil, 706
Cool carrots from garden to table: how to plant, grow, and prepare carrots, 707
Cool green beans from garden to table: how to plant, grow, and prepare green beans, 708
Cool leaf lettuce from garden to table: how to plant, grow, and prepare leaf lettuce, 709
Cool potatoes from garden to table: how to plant, grow, and prepare potatoes, 710
Cool tomatoes from garden to table: how to plant, grow, and prepare tomotoes, 711

Cool health and fitness (ABDO)

Cool body basics: healthy and fun ways to get your body moving, 866
Cool eating: healthy and fun ways to get your body moving, 867
Cool exercise: healthy and fun ways to get your body moving, 389
Cool relaxing: healthy and fun ways to get your body moving, 868
Cool sleeping: healthy and fun ways to get your body moving, 869
Cool thinking: healthy and fun ways to get your body moving, 870

Cool science projects with technology (Enslow)

Electric motor experiments, 1467
Radio-controlled car experiments, 1469
Robot experiments, 1470
Solar cell and renewable energy experiments, 1471

Cool stuff (ABDO)

Cool stuff for bath & beauty: creative handmade projects for kids, 1380
Cool stuff for family & friends: creative handmade projects for kids, 1381
Cool stuff for reading & writing: creative handmade projects for kids, 1382
Cool stuff for school: creative handmade projects for kids, 1383
Cool stuff for your garden: creative handmade projects for kids, 1384
Cool stuff for your room: creative handmade projects for kids, 1385

Cool trash to treasure (ABDO)

Cool fabric projects: creative ways to upcycle your trash into treasure, 1374
Cool glass and ceramic projects: creative ways to upcycle your trash into treasure, 1375
Cool metal projects: creative ways to upcycle your trash into treasure, 1376
Cool odds and ends projects: creative ways to upcycle your trash into treasure, 1377
Cool paper projects: creative ways to upcycle your trash into treasure, 1378
Cool plastic projects: creative ways to upcycle your trash into treasure, 1379

Cool world cooking (ABDO)

Cool African cooking: fun and tasty recipes for kids, 1632
Cool Chinese and Japanese cooking: fun and tasty recipes for kids, 1633
Cool French cooking: fun and tasty recipes for kids, 1634
Cool Italian cooking: fun and tasty recipes for kids, 1635
Cool Mexican cooking: fun and tasty recipes for kids, 1636
Cool Middle Eastern cooking: fun and tasty recipes for kids, 1637

Craft library (Hamlyn)

Crafts for kids, 383

Craft of writing (Marshall Cavendish)

Fiction, 429
Plays, 430
Poetry, 1166
Screenplays, 431

Craft star (Walter Foster)

Green crafts: become an earth-friendly craft star, step by easy step!, 508
Pet crafts: everything you need to become your pet's craft star!, 509
Rockin' crafts: everything you need to become a rock-painting craft star!, 486

Crafts (Capstone)

Beading: bracelets, barrettes, and beyond, 179
Beginning knitting: stitches with style, 1186

Discover your world (Nomad Press)

Discover national monuments: national parks, 203

Discover the Amazon: the world's largest rainforest, 145

Discover the desert: the driest place on Earth, 255

Discover the oceans: the world's largest ecosystem, 146

Disgusting & dreadful science (Crabtree)

Ear-splitting sounds and other vile noises, 297

Electric shocks and other energy evils, 298

Glaring light and other eye-burning rays, 299

Gut-wrenching gravity and other fatal forces, 300

Do it yourself projects! (PowerKids Press)

Make your own books, 369

Make your own creative cards, 1515

Make your own masks, 370

Make your own musical instruments, 371

Make your own puppets, 372

Make your own purses and bags, 373

Make your own slippers and shoes, 374

Make your own toys, 1516

Dog ownership (Capstone)

Dog obedience: getting your pooch off the couch and other dog training tips, 1217

Dog tricks: teaching your doggie to shake hands and other tricks, 1218

Doodle books (Child's World)

How to draw aircraft, 333

How to draw cars and trucks, 334

How to draw Christmas things, 335

How to draw dinosaurs, 336

How to draw flowers and trees, 337

How to draw food, 338

How to draw Halloween things, 339

How to draw Independence Day things, 340

How to draw jungle animals, 341

How to draw people, 342

How to draw sports things, 343

How to draw underwater animals, 344

How to draw watercraft, 345

Draw 50 (Broadway Books)

Draw 50 princesses: the step-by-step way to draw Snow White, Sleeping Beauty, Cinderella, and many more, 38

Draw the magic fairy (Enslow)

Draw the magic blue fairy, 350

Trap and skeet shooting for fun!, 505
Yoga for fun!, 1528

For kids (Chicago Review Press)
Albert Einstein and relativity for kids: his life and ideas with 21 activities and thought experiments, 1240
Beethoven for kids: his life and music with 21 activities, 76
Beyond the solar system: explaining galaxies, black holes, alien planets, and more: a history with 21 activities, 249
California history for kids: missions, miners, and moviemakers in the Golden State; includes 21 activities, 406
Charting the world: geography and maps from cave paintings to GPS with 21 activities, 1219
Frederick Douglass for kids: his life and times with 21 activities, 1356
Harry Houdini for kids: his life and adventures with 21 magic tricks and illusions, 247
Isaac Newton and physics for kids: his life and ideas with 21 activities, 733
Native American history for kids: with 21 activities, 579
New York City history for kids: from New Amsterdam to the Big Apple with 21 activities, 1220
Rightfully ours: how women won the vote: 21 activities, 734
Van Gogh and the Post-Impressionists for kids: their lives and ideas, 21 activities, 1350
Verdi for kids: his life and music with 21 activities, 77

From couch to conditioned (Rosen)
Pilates for beginners, 815
Tai chi for beginners, 848

Fun adventure crafts (Enslow)
Fairy tale adventure crafts, 971
Haunted house adventure crafts, 972
Medieval castle adventure crafts, 973
Pirate ship adventure crafts, 974
Space adventure crafts, 975

Fun and easy drawing (Enslow)
Fun and easy drawing at sea, 354
Fun and easy drawing fantasy characters, 355
Fun and easy drawing on the farm, 356
Fun and easy drawing storybook characters, 357

Fun art projects (PowerKids Press)
Having fun with collage, 1094
Having fun with paint, 1095
Having fun with paper, 1096
Having fun with printing, 1097

Fun food for cool cooks (Capstone)

Fun projects for curious kids (Capstone)

Fundamental experiments (Bearport)

Games handbook (QEB)

Get crafty outdoors (PowerKids Press)

Get dancing (Sea to Sea)

Get outdoors (PowerKids Press)

Cool crafts with newspapers, magazines, and junk mail: green projects for resourceful kids, 790

Cool crafts with old CDs: green projects for resourceful kids, 1451

Cool crafts with old jeans: green projects for resourceful kids, 1452

Cool crafts with old t-shirts: green projects for resourceful kids, 1453

Cool crafts with old wrappers, cans, and bottles: green projects for resourceful kids, 1454

A green kid's guide to gardening! (Magic Wagon)

A green kid's guide to composting, 927

A green kid's guide to garden pest removal, 928

A green kid's guide to organic fertilizers, 929

A green kid's guide to preventing plant diseases, 930

A green kid's guide to soil preparation, 931

A green kid's guide to watering plants, 932

Gross guides (Capstone)

Gross pranks, 942

Gross recipes, 1557

Gross science projects, 1654

Halloween extreme (Capstone)

How to build hair-raising haunted houses, 1233

How to carve freakishly cool pumpkins, 1391

How to create spectacular Halloween costumes, 212

How to make frightening Halloween decorations, 758

Hands-on science (Kingfisher)

Electricity and magnets, 45

Forces and motion, 46

Sound and light, 263

Hands-on ancient history (Heinemann)

The history and activities of ancient China, 40

The history and activities of the Aztecs, 855

The history and activities of the Islamic Empire, 71

Hands-on heritage (Edupress)

Ancient Greece, 812

Mexico, 813

Hands-on history (Armadillo)

The Ancient Egyptians: eat, write, and play just like the Egyptians, 1005

Art & craft: discover the things people made and the games they played around the world, 1292

Aztecs: eat, write, and play just like the Aztecs, 1006

Celts: eat, write, and play just like the Celts, 512

Hands-on history! Ancient China: step into the time of the Chinese Empire, with 15 step-

Hands-on science (Kingfisher)

Hands-on science fun (Capstone)

Have fun with arts & crafts (Franklin Watts)

Language arts explorer junior (Cherry Lake)

How to write a biography, 1113
How to write a book report, 1114
How to write a business letter, 1115
How to write a comic book, 1687
How to write a fairy tale, 1116
How to write a fractured fairy tale, 1688
How to write a how-to, 1117
How to write a journal, 1118
How to write a lab report, 1689
How to write a letter, 1119
How to write a memoir, 1690
How to write a mystery, 1120
How to write a news article, 1121
How to write a play, 1122
How to write a poem, 1123
How to write a report, 1124
How to write a review, 1125
How to write a thank-you letter, 1126
How to write about your adventure, 1127
How to write an ad, 1128
How to write an e-mail, 1129
How to write an essay, 1130
How to write an interview, 1131
How to write and give a speech, 1132

Last minute science projects (Enslow)

Atoms and molecules experiments using ice, salt, marbles, and more, 535
Electricity and magnetism experiments using batteries, bulbs, wires, and more: one hour or less science experiments, 539
Energy experiments using ice cubes, springs, magnets, and more: one hour or less science experiments, 541
Human body experiments using fingerprints, hair, muscles, and more: one hour or less science experiment, 547
Simple machine experiments using seesaws, wheels, pulleys, and more: one hour or less science experiments, 555
Solids, liquids, and gases experiments using water, air, marbles, and more: one hour or less science experiments, 558
Tundra experiments: 14 science experiments in one hour or less, 561

Learn to draw (AV2 by Weigl)

How to draw Teenage Mutant Ninja Turtles: learn to draw Leonardo, Raphael, Donatello, and Michelangelo step by step!, 1169
Learn to draw American landmarks & historical heroes, 1104
Learn to draw ancient times: step-by-step instructions for 18 ancient characters and civilizations, 147

Learn to play (Eldorado Ink)

Let's do art (Wayland)

Let's draw (Windmill Books)
  Animals, 731
  Bugs, 1289
  Cars, 246
  Dinosaurs, 732

Let's get active (PowerKids Press)
  Let's learn martial arts, 1069
  Let's play baseball, 1070
  Let's play basketball, 1071
  Let's play football, 1072
  Let's play ice hockey, 1073
  Let's play soccer, 1074

Let's get cooking! (PowerKids Press)
  Fun with Chinese cooking, 939
  Fun with French cooking, 599
  Fun with Mexican cooking, 1644

Let's play dress up (Windmill Books)
  I want to be a fairy, 1430
  I want to be a knight, 1431
  I want to be a pirate, 1432
  I want to be a princess, 1433
  I want to be a robot, 1434
  I want to be an astronaut, 1435

Life science projects for kids (Mitchell Lane)
  Exploring Earth's biomes, 1187
  A project guide to fish and amphibians, 1463
  A project guide to mammals, 1231
  A project guide to reptiles and birds, 845
  A project guide to sponges, worms, and mollusks, 846
  Projects in genetics, 1190

Little hands! (Williamson)
  Little hands celebrate America: learning about the U.S.A. through crafts and activities,
    692

Mad science (Sterling)
  Kitchen science experiments: how does your mold garden grow?, 60
  Nature science experiments: what's hopping in a dust bunny?, 61

Magic handbook (Firefly Books)
  Card tricks, 511
  Coin and rope tricks, 513
  Magical illusions, 1566

Prepare to survive (Capstone)
How to survive in the wilderness, 1197
How to survive on a deserted island, 1198

QEB rock your . . (QEB)
Rock your party, 1560
Rock your room, 1561
Rock your school stuff, 1562
Rock your wardrobe, 1563

Quick draw (Kingfisher)
Quick draw cats and dogs, 223
Quick draw creepy crawlies, 224
Quick draw fairies and princesses, 225
Quick draw transportation, 226
Quick draw under the sea, 227

Ready, set, draw! (Millbrook Press)
Airplanes and ships you can draw, 187
Cars, trucks, and motorcycles you can draw, 188
Cats you can draw, 189
Cool boy stuff you can draw, 190
Cool girl stuff you can draw, 191
Dinosaurs and other prehistoric creatures you can draw, 192
Dogs you can draw, 193
Extinct and endangered animals you can draw, 194
Horses you can draw, 195
Insects you can draw, 196
Sea creatures you can draw, 197
Spaceships, aliens, and robots you can draw, 198

Real world math, personal finance. (Cherry Lake)
Starting your own business, 1133

Recreational sports (Smart Apple Media)
Biking, 1040
Fishing, 1042
Hiking and camping, 1044
Rock climbing and rappeling, 1048
Snorkeling and diving, 1050

Rockin' Earth science experiments (Enslow)
Super science projects about Earth's soil and water, 560

School projects survival guides (Heinemann)
Oral reports, 1472
Studying and tests, 1473

Team projects, 1474
Written reports, 1475

Science experiments with simple machines (Windmill Books)

Simple experiments with inclined planes, 1214
Simple experiments with pulleys, 1215
Simple experiments with wheels and axles, 1216

Science explorer (Cherry Lake)

Super cool science experiments: bugs, 629
Super cool science experiments: cells, 1162
Super cool science experiments: circulation, 1193
Super cool science experiments: compounds and mixtures, 1444
Super cool science experiments: digestion, 1194
Super cool science experiments: ecosystems, 1163
Super cool science experiments: electricity, 978
Super cool science experiments: erosion, 1445
Super cool science experiments: light, 1287
Super cool science experiments: magnets, 1543
Super cool science experiments: minerals, 979
Super cool science experiments: planet Earth, 1164
Super cool science experiments: plants, 630
Super cool science experiments: respiration, 1195
Super cool science experiments: rocks, 980
Super cool science experiments: seeds, 631
Super cool science experiments: soil, 500
Super cool science experiments: solar energy, 1544
Super cool science experiments: sound, 1545
Super cool science experiments: states of matter, 1165
Super cool science experiments: water, 1446
Super cool science experiments: weather, 1196

Science explorer junior (Cherry Lake)

Junior scientists: experiment with bugs, 626
Junior scientists: experiment with heat, 976
Junior scientists: experiment with liquids, 1161
Junior scientists: experiment with magnets, 1541
Junior scientists: experiment with plants, 627
Junior scientists: experiment with rocks, 977
Junior scientists: experiment with seeds, 628
Junior scientists: experiment with soil, 499
Junior scientists: experiment with solar energy, 1542
Junior scientists: experiment with solids, 637
Junior scientists: experiment with water, 1443
Junior scientists: experiment with weather, 1191

Science fair winners (National Geographic)

Bug science: 20 projects and experiments about arthropods: insects, arachnids, algae, worms, and other small creatures, 1692

Science fair winners: crime scene science: 20 projects and experiments about clues, crimes, criminals, and other mysterious things, 1693

Science in motion (Chicago Review Press)

The flying machine book: build and launch 35 rockets, gliders, helicopters, boomerangs, and more, 1106

The hot air balloon book: build and launch kongming lanterns, solar tetroons, and more, 253

The motorboat book: build and launch 20 jet boats, paddle-wheelers, electric submarines & more, 1468

The science of (Macmillan Children's)

The ultimate survival guide, 488

Score! Sports science projects (Enslow)

Goal! Science projects with soccer, 611

Home run! Science projects with baseball and softball, 178

Slam dunk! Science projects with basketball, 556

Wheels! Science projects with bicycles, skateboards, and skates, 614

Secrets of magic (Smart Apple Media)

Card tricks, 1605

Close-up tricks, 1608

Mind-reading tricks, 1612

Prop tricks, 1613

Vanishing tricks, 1614

Sharpen your writing skills (Enslow)

Sharpen your business letter writing skills, 1337

Sharpen your debate and speech writing skills, 1338

Sharpen your essay writing skills, 1339

Sharpen your good grammar skills, 1340

Sharpen your report writing skills, 1341

Sharpen your story or narrative writing skills, 1342

Show me how (Armadillo)

I can cook: recipes for kids shown step by step, 1058

I can grow things: gardening projects for kids shown step by step, 1642

Simply dance (Franklin Watts)

Jive and street dance, 1512

Samba and salsa, 1518

Tango and paso doble, 1519

Waltz and quick step, 1522

Starting art (Kids Can Press)

1-2-3 I can build!, 998

1-2-3 I can collage!, 999

1-2-3 I can draw!, 1000

1-2-3 I can make prints!, 997

1-2-3 I can paint!, 1001

1-2-3 I can sculpt!, 1002

Starting sport (Franklin Watts)

Athletics, 746

Basketball, 747

Gymnastics, 748

Rugby, 590

Swimming, 750

Tennis, 751

Step-by-step crafts (Boyds Mills)

Step-by-step crafts for gifts, 1334

Step-by-step crafts for summer, 1335

Step-by-step experiments (Child's World)

Step-by-step experiments with electricity, 645

Step-by-step experiments with insects, 1023

Step-by-step experiments with life cycles, 1024

Step-by-step experiments with light and vision, 762

Step-by-step experiments with magnets, 646

Step-by-step experiments with matter, 647

Step-by-step experiments with plants, 407

Step-by-step experiments with simple machines, 648

Step-by-step experiments with soils, 649

Step-by-step experiments with sound, 650

Step-by-step experiments with taste and digestion, 1025

Step-by-step experiments with the water cycle, 408

Step-by-step stories (Capstone)

Recycling, step by step, 996

Steve Spangler science (Greenleaf Book Group)

Fire bubbles and exploding toothpaste: more unforgettable experiments that make science fun, 1484

Naked eggs and flying potatoes: unforgettable experiments that make science fun, 1485

Super simple cooking (ABDO)

Super simple breakfasts: easy no-bake recipes for kids, 1594

Super simple desserts: easy no-bake recipes for kids, 1595

Super simple dinners: easy no-bake recipes for kids, 1596

Super simple holiday treats: easy no-bake recipes for kids, 1597

Super simple snacks: easy no-bake recipes for kdis, 1601

Super simple crafts (ABDO)

Super simple art to wear: fun and easy-to-make crafts for kids, 833
Super simple clay projects: fun and easy-to-make crafts for kids, 834
Super simple jewelry: fun and easy-to-make crafts for kids, 835
Super simple magnets: fun and easy-to-make crafts for kids, 836
Super simple masks: fun and easy-to-make crafts for kids, 837

Super simple cultural art (Abdo)

Super simple African art: fun and easy art from around the world, 876
Super simple American art: fun and easy art from around the world, 877
Super simple Chinese art: fun and easy art from around the world, 878
Super simple Mexican art: fun and easy art from around the world, 879
Super simple Native American art: fun and easy art from around the world, 880
Super simple South and Central American art: fun and easy art from around the world, 881

Super simple exercise (ABDO)

Super simple bend and stretch: healthy and fun activities to move your body, 1593
Super simple hop and jump: healthy and fun activities to move your body, 1598
Super simple move and shake: healthy and fun activities to move your body, 1599
Super simple punch and kick: healthy and fun activities to move your body, 1600
Super simple throw and catch: healthy and fun activities to move your body, 1602
Super simple walk and run: healthy and fun activities to move your body, 1603

Super simple recipes (ABDO)

Let's cook with apples! Delicious & fun apple dishes kids can make, 1587
Let's cook with cereal! Delicious & fun cereal dishes kids can make, 1588
Let's cook with cheese! Delicious & fun cheese dishes kids can make, 1589
Let's cook with eggs! Delicious & fun egg dishes kids can make, 1590
Let's cook with noodles! Delicious & fun noodle dishes kids can make, 1591
Let's cook with popcorn! Delicious & fun apple dishes kids can make, 1592

Super simple science (ABDO)

Super simple things to do with balloons: fun and easy science for kids, 391
Super simple things to do with bubbles: fun and easy science for kids, 392
Super simple things to do with plants: fun and easy science for kids, 393
Super simple things to do with pressure: fun and easy science for kids, 394
Super simple things to do with temperature: fun and easy science for kids, 395
Super simple things to do with water: fun and easy science for kids, 396

Super skills (Smart Apple Media)

Circus skills, 1607
Craft skills, 1610
Cooking skills, 1609
Magic skills, 1611

Top 25 football skills, tips, and tricks, 1559
Top 25 gymnastics skills, tips, and tricks, 1371
Top 25 hockey skills, tips, and tricks, 1372
Top 25 soccer skills, tips, and tricks, 1373

Try this at home; don't try this at home (Capstone)

Amazing bike tricks, 889
Cool board tricks, 890
Fun magic tricks, 744
Impressive dance moves, 893
Silly circus tricks, 745

Velocity (Capstone)

Hip-hop dancing volume 1: the basics, 570
Hip-hop dancing volume 2: breaking, 571
Hip-hop dancing volume 3: popping, locking, and everything in between, 572
Hip-hop dancing volume 4: dancing with a crew, 573
How to draw the coolest, most creative tattoo art, 1167
How to draw the darkest, baddest graphic novel, 1449
How to draw the meanest, most terrifying monsters, 1168
How to draw the most exciting, awesome manga, 1450
Motocross: how to be an awesome motocross rider, 1533
Self-defense: be a master at self-defense, 1049
Skateboarding: an awesome skateboarder, 1546
Survival skills: survive in the wild, 432

Watch me draw (Walter Foster)

Watch me draw a boy's adventure, 1662
Watch me draw Disney's Mickey Mouse clubhouse, 1345
Watch me draw Dora's favorite adventures, 24
Watch me draw favorite pets, 1663
Watch me draw Spongebob's underwater escapades, 607
Watch me draw things girls love, 1664

Whizzy science (Wayland)

Make it bang!, 301
Make it change!, 302
Make it glow!, 303
Make it grow!, 304
Make it splash!, 305
Make it zoom!, 306

Who dunnit? Forensic science experiments (Enslow)

Who can solve the crime? Science projects using detective skills, 563
Who forged this document? Crime solving science projects, 564
Whose bones are these? Crime solving science projects, 565

Keyword Index

~~~~~~~~~~~~~~~~~~~~~~~~~~~~~~~~~~~~~~~

References are to entry numbers, not page numbers.

A

~~~~

ABC   688, 804, 1245
Aboriginal   1033, 1303
Abseiling   269
Abyssinian   189
Acceleration   524, 1240, 1533
Accordion   676
Acid   177, 211, 413, 520, 527, 532, 533, 912,
    1018, 1294, 1627, 1640
Acid rain   532, 533, 912
Acidity   536, 557, 562
Acids and bases   211, 413, 1223, 1627
Acrobatics   739, 745, 1553
Acrostic   1350
Acting   826, 1615
Adinkra   258, 567, 876, 1140
Afghanistan   1414
Africa   567, 860, 1140
African   38, 59, 371, 567, 860, 876, 1066,
    1080, 1140, 1362, 1632
Aikido   152, 1175
Air cannon   324
Air pressure   520
Airbender   785
Aircraft   333, 450, 651, 676, 850
Akuaba   1107
Akwadu   31
Albertosaurus   1067
Algonquian   726
Alien   59, 127, 138, 198, 239, 249, 400, 758,
    765, 820, 882, 1134, 1168, 1265, 1308,

1357, 1361, 1435
Alligator   18, 399, 716, 843, 1066, 1330,
    1465
Allosaurus   308, 732, 1067
Almond cookies   1054, 1633
Almond milk   184
Aluminum   551, 1018, 1468
American paint horse   195
American quarter horse   195
American shorthair   189
Amphibians   485, 779, 1463
Anaerobic   610
Anatomy   1243
Ancestor   1220
Andes   861
Anemometer   43, 163, 251, 1293
Angel   959, 1056, 1076, 1246
Angel food cake   1246
Angle   62, 532, 556, 610, 611, 1068
Animal   266, 719
Animal masks   1107, 1250
Animal tracking   216, 577
Animation   426, 1134, 1540
Anklet   1277
Anko   690
Ankylosaurus   89, 119, 130, 192, 732, 1067,
    1309
Ansel Adams   693
Antarctic   1617
Antelope   1140
Antenna   213, 1469
Anthrax   1693

B

C

D

E

F

G

H

I

J

K

L

M

N

Q

R

S

U

V

W

About the Authors

CATHARINE BOMHOLD is an assistant professor of library and information science at the University of Southern Mississippi.

TERRI ELDER is a school media specialist with the Birmingham (AL) Public School district.